**Paul Willetts** is the author of two previou
*Loathing in Fitzrovia* and *North Soho 999.*
four much-praised collections of writing b          ........ dandy, Julian
Maclaren-Ross. He also devised and worked as co-photographer on
*Teenage Flicks*, a jokey celebration of Subbuteo, featuring contributions
by Will Self, David Baddiel and others. His journalism has appeared in
the *Independent, Guardian, The Times, Spectator* and elsewhere.

## Praise for *Fear and Loathing in Fitzrovia*:

'Very striking, very strange and altogether fascinating' Richard Holmes,
author of *The Age of Wonder*

'[It] breaks new ground and revives a remarkable writer in the context of
his times...' Philip French, *Observer*, 'Books of the Year, 2003'

'[An] entertaining chronicle of the '40s literary legend J. Maclaren-Ross'
D. J. Taylor, *Spectator*, 'Books of the Year, 2003'

'His book evokes not just the seedy flamboyance of a man who slept in
Turkish baths... but also a long-vanished bohemian world' Michael
Arditti, *The Times*, 'Books of the Year, 2003'

'An inspiring read' John King, *New Statesman*, 'Books of the Year, 2003'

'...an inventory of flits from boarding houses, unpaid bills, drinking
clubs, unfulfilled hopes. It should deter anyone who reads it from
becoming a writer' Jonathan Meades, *Evening Standard*, 'Books of the
Year, 2003'

'Willetts's gloriously readable biography paints a picture of a life which, for all its disappointments, was richly lived' *Mail on Sunday*

'[This] wonderful book is so informative and so psychologically perceptive...' Francis King, *Spectator*

'Diligent, painstaking and bleakly hilarious' *Guardian*, 'Book of the Week'

'Amusing and ultimately tragic...' Anthony Daniels, *Sunday Telegraph*, 'Summer Books Recommendations, 2003'

'A cracking portrait of London bohemia' *Independent*

## Praise for *North Soho 999*

'This book is like one of the best black and white films... Unputdownable' *Independent*, 'Books of the Year, 2007'

'[An] immensely well-researched evocation of late '40s London gangland...' D. J. Taylor, *Spectator*, 'Books of the Year, 2007'

'I urge you to read *North Soho 999*... It's the absolutely gripping true story of an armed raid on a Fitzrovia jewellers/pawnbrokers that escalated into a huge manhunt' Mark Gatiss, *Independent on Sunday*

'Fitzrovia is the setting of Paul Willetts's tour-de-force *North Soho 999*... a fascinating account of a vanished Britain' Philip French, *Times Literary Supplement*

# Members Only

THE LIFE AND TIMES OF
## PAUL RAYMOND
Soho's billionaire king of burlesque

Paul Willetts

A complete catalogue record for this book can
be obtained from the British Library on request
The right of Paul Willetts to be identified as the author of this work
has been asserted by him in accordance with the
Copyright, Designs and Patents Act 1988

First published in 2010 by Serpent's Tail,
an imprint of Profile Books Ltd
3A Exmouth House
Pine Street
London EC1R 0JH
website: www.serpentstail.com

ISBN 978 1 84668 715 0

Designed and typeset by folio at Neuadd Bwll, Llanwrtyd Wells

Printed and bound in Great Britain by Clays, Bungay, Suffolk

10 9 8 7 6 5 4 3 2 1

The paper this book is printed on is certified by the © 1996 Forest
Stewardship Council A.C. (FSC). It is ancient-forest friendly. The printer holds
FSC chain of custody sgs-coc-2061

**FSC**
**Mixed Sources**
Product group from well-managed
forests and other controlled sources
Cert no. SGS-COC-2061
www.fsc.org
© 1996 Forest Stewardship Council

For V.

# CONTENTS

# LIST OF ILLUSTRATIONS

**Author's Note**

You need only flick through *Members Only* to realise that it features more speech than some novels. This isn't because I've resorted to the type of fraudulent 'imaginative reconstructions' favoured by a disconcerting number of contemporary writers of what masquerades as non-fiction. The speech is, instead, drawn from a range of historical sources, all identified in the notes at the back of this book. My sources include newspaper reports, recordings, memoirs, interviews, witness statements, police transcripts and hitherto secret phone taps, obtained under the Freedom of Information Act.

*Overleaf: Paul Raymond, backstage at the Raymond Revuebar, 1 January 1960*

A S I WALKED through the night I got to thinking about what I had seen... I got to thinking why things happen in London at night. For twenty-five years I had seen these topsy-turvy people come into clubs at the hour when respectable people are going to bed. For twenty-five years I had seen men and women do crazy and unlawful things in the hours between midnight and four or five o'clock in the morning... I thought, too, that maybe these queer and sometimes frightening hours were the cause of all the crazy things I had seen. Perhaps when midnight passes and you're sitting in a club listening to the music, drinking too much, and watching sexy floor-shows while some painted harlot with her eye on your pocket-book is pressing her thighs against yours; perhaps at these times there's a madness steals over you, a derangement of the brain that vanishes with the dawn.

Jack Glicco, *Madness after Midnight*

# 1  AN AUDIENCE WITH THE KING

FOR MOST MEN it was the raw material of pulse-quickening fantasy. But these auditions had, by the closing months of 1960, become little more than a tiresome ritual for the man sitting near the stage that morning at the Raymond Revuebar, the upmarket strip-club he'd opened just over two years earlier. Destined to establish himself as one of the world's wealthiest people, his face familiar to British newspaper readers, the man in question was a thirty-five-year-old Northerner who had changed his name to Paul Raymond, a durable memento of his own abortive stage career. His sharp suit, cut in the continental style worn by Marcello Mastroianni in the previous year's hit movie *La Dolce Vita*, contributed to an impression of well-groomed prosperity and suave self-assurance. Such was his fastidious poise, you could almost have been persuaded that he also shared the Italian actor's dark good looks. Instead, he possessed the long, clean-shaven, pallid features of a medieval effigy. Any fleeting associations with the frigid hush of some bucolic parish church were, however, dispelled by the cigarette between his lips and the sight of his receding, wavy brown hair which he oiled into a crisply parted quiff, resembling the spirals of whipped cream piped on to the desserts served in the fashionable restaurant downstairs. Recurrent doses of cod liver oil and malt extract had failed to vanquish his unhealthy facial puffiness.

Smoke rings unspooled above Raymond as his doleful, dog-at-the-dinner-table eyes scrutinised the hesitant young girl who had ventured onto the otherwise empty stage. It extended fifteen feet into the terraced auditorium, around which tables and chairs had been arranged. Those seats would soon be filled by the usual attentive, smartly dressed crowd: film producers, businessmen, aristocrats, politicians, singers, gangsters, barristers, movie stars, quaffing overpriced drinks while they watched the show. At present the audience was sparse, just the inevitable technicians, plus Raymond and the journalist who had come to interview him about his controversial club.

Raymond had grown accustomed to encounters with the press. His latest interviewer was Ernest Dudley, courteous, fruity voiced and almost two decades his senior, though the age gap seemed greater because Raymond shaved off a few years whenever journalists asked how old he was. Until recently, Dudley had enjoyed nationwide fame as a BBC radio presenter. Nowadays he concentrated on working as a novelist and screenwriter. In between, he'd picked up a commission from *Today* – a popular weekly news magazine – to write a three-part feature about Raymond.

Had Dudley requested a press clippings file on his interviewee, he'd have been presented with a sheaf of yellowed articles from national newspapers. These bestowed on Raymond a range of flippant titles, including 'Mr Striptease' and 'the King of the Keyhole Shows', the latter rendered doubly pertinent because Raymond claimed to have obtained his first sight of naked female flesh by peering through a keyhole. The object of King Paul's bug-eyed scrutiny was one of his unsuspecting aunts, gingerly lowering herself into her bath.

Flavoured with disdain, the newspaper cuttings portrayed Raymond as a stereotypical wide-boy. But Dudley's interviewee bore no resemblance to the brash and sleazy profiteer who emerged from so many of these. Contrary to the stereotype, Raymond had manners as immaculate and formal as his custom-made suits. He had a gruff, carefully modulated voice with a slight stammer that hinted at vulnerability, only a trace of what could have been mistaken for a

Manchester accent discernible in his nasal, constricted delivery. He had a temperament that was phlegmatic, guarded, watchful, initially even a little shy and abrupt with strangers, his old-fashioned decorum prone to be misinterpreted as coldness. And he had practised charm with which he kept journalists at a distance while purveying an illusion of intimacy, of privileged access. He'd woo them with his self-deprecation, his bracing, ostensibly guileless candour, his ample stock of dryly humorous stories about his rackety past, stories garnished by a catchy laugh redolent of a misfiring lawnmower. Mouth realigning itself into a contagious half-smile, cigarette waved with a theatrical flourish, he'd say, 'I've never had a good write-up and I don't expect yours to be the first.'

It was part of a repertoire of lines Raymond trotted out during interviews, his delivery displaying all the brisk confidence of a former top-of-the-bill performer in provincial variety shows.

'I have read parts of a book, but never an entire book,' he delighted in telling reporters. 'Maybe I attempted to read the *wrong* sort of book.' Sometimes he'd justify this tone of gleefully mischievous philistinism by adding, 'Reading could destroy my instinct for what's popular. The average man doesn't read books. And *I* understand the mass trade. I believe I have the touch that the ordinary man in the street wants.'

On other occasions he'd strike a rare note of self-congratulation by gesturing to his luxurious surroundings and saying, 'Not bad for a lad who arrived from Liverpool with five bob in his pocket...'

Questions about the future of his lucrative, red-plush-adorned realm elicited the pronouncement, 'There'll always be sex – always, always, always.'

Forced to defend the nature of his business, he'd dispense another of his old favourites: 'It's simply that a normal, healthy chap likes to see a pretty girl without any clothes on.'

Raymond's routine captivated his current interviewer, who was fascinated by the contradictions of his personality, by what Dudley later described as 'his breathless audacity'. The first instalment of the eventual feature series would pose the question 'Is his sort of entertainment harmless or a moral menace?' To counter the predictable accusations of immorality, Raymond – or maybe his publicist – fed Dudley a line about him being a devout Roman Catholic, spiritually at ease despite the apparent incompatibility between his religious faith and his chosen career.

Quizzed about the titillating contents of his newest show, which featured a naked woman dancing with a boa constrictor, Raymond shrugged his well-padded shoulders and said, 'But what harm can there be in showing beautiful girls in interesting acts? Everything is clean, wholesome and above board.'

Right then, Dudley was studying Raymond as intently as Raymond was studying the girl he was about to audition. Regular letters from girls like her arrived at the Revuebar: girls who fancied reinventing themselves as gypsy seductresses, Nordic goddesses or South American sexpots, girls from any social class, their letters enclosing a snapshot more often than not taken by an obliging boyfriend or brother on some windswept British beach. Frequently, Raymond's wife Jean – responsible for choreographing and producing the shows as well as designing the costumes – would attend the subsequent auditions and rehearsals with their four-year-old daughter Debbie, who'd throw tantrums unless Jean brought her along.

Since his wife wasn't there to help him reach a verdict on the current would-be recruit, Raymond had to rely on his own judgement. Not that he lacked belief in his ability to select the appropriate candidates. He told people that he always looked at a stripper's face first because that's 'what makes everything come alive on a girl's body'. The attributes of a perfect stripper had, he believed, the immutable authority of Old Testament scripture. Call them the Four Commandments. Thou shalt be between eighteen and thirty years old. Thou shalt be five feet eight inches tall. Thou shalt weigh nine stone. And thou shalt not have excessively large breasts, the preferred dimensions being between thirty-six and thirty-eight inches. If they were bigger than that, he reasoned they'd be too floppy. Perhaps as a legacy of his strict upbringing, Catholic dogma mingling with middle-class squeamishness, Raymond was in those days reluctant to refer to them as 'breasts', let alone 'tits', 'bazookas' or any such lustful epithets. Betraying a streak of prudishness that Dudley found anomalous in a strip-club owner, Raymond insisted on calling them 'busts' or 'bosoms'.

His regal position within the club gave him the mandate for expressing absurd generalisations about the girls he auditioned. 'Very pretty girls', he was fond of declaring, 'often have bad figures, but girls with attractive figures invariably have pretty faces.'

In a reflection of changing fashion and his own changing tastes, what he defined as a pretty face and an attractive figure were remote from their equivalents thirty years later. Back in 1960, these paradigms of feminine allure could have subtly rounded stomachs, broad hips, pasty complexions, asymmetrical breasts and arms that didn't appear as if they were equipped to bench-press 100 lb. weights

Whenever Raymond scheduled auditions, he liked to claim that he wasn't just looking for the obvious attributes. No, *he* was looking for girls who were unselfconscious and capable of walking gracefully. As a rule, performers with at least a smidgen of showbusiness experience were favoured because he thought they lacked any offputting coyness. He said he was keen to recruit girls from what he termed 'good homes', girls from the quieter suburbs who, he felt, made the best strippers. He also said he wasn't, unlike some of his European colleagues, trying to find girls who derived a sexual thrill from what they did. His shows, he insisted, had nothing to do with sex. They were just 'two hours of refined, family-style entertainment'.

Eager to impress her potential employer, the girl currently onstage was wearing an unseasonal summer dress and a bit too much make-up, designed to give her the appearance of someone older, more sophisticated. Far from achieving the desired effect, the make-up emphasised her callowness. You could tell she'd never been auditioned before. Nor had she, in all likelihood, previously set foot inside the Revuebar or any other strip-club.

She flashed a nervous, ingratiating smile at Raymond. He responded with a slight nod.

The girl glanced into the wings, as if seeking further instructions. Then she peeled off her dress. Now wearing nothing but her bra, panties and slip-on shoes, she stood awkwardly beneath a proscenium arch embellished by Raymond's gilded, cursive monogram.

Another uncomfortable pause ensued before she swivelled round and paraded in front of both Raymond and his interviewer. She could have done with some music to lend her movements rhythm. Ordinarily, a three-piece band accompanied the performers. In the band's absence, noises from the surrounding central London streets tended to leak into the theatre: shouts, wolf-whistles, the hum of cars and lorries, the angry insectoid buzz of scooters.

Under Raymond's direction, the girl was soon mincing round the stage and striking the requisite poses, shedding her initial reticence more slowly than her dress. Next time she met his genial, non-committal gaze, her expression had acquired a new-found coquettishness.

Speaking softly, he asked her to take off her remaining clothes. As she followed his instructions, he watched with the detachment of an antique dealer appraising a piece of china. Almost a decade in the skindustry had left Raymond blasé about female nudity. For him, this wasn't about ogling pretty young girls. It was about his abiding obsession – not sex, but *money*. It was about business, about profit and loss, about contributing to the cost of his next Bentley, his Savile Row suits, his daughter's school fees, his wife's haute couture outfits.

'Believe me, I get no special kick out of the job I do,' he assured Dudley. 'To the girls, I am no more than a doctor examining his patients.'

# 2  EDUCATING GEOFFREY

RAYMOND OFTEN DESCRIBED himself as a self-made man. Infused with an undercurrent of immodesty, it led many people who met him during the 1960s to assume he was part of the influx of predominantly northern working-class talent energising the London art and show business scene and pushing at the boundaries of what was deemed acceptable. His well-advertised past as an itinerant market stallholder and variety artiste, together with the vestiges of a North Country accent, conspired to reinforce that misapprehension. Here was someone whose name appeared to belong in a roll-call spanning actors, writers, fashion designers, photographers, musicians and painters, among them Michael Caine, David Hockney, Ossie Clarke, Joe Orton and John Lennon. If pressed on the subject, however, Raymond would admit to being *middle* class, yet that label conceals as much as it reveals.

He was the second child of socially and temperamentally mismatched parents. His gregarious, roistering father Francis – known as Frank – Joseph had grown up in godless poverty amid the slums of the West Derby area of Liverpool. Raymond's paternal grandfather had worked on the city's docks during the nineteenth century, where he installed rigging on sailing ships. Defying the handicaps of this impecunious background, the future strip-club maestro's father had ended up running his own Liverpool-based 'forwarding agency' – what would now be called a haulage company. In 1921, aged twenty-six, Frank Joseph married a middle-class girl named Maud McKeown. Prior to their marriage, she'd been living with her Irish-born parents and her nine well-educated siblings, two of whom were schoolteachers. Maud had grown up in a spacious house in nearby Toxteth, a district far removed from its 1980s incarnation as a symbol of urban decay. The rigidly stratified class system of the period meant that her elderly father, who had, by his retirement, achieved the exalted rank of superintendent in the Liverpool Constabulary, was unlikely to have welcomed her choice of husband. There was also the contentious matter of religion, the McKeowns being such staunch Roman Catholics that Maud's brother, Charles, had become a Jesuit priest.

Probably as a way of appeasing his in-laws, Frank Joseph agreed to let his children be brought up as Catholics and to change his palpably Jewish surname. Duplicating the middle name of another of Maud's brothers, Felix Quinn McKeown, he became Frank Quinn, ersatz Gentile. He and Maud liked his new name enough to bestow it on the son she bore him during the winter of 1923.

In view of Maud's unstinting religiosity, which surely extended to a horror of contraception, her relationship with her husband can't have been a great sexual success, otherwise there wouldn't have been such a gap between the birth of Frank Quinn, Jr and her next pregnancy. On Sunday, 15 November 1925 their second child was, along with a high proportion of children at that time, born at home. Maud's labour must have been accompanied by the echoey noise of tannoy announcements from the railway station not far beyond the end of their small back garden. The scene of his birth was 'Brentwood', a large semi-detached house at 20 Rathmore Avenue. His family's home formed part of a new development, set in the grassy, tree-dotted south Liverpool suburb of Mossley Hill, byword for prim respectability.

Like his father, whose reputation as a boozy womaniser he'd inherit, Raymond didn't begin life with the name by which he came to be known. He was, instead, baptised Geoffrey Anthony Quinn – a name better suited to a Whitehall mandarin than a nightclub owner.

☆

His mother was a reproachful woman of puritanical thrift and severity, reflected in one of her favourite maxims – 'Much wants more...' This frugality encompassed both the material and emotional worlds. Perpetuating the aloof style of parenting favoured by so many middle-class parents during the nineteenth century, the era of her birth, she avoided physical contact with her children. Public displays of affection were, in any event, something she regarded as 'common'. She was, according to her second child, 'a terrible snob'. Lest it reflect badly on her, she wouldn't even permit her husband to bring copies of the downmarket *News of the World* home from work.

Statues of the Virgin Mary were distributed round their house, presenting an inescapable reminder of her oppressive piety. She's likely to have been behind the decision to send Geoffrey – and presumably his elder brother Frank as well – to a local fee-paying infant school, run by the Notre Dame order of nuns. Geoffrey would remember the experience with great fondness. He said they taught him to be 'polite and forgiving'. While he seldom forgot their lessons in politeness, he had trouble with the concept of forgiveness, his natural inclinations being closer to the vengeful eye-for-an-eye creed of the Old Testament.

Two years before completing his primary schooling, he acquired a younger brother named Philip, the arrival of whom in 1931 appears to have accelerated the dissolution of his parents' marriage. His father moved out of the house on Rathmore Avenue soon afterwards, leaving his mother in what was, during the early 1930s, the rare and socially awkward position of being a single parent. Nonetheless she refused to divorce her husband because that contravened the teachings of Catholicism.

Geoffrey's aunts on his mother's side of the family – Sarah, Winifrid, Josephine, Mary and Catherina – did their best to make up for the absence of his father, their ubiquity teaching him to feel comfortable around women. The support from the McKeown family may also have been financial.

He and his elder brother were told to respond to enquiries about their dad's whereabouts by saying that he was working abroad. In reality their errant father was living with a girlfriend in a house on the waterfront at New Brighton, just across the river from Liverpool docks. Decades from then, Geoffrey would reminisce about a melancholy occasion when his embittered mother had taken him there and pointed out the house's lighted windows.

His father's departure and the subsequent dissembling must have provided a hurtful introduction to the world of adult duplicity. Tears were an obvious release for the pain endured by Geoffrey. But he had, under the influence of his emotionally straitened mother, been brought up to believe men shouldn't cry. As an adult, he declared, 'I think it's absolutely appalling to see a man cry. That's the most terrible, terrible thing of all time.'


After primary school Geoffrey moved on to St Francis Xavier's College, the Catholic boys' private school where his brother Frank was already in the third year. Referred to by pupils and staff alike as 'SFX', it was a Jesuit-run institution, located on the fringe of the city centre. It had a reputation for offering its 600 pupils a route into the prestigious civil service or even to university, higher education at that stage being a privilege available to a tiny percentage of the population.

Maybe as a consequence of some childhood illness, Geoffrey – generally addressed as 'Geoff' – missed the start of the academic year, only attending his first lessons on Thursday, 9 November 1933. Arriving there would have been an intimidating experience for him – fear of the unknown, of mingling with older boys, of coping with its harsh discipline compounded by its dismal architecture. The arched entrance to the school pierced the flank of a huge red-brick French Gothic-style building, the monumental buttresses of which resembled the ribs of a dinosaur. Not exactly guaranteed to soothe any ripples of anxiety endured by the seven-year-old Geoff, attired in his unfamiliar new school uniform – cap, tie, grey blazer, knee-length shorts and long socks.

With no defined catchment area, SFX drew boys from as far away as south Manchester. Geoff joined a mixture of other fee-paying pupils and a smattering of poor boys who had won scholarships, shared religion tending to smooth out the social differences that caused friction at other schools. In imitation of the public school system, he and his fellow new boys were assigned to one of four houses – Briant, Campion, Ogilvie or Southwell. Captained by urbane, Brylcreemed senior pupils who wore double-breasted suits and brogues that made them appear older than they were, each of these houses competed against the others for an array of sporting trophies.

Under the dog-collared headmastership of Father Woodlock, athletic excellence was prized almost as much as scholastic achievement. An ageing but vivacious former army chaplain who had served in the trenches during the First World War, Woodlock combined his administrative duties with teaching Latin and running the school boxing club, not to mention coaching football and cricket. He was a lanky man with a scrape-over hairdo, round wire-rimmed glasses and an unassuming manner that belied his double first from Oxford University. By the standards of the period he was kindly and humane, making a point of learning the names of all the boys. Corporal punishment was nevertheless administered with brutal frequency.

Sitting at their desks in Victorian classrooms which were seen as antiquated and inadequate, Geoff and the other boys could be disciplined for not paying attention, talking during a lesson, or failing to answer a question correctly. As if the looming possibility of punishment didn't already exert enough pressure on Geoff each time a teacher pointed at him and asked a question, he also had to contend with a stammer sufficient to make teachers impatient and induce derisive laughter from classmates.

Punishment must have been a regular occurrence for Geoff who, as an adult, confessed to having struggled with schoolwork, invariably finishing bottom of his class's league table of scholastic attainment. Quite a contrast to his more academically inclined brothers, the younger of whom would follow their Uncle Felix into a career as a GP. Coloured though Geoff's confession may have been by rebellious, anti-intellectual bravado, it was lent credence by his presence in the lower of the school's two academic streams.

Whenever Geoff or his schoolmates committed some misdemeanour, their teacher wrote out what was known as 'a bill'. These small invoices stated the offence that had been committed, the offender's name, the date and the requisite number of blows, usually in multiples of three, extending up to twenty-four. The offender then took his bill to be countersigned either by one of the senior teachers or a sleekly besuited prefect. After that, the bill-holder trudged up to the first-floor storeroom which doubled as the place of execution. Holding out both hands, the victim received the specified number of blows on each palm. This stinging punishment was administered with a ferula – a pliable, foot-long bat, made from a wooden composite material.

Geoff's long-fingered, boney hands would, courtesy of his lack of distinction in the classroom, have been a ferula magnet. Some of his similarly unacademic contemporaries redeemed themselves through sporting excellence, but the school playing-fields merely offered Geoff another arena for mediocrity, if not outright failure.

Sport and scholarship weren't the only components of the timetable at SFX. Besides being taught the catechism by rote, he attended mass once a week and received religious education lessons. Every fortnight he also had to go to confession in the local parish church. Juxtaposed with this diet of religion were elocution lessons, the ability 'to speak properly', to mimic what was sometimes caricatured as the 'lah-di-da' pronunciation of BBC presenters, being considered a prerequisite for social and professional advancement. His elocution teacher was the wonderfully named Miss St George-Yorke, the name itself akin to some lip-flexing exercise in pronunciation. She must have contributed to the adult Geoff's precise, rather clipped – yet still perceptibly Northern – diction, its precision indicative of someone for whom every syllable was an obstacle that had to be scaled with care.

Extending the impressive breadth of education on offer were all sorts of extracurricular activities. There was a swimming club, a photography club, a debating society and a literary society, though the resolutely unbookish Geoff wasn't likely to have relished the opportunity to discuss the novels of P. G. Wodehouse or Evelyn Waugh. As well as the clubs and societies hosted by the school, there were theatrical productions and annual trips – camping expeditions to North Wales and holidays in France where the boys had the chance to go round the cultural landmarks. If Geoff ever visited Paris on one of these trips, his Jesuit guide failed to instil in him so much as a flicker of interest in art and architecture. His adult self came to equate Paris not with the Louvre or Notre Dame Cathedral but with the Crazy Horse Saloon and other temples of French striptease.

Since his separation from his wife, Frank Quinn had played little if any role in the lives of his three sons. By 1936, his business had buckled under the weight of the Depression. Now he was living in a rough part of Liverpool and working as a lorry driver. Most evenings, his son Geoff recalled, he could be found chatting up women in the Bear's Paw pub in Kensington, a district to the east of the city centre.

The latest intake of pupils at SFX that year included a Scottish boy six years older than Geoff. His name was John Gregson and, like Geoff, he'd go into show business – not as an impresario, but as the amiable star of *Genevieve* and other popular British movies. While he and Geoff and their fellow pupils were reacquainting themselves with the insular rhythms of school life, the worrying political situation in Europe further deteriorated. This violent polarisation between right and left even extended into the corridors of SFX. Instinctively tribal and quarrelsome, many of the boys sided with either pro or anti-fascist cliques, disputes between the two factions resulting in widespread lateness for lessons. The conflict found more cerebral expression within the Debating Society, where a mock Parliament was created.

Pupils were encouraged to treat school drama productions with comparable seriousness. What might have appeared an inconsequential exercise in self-indulgence was viewed by the Jesuits as a valuable facet of education which honed their pupils' public speaking skills. Few of the boys at Geoff's school were, however, prepared to relinquish their free time in order to take part in rehearsals.

Affording a sneak preview of his theatrical leanings, Geoff enlisted in the school's Glee Club, which staged an annual Shrovetide production. Not many weeks into the autumn term of 1938, by which time he was a comparatively tall, style-conscious thirteen-year-old with a dark, greasy quiff and a cheeky demeanour, he volunteered for the cast of *Columbus in a Merry Key*, an operetta about Christopher Columbus's arrival in the New World. Geoff failed to land a leading role, instead finding himself part of the sailors' chorus, his stammer apparently disappearing whenever he was required to perform. Together with a small orchestra, he and the other cast members attended after-school rehearsals in the Music Room, from where a contemporary of theirs reported hearing a cacophony that didn't bode well for the scheduled public performance.

But the production ran into far greater problems just before Christmas when two of its stars pulled out. The possibility of cancelling the show was discussed. Eventually the producers decided to go ahead, prompting them to audition replacement singers. Once the vacant roles had been filled, rehearsals began again, though there were complaints from boys working backstage about the limited preparation time.

Costumes and a large painted backdrop depicting the deck of a Spanish galleon were nevertheless ready for the show's solitary performance on Tuesday, 7 February 1939. Geoff and the rest of the sailors' chorus donned matching jackets, white shirts, dark shorts and white bandanas. Three of their schoolmates, meanwhile, had to appear in drag and eleven others – cast as 'savages' – blacked-up, the uneven make-up lending them the grubby-faced look of miners at the end of a shift.

On the night of the show, parents and relatives were well represented

*Geoff Quinn (inset close-up) pictured with the rest of the cast of* Columbus in a Merry Key. *He is fourth from the right on the third row from the back*

in the audience that awaited Geoff and the rest of the cast. 'The principals were excellent,' reported the school magazine. 'Columbus, though stiff in movement, sang in a clear and sweet voice.' The magazine's anonymous correspondent reserved his scorn for the three choruses – the sailors, savants and savages. 'When a complicated movement was in progress, there was always a "savant" endeavouring to find his relations in the audience. A desire among some to be prominent in the front row robbed some of the groupings of their full effect.'

It wasn't the most auspicious of preambles to Geoff's career in show business. At that age, however, he doesn't seem to have had any intimation of the path his life would take. He later claimed that, as a thirteen-year-old, he'd wanted to become a priest and that he and his elder brother – probably encouraged by their mother – would play what they called 'altars', dressing up and pretending to conduct mass.

# 3   PHWOAR AND PEACE

**A**LL BUT THE MOST NAIVE optimists were aware of the imminent military conflict in Europe. The devastation already wreaked by German bombers during the Spanish Civil War had alerted the British populace to the destructive potential of aerial bombardment. With its teeming docks, Liverpool was a certain target for similar raids. By that summer Maud had arranged for herself, her sons, one of her sisters and her recently widowed octogenarian mother, Hannah, to move out of the city.

In mid-July 1939, when the school year ended, Geoff left SFX. So did his sixteen-year-old brother Frank, who had just passed half a dozen School Certificate exams – the equivalent of GCSEs. Along with seven-year-old Philip and the rest of their immediate family, they'd been invited to live with their mother's unmarried brother, Felix, described by Geoff as 'a marvellous, kind uncle'.

His Uncle Felix was a First World War veteran who had won the Military Cross before going on to run his own medical practice. The setting for this was the small industrial town of Glossop, a freckle on the buxom contours of the High Peak District, thirteen miles to the south-east of Manchester.

Like the majority of his colleagues in the pre-National Health Service era, Felix McKeown charged for his services. They were lucrative enough to provide him with a home of sufficient size to accommodate not only a surgery but also the six evacuees. Geoff's new home was Moorbank House, a three-storey stone building with high-ceilinged rooms, plaster cornices and elaborate ceiling roses.

Situated near the foot of Victoria Street, which sloped past the town hall and into the high street, it shared the soot-blackened appearance of Glossop's other predominantly stone buildings. The soot had been disgorged by numerous mill chimneys that spiked the town's skyline. These included a paper mill and a chemical works, both of which sent peculiar smells wafting through the streets.

Instead of trying to smooth the transition between Liverpool and Glossop by befriending the locals, Geoff's mother and his aunts coalesced into a self-sufficient group, mistrustful of the motives of other women, that suspicion perhaps deriving from his father's extramarital dalliances. Nurture bolstering nature, the boy who'd become Mr Striptease must have acquired some of his habitual wariness from his mother and aunts. Even with his friends, he was reluctant to disclose much about himself or betray any sign of weakness. As several of them have testified, he always gave the impression that he was withholding things, that they knew only what he *wanted* them to know.

For Geoff and his displaced family, religion offered a potentially comforting sense of continuity. Free to choose between three Catholic churches, his mother – true to form – opted for the grandest of them: Sumner Memorial Church, usually known as St Mary's. It possessed the added cachet of a senior priest, the Very Reverend Canon W. R. Winder, officiating at mass.

Maud must have been annoyed that the town had no Catholic school comparable to SFX. Ready for the new academic year, her sons were enrolled at the best available alternative: Glossop Grammar School, known throughout the area as 'GGS'. In common with SFX, it was a fee-paying establishment that admitted a limited proportion of scholarship boys and had a reputation for steering its pupils into the professions and, in a few cases, university.

During the summer of 1939, Geoff and his brothers were kitted out in the GGS uniform. This featured a snazzy blazer and tie, which incorporated blue, red, green and black stripes, trimmed with gold thread. Sewn to the breast pocket of the blazer was the town crest, paired with the motto 'Virtus, Veritas, Libertas' – 'Virtue, Truth, Liberty'. Geoff would, in subsequent years, take only the latter to heart.

Germany's invasion of Poland that September triggered the outbreak of what would escalate into the Second World War. Those opening weeks of the conflict overlapped with the beginning of the autumn term at Geoff's new school.

Built in 1910 at the junction between Talbot and Fitzalan Streets, GGS was within easy walking distance of Moorbank House. To Geoff, accustomed to a school with twice as many pupils, GGS must have felt small and, possibly, less daunting in consequence. Its shabby classrooms, condemned by the Ministry of Education as 'utterly unsatisfactory', were crammed into two floors and a basement. Further teaching space was provided by five dilapidated and even shabbier wooden huts. Owing to the lack of a suitable room, morning assembly had to be held in the entrance hall.

On the Quinn brothers' first day at GGS, their fellow pupils would have been packed into the lobby. Being in such close proximity to the girls who made up half the school's intake would have been a novel experience for Geoff and his brothers. Assemblies were usually presided over by the middle-aged headmaster, Cecil Lord, nicknamed 'Joe', a benign soubriquet that obscured sadism sufficient to make even the Jesuits flinch. He'd recently inaugurated an annual cross-country race, would-be entrants to which had to prove their athleticism by dangling for two minutes from an improvised trapeze, suspended from the ceiling of the woodwork room. His malevolent streak also manifested itself through his habit of making disparaging remarks about the boys from poorer families. It was a habit that fostered what one pupil called a 'them and us' atmosphere, dividing the scholarship pupils from the rest of the school whose families paid fees of £10 10s a year.

Geoff and his brothers weren't the only evacuees to enrol that term. They were joined by children from Manchester, Bolton and Surrey. The war soon made itself felt within GGS in other ways, too. All sports fixtures against schools outside Glossop were cancelled. In the spirit of the famous 'Dig For Victory' propaganda campaign, an allotment was created at one end of the playing fields, situated well away from GGS's main buildings. Trenches were dug elsewhere around the edges of the sports pitches, offering pupils shelter from bomb blasts. Gas masks were issued to everyone. These hung from row upon row of pegs in the basement, which had been turned into an air-raid shelter. And the Stationery Room was transformed into the First-Aid Room, equipped with basic medical supplies. To provide some security from explosions for the building's occupants, brick walls were constructed in front of the ground-floor windows. As a safeguard against flying glass, heavy felt curtains, which could be quickly unfurled, were hung on the other side. For additional protection, brown paper was glued to the glass, necessitating electric lighting even on the brightest of days.

In the early months of the war, air-raid drills and first-aid lessons became an intermittent feature of Geoff's schooling. When a drill was announced, the caretaker rushed round the classrooms lowering the safety curtains while the pupils hurried down to the basement, where they had to sit beneath their pegs, attention diverted by prefects under instructions to organise word games. The pupils and staff remained in the basement for an hour at most, their improvised shelter rendered uncomfortable by lack of ventilation.

At assembly, the occasion as yet free from sobering references to former pupils who'd been killed fighting for king and country, there began to be recurrent allusions to ways in which GGS could contribute to the war effort. Campaigns to collect aluminium, scrap metal and paper were launched. Fund-raising drives were held for the British Red Cross Society. Parcels of spare clothes were put together. The girls were expected to knit blankets for the women in the Auxiliary Territorial Service, and the boys encouraged to work on the school allotment, where the soil turned out to be so poor that it yielded potatoes no bigger than marbles.

Myriad changes were wrought on life outside school as well. Everyone started carrying ration books and identity cards. Water tanks, installed just in case the mains were severed by bombing, popped up all over the town. Cast-iron railings round parks and gardens began to be recycled. Dustbins were placed on street corners, so food scraps could be donated for use as pig swill. And meals began to incorporate unfamiliar, often unappetising ingredients – condensed milk, dried eggs, Spam – the dawn of rationing and food shortages bestowing official sanction on Maud Quinn's censorious thrift.

Most of the teachers at GGS were approaching the age when they would, under normal circumstances, have retired. Age hadn't, however, diminished the effectiveness of several of the staff, including Miss Norris, a Londoner who had taught English there for more than a decade. But even *she* failed to inspire Geoff, the quality of whose schoolwork can't have been improved by the distraction of sharing a classroom with girls. He later recounted how his burgeoning interest in them gave him abundant raw material for his visits to the confession booth at St Mary's, these leading the Reverend Winder to warn his mother that she'd have to keep an eye on him because he was 'wild'.

Neither his mother nor his aunts liked the idea of him going out with girls until he'd taken his School Certificate exams. Girls would lead him astray, he remembered being cautioned. Yet he had, by the age of fourteen, acquired a girlfriend. As a contemporary of his recalled, their courtship soon landed him in trouble.

Under cover of the blackout Geoff and his girlfriend were canoodling in the pavilion at Manor Park recreation ground when one of the local air-raid wardens, responsible for patrolling the area, shone a torch at them. Geoff was convinced that a jealous schoolmate had informed on him. The escapade provoked a ticking off from the headmaster who threatened to expel him.

In late January 1940, only a few months into his second year at GGS, Geoff received what may well have been his first taste of a High Peak District winter. At about 10 p.m. on the last Friday of that month, heavy snow began to fall across the town. Over the next forty-eight hours, the blizzard intensified. When Geoff's school opened at 8.40 a.m. on Monday morning, snow was still coming down. Except for GGS pupils trudging in the direction of Talbot Road, few people were on the town's streets and few of its shops and other businesses showed any inclination to open. Before the snowfall relented that Wednesday, the drifts had become so deep that children were using them to clamber onto the crossbars at the top of lamp-posts.

Geoff and the rest of Glossop's population didn't just have to endure blizzards. For numerous nights that summer the sound of air-raid sirens could be heard across the town. Many local families, the occupants of Moorbank House probably among them, were too frightened to make their way to the public air-raid shelters. Instead, they stayed at home, often huddled in under-stair cupboards, terrified by the deceptively close-sounding drone of German aircraft twenty or thirty miles away.

Vindicating the Quinns' self-imposed evacuation from Liverpool to Glossop, the town would remain untouched by bombing throughout the war. Substantial areas of Liverpool as well as other British towns and cities were, in the meantime, gutted by incendiary bombs.

The destruction of one of the main naval depots in Portsmouth encouraged the Admiralty to transplant its workforce to Glossop. They took over Wood's Mill, a huge disused factory on the same street where Geoff and his family lived. Each morning the pavements outside their house were crowded with hundreds of naval workers en route to the mill.

After the capitulation of France midway through GGS's summer term, evacuees from Suffolk also poured into Glossop. As the threat of a

German invasion escalated, the town formed its own Home Guard unit, which could be seen marching round the streets. Its recruits included Cecil Lord, stewing with resentment because he'd only been assigned the rank of private. At school, though, he'd landed an even less desirable title, his nickname amended from 'Joe' to 'Gauleiter'.

That academic year must have felt endless for Geoff. Under the school's new wartime schedule, the final term had been extended into August 1940, reducing the summer holiday to a mere fortnight. On his return to GGS, Geoff should have been preparing for his School Certificate exams the following summer but, as one of his contemporaries said, 'He was in a hurry to begin adult life.' Much to the disapproval of his family, who had made a substantial investment in his education, he left school at the earliest opportunity: on – or soon after – his fifteenth birthday.

# 4  FIDDLER ON THE HOOF

**G**EOFF'S FIRST JOB was in Manchester, only a short train or bus ride from Glossop. Paying no more than about fifteen shillings a week, the job appears to have been as an office boy, running errands and making cups of tea in a cotton mill. He remembered his mother being so embarrassed by this lowly employment that she insisted on telling people he was 'a junior clerk'.

Like a lot of boys his age, he'd become a fan of big band dance music, tuning in to BBC radio programmes such as *Swing Boys Swing*. These inspired him to learn to play the drums by practising on a friend's drum kit. Years afterwards, he revealed how his mother had disapproved of the friendship because his pal lived in a tiny terraced house. Geoff and his chum ended up playing at local dances where they could each earn as much as £1 a night.

Offered the chance to join Louis Gold and His Monarchs of Melody, the house band at the Grand Pavilion in the Yorkshire seaside town of Withernsea, he gave up his job and moved there. It was a decision which, he recalled, horrified the McKeown family, his maternal grandmother referring to him disdainfully as a 'common drummer'. They can't have been too happy about the accent he'd acquired either: a nasal Glossop inflection redolent of Manchester rather than his adoptive county of Derbyshire.

Declaring itself 'Withernsea's Brightest Spot', a dubious accolade during that forlorn period, the Grand Pavilion was open every night. It didn't just host dances. It hosted cabaret evenings and heavily discounted 'Crazy Nights'. There were also Sunday evening concerts at which Geoff and his fellow Monarchs of Melody performed alongside guest stars – generally baritones and mezzo-sopranos, familiar from appearances on the radio.

For the purpose of the bandleader's preliminary patter, in the course of which each musician was introduced to the audience, Geoff dropped his real name and devised a series of more catchy pseudonyms. First there was 'Ray Carlton'. Then there was 'Gene Raymond', but he felt obliged to drop this when he discovered it was the name of a Hollywood actor. Finally, he settled on 'Geoff Raymond'.

During the daytime Geoff could sample the rival entertainments on offer in the town. Though he was too young to use the pubs, he could go to the cafés, the amusement arcade, the Glitterdromes roller-skating rink and the three cinemas where, under wartime regulations, customers had to show their gas masks before being allowed inside.

His stint at the Grand Pavilion came to an end when the Military Police raided the place one evening and hauled off his employer, who was an army deserter. Geoff had, by then, reached the disappointing conclusion that he wasn't talented enough to make a career as a drummer. Compelled to devise an alternative way of earning a living, he became a self-confessed spiv, running market stalls in the Lancashire towns of Rochdale and Oldham. He specialised in shoelaces, hairnets, perfume and nail varnish – a banned product because it wasted scarce supplies of oil. To get round the regulations, it was sold as 'Ladderstop', ostensibly for repairing laddered stockings.

Still making his living from market stalls, Geoff celebrated his eighteenth birthday in November 1943, seemingly inevitable conscription into the armed forces perhaps tarnishing the occasion. Instead of being funnelled into the military, though, he was called up to serve as a so-called Bevin Boy. Named after Ernest Bevin, Minister of Labour in the wartime coalition government, the Bevin Boys' Scheme had recently been set up to recruit the 20,000 miners necessary to sustain the existing level of coal production. From an inventory of every man under the age of twenty-five who hadn't yet been conscripted, 10 per cent were randomly selected by the government.

As instructed, Geoff reported to Manvers Main Colliery near the town of Mexborough in south Yorkshire. Most likely gathered in a fretful crowd beneath the pit wheel which glowered across that part of the Dearne Valley, he and the latest batch of recruits would have been herded round the bleak site. On their first day they'd not only have been given pep-talks about the importance of coal to the war effort but also issued with weighty boots, ill-fitting helmets and other equipment. Recruits were typically given about a month's instruction in the rudiments of mining, the prelude to which was a fortnight spent perched on a slag heap shovelling stone for eight hours a day, every gust of wind scouring their faces with grit and coal dust.

Geoff subsequently admitted that he'd got through no more than a week's training which, he said, included a spell underground. 'I didn't like it at all down there,' he admitted. 'Not at all, so I walked out. I wouldn't have minded the merchant navy, but the mine was terrible.'

He wasn't alone in disliking his new role as a trainee pitman. Absenteeism from the Bevin Boys' Scheme was high. If he returned to Glossop, he risked immediate arrest, so he drifted down to London, the capital's anonymity offering him a greater chance of evading the authorities. Disembarking there in late 1943, his journey taking him through drab, bomb-damaged streets, he'd have found the bus and train stations packed with diversely uniformed men and women.

Besides playing host to a transient population of service personnel, the majority of them converging on the West End, London was home to a vast shadow army of conscription dodgers and deserters. By the end of the war, around 20,000 of these fugitives, not just British personnel but overseas servicemen as well, were estimated to be on the run, most of them in the capital. Unable to claim the ration-books that would have permitted them to purchase the necessities of life through conventional channels, they had to rely on the flourishing black market for those necessities and, more often than not, as a source of income, too.

Rationing and government restrictions on the sale of certain goods had spawned a feverish demand for such scarce commodities as clothes, handbags, cigarettes, meat and whisky, large quantities of which were being purloined from shops, warehouses and rail depots. Also there was a trade in forged and stolen ration coupons, which could be used to buy most of these goods. Street markets afforded convenient cover for this surreptitious trade.

Already well acquainted with the bantering, rough-and-ready world of outdoor stallholders, Geoff became a ubiquitous presence on Cambridge Market, which lined Moor and West Streets, two narrow roads on the periphery of the central London district of Soho. There, he established a reputation for being what was, in the days before the term 'spiv' gained widespread currency, known as 'a fiddler', 'a pavement pusher' or sometimes 'a kerb boy'. Dawdling among the wooden barrows, he became friendly with Frank Fraser, a short, thickset, deceptively polite and mild-mannered young south London criminal who'd absconded from the army.

'People like me knew he was on the run,' Fraser remembered. 'He dealt in everything, petrol coupons, clothing coupons, you name it. He was a lively bloke. Good at what he did. He was the type who could always get hold of things you needed.'

Unlike clothing coupons, which could be handed over in shops with minimal risk, petrol coupons couldn't be used without attracting scrutiny. After all, few civilians were, under wartime regulations, entitled to purchase petrol. Only professional criminals tended to be willing to take the associated risk. Among them was the West End pimp Gino Messina, who needed his car to cruise round the blacked-out streets, checking on his girls.

Often Geoff would be seen in the pubs and cafés of Soho, now synonymous with the black market, with fiddlers of the unmusical variety, generally recognisable by their dress sense and conversation, which could be termed 'flash' or 'wide'. They usually went in for gleaming shoes, chunky rings, broad-lapelled bum-warmer jackets, and hats with narrow curly brims, worn at an angle. The archetypal fiddler also sported a pencil moustache – an accoutrement Geoff had already acquired – and hair slathered in enough Brylcreem to deep-fry a couple of portions of cod and chips.

Fiddling was just one of several businesses turning a fat profit in wartime Soho. The other beneficiaries of circumstance included publicans, restaurateurs, pimps and prostitutes, as well as the owners of clubs, cafés, theatres and cinemas. Each night hordes of service personnel and civilians stumbled through the blackout, seeking a few hours' solace from the war, heightened awareness of their own mortality fostering a live-for-the-moment ethos. By far the most famous destination for male revellers was the Windmill Theatre on Great Windmill Street, a visit to which Geoff later recalled.

Originally opened in 1909 as a cinema, the Windmill had, since 1932, been hosting *Revudeville*, a production conceived by its manager, Vivian Van Damm. In creating the show, he'd modified a theatrical genre popular on both sides of the Atlantic. That genre was 'revue', itself an offshoot of so-called 'variety theatre', the latter-day incarnation of music hall which had enjoyed its golden age in the late nineteenth and early twentieth centuries. Like variety, revue consisted of numerous sketches and other routines. These could encompass singers, magicians, jugglers, dancers, comedians and even novelty acts. Where revues diverged from variety shows was in their thematic cohesiveness, often signposted by their titles.

Assimilating the words 'revue' and 'nude', *Revudeville* hinted at both the show's preoccupation with sex and its star turn – a troupe of attractive young girls, minus their clothes. At the insistence of the Lord Chamberlain, who had the power to censor theatrical productions in

*A wartime performance at the Windmill Theatre*

Britain, the girls had to remain motionless, their naked bodies subtly lit. To comply with these stipulations, Van Damm had devised what he'd portray as the revolutionary concept of 'living tableaux'. Beneath subdued lighting, goose-pimpled models, invariably positioned at the back of the stage, maintained static poses that mimicked Grecian friezes, famous paintings or classical statuary, these high cultural allusions offering convenient camouflage for low cultural prurience. The girls' genitals were hidden by a combination of cunning poses, discreet items of drapery and lighting that cast shadows deep enough to prompt men in the audience to pucker their faces in squinting, monobrowed concentration. Whenever front-row seats were vacated, remaining members of the audience would compete in what was waggishly dubbed 'the Windmill Steeplechase'. Desperate to claim the empty seats, from where they'd get a better view, they would vault the chairs ahead of them.

*Cover of the 1943 'Revudeville' souvenir programme*

The nude tableaux were punctuated not only by variety acts but also dance numbers featuring the scantily dressed resident chorus line. All this exposed female flesh was too much for some customers, who furtively masturbated despite the risk that they'd be spotted by staff employed to scan the audience through binoculars. Those staff had once included the future film star Kenneth More.

Except for the period during September 1939 when the government forced all theatres to close, the Windmill, unlike London's forty-one other theatres, remained open throughout the war. For thousands of Allied troops converging on the capital, a trip to the Windmill – hailed by several American newspapers as 'the best-known theatre in the world' – was obligatory. By 1943 its small auditorium was routinely packed with gum-chewing US servicemen eyeballing performers such as 'the Platinum Goddess', whose bra and skirt were torn off by actors dressed as loin-clothed tribesmen. Back home, many of those servicemen must have sampled genuine striptease in the far less sedate surroundings of the big-city burlesque houses. The Americans responded to the Windmill's pallid offerings with uninhibited whoops and futile shouts of 'Shake it, sister!' – futile because, as the manager's daughter boasted, the only time any of the nudes moved appreciably was on the day that a V-1 rocket exploded fifty yards away.

When Geoff walked into the foyer of the Windmill during 1943, posters for the show bore the proud declaration 'We Never Closed'. Jokers persisted in quipping that it should've read, 'We Never *Clothed*'. Propelled by this amalgam of stoic humour and defiance, the Windmill would become part of the burnished, cliché-ridden vision of wartime England: a vision of Spitfires, air-raid shelters, communal sing-songs, powdered egg, bumbling Home Guardsmen and the plangent wail of sirens. Yet Geoff's recollection of his visit to the theatre defied nostalgic folk-memory. 'It was not a wonderful experience,' he insisted, 'and the comics were ghastly.'

# 5  PRIVATES ON PARADE

ONCE THE WAR in Europe had ended, Geoff assumed it was safe to rejoin his family in Glossop where, most likely, he continued his career as a market trader. According to an account he gave twenty-five years later, the illusion of safety was destroyed by an unexpected phone call from the police in late 1946. He remembered the policeman saying, 'You should be down the mine,' to which he replied, 'Well, I've been ill.'

As a deserter, he faced a potentially long prison sentence. But the authorities opted instead to call him up for National Service, a new obligation for boys when they reached their eighteenth birthday. Two years' compulsory peacetime conscription had been introduced by the post-war Labour government, not as a means of instilling delinquent youth with discipline but as a way of meeting the country's military commitments. Those included garrison duties in West Germany and Austria, plus assorted colonial outposts, the most dangerous of these being Palestine, where British troops were caught in a guerrilla war between Jews and Arabs.

Even though Geoff had received the letter summoning him to the Medical Examination and Written Test, held at the local Ministry of Labour offices, there was still a chance that he could avoid the boredom, danger and inconvenience of conscription. Sixteen per cent of conscripts were, after all, rejected because they were homosexuals or because they had some disability, illness or psychological problem.

Most eighteen-year-olds seem to have accepted and sometimes welcomed conscription as an unavoidable rite of passage, offering a chance to leave home, escape from dull jobs and travel abroad at government expense. With several years of independence behind him, Geoff was out of kilter with the majority. Among those conscripts who, like him, hoped to sidestep military service, urban myths about how to fluff the medical proliferated. You could pretend to have a fit. You could douse yourself in perfume, flutter your eyelashes and adopt effeminate mannerisms. Or, if you were *really* desperate, you could puncture one of your eardrums with a knitting needle. Decades from then, Geoff would relish telling the story of how he'd heard that you could induce a temporary heart murmur by force-feeding yourself sugar butties. He followed the advice yet, unable to deceive the medical officer's stethoscope or X-ray machine, he was graded 'A-1' – fit for all duties.

After the medical examination which lasted a couple of hours, he was put through the written test, spanning half an hour or so. Its title was misleading, however, because it didn't entail much writing. In common with the IQ tests on which it was modelled, it mainly consisted of arranging sequences of numbers, words and symbols.

Geoff's test results led to him receiving another official envelope in the post. This contained an Enlistment Notice, giving the date and time when he was expected to report to his unit. Probability decreed that he'd be assigned to the army rather than the RAF. As an infantryman, he could have ended up patrolling some dusty street in Palestine, a sweat-beaded target for gunmen from both warring factions, so his allocation to the air force must have been a source of immense relief.

Reporting for duty at the specified base, he and his fellow recruits, young men from diverse regions and social classes, were kitted out. As they moved from one queue to another, they collected different items – boots, jackets, coats, mess tins, trousers – from different counters. Now in often ill-fitting blue-grey RAF uniforms, they joined a long queue that filed past a row of tailors who indicated any necessary alterations with swift chalk marks.

During what amounted to a brief interregnum between their lives as civilians and as servicemen, recruits were given regulation short haircuts of the type Geoff loathed. They were also schooled in the basics of service life. Their undemanding schedule left them with enough spare time to smoke their way through generous cigarette rations while they acclimatised to life in uniform.

Compared to many conscripts Geoff was better equipped to make the transition from so-called 'civvy street' into the military. Unlike a lot of middle-class recruits, he was accustomed to living away from home, to material hardship, to the habitual profanities of some working-class banter. Yet he appears to have had trouble adapting to service life, perhaps because he had, since leaving his office job in Manchester, pursued an individualistic existence remote from the rigidly structured, hierarchical, disciplined ethos of the RAF.

On the fourth or fifth day he and the other recruits were transferred to a Primary Training Centre, probably at Driffield in Yorkshire, where they were divided into large groups, known as 'flights'. Over the next eight weeks they were given courses of compulsory vaccinations, administered in the station sick quarters. And they were subjected to an arduous training regime, often lasting seventeen hours a day, its rigours magnified by the possibility of bullying, psychological or physical, a commonplace prank involving a recruit having his trousers pulled down and his genitals daubed with boot polish. Irrespective of the weather, recruits were drilled on the parade ground, sent round the assault course and put through sessions of physical training, anything from jogging to push-ups, supervised by bellowing corporals who had a reputation for swearing at conscripts, humiliating them and even assaulting them. The corporals, clutching heavy drill-sticks that added to their menace, also taught recruits how to clean and fire a Lee Enfield rifle.

Primary training completed, Geoff and the others were split up and allocated to different units. Only a tiny proportion of each intake was selected for tuition as potential aircrew. The rest, Geoff among them, were assigned to more mundane duties. Under his new identity as

Aircraftsman Quinn, he was posted to RAF Tern Hill, just to the south-west of the Shropshire town of Market Drayton. Home to No. 6 Service Flying Training School, which had moved there only a few months earlier, Tern Hill was one of the oldest and most picturesque of military airfields. Not that Quinn, who had little interest in the countryside, would have appreciated the sylvan setting. Perched on a wooded hillside, the main buildings, including accommodation that dated from the mid-1930s, overlooked the runways along which small training aircraft regularly took off and landed.

Quinn's earlier experience as a musician garnered him a comparatively cushy berth playing the big drum in the unit's marching band. Like some prototype of the skiving, wheeler-dealing character portrayed by Richard Attenborough in the Boulting Brothers' 1956 National Service comedy *Private's Progress*, Quinn soon wangled a transfer to an even cushier job as a switchboard operator. He and his colleagues worked a shift system. Usually he was on the night shift, during which he could catch up with his sleep, interrupted by only the occasional phone call. Better still, his new job gave him the chance to resume his pre-RAF career as a spiv.

Three years older and more worldly than most of his fellow recruits, he took to organising dances at a church hall in Market Drayton, where he could work his charms on the local girls. To enable him to supervise these dances, sometimes staged on alternate evenings, netting him up to £80 a week, he'd pay a colleague ten shillings for covering his shift. 'I was never really in the RAF more than three days a week,' he admitted years afterwards.

Brimming with moneymaking schemes, he supplemented his income from the dances by staging a raffle. The prize for this was a bicycle owned by an obliging sergeant. 'We just had to make sure he won the bike,' Quinn recalled.

His commercial activities extended before long to flogging second-hand cars, presumably bought with the cash he'd earned from the dances. For 10 per cent of the sale price of each car, he talked a noncommissioned officer into showing them to customers whenever a stint of guard duty left him unavailable.

The success of his various schemes, which provided an early example of his genius for identifying and then seizing business opportunities, gave him his first taste of what it felt like to enjoy a relatively large income. This could have bankrolled his return to civilian life. Succumbing instead to the improvidence of youth, the lure of short-term pleasure triumphing over long-term planning, he got into the habit of blowing his earnings, mainly on extravagant nights out with girlfriends.

However easy and profitable his spell in the RAF had been, he was nevertheless impatient for the day his demob papers were due. In that sense he was, once again, out of synch with his fellow conscripts, the majority of whom, according to a contemporary survey, enjoyed service life.

When Quinn was at last discharged from the RAF during 1948, he moved to Manchester and set up his own business in the city centre. Based at 23 Brazennose Street, part of a maze of tall nineteenth-century industrial buildings, his firm was called the Raymond Shirt Company. Contrary to its name, his business wasn't dedicated to manufacturing shirts. It was, instead, a front for the sale of black-market cloth, rendered scarce by the rationing which continued to make life as monochrome as most of the footage screened at neighbouring cinemas. That cloth would probably have come from the docks at Birkenhead where criminal gangs were stealing unprecedented quantities of it.

Quinn later told the story of how the police had once visited him after a tip-off about some missing rolls of fabric. He said that the coppers must have believed him when he feigned ignorance of it. Fortunately for him, they didn't bother to look behind the curtain where the stolen cloth was hidden.

Disturbed perhaps by this near-miss, he went on to run a second-hand pram shop in the city. Local residents would often see him wheeling old prams back to his shop where he cleaned them up, ready to sell. But the business doesn't seem to have lasted more than a few months. He was now in such desperate circumstances that he was willing to take a job as assistant to a self-styled 'psychic healer' touring Northern towns. Clad in a white coat, Quinn would guide members of the audience onto the stage where his employer performed ostensibly miraculous cures.

His experience of organising regular dances must have buttressed Quinn's innate belief in his own business acumen. Such confidence encouraged him to scrape together enough money for a fresh venture – promoting a beauty contest in Blackpool. The event turned out to be a commercial disaster, forcing him to take another poorly paid job. His new employment consisted of running a lottery machine on the pier at the Essex resort of Clacton-on-Sea during the holiday season.

Among Britain's most popular seaside destinations in the 1930s, the town was just beginning to recover from the Second World War. Peeling paintwork had been renewed; all the lighting had been switched on for the first time in years; and the streets were looking neater than most dowdy British towns and cities of that period. Over the bank holiday weekend of Easter 1949, warm sunshine helped the season get off to its best start in three decades. Nearly eleven thousand visitors arrived by rail, others making the journey by coach. Some headed for the congested seafront, with its 'Tell Your Weight' machine, ice-cream stalls and stacks of deckchairs for hire. Others made a beeline for the pier and joined the constantly replenished fifty-yard queues stretching out from the turnstiles. Once those holidaymakers had clicked through these and sauntered onto the huge, spoon-shaped pier, they could make use of the swimming pool, the Cresta Run Helter Skelter and the Blue Lagoon Café, where they could have afternoon tea and dance to the music of Teddy Dobbs and His Orchestra. They could, of course, also visit the funfair on which Quinn worked, the air filled with the metallic clatter of pinballs, the shrieking of children, the hum and sputter of dodgems, all overlaid by the musical tinkle of coins disappearing down the digestive tracts of gluttonous slot machines.

The Easter crowds served as the frenetic prologue to a busy holiday season which entered its peak period in mid-June when tourists flooded into the town, many of them travelling from London on seagoing steamers. By then, the pier's attractions had been augmented by the opening of a cabaret show at the Ocean Theatre. While Quinn was working nearby, he got to know a man, also employed on the funfair, who had been part of an old variety double-act: a mind-reading turn called 'Mr and Miss Tree', its title a jokey reference to the raffish slang for a homeless runaway girl – 'a mystery'. Quinn ended up paying him the considerable sum of £25 for a trunk full of pre-printed astrological predictions and, more importantly, the secrets to the act. Those secrets enabled the mind-reader and his female assistant to perform an impressive-looking trick which had scope for numerous variations. The trick involved the assistant blindfolding the mind-reader, then going up to someone in the audience and holding up an item borrowed from that person, a fountain pen perhaps. Using seemingly innocuous everyday phrases, listed in a code book, she'd help the mind-reader to pull off a feat of apparent telepathy by naming the borrowed item.

After the holiday season, Quinn returned to Glossop. With his hair extending below his collar and his shoes so battered that he was reduced to stuffing pieces of cardboard inside them to fill the holes, he must have embarrassed his rigidly conventional mother. Back in what he now regarded as his home town, he set about launching himself as a stage performer – an odd choice of career for someone who preferred cinema to theatre. Then again, his motives for wanting to get into show business were unusual. 'The love of the theatre and the footlights is nil to me,' he readily conceded. 'I'm in it purely to make money.'

He began by placing a newspaper advert, soliciting applications for the job of assistant to a variety artiste. The advert precipitated a reply from a seventeen-year-old named Noreen O'Horan. When he auditioned her, he found she was perfect for the role of glamorous sidekick. She had a soft Yorkshire accent, together with a pert-nosed, photogenic face, inclined towards plumpness. Shapely legs, a curvaceous figure and long, dark hair, worn in ringlets, set the seal on her vampish allure.

Soon Quinn and his assistant, whose mature good looks concealed a spirit of adolescent waywardness, were rehearsing their act. Gradually, he incorporated his own refinements into it, though it remained third rate by his own admission. Too proud to concede that he was just as much of a theatrical novice as O'Horan, he strove to give her the impression that he'd been treading the boards for years. In preparation for their debut, both of them changed their names. O'Horan became 'Gay Dawn' and Quinn, sensing that his baptismal name was 'not commercial', assumed the suave moniker of 'Paul Raymond', his choice of initials coincidentally hinting at his yet-to-be-exploited flair for public relations.

Without significant competition from television, only 126,000 of which had been licensed for use in Britain, variety theatre was reaching the apex of its final boom period. Even so, Raymond – who billed himself as 'The Modern Man of Mystery' – struggled to secure theatrical bookings for their act. He and O'Horan found themselves working on the pier at Clacton, and then in what was known as 'cine-variety'. This consisted of live shows performed in cinemas during the interval between the supporting programme – adverts, newsreels, trailers, plus a short film – and the main feature. To supplement the derisory fee they were paid by the cinema's management, they also went round the audience selling astrological predictions. For these, they charged one shilling each. So hard up that he often couldn't afford the bus fare home from his shows, Raymond had no choice but to hitchhike or trudge long distances back to his uncle's house.

All the hours he and O'Horan were spending together in fleapit cinemas and decrepit theatres contributed to their professional partnership turning into a sexual relationship. But their physical intimacy didn't extend to spiritual intimacy. Raymond refrained from confiding in her or exposing the more painful aspects of his past. Looking back on their relationship, she said, 'You never heard him mention his father. Never once. I think somewhere along the line there was some real hurt there.'

O'Horan sensed that her romance with him was just an ephemeral pleasure, that she and Raymond didn't have enough in common to endow it with longevity. Her attitude seems to have been shared by her boyfriend. Weeks of penury, of performing in front of small audiences, convinced him that the prospects for their double-act were no rosier onstage than off. His show-business future, he decided, lay in becoming a solo artiste, so he severed their theatrical partnership around June 1950. Matters were complicated, though, by the news that O'Horan was pregnant. Undeterred by the disruption this would wreak on his plans, Raymond dutifully proposed marriage, a proposal couched, according to O'Horan, in the unromantic declaration that 'I'm quite willing to do the right thing'.

Her account of the conversation culminated in her saying that it had never been her intention to marry him, that she was going to bring their child up herself, that she'd make sure he contributed to the child's upbringing. Despite her preparedness to defy the norms of the period by becoming a teenage single parent, Raymond – probably under pressure from the redoubtable Maud Quinn – didn't accept O'Horan's response. Instead, he schemed with her mother to arrange a hasty marriage. Their machinations, however, came to nothing.

Raymond then set off for London, centre of the British show-business world. As he never tired of telling receptive journalists who interviewed him after he'd become famous, he hitched a ride on a lorry down to the capital with only a few shillings in his pocket. Energetic self-mythologiser that he was, he'd sometimes endow himself with hobo chic by telling people that he'd travelled on the *back* of the lorry. But the romance of the story is diminished by the knowledge that the intrepid adventurer could, like many a latter-day backpacker, have been bailed out, if necessary, by his prosperous extended family.

# 6 NUDE AWAKENING

THE CAPITAL STILL hadn't shaken off the legacy of the war. It remained the city depicted in smudgy black-and-white newsreels, a city pocked by bomb sites, many of them now used as car parks; a city where the streets echoed to the hoarse shouts of newsvendors; a city whose arteries hadn't yet been clogged by vehicular cholesterol; a city with riverbanks fringed by dockside warehouses and cranes; a city of dreary furnished rooms with carpets as worn as their tenants; a city of all-night coffee stands; a city of hats, suits and overcoats; a city of smoke. Not for nothing was London nicknamed 'the Smoke'. There was smoke almost everywhere. Sulphurous clouds of the stuff billowed from the chimneys of factories and houses. It spiralled upwards from bonfires. It curled from the tips of cigarettes, pipes and cigars, plumes of it also snaking from people's mouths and noses. Its odour scented the air and often made the capital look as if it was being viewed through a flyblown net curtain, softening the hard edges of its predominantly low-rise skyline.

On arrival there, Raymond was lucky enough to find a job that provided him with food and accommodation, along with a weekly wage of between £4 and £5. His new job was in a pub in the north-eastern suburb of Walthamstow, where he was employed as barman and general dogsbody. He soon discovered that the position came with an unforeseen bonus – customers would buy him drinks.

Left with minimal expenses, it didn't take Raymond long to build up sufficient funds to stake himself to another round of the show-business game, his self-belief apparently unshaken by past failures. On the advice of a helpful Northern theatrical agent, he went for a different approach this time. Since he'd previously had trouble securing bookings in theatres, the agent had suggested an ingenious solution. It entailed creating his own shows and dovetailing himself into the line-up. His new strategy followed a fashion that dated back to the war. Seeking to deflect the financial risks, variety theatres had started using agents as surrogate producers, responsible for putting together shows.

Raymond assembled a revue which he called *Vaudeville Express*. Promoted as 'The Quick-fire, Fast-Moving Road Show Carrying The Goods of The Entertainment World', it combined a motley selection of acts. Top billing was shared between himself – 'The Man Who Baffles The Press' – and Billy Scott-Coomber, the has-been 1930s big band vocalist. Their supporting line-up included Evelyn and Her African Pigeons, Walter's Dogs and Monkeys, as well as a drag re-enactment of Little Red Riding Hood.

Predictably enough, the venue for *Vaudeville Express* was a lower-echelon provincial theatre – the Hippodrome in the Suffolk seaside town of Lowestoft. Seven performances were booked there, extending from Monday, 13 November 1950 to the following Saturday, but the prognosis for these wasn't good. Besides being scheduled for when there were no holidaymakers around, Raymond's revue faced competition from a repertory theatre and four cinemas. Worse still, attendances at the Hippodrome had been declining to the point where its management was poised to abandon full-time variety in favour of a programme of films, interspersed by the occasional stage show. Yet *Vaudeville Express* generated healthy box-office returns, aided by a shamelessly dishonest advertising campaign that claimed Raymond was on his 'Direct From America Tour'. Direct From Walthamstow would have been more accurate.

The takings from *Vaudeville Express* enabled Raymond to contemplate a viable career as a variety performer and producer. In the following months, his show moved on to theatres in Blyth, Gateshead, Hulme and West Hartlepool, bringing him a decent income of between £5 and £12 a week, though he possessed enough self-awareness to realise that his act was 'not a great success'. There was certainly little chance of it bringing him the wealth and approbation he craved, so he began to place increasing emphasis on the production side of the business.

Over in Salford, meanwhile, another potentially significant development in his life occurred – Noreen O'Horan gave birth to their son. She named the child Darryl Gabriel. But Raymond, manifesting a selfish streak, was too preoccupied by his career either to attend the birth or meet his son. Determined to ensure that Raymond made a financial contribution to their child's upbringing, O'Horan applied to Salford Stipendiary Magistrates' Court, from where she obtained a court order forcing him to pay her twenty shillings a week, the statutory minimum maintenance payment, applicable until the child's fifteenth birthday.

Around the spring of 1951 Raymond produced an untitled touring show featuring two female tap-dancers and a collection of obscure support acts, all doomed to remain that way. The prime attraction was the West Indian singer Uriel Porter, who had performed a few times on BBC radio programmes and in tiny roles in low-budget British movies.

Once the artistes had been signed up, the next step was for Raymond to ring round and obtain bookings for the show. To that end, he contacted Fred Radley, manager of the Queen's Park Hippodrome in Manchester. The two men were on good terms, but Radley refused to book the show unless it incorporated a nude act.

Since the advent of static nude tableaux at the Windmill Theatre nineteen years earlier, naked female flesh had become a frequent component of the revues that toured second- and third-rate variety theatres. These so-called 'tat shows', incorporating nudes into a miscellany of dance numbers, comic sketches, conjuring tricks and other acts, revelled under titles such as *It's Naughty and Ever So Saucy, Toujours*

*L'Amour, The French Peep Show* and, best of all, *Oooh, La, La, Oui, Oui* – titles designed to appeal to a teenage and adult male audience in search of risqué entertainment.

A typical act of this kind was Rita Atkins's Eight International Nudes, the internationalism of its participants extending no farther than Wigan. They specialised in group poses based on famous works of art, each pose introduced by their posh-voiced, professorial master of ceremonies – 'First, ladies and gentlemen, the lovely Natalya and the charming little Renée offer you "The Toilet of Venus" by Diego Velasquez from the National Gallery here in London...' The tremulous pose was then sustained for about ten seconds before the curtain came down.

Frustrated by the Lord Chamberlain's continued insistence that nude theatrical acts should remain motionless, a tongue-in-cheek lobbying group had been set up. The organisation called itself the Society for Ecdysiasts. An ecdysiast was the facetiously abstruse synonym for a stripper which the *New Yorker* critic and humorist H. L. Mencken, responding to the celebrated American burlesque performer Gypsy Rose Lee's intellectual pretensions, had coined from '*ekdusis*', the Ancient Greek word for 'shedding'. Members of the society sought to legalise striptease, currently thriving in Paris and Tokyo as well as in Gypsy's homeland. Their organisation's learned-sounding title hadn't, however, been sufficient to persuade the Lord Chamberlain to relax his regulations. For the moment British audiences had to be content with static tableaux. These were nevertheless growing increasingly popular, not just in the provinces but in London, where trade at the Windmill was so brisk that it started opening at noon.

At the time Raymond got in touch with Fred Radley, the owners of the Hippodrome chain of theatres were about to exploit this popularity by relaunching the Queen's Park venue as 'The Windmill of the North'. Rather than lose the chance of a booking there, Raymond – ever the opportunist – offered two tap-dancers, already signed up for the tour, an extra ten shillings if they agreed to pose topless as part of his show.

They'd otherwise be paid only £5 10s a week, from which they had to cover their bus fares to and from the theatre, so both girls agreed, enabling Raymond to secure a six-day booking.

The show opened at the Queen's Park Hippodrome on Monday, 18 June, promoted by posters and advertisements in the local press. Exhibiting his gift for what a later generation would call 'hype', Raymond billed Uriel Porter as 'The Famous West Indian Stage and Radio Singing Star'. He called his freshly acquired act 'Nudes in the Night'. Each striking a topless pose, the two erstwhile tap-dancers appeared separately during the first half of the show. After the interval, they briefly posed together. While they were straining not to move, they wouldn't have realised they were contributing to an event that would transform their employer's life and career which would, in turn, contribute to changes in British society few would have predicted.

# 7  MAMMARY MAN

THERE WAS SOMETHING paradoxical about a man as guarded and secretive as Raymond involving himself in a business that dissolved the boundary between public and private. Still, he found that the decorous posing of the 'Nudes in the Night' dramatically boosted ticket sales at the Queen's Park Hippodrome. His share of the box office was more than enough to justify the extra fee he'd paid the two dancers. Even a mind-reader of his circumscribed talents could tell what the audience was thinking. By chance he'd stumbled across a formula that promised to yield the profits that had so far evaded him. Reviewing it from the perspective of 1989, he characterised this formula as 'the comic, the conjurer and the girl with her tits out'.

For Raymond, the show at the Queen's Park Hippodrome proved a eureka moment, yet the occasion was akin to a physics student recreating the calculations behind some epoch-making experiment. Static nude tableaux were, after all, nothing new in the British theatre. Despite the efforts of Vivian Van Damm to take credit for the innovation, it predated *Revudeville* by almost a century.

The first recorded shows of this type held in Britain were staged in about 1847 at the Walhalla Gallery in Leicester Square. There, customers could admire Madame Warton's 'Tableaux Vivants and Poses Plastiques'. So-called 'Poses Plastiques', sometimes described more prosaically as 'living statues', usually recreated paintings and classical sculpture. To avoid prosecution for indecency, the performers – men as well as women – wore body stockings that gave the appearance of full or partial nudity. Visitors to the Walhalla Gallery, located on the site currently occupied by the Empire Cinema, were promised 'perfect and complete living embodiments of the works of the most celebrated Ancient and Modern masters both in painting and sculpture'.

Such mildly arousing tableaux had, by the late nineteenth century, become a common ingredient of music-hall bills. Suffice to say the shows at the Windmill merely reanimated a dormant tradition, rapidly spawning imitators.

Before he could capitalise on his eureka moment, Raymond had to travel to the Plaza Theatre in the Birmingham suburb of West Bromwich, where he'd persuaded the management to book one of his old-style revues for a dozen twice-nightly performances. It was called *Gay, Chez, Paree*, punctuation and meaning sacrificed to the cause of conveying unmerited exoticism. The show featured himself in the role of headline act, alongside a singer and the home-grown Ballet Montparnasse chorus line.

As the producer, he was eligible for a share of the box-office receipts. From these, he arranged to pay the entertainers appearing with him. But the revue provoked disappointing ticket sales, resulting in his share of the takings being insufficient to cover what he owed the cast.

On the strength of the production at the Queen's Park Hippodrome, Raymond signed up some more nudes, together with half a dozen conventional variety performers, for a follow-up show. This was booked into the Hippodrome as well as a string of other provincial venues – subject to the approval of each local council's Watch Committee. Since nudes were clearly responsible for all those extra ticket sales, he called his show *The Festival of Nudes*, a playful nod towards the widely publicised Festival of Britain, which had just opened on London's South Bank. While visitors to the metropolitan event marvelled at the Dome of Discovery and the futuristic Skylon, the audience for Raymond's show was left to gawp at topless girls and guffaw at the comic antics of Tubby Turner & Florence.

His show reached Manchester the week before Christmas 1951, the accompanying adverts proclaiming it 'A Paul Raymond Production'.

Inevitably, his mother soon heard about the salacious direction his business had taken, a direction unlikely to receive the stamp of maternal approbation. 'To think that a son of mine could have anything to do with a show like that!' she is reputed to have told him. Much as she disapproved of what he was doing, the two of them remained close.

Single minded enough not to be put off by his mother's censure, he approached Leslie and Lew Grade, the country's foremost theatrical agents, with a view to employing a prominent client of theirs, namely Chrystabel Leighton-Porter, one of the best-known stars of nude revue. Her fame rested on having been the life model for the cartoonist who had created 'Jane', the glamorous blonde secret agent whose tussles with Nazi spies and assorted fascist bogeymen were chronicled in the

*A publicity photo of Chrystabel Leighton-Porter, a.k.a. 'Jane'*

*Daily Mirror*'s hugely popular 1940s cartoon strip. Each instalment tended to culminate in her somehow losing her clothes and wearing only a bra and frilly knickers. Among British servicemen, Jane had been a favourite pin-up, her image painted on the turrets of tanks and the fuselage of aircraft, its morale-boosting effect reputedly leading Winston Churchill to hail her Britain's secret weapon against the Nazis.

Parlaying this fame-by-proxy for first-hand celebrity, Leighton-Porter had built a career in post-war variety shows. For these, she posed in the nude, danced in her underwear and mangled a repertoire of songs. Such was her box-office appeal that Raymond gave her a rolling contract guaranteeing her forty-eight weeks' work every year. Alongside the usual blend of fully clothed artistes, he cast her in his latest show, the catchily titled *We Strip Tonight*. But this time he expanded the nude element through the inclusion of a troupe called the Palm Beach Models.

Far from trying to conceal his murky background as a black marketeer, Raymond – now twenty-six years old – cultivated an appearance that didn't suggest he was in show business. Instead, he resembled a caricature of a spiv, his broad-shouldered suits and pencil moustache offering a pungent reminder of street-corner salesmanship.

Still plugging away with his career as a stage clairvoyant, he got to know many of the often idiosyncratic characters who populated the world of provincial variety. One of these was the black Jamaican singer Archie Lewis, who specialised in slow-tempo romantic ballads. Another was Phyllis Dixey, then in her early forties, her wartime celebrity ebbing fast. Sometimes mistakenly hailed as the first British star of striptease, she'd imported the American craze for fan dancing. Naked apart from a couple of huge feathered fans, Dixey would prance round the stage, using the fans to restrict the audience to occasional glimpses of flesh.

'She never allowed anyone backstage while she was on,' Raymond recollected. 'She looked like a schoolteacher, you know. Very prim and proper, with her hair in a bun. And she could always get round the Watch Committees if she ever went a bit far.'

Of all the people Raymond encountered backstage in provincial theatres, none would have a more far-reaching effect on his life than Jean Bradley, an auburn-haired dancer who, during March 1952, appeared with him on a variety bill he was promoting. Six years his junior, she had a Nottinghamshire accent, delicately beautiful, dark-eyed features, plus an attractive figure and a personality exuding vivacity and intelligence. Together with her skill as a dancer, these earned her the role of head chorus girl in the Ballet Montparnasse. She was an obvious target for the advances of Raymond and other heterosexual male colleagues.

With sexual vanity common to his age group, Raymond often claimed that he never had to pursue women, that they were just naturally attracted to him, yet Bradley seemed impervious to his self-professed magnetism. If he was going to have any chance to win her over, he had to adopt a less passive approach, so he launched a seduction campaign. The trouble was, she disliked his spivvy get-up. That month, before his efforts could make much headway, she left the show and set up a dance

*Phyllis Dixey striking a pose sufficiently unrevealing to use on posters for her shows*

act with another girl. But she remained within his orbit because she asked him to be her agent. In that guise he secured some bookings for her new act, his work as an agent yielding more rapid dividends than his efforts as a seducer. Despite the lack of encouragement, he persisted with his amorous pursuit of Bradley. By the time she took up a booking as an entertainer at a Butlin's holiday camp in Wales that summer, he'd won her over. When he met some friends of hers – a married couple named Jan and Joan Harding – who were also performing there, Raymond was introduced as her boyfriend.

Unconsciously echoing the cross-class relationship between Raymond's parents, Bradley turned out to come from a staunchly working-class family. Her mother was a cleaner and her father was an unskilled labourer, living in a poky house in the north Nottinghamshire coalfields – facts scarcely calculated to endear her to Raymond's snobbish mother. As a means of compensating for a sense of social inferiority, Bradley took to fibbing about how she'd been a dancer with the Sadler's Wells Ballet.

Intimate though she and Raymond had become, *he* resorted to a more corrupting brand of dishonesty. This took the form of not telling her about his son, Darryl. Nor did he mention that Darryl's aggrieved mother, aware of the upturn in his professional fortunes, had just taken legal action against him.

While Raymond was enjoying his summer romance with Bradley, Noreen O'Horan attended Salford Stipendiary Magistrates' Court, where she applied for an increase in his maintenance payments. Citing his improved financial position, she won her case, the judge ordering Raymond to pay her £1 10s a week.

Victory was achieved at a high psychological cost for her. In the wake of the court hearing, she became terrified that Raymond might develop a possessive interest in their infant son and fight to obtain custody. Nothing could have so eloquently demonstrated just how little she knew Raymond, who was content to replicate his own absent father's lack of curiosity about his son.

# 8 STRIP! STRIP! HOORAY!

**F**ROM THE EARLY SUMMER of 1952, *We Strip Tonight* toured Britain. Towards the end of that year, the income from the show allowed Raymond, who had finally retired from the stage, to install his business – now trading as the Paul Raymond Variety Agency – in offices on Charing Cross Road. This was a street associated with three things: bookshops, sheet-music publishers and showbiz agents. A Charing Cross Road address projected a reassuring message that Raymond was at the epicentre of his chosen profession. Not that there was anything particularly reassuring about the offices themselves. These were above Ferrari's Milk Bar at No. 156, a four-storey building no more than a minute's walk from Tottenham Court Road tube station. He also shared the address with three other theatrical agents and a sheet-music publisher.

Each day he had to thread his way past performers loitering on the pavement outside, killing time before appointments with his neighbours. Reached by a series of narrow staircases, probably sheathed in brown lino that had been scuffed by the shoes of countless visitors, his new offices consisted of three attic rooms. The back room overlooked St Giles Circus while the front one had a view of the Astoria Cinema as well as the busy junction with Oxford Street. Like other producer/agents, Raymond would have been approached by a stream of hopefuls, buoyant youngsters interspersed with 'resting' veterans whose nicotine-stained fingers and routines were every bit as threadbare as their clothes, to which the fried-fish odour of provincial digs still clung. Song-and-dance teams, conjurors, acrobats, nudes, comedians, memory men, trick cyclists, ventriloquists, singers, mimics, jugglers, tap-dancers and all manner of novelty acts would have trooped through his offices, some brandishing crumpled press clippings, others bragging about how their last show had gone down a storm.

By the autumn of 1952 Raymond's romance with Jean Bradley had progressed to the point where she'd stayed overnight with him several times. Since they were sleeping together on a regular basis, he suggested that she move in with him. But she wouldn't countenance his proposal, cohabitation not yet being a socially acceptable alternative to wedlock. She was insistent they should get married, though she must have known that marriage to Raymond would be tantamount to becoming part of a *ménage à trois*, the role of marital interloper, of wheedling mistress taken by the Paul Raymond Variety Agency.

He was never entirely off duty – even at night. Next to the bed he kept a notepad on which he'd scribble ideas for revue titles. Neither he nor the majority of his rivals, however, possessed the verbal dexterity to challenge their New York counterparts, whose shows bore inspired titles such as *Anatomy and Cleopatra*, *Julius Teaser* and *Panties' Inferno*.

That November, less than a year after they'd met, Raymond acceded to his girlfriend's demands and married her. He couldn't, however, afford to present her with anything more than a plain gold wedding ring. After their marriage they set up home in a flat at 34 Cambridge Court, a giant, six-storey interwar block on the West End stretch of Edgware Road, one of London's busiest streets. Even with the windows shut, their flat remained noisy, the sound of traffic punctuated by the electrical whirr and clatter of trains passing through Edgware Road underground station.

His appetite for work undiminished by marriage, Raymond put in long hours at his offices. Visitors to these were reminded of his credentials by the framed posters for his suggestively titled revues, lining the room where he conducted most of his business. The posters advertised shows such as *Abreast of Beauty*, numerous permutations of the words 'folies', 'nudes', 'striptease' and 'Paris' garnishing them.

For the 1950s British male, the words 'Paris', 'French' and 'Continental' were instilled with sexual connotations, partly because so many pornographic books had either been imported from across the Channel or translated from French that they had acquired the generic label 'French books'. The large number of French prostitutes, nicknamed 'Fifis', who had plied their trade in pre-war London must also have served to give these words sexual associations so calculatedly exploited by Raymond and his fellow tat-show impresarios.

Though the posters for his shows still bore the line 'Paul Raymond Presents', his business had evolved into a joint enterprise since his wedding. In recognition of this, he installed Jean as a company director. There can't have been many firms with board members required to fulfil her range of responsibilities. Besides producing and choreographing the revues for her husband, the sense of professional collaboration apparently nourishing her marriage, she chose the models for them and even appeared in several shows. These toured such exotic locations as Margate, where, under the guise of 'Zsa-Zsa, the Brazilian Bombshell', she performed the Tassel Dance, a routine originated in the burlesque theatres of 1920s America. It required her to wiggle her breasts until the tassels spun so fast they resembled the propellers on the twin-engined planes Raymond would have seen taxiing along the runway at Tern Hill.

Collins Music Hall in north London staged the final night of a week-long run of *Scanties and Fancies* on Saturday, 25 April 1953. Two days later this historic venue, scene of many performances by Victorian and Edwardian music-hall luminaries, hosted another nude revue, this time one of Raymond's productions, billed as 'The Sauciest Show of the Century'.

Here Raymond began an improbable friendship with someone worthy of portrayal by Alec Guinness or, perhaps, Wilfrid Hyde-White in an Ealing comedy. That person was the Reverend Edwyn Young, a forty-year-old High Church Anglican vicar who held the post of chaplain to Collins Music Hall. Cutting an incongruous but chatty figure amid the showgirls, singers, nudes and comedians, Young wore clerical robes and black-framed glasses that contrasted with his prematurely grey hair. Like Raymond, he was an improbable middle-class intruder in this shabby theatrical milieu with which he'd long been fascinated. Even though he strongly disapproved of nude shows, he didn't let that get in the way of either his emergent friendship with Raymond or his job of counselling troubled performers.

Inculcated with his mother's staunch royalist sentiments, Raymond would have been looking forward to the coronation of Queen Elizabeth II, due to take place in June 1953. But he'd surely have been oblivious to its long-term effect on his business. The prospect of being able to watch live coverage on the BBC acting as a potent lure, television ownership almost doubled. Though there were still only 2,142 British households with televisions, the small screen was threatening to challenge other forms of entertainment, notably the cinema and theatre. For now, that challenge was no clearer than the fuzzy images on those television screens – nothing to panic Raymond and his colleagues.

Business carried on much as before. The main difference was that nude shows were becoming an ever more prominent constituent of variety bills in all except top venues such as the London Palladium, where the management could afford to import American showbiz stars of the calibre of Frank Sinatra and Danny Kaye. With so many rival nude revues vying for bookings and ticket sales, Raymond and his wife endeavoured to fend off their competitors by devising shows that embraced some distinctive novelty. The earliest of these was *Nudes in Ice*, one of four Raymond productions simultaneously touring the country during 1953. Its title attraction comprised an igloo constructed out of blocks of ice obtained from a fishmonger. Inside were two unfortunate nudes, shivering while a third balanced precariously on a rubber mat laid across the crown of the igloo.

For inexplicable reasons the show proved more popular in the North than elsewhere in the country. Raymond quickly became accustomed to such inconsistencies. As a jocular rule of thumb, he said the most picturesque English towns offered the best venues, Bath and Chester being especially profitable.

The attitude of local councils also differed from place to place. Certain councils insisted on him altering the wording on his posters, so that specific words were transposed, 'glamour' replacing 'striptease', and 'girls' replacing 'nudes'. There were even a few councils, Sunderland among them, which wouldn't allow nude shows to appear within their boundaries.

Audience behaviour offered another perplexing variable. At some venues the audience would sit in rapt silence. At others nudes would be sprayed with soda fountains or reduced to shrieking, breast-quivering hysterics when mischievous customers released mice onto the stage. Worst of all was the Glasgow Empire, which lived up to its intimidating reputation when Raymond's nudes were pelted with beer bottles and assorted missiles.

In spite of these problems, not to mention the ferocious competition, his business was flourishing. According to Raymond's old friend Frank Fraser, word of his success filtered through to the gangster Jacob Colmore, alias Jack Comer but better known as Jack Spot. The child of Polish immigrants who had settled in the East End, Spot was only in his early forties yet he'd been the dominant figure in the London underworld for the best part of two decades. Backed by his feared enforcer, Morris Goldstein, aka 'Moishe Blue Boy', he intimidated anyone who dared to stand up to him or try to snatch a share of the capital's protection racket, nowhere more lucrative than in the West End. Small businesses, typically restaurants, pubs and drinking clubs, were the favoured targets. So-called 'strong-arm boys' would be sent round to smash up the place or start a fight with the customers. Once the owner had tasted the disruption this could cause, Spot or one of his sidekicks would, in exchange for a regular payment, offer to 'mind the premises' and stop any recurrence of whatever trouble they'd orchestrated. Alternatively, the racketeers sometimes dispensed with the preamble and concentrated on extorting weekly envelopes full of cash. 'The fact that the proprietors of these types of businesses were often skating on thin ice as far as the licensing and other laws were concerned made them reluctant to complain to the police,' one former officer recalled. Besides, the West End police had an appalling reputation for running their own protection rackets.

Fraser remembered Raymond complaining that Spot had visited his Charing Cross Road offices and demanded a regular cut from the money generated by his touring shows. Instead of paying up or going to the authorities, Fraser said Raymond sought help from Billy Hill, now beginning to surpass Spot as the capital's top mobster.

In most senses Hill, who specialised in armed robberies, conformed to the Hollywood image of a gangland boss. He was a sharp dresser with a fondness for dark suits, trilbies and white display handkerchiefs. He usually had a cigarette drooping from the corner of his mouth. He had a polished manner and a soft voice that amplified the menace radiated by his battered but still handsome features. He had the capacity to inflict cold-blooded violence, his preferred weapon being a knife. And he possessed a flair for meticulous planning, recently manifested in the successful ambush of a Royal Mail van carrying £287,000 in used banknotes.

'Raymond knew that Bill's star was on the rise, so he went to Bill for help,' Fraser said. 'Bill gave Raymond the assistance he needed – at a cost, of course. Just a one-off payment instead of the regular payments Jack Spot wanted.'

# 9 STRIPTEASEY-WEASY RAYMOND

FEMALE NUDITY WAS the main selling point of Raymond's shows, yet he didn't *just* employ nudes. He still hired other types of variety artistes. One such performer was Jean's friend Jan Harding, whom Raymond engaged as a comedian. Another was a hip-wiggling, finger-snapping Welsh teenager named Shirley Bassey, a former factory worker slogging her way up the foothills of her singing career. For a salary of £18 a week, almost half that of the four top-line acts, Raymond booked her to appear seventh on the bill of a nude-free revue called *Hot From Harlem*, assembled in collaboration with Joe Collins, father of the actress Joan Collins. Predominantly a comedy and dance show, it visited the Palace Theatre, Leicester, and comparable provincial venues. There, Bassey was given spurious billing as 'Broadway's New Singing Sensation'.

Courtesy of countless posters displayed in theatres and on hoardings across the country, each emblazoned with the prefix 'Paul Raymond Presents', *Hot From Harlem*'s co-producer was on the way to transforming his name into a well-known brand, synonymous not with singers, dancers and comedians but with semi-naked women. His self-applied surname had, at the same time, acquired a serendipitous sheen of Gallic sophistication and, by extension, *Gallic sauciness*. The element of sophistication derived from the unlikely figure of Raymond Bessone, a hairdresser who ran a chain of ultra-fashionable West End salons. Despite being a heterosexual, working-class Cockney, Bessone had adopted a French accent, an effeminate manner and a foppish dress sense. In the course of a 1954 television appearance, he'd demonstrated his haircutting technique by mincing round the model, snipping off a 'teasy-weasy bit' here and a 'teasy-weasy bit' there. A catchphrase was born. From then on, Bessone became 'Teasy Weasy' Raymond, pronounced '*Ray*-monde'. Over the next decade or more, there would be a subliminal and – for Paul Raymond at least – advantageous connection between them, between the 'Toscanini of hairdressing' and his namesake.

As the summer of 1954 approached, Raymond made plans for his next production. He called it *Bal Tabarin* in honour of the risqué Paris music hall of the same title. The show, which was booked to open in Morecambe that June, featured a dance number entitled 'Paris By Night'. In preparation, Raymond ordered a set of can-can outfits from Granon Stage Productions, a Tooting-based theatrical costumier. He also placed an order from the same company for the other costumes he needed, gypsy blouses and G-strings among them. Altogether the order set him back £85.

Only a couple of days before the show was due to premiere, the clothes were sent directly to Morecambe, where the chorus girls were rehearsing, presumably under the tutelage of his wife. News then reached Raymond that the girls were refusing to wear the G-strings and grumbling about many of the other garments they were expected to wear. They said the costumes were far too brief, the gypsy blouses were transparent, the skirts bore no relation to traditional frilly can-can skirts, and the G-strings would snap as soon as whoever was wearing them walked across the stage. This led Raymond to insist on the costumier paying to despatch the offending items back to London for inspection.

When Raymond saw the can-can costumes, he realised these were 'quite useless'. Since there wasn't enough time to obtain replacements, he was forced to drop the 'Paris By Night' number from the Morecambe show. Furious about what had happened, he sued the costumier. But his problems with the wardrobe for *Bal Tabarin* represented a comparatively minor setback for his thriving business. The same could be said of Wigan Town Council's decision to ban one of his revues from being staged there.

In a money-spinning demonstration of his talent for providing the public with just what it wanted, that summer his shows played to packed houses in provincial theatres across the country. *Paris After Dark* – not to be confused with the ill-fated 'Paris By Night' dance routine – was among those shows. Lest the reference to nocturnal Paree should fail to conjure suitably lewd images, the show was subtitled 'The Web of Desire', and adverts for it drew attention to 'The Fabulous G-String Girl', who promised to 'show you what happens in a French bedroom'.

Other revues touring Britain under the Raymond banner included *Piccadilly Peepshow*, *Folies Parisienne* and *The Jane Show*, the latter starring Chrystabel Leighton-Porter, who was justifying her salary. 'She would play two weeks in a town,' Raymond said. 'She would go back two or three times – and every time she went back she played to more money than she had in the first place.'

Constantly on the lookout for ways to refresh the nude-show genre and satisfy jaded audiences, Raymond came up with a cunning innovation, first deployed in *Folies Parisienne*. By presenting the models on rotating stages, he could promote them as 'the only moving nudes'.

Yet he could – in a legalistic sense – still comply with the Lord Chamberlain's ruling about nudes remaining motionless.

*Folies Parisienne* was also marketed on the basis of 'The Eurasian Voodoo Dance', described as 'A Raging Torrent of Emotion Which Even Nature Cannot Control'. If that wasn't alluring enough, there was 'The Banned Reefer Dance, performed by The Dangerous Girl

With The Low Neckline'. And there were the 'Harlem Nudes', who would treat audiences to the 'taunting, scantily clad Native Mating Dance', seen in 'stark-naked reality'.

Though Raymond had no hesitation in pocketing the generous rewards from such unequivocal theatrical sexploitation, he still valued the tenets of middle-class propriety enough to deny the true nature of his business. In his eagerness to dispel the notion that his shows were the natural habitat of goggle-eyed masturbators, he assured a sceptical journalist from the left-wing *Daily Herald* that his revues were attracting 'family audiences', that 'children rising from infancy to the teens' were 'taken to his shows by their doting elders'.

The consequent newspaper article provided his business with free publicity and fed his growing fame. Just under three months after his first appearance in the national press, his legal action against Granon Stage Productions reached Westminster Crown Court. Raymond turned up there with a hamper full of garments supplied by the company. Called to give evidence, he proffered a can-can outfit and a pair of chorus girls' knickers as examples of sub-standard workmanship. When he explained to the court that these unsatisfactory costumes had led to the cancellation of the performance of 'Paris By Night', the judge asked – with a hint of facetiousness – whether the show could have been staged *without* costumes.

Raymond was followed into the witness box by twenty-two-year-old Bunty Colwyn, the first of two chorus girls from the troupe that had appeared in Morecambe. She said the costumes had provoked a mutiny. 'They were more what a nude would wear than for girls to dance round the stage in,' she added. To illustrate what she'd said, she flourished a pair of panties, made from little more than multicoloured feathers.

'Is that the *whole* costume?' the judge enquired. 'Are you complaining it is too big or too small?'

Colwyn replied that the costumes were so small none of the girls could get them on, and the G-strings were badly made.

After he'd heard the costumier's defence, which proved as flimsy as the costumes, the judge declared, 'Two chorus girls, who seem very decent and straightforward, have said the garments were so brief that they felt they looked naked in them. Whether they would have felt completely dressed if the garments had been an inch bigger, I do not know.' He then awarded £39 10s damages to Raymond and dismissed a counter-claim against him for the expense of transporting the costumes from Morecambe to London.

While Raymond savoured the verdict, Noreen O'Horan settled into the routine of a single parent, struggling to support their son by working at Belle View Zoo & Amusement Park in Manchester. She held jobs that ranged from selling horoscopes to riding on the handlebars of a motorbike as it circled the Wall of Death. Even though her erstwhile boyfriend hadn't so far made any attempt to see their infant son, she still feared that Raymond might seek custody of him. In an effort to make Darryl hard to trace, O'Horan kept him out of formal education.

She needn't have gone to these lengths because her ex-boyfriend was far more interested in himself and his career. Pursuing fresh markets for his shows, he took one of them to the Continent around the end of 1954. At the beginning of the following year he repeated the experiment. Second time round he transported what appears to have been a large, well-paid variety troupe to Vienna. But their show, popular in Britain, didn't appeal to the Austrian audience. Raymond found himself saddled with such a whopping bill that he was on the verge of bankruptcy. Unable to cover his losses and survive on the income from his other shows currently touring Britain, he applied for the post of managing director of the Savoy Theatre, a council-owned former-cinema-turned-variety-theatre not far from the middle of Clacton-on-Sea. During the third week of April 1955 he was appointed to the job. It embraced not only management duties but also responsibility for booking shows. Like the town's other variety theatres, the Savoy – which he was permitted to rebrand as 'A Paul Raymond Theatre' – only operated during the summer.

Since commuting from London wasn't a viable option, the Raymonds decamped from their Cambridge Court flat to a large semi-detached house at 91 St Osyth Road, close to the Savoy. With the summer looming, he had little time in which to secure a suitable show. He booked a touring revue of the type he'd often compiled in collaboration with his wife. The booking had been left so late, however, that the show wasn't available until well after the beginning of the holiday season. And it was already booked elsewhere from mid-August onwards.

Despite its scant Gallic connections, the show was billed as being 'From Paris' and called the *Fabulous Montmartre Revue*. It starred Frederick 'The Voice' Ferrari, a veteran tenor famous for his lush renditions of sentimental songs. The line-up also featured a singer, a pair of slapstick acrobats, two female impersonators, a comedian, some nudes and a troupe of showgirls advertised as 'Les Beaux Mannequins de Montmartre'.

Tickets went on sale during the first week of June, though the *Fabulous Montmartre Revue* wasn't due to open for another fourteen days. Its takings can't have been improved by the rail strike which reduced the normal flood of tourists, making competition for customers even hotter than usual. Around then, Jean discovered she was pregnant. She and Raymond could hardly have chosen a less auspicious moment to become parents. They were already facing enough problems without the added pressure of raising a child. To compound these, Jean turned out to be expecting twins. In spite of the difficulties that beset her and Raymond, she regarded their marriage as being 'very good'.

On the evening of Monday, 20 June, the *Fabulous Montmartre Revue* received its Clacton premiere. 'It's a bright show, dominated – naturally – by the female form,' pronounced the local paper.

The timing of the show's belated opening was fortuitous, a combination of fine weather and the resolution of the rail strike having coaxed holidaymakers back to the town. Though the Savoy's show was in direct competition with three other summer revues – *Joys Bells* at the West Cliff

Theatre, *Showtime* at the Jolly Roger Theatre and *Ocean Revue of 1955* at the Ocean Theatre – it had one distinct advantage. None of its rivals boasted nudes. Even so, its box-office receipts weren't too impressive.

Three years earlier, Clacton Urban District Council had employed a publicity manager who spent each close season promoting the resort in cities across Britain. His work helped to lure vast crowds to the town that summer. These reached their zenith during the first weekend of August, when about 100,000 visitors arrived, prompting the joke that the beach was so crowded there was no room for the incoming tide. Unable to find accommodation, hundreds of people slept in the seafront shelters and beneath the pier. Offended by the sight of nudes on stage at the Savoy, one of the holidaymakers complained that Raymond's show should be banned.

There were still several weeks of the season remaining when the *Fabulous Montmartre Revue* ended its Clacton run on Saturday, 20 August, yet Raymond hadn't been able to find a replacement show. Instead, he'd taken the imaginative step of booking the most novel of novelty acts: a rotund, forty-year-old Manchester housewife named Marie Austin who, under the name of 'Musical Marie', performed as a 'non-stop pianist'.

Sitting on stage at 10 a.m. the following Monday, she began her attempt to break what, she claimed, was the world record for playing the piano continuously – 132 hours, set by a West German pianist the previous March. Her audience included not only paying customers but also her manager and trainer, plus members of the Clacton Red Cross and St John's Ambulance Brigade, who were there just in case she required medical assistance. During the evenings the audience sang along to her heavy-fingered renditions of tunes by Ivor Novello and others.

'Good thing I'm not musical, otherwise I'd never stand it,' her trainer quipped to a reporter.

She kept herself going with a daily allocation of about a gallon of tea and 100 cigarettes, interspersed with soup, boiled eggs, fruit juice and glasses of brandy. Whenever she needed to use a chamber pot or put on fresh clothes, she'd continue playing one handed. The audience was, meanwhile, briefly ushered out.

To stimulate interest in her feat of endurance, periodic press releases were issued. At 6 a.m. on the fourth day, she was visited by a journalist from the *East Essex Gazette*. Her fatigue manifesting itself in her lethargic playing, she announced that she wanted a change of clothes. Arthur Lea, her trainer, told everyone to 'Hop it!' By the time they returned, she'd swapped her nightie and silk dressing gown for a voluminous evening dress made from fabric that resembled tinfoil.

That afternoon a press release was issued stating, 'She is almost exhausted and depressed. Doctor to examine her today.'

Musical Marie aimed to finish her marathon at 11 p.m. on Saturday, 27 August. As she neared her 133-hour target, so many people wanted to see her that the audience wasn't permitted to linger. In a seemingly endless procession, they perambulated round the theatre, gawping at her.

A reporter from the *East Essex Gazette* had, by then, discovered that her world-record claim was invalid because she'd achieved an identical feat in Cornwall two weeks earlier. Raymond was probably behind the astute decision to ban the press from talking to her, in the process sparing her any awkward questions.

Half an hour before Marie finished playing, spectators were allowed to sit down. The theatre rapidly filled, bringing her total audience that week to more than twenty thousand. When the clock in the auditorium showed 11 p.m., the people watching her cheered, then sang 'Rule, Britannia' and the National Anthem.

Such a large crowd had gathered outside that the road was blocked. A spontaneous round of 'For she's a jolly good fellow' greeted her as she emerged from the theatre, braced by St John's Ambulancemen.

# 10 BREAST OF BRITISH

JUST WHEN RAYMOND and his wife, now five months pregnant, could have done with a period of stability, their interlude on the Essex coast was cut short. Though the town councillors who had appointed him should have known what to expect once he took charge, they were so horrified by the inclusion of nudes in his show that they dispensed with his services.

At the end of that summer he and his wife returned to London, where he speedily revived his business as a promoter. Soon he had eight nude revues on the road – almost half the total number of such shows touring Britain. His recent bitter experience with the costumes for *Bal Tabarin* led him to set up his own wardrobe department. He also hired staff to design and construct scenery for his shows. And he acquired a fleet of second-hand buses, used to ferry his employees between theatres.

Often Raymond would accompany his productions as they travelled the country. Prior to the creation of a motorway network, those journeys were tiringly elongated. Stopping for a toilet break and a meal at various transport cafés, he kept bumping into Paul Lincoln, an Australian wrestling promoter who appeared in his own shows under the *nom de guerre* of 'Doctor Death'. 'Raymond was a very nice, likeable chap,' Lincoln remembered. 'We got on well and always had a laugh.'

Lincoln – a burly but otherwise surprisingly small man – doubled as co-owner of the 2i's, the most famous and fashionable of the new Italian-style coffee bars popping up all round Soho. Along with his business partner, Lincoln had transformed the cellar of the 2i's, self-styled 'Home of the Stars', into Britain's pre-eminent venue for teenagers to dance and listen to live skiffle as well as rock 'n' roll, played by the likes of Tommy Steele and Joe Brown. Talking to Lincoln about the 2i's may have influenced Raymond not only to consider setting up his own Soho venue but also to look for a comparable trend to exploit.

In expanding the number of revues he was packaging, there was a danger that their quality might suffer. Aware of this, Raymond and his pregnant wife lavished considerable attention on each show. He even paid for specialist advice from the female impersonator Danny La Rue, whom he'd known for several years. Raymond had still been working as a mind-reader when he'd first got to know the vivacious La Rue, who was at that point employed as a window-dresser in a London department store. Now in his mid-twenties, La Rue was performing a popular drag act at Churchill's, a glamorous cabaret club at 160 New Bond Street, which attracted celebrity customers from all over the world. La Rue always insisted that he *imitated* women rather than parodying them. Ironically, Raymond asked La Rue to teach some of his chorus girls and nudes how to be more ladylike in the way they walked, posed and conducted themselves.

Describing the ideal nude, Raymond said, 'She must be refined and artistic – and dress well off-stage. The men recognise our girls in the street. If they were flashily dressed and hung round milk bars, it would give the show a bad name. They must be respectable.'

Girls who failed to conform to the requisite standards were liable to provoke his favourite, somewhat camp expression of disapproval: 'You'd never see the Queen doing *that*.'

The increased scale of his business encouraged him to turn it into a limited company. He called his firm the Paul Raymond Organisation, a title modelled on the J. Arthur Rank Organisation, one of the companies founded by Britain's leading movie magnate. With the profits from his touring revues, Raymond was able to swap his seedy Charing Cross Road offices for smart new premises. In keeping with these, he gave his agency a smart new name which conveyed an image entirely at variance with reality. The new name was the Paul Raymond *Theatrical* Agency. You'd think he was dealing with Laurence Olivier, Ralph Richardson and John Gielgud rather than the Two Rexanos, Coral 'The Body' Gaye and Viki 'The Bust' Lorraine.

His latest offices were at 45–46 Chandos Place, a four-storey, Dutch-gabled building that backed on to the Coliseum Theatre. From there, bent over a paper-strewn desk, overlooked by a plaster bust of Shakespeare, who was yet to inspire any nude tableaux, Raymond wrote poster copy, secured bookings and made plans to add two more shows to his inventory of touring productions.

As a gauge of his rising status within the variety business, during mid-January 1956 he received a visit from Arnold Russell, a newspaper columnist who wanted to profile him. Asked about his revues, Raymond referred to a show currently in rehearsal which featured 'a sensational knife-throwing act in which knives are thrown around the nudes'. Unable to suppress his pride, Raymond informed Russell that another of his forthcoming shows included an act in which nudes posed in a lions' cage while the trainer put the animals through their paces. 'And there's no fake about it either,' Raymond told him.

'What happens if a nude in the lions' den has a mouse run over her foot and in the uproar a lion eats the trainer?' Russell enquired.

'I have just told you,' Raymond answered tetchily. '*Nudes make news.* Provincial bookings are terrific because the customers are waiting for something to happen.'

Mention of the nudes in the lions' den and the knife-throwing act led Russell's article to raise the light-hearted yet ultimately prescient question, 'Surely there should be a Society for the Protection of Nudes?'

Six days after the profile of Raymond had been published, hailing him as 'the most go-ahead impresario in the variety business', Jean gave birth to twins. But the Raymonds' joy was tempered by the fact that one of the

------PROGRAMME------
Week commencing MONDAY, SEPTEMBER 5th, 1955

PAUL RAYMOND Presents

## "BURLESQUE"

1 OVERTURE

2 WELCOME TO HOLLYWOOD
  Denis Brothers & June, Kenny Noble, The Sex-Appeal
  Girls and Company

3 NEVER A DULL MOMENT
  Harry Shiels, Jan Harding and Co.

4 THE LEGEND OF THE GLASS MOUNTAIN
  Denis Brothers & June, Kenny Noble, The Sex-Appeal
  Girls and Nudes in the Glass Mountain

5 HARRY SHIELS & JAN HARDING

6 MUSIC FOR MODERNS ... Kenny Noble & Del Denester

7 GALAXY OF GLAMOUR
  Miss Blandish and Her Famous Moving Nudes

8 DRUMMING OUT THE LAFFS... ... Harry Shiels

9 MAMBO MEXICANA
  Billy & Brian Denis with June, Kenny Noble, The Sex-Appeal
  Girls, The Glamorous Nudes and Ensemble

10 INTERVAL
  IVAN DOZIN AND THE PALACE PLAYERS

Visit our Bars for Refreshments at Popular Prices
Chocolates and Ices on Sale from the Attendants

---

11 ARTISTRY IN DANCE
  Denis Brothers, The Sex-Appeal Girls, The Artistic Models

12 THE AERIAL DAREDEVIL ... ... Saballa

13 TREBLE ROMANCE Harry Shiels, Jan Harding and Co.

14 MODERNISTIC MOODS
  The Sex-Appeal Girls with The Four Vogues

15 MAGICAL MANIACS Harry Shiels, Jan. Harding and Co.

16 STARS OF SEX-APPEAL
  Glamorous Nudes in Poses which brought Famous Film Stars
  fame. These are not intended to depict or impersonate the Film
  Stars themselves.
  SIMONE SILVA'S Nude Pose, from the waist upwards, with
  Robert Mitchum.
  HEDY LAMARR'S Pose from the film "Ecstasy".
  GIPSY ROSE LEE, Famous Pose of America's Queen of
  Glamour.
  MARILYN MONROE'S Internationally Known Calendar Pose.
  SABRINA'S Nationally publicised Nude Photographic pose.

17 THE MINISTER OF ENJOYMENT ... Harry Shiels

18 AMERICAN CABARET
  The Sex-Appeal Girls, The Glamorous Models and featuring
  The Denis Brothers and June

19 THE COMPANY WISH YOU ALL GOODNIGHT

Production and Choreography : JEAN RAYMOND
Decor : Paul Raymond Scenic Studios (designed and constructed by George Flowers).
Costumes : Paul Raymond Theatrical Costumiers (designed and executed by Vicky
Raymond). Comedy material by Harry Shiels. Stockings by Kayser Bondor. Stak-
a-bye and Fold-a-bye steel furniture by Sebel Products Ltd.

| Company Manager | ... | For | ... | JAN HARDING |
| Stage Director | ... | PAUL RAYMOND | ... | VICTOR SABALLA |
| Musical Director | ... | PRODUCTIONS | ... | DEL DENESTER |

See the "Evening News", "Star" and "Evening Standard" for
our attractions

The Management reserve the right to refuse admission to the Theatre and cannot be
responsible for the absence of any Artists through illness or any other circumstances.

Production and Variety Acts being copyright, Photographing in this Theatre is forbidden.

n accordance with the requirements of the London County Council—
  1.—The public may leave at the end of the performance or exhibition by all exit doors
and such doors must at that time be open. 2.—All gangways, corridors, staircases and
external passageways intended for exits shall be kept strictly free from obstruction, either
permanent or temporary. 3.—Persons shall not be permitted to stand or sit in any of the
gangways intersecting the seating, or to sit in any of the other gangways. If standing be
permitted in the gangways at the sides and rear of the seating, it shall be strictly limited to
the number indicated in the notices exhibited in these positions. 4.—The safety curtain
must be lowered in the presence of each audience.

In the interest of Public Health, this Theatre is disinfected throughout with JEYE'S FLUID

---

*Programme listings for a Paul Raymond Production at the Chelsea Palace Theatre in London. Billing one of the performers as 'Miss Blandish' is a potentially titillating allusion to the heroine of* No Orchids For Miss Blandish *(1939), James Hadley Chase's bestselling, sexually sadistic hardboiled novel. Another reference that has, for most people nowadays, lost its erotic fizz is the act based on a 'nationally publicised nude photographic pose' by 'Sabrina', pseudonym of Norma Sykes, the buxom teenage precursor of Jordan and other pin-ups. Hidden in the small-print, there's an unsavoury announcement that dispels any doubts about the masturbatory habits of the show's audience. 'In the interest of Public Health,' the programme declares, 'this theatre is disinfected throughout with Jeye's Fluid'* babies was stillborn. The other was a healthy girl, on whom Raymond doted. He and Jean named her Deborah Jane.

His daughter's birth prompted Raymond to move his family into a new £8,000 house at 49 Nassau Road, a pleasant street in the well-heeled south London riverside suburb of Barnes. The Raymonds offered a conspicuous contrast to their immediate neighbours. Two of those neighbours were unmarried, Oxbridge-educated sisters living bookish and cerebral lives. Nearly thirty years later, the elder sister would describe her first sighting of Raymond. 'Some people moved into the house next-door, and one afternoon I saw a tall, balding, rather academic-looking man walking in the garden, holding in his hand what appeared to be an ostrich feather,' she wrote. Adding an extra layer of incongruity to the juxtaposition, the younger of the sisters was Barbara Pym, a novelist beginning to acquire a small readership who appreciated her subtle portraits of chaste spinsterdom. Not that either Raymond or Jean would have been remotely conscious of her work.

Fatherhood doesn't seem to have distracted Raymond from his growing business, his deeply ingrained ambition sharpened perhaps by a sense of financial responsibility towards Deborah. Just as he'd planned, he had ten revues touring the country within weeks of her birth. He'd also succeeded in getting four of those shows into the two biggest theatre circuits, run by Moss Empires and Stoll, companies once reluctant to programme his revues. Those four productions would consequently be playing in theatres which, in some cases, accommodated more than two thousand customers.

On the surface at least, Raymond had abundant justification for feeling bullish about the future. 'A good show will always pack 'em in despite television or cinema,' he told one journalist. And he said to another, 'The public want to see something they can't see on TV. They *can't* see nudes on TV.'

Yet it would soon become apparent that the opening months of 1956 were not the prelude to an ever more successful career as a promoter of touring shows. They were, instead, the summit of that career. In expressing his faith in the all-conquering power of 'a good show', he'd either ignored or underestimated the looming threats faced by his business.

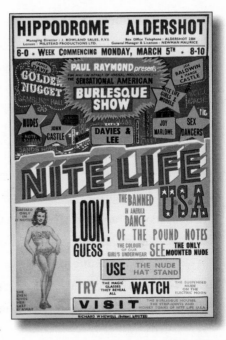

Many variety theatres were closing, the decline in their box-office receipts encouraging their owners to convert them into cinemas or demolish them. At the same time, the launch of independent television in September 1955 had advanced the mounting challenge from the small screen.

For the moment, though, Raymond had other things to occupy his attention. During the final week of April 1956 British Rail refused to display one of his posters at its stations. As always, Raymond had devised the offending advert. A picture of a semi-naked brunette was accompanied by the words 'Look! The Dance of the Pound Notes. Dressed Only In Pound Notes… She Even Gives Her Last Pound Note Away'. Further down the poster he'd listed the supporting attractions which included 'the Nude Hatstand' and 'Guess the colour of our girl's underwear'.

Cannily exploiting British Rail's decision, he whipped up a public row with the company, a row that brought him advantageous publicity in the form of a full-page article in the *Daily Mirror* which struck the classic scandal-sheet pose, voyeuristic fascination masquerading as moralistic revulsion. But this publicity bonus couldn't prevent the trajectory of

Raymond's business from levelling out. By the third week of June, he was back to running eight revues, each of them nevertheless employing seventeen or eighteen showgirls, a dozen other performers, plus backstage staff and a manager.

His current productions included *Les Nuits de Paris*, a title suggestive of the Folies Bergère, of camiknickered, can-can-dancing Continental naughtiness, though the performers were no more Parisian than the venues in which they performed. Its star attraction was the nudes in the lions' den routine. Supervised by a former comedian named Dickie Arnold, its cast and crew, incorporating three ageing lions and a fifty-one-year-old freelance lion-tamer, had been on the road since mid-May.

On Sunday, 24 June they rolled up in Nottingham. Ahead of the troupe's arrival, there had been the customary advertising campaign. It hailed *Les Nuits de Paris* as 'the most daring and fearsome revue ever staged'.

The show was scheduled for a six-day run at the Nottingham Empire, a flamboyantly pinnacled late Victorian confection, operated by the Moss Empires chain. Every performance of *Les Nuits de Paris* culminated in an act billed as the 'Nudes de Paris'. It began with twenty-year-old Phyl Edmond and twenty-three-year-old Zelda Lamone standing motionless on three-feet-high pedestals inside a giant metal cage. Both girls were naked apart from sequinned G-strings, high-heeled shoes and plumed headdresses. They shared the cage with two male lions and a lioness. To add to the sense of danger, the performers were locked inside. Under the command of Nikolai, a veteran Greek lion-tamer, the animals leapt on and off three stools. It was a routine which, by Friday of that week, the troupe had gone through nearly two hundred times.

Lending validity to Raymond's optimism about variety theatre, the second performance that Saturday evening attracted a full house of 1,800 people. From the cheapest seats in the uppermost gilt-encrusted balcony, the lions on the stage appeared no more menacing than a set of animals from a toy Noah's Ark. As the show reached its well-choreographed climax, the audience would have had no intimation that anything out of the ordinary might be about to occur.

Lamone and Edmond posed calmly on their pedestals while the white-gloved, cane-swishing Nikolai strutted round the cage, issuing commands to the lions, which jumped and roared on cue. Midway through the act, he ordered all three animals to get down from their stools. A couple of them obeyed, but the fiercest of the group – a nine-year-old lioness named Rana – stayed where she was, snarling and clawing the air. Then she bounded towards Nikolai and lashed out with one paw. Her claws snagging his left hand, she ripped open his glove and two fingers beneath. When the audience realised what they were witnessing, entertainment shape-shifting into potential tragedy, they lapsed into a shocked hush. This was broken by the communal gasp at the sight of Nikolai wrenching his injured hand free. As he did so, his cotton glove changed colour with the rapidity of litmus paper exposed to some acidic chemical. One second the glove was white, the next it was crimson.

Only the customers sitting at the front of the stalls would have been able to hear what Nikolai said to the two near-naked showgirls, perched on their pedestals. 'Don't move!' he murmured.

Knowing that the slightest sign of fear would encourage Rana to renew her attack, he ignored the pain and shouted the usual commands as he advanced on her.

At first the lioness refused to back down, her growls counterpointed by the roar of the other animals. Gradually, though, she retreated – still snarling – to where the other two were waiting.

Despite the injury Nikolai had suffered, he went through the remainder of his act. Not until the final curtain was he rushed to Nottingham General Hospital, where he had seventeen stitches inserted into his unzipped fingers. He then returned to the theatre.

'I consider myself very fortunate indeed to have escaped so lightly,' he informed a journalist from the *Nottingham Guardian*. 'If the lioness's paw had gripped my wrist, I would not have been able to free myself and she would have come in for the kill.'

Word of how a fatality had been narrowly averted soon reached the *Daily Mail* and other national newspapers. They sent reporters to interview Nikolai, Edmond and Lamone, as well as Dickie Arnold.

Nikolai gave a devil-may-care shrug as he told one of the reporters, 'It was no use backing away. I had the girls to think of…'

Suitably appreciative, Lamone cooed, 'He was terribly brave.' She added that she and Phyll Edmond must be 'the craziest girls in showbusiness' to do what they did.

'I was not frightened,' Edmond – a diminutive brunette from Scarborough – declared. 'Zelda and I are so confident in Nikolai. We didn't move when the lion struck. It's against the law to move, of course. *And* it's dangerous. Besides, all we had to defend ourselves with were high-heeled shoes.'

The day after Nikolai's ordeal, he and the rest of the troupe headed for Southampton, where they were due to perform the following Wednesday. Lamone and Edmond had permission to stop off in London and recuperate before rejoining the tour party on Tuesday.

Paul and Jean Raymond must have been delighted by the free publicity *Les Nuits de Paris* received in Monday's newspapers. Both the *Daily Mail* and the *Daily Express* ran dramatic front-page stories about the previous weekend's incident.

Next day less welcome news reached Raymond. He discovered that Lamone, for all her professed trust in Nikolai's abilities as a lion-tamer, had failed to turn up at the Grand Theatre in Southampton, where the cast was preparing for the opening night. Since there was too little time to recruit a replacement, Jean offered to take her place. Raymond accepted Jean's offer, even though it carried a significant qualification. She stressed that, being a married woman and the mother of a baby, she shouldn't appear in the nude. If she *had* to fill in for Lamone, she would only do so while wearing her bikini.

Together with Raymond, she travelled down to the south coast, where the weather promised good box-office takings, the unseasonal chill, monotonous cloud cover and sporadic showers likely to drive people in search of indoor entertainment. After the Raymonds arrived at the Grand Theatre, Dickie Arnold tried to drum up even more coverage for *Les Nuits de Paris* in the national press. He phoned George Clegg, a locally based stringer for the *Daily Sketch*, just the type of salacious newspaper that might have been expected to appeal to the show's potential male audience. Arnold told Clegg that Mrs Raymond would be taking the place of the missing girl, though Arnold's exact choice of words was destined to become the focus of intense debate.

If the Southampton public wasn't already aware of the imminent show, a sequence of adverts had been booked in the *Southern Daily Echo*, the city's principal local paper. Raymond prided himself on his attention to the minutiae of his business, so there's every chance he would have skimmed through the *Echo* to check his advert was there. In the process he'd surely have noticed the front-page headline – 'Two Remanded on Charge of Wounding Jack Comer' – and taken quiet satisfaction in the violence meted out against the gangster who had previously threatened him.

The story related to an incident when, just over two months earlier, a couple of armed men had attacked Comer – alias Jack Spot – on a London street. They'd sent him crashing to the pavement before kicking and slashing him. What the *Echo* failed to mention was the identity of the men facing a charge of malicious wounding with intent to cause grievous bodily harm. One of them was Frank Fraser who had, by then, accrued fifteen convictions and twice been certified insane.

A solicitous husband at that point, Raymond would have shared his wife's relief that her subsequent appearance in the lions' cage involved no repeat of the Nottingham mishap. Her feelings were tempered by the sight of Thursday morning's edition of the *Daily Sketch*. Clegg's article stated that she had 'posed as a nude in a lions' cage at Southampton last night'. Oddly enough, in view of the handsome income she and her husband made from nudity, she was infuriated by the story because she knew that nudes were, within the theatrical profession, 'not looked upon as [having] much class'. After all, as she explained, 'A nude does not require any talent and a person with talent just does not want to display her body.'

Similarly irate, Raymond – whose stammer belied his often combative manner – supported her by phoning the paper's news desk and demanding they print a retraction or at least a correction. Neither was forthcoming, so his wife threatened to take legal action against Associated Newspapers, the influential company that owned the *Daily Sketch*.

Possibly because Raymond wanted to deter her from going ahead with her threat, he refused to be responsible for the cost of hiring a barrister. Her sense of grievance, however, outweighed the financial risk, prompting her to initiate the mooted libel action.

# 11  CRUMPET VOLUNTARY

**B**Y THE BEGINNING of 1957 Raymond still had eight touring revues in circulation, generating an annual turnover of £400,000, yet he'd come to realise just how misguided his optimism about the future of variety theatre had been. Over the past few years, 150 venues throughout Britain had closed. Dwindling attendances, combined with the increasingly punitive Entertainment Tax, had rendered a lot of the smaller theatres unviable. In the case of many of the larger venues, typically situated in city centres, their sites had become more valuable to the owners than the theatres themselves, the end of wartime building restrictions having encouraged the rise of speculative development.

Some theatres were converted into cinemas, some turned into bingo halls, some were burnt down in insurance scams, others were demolished, making way for new buildings. Even the once mighty Moss Empires circuit wasn't impervious to the trend, its rapid contraction hastened by the covert relationship between its managing director, Val Parnell, and the boss of a prominent property company. A joke went round the variety business about how, at a meeting of the board of directors of Moss Empires, Parnell had stood up and said, 'Gentlemen, as an experiment we are going to close the Swansea Empire and if that is a success we'll close the bloody lot.'

Raymond found himself being blamed by disgruntled artistes for the sudden decline of variety theatre. They complained that nude shows, however well presented, had driven away family audiences. But that was to ignore the truth: family audiences were already drifting away from variety theatre. 'Look, there's no such thing these days as a family audience,' Raymond had conceded the previous year. If anything, the nude shows were keeping the variety circuit alive.

Television was also widely – and justifiably – held responsible for the decline. There's no doubt that the small screen offered a general distraction. And it even offered a direct challenge in the form of programmes such as *Sunday Night at the London Palladium*. These gave people the chance to see top variety performers without paying for a ticket or leaving their sitting rooms. Improved housing standards must have contributed to the trend, too. Evenings at home were, generally speaking, now much more enticing than they'd ever been.

His wounding experience with the *Daily Sketch* led Raymond to hire a freelance public relations expert. For this role he chose Connor Walsh, a husky-voiced, impeccably mannered, neatly turned out Yorkshireman who was a few years younger than him. Otherwise down to earth, Walsh smoked through a cigarette-holder used to italicise salient points in whatever he was saying. Previously he'd held down a series of newspaper jobs for publications that included the *Daily Sketch* and the *Sunday Pictorial*, where he'd been the chief crime correspondent. He'd also worked as a PR man for the Windmill Theatre. Perhaps because he and Raymond were from similar Northern backgrounds and had both worked on market stalls and as salesmen, they soon established a rapport. They'd frequently be together in Raymond's office discussing the ideas Walsh dispensed with nonchalant profligacy.

'I did a trip to Paris to the Folies Bergère and came back and described to him what was going on there and he was fascinated by that,' Walsh recalled. Mindful of the need to find an escape route from the dying variety business, Raymond began to consider the possibility of setting up an English equivalent, trading on the nude revue brand he'd created.

Further inspiration must have come from the success of Britain's first legal striptease club. Despite the notoriety of Gypsy Rose Lee and Lili St Cyr, America's two most celebrated strippers, and despite the hollow promise of 'striptease' on posters for Raymond's nude revues, few British people had witnessed a performance before October 1956, when London acquired its first strip-club. Until then, striptease had been available in Britain only on an illegal basis.

It could be sampled in the rare pubs and clubs prepared to flout the law. But it was more readily available as a celluloid experience. For some people, this came via short 16mm American films such as *Hollywood Peep Show*, smuggled into Britain and sold at wince-inducing mark-ups. For others, it was purveyed by home-grown 8mm films lasting no more than two and a half minutes, the anonymous performers sometimes ending disappointingly short of full nudity. These British offerings could be purchased by mail order from companies that advertised in *Photo Studio* and other comparatively chaste nudie magazines available in Soho and under the counter through certain local newsagents. At the height of this trade, one such company was selling 1,000 prints a day.

Striptease had, of course, also been available to people determined or wealthy enough to cross the Channel or even the Atlantic prior to the advent of cheap air travel. Both the art of striptease and the word itself were American inventions, though it had French antecedents. In its most rudimentary guise, female undressing appears to have made its debut as a form of theatrical entertainment in Paris during March 1894. The venue for that landmark performance was an after-hours nightclub at 75 rue des Martyrs, where Blanche Cavelli performed *Le Coucher d'Yvette*. Her act began with her sitting beside her bed, wearing everyday apparel. A piano played in the background as she took off layer upon layer of clothes until she was wearing only a nightdress. She then climbed into bed and the lights dimmed.

The earliest recorded undressing show on this side of the Atlantic was staged for a three-month period no later than 1925 and possibly as early as 1916. It took place at the posh Venice Café at 14 Soho Street. Genuine striptease, incorporating the hip-swaying sensuality of the shimmy and other Jazz Age dances, didn't arrive, however, on either side of the Atlantic until a few years later. Hinda 'The Blonde Bombshell' Wausau appears to have performed the initial show in one of Chicago's burlesque theatres between 1927 and 1928 – the year when the word 'striptease' made its debut appearance in print. Like innumerable other American cultural phenomena, this offspring of Roaring Twenties Chicago would ultimately take root in Britain, in the alien soil of Harold Macmillan-era London.

Britain's first strip-joint, which went some way towards proving Macmillan's oft-quoted claim that his countrymen had 'never had it so good', was situated above an Indian restaurant at 17 Irving Street, just off Leicester Square. It was called the Irving Strip Club. When it opened, advertising 'non-stop striptease' and billing itself as 'the only theatre in London where the nudes can move', it attracted long queues of would-be customers prepared to pay the hefty twenty-five-shilling membership fee. Its owner, a bespectacled Bengali former barrister named Dhurjati Chaudhuri, had taken advantage of a legal loophole formerly exploited by theatre clubs to enable them to stage controversial plays banned by the Lord Chamberlain. Casting round for an alternative use for his Asian Institute art gallery and theatre, which had been sustaining heavy losses despite enjoying the patronage of Laurence Olivier, Jacob Epstein and other cultural heavyweights, Chaudhuri had converted the place into a ninety-eight-seat club. By making it a members-only venue, he rendered the Lord Chamberlain's edict on nudes irrelevant.

But there were two drawbacks to Chaudhuri's inspired wheeze. The first of these involved the licensing regulations, which required an inconvenient forty-eight-hour gap between a customer completing a membership form and being allowed to watch a performance. On top of that, Chaudhuri and future strip-club owners found themselves in a Catch-22 situation. To operate legally, they needed a Public Music and Dancing Licence, yet London County Council refused to grant these to strip-clubs. Monthly £100 fines therefore became part of the overheads of Chaudhuri and his imitators.

As Raymond probably discovered, more imagination had gone into circumventing the law than into staging the shows at the Irving. Nonetheless, the audience remained hynotised by the sight of the G-stringed strippers ploughing through perfunctory routines to the accompaniment of a drummer and a pianist. In between the stripping were revue sketches, performed by the young dinner-jacketed, bow-tied Victor Spinetti. These ranged from an impersonation of Al Jolson to a song called 'I'm An Angry Young Man With A Bank Roll', which sent up the voguish playwright John Osborne. Spinetti remembered catching sight of the writers Kingsley Amis, Philip Larkin and Alec Waugh in the audience. Yet the spectators mainly comprised 'executive-looking types', many of them probably frustrated by the stern warning in the programme that read, 'Artificial Aids To Vision Not Permitted'.

If a show like *this* could attract full houses, then surely an extravagant cabaret-style presentation in a luxurious setting would reap even greater rewards? With that in mind, Raymond set about finding not only suitable premises but also a business partner prepared to share the substantial expense of refurbishing those premises. He and a wealthy shoe manufacturer were soon in discussion about going into partnership. Their negotiations yielded a verbal agreement that the profits from the club would be divided 60/40 per cent in Raymond's favour.

Locating appropriate premises for the club wasn't so straightforward. Whenever the word 'striptease' was mentioned, landlords had a tendency either to refuse to discuss leasing the property or to name a price quadruple the market value. While Raymond was still searching for premises, there was a danger that other astute businessmen might exploit the commercial possibilities of striptease, making it hard for him to establish his club.

Sure enough, by the summer of 1957 Michael Klinger and Jimmy Jacobs, owners of the once prestigious but now ailing Gargoyle Club in

Soho, had turned the club's 'Nell Gwynn Room' into a popular strip-club called 'The Nell Gwynn Revue'. It hosted what they advertised as 'the Dance of the Seven Veils', for which the target audience was provincial businessmen visiting London.

Additional uncertainty was heaped on Raymond's scheme when he and his investor met to sign their partnership agreement. According to Raymond, the investor said, 'You've got it the wrong way round. It should be 60% for *me*.' To which Raymond replied, 'If that's the way you behave now, what are you going to be like later?'

Raymond claimed to have 'torn up the contract there and then'.

# 12 GENTLEMEN PREFER NUDES

FOUR DAYS SHORT of the first anniversary of the publication of the *Daily Sketch* article that had so affronted Jean Raymond, her legal action reached the High Court of Justice. In this cluster of Gothic Revival buildings, akin to an Oxbridge college transplanted into central London, she was joined by her husband and legal team, led by W. A. Fearnley-Whittingstall, whose expertise had been utilised by many other show-business clients. Jean's counsel faced Gilbert Beyfus, a veteran barrister with beaky-nosed features that looked as if they were sliding down his skull. Nicknamed 'The Old Fox', Beyfus was a daunting adversary famous for his droll belligerence.

Under the direction of the septuagenarian Mr Justice Hilbery, the jury took their seats and heard the allegedly libellous passage. On behalf of Associated Newspapers, Beyfus admitted publication of it but denied that it constituted libel. He said the sentences in question had been 'published with the leave and license of the plaitiff'. Moreover, 'they were true in substance and fact'.

Fearnley-Whittingstall was now free to address the jury: 'In the early stages, this case had been a nasty libel, maybe as a result of gross carelessness or sensation-seeking and gossip.' But he argued the offence had been aggravated by the defendants' insistence on the truth of the allegedly libellous passage. He said this amounted to 'an attack on the plaintiff's seemliness and propriety, which was absolutely wanton and thoroughly nasty'.

He went on to outline the grounds for his client seeking damages from Associated Newspapers, then described how Jean had ended up appearing in *Les Nuits de Paris* – 'the name', he observed, 'being more electrifying than the spectacle.' He emphasised that she'd only agreed to feature in the show if she was permitted to wear a bikini. In referring to this, he brandished the sequinned garment.

'You had better hold it up and show the jury how it is worn,' Hilbery said.

'My Lord, it would not fit me.'

Seeing the bikini, Hilbery couldn't resist passing a Blimpish comment on how it resembled an old pair of three-cornered bathing drawers.

No sooner had Fearnley-Whittingstall set out the rudiments of his case than he summoned Jean to the witness box. He asked her to tell the court what the showgirls in her husband's touring revues normally wore.

She said they wore a G-string.

'A G-*skin*?' the baffled judge asked. This provoked an indulgent smile from his wife, who was sitting in the public gallery, alongside several journalists, attracted to the case by its risqué ingredients.

'A G-*string*,' Jean repeated before explaining what it was.

Hilbery said, 'Is that immodest?'

'No, I don't think so.'

'There is nothing immodest about girls being nude in that type of show?'

'Not if they choose to do it.'

'These girls in your husband's show were exhibited in that way to the public to make the show pay, I gather?'

'Of course. We have to give the public what they like. It depends—'

'If they like indecency, would you provide that?'

'It just depends on what is called "indecent".'

Now came the opposing barrister's chance to display the cross-examination skills that ensured his services were in such demand. Beyfus put it to Jean that her husband had resorted to nude revues only after he'd failed as a producer of conventional shows.

He hadn't been a failure, she replied, but she had to admit the nude shows were more profitable. She added that her husband insisted on the showgirls being refined, artistic and well dressed offstage.

In a bid to undermine her case, Beyfus quizzed her about her 1953 performance at the Theatre Royal, Margate where she'd appeared as 'Zsa-Zsa, the Brazilian Bombshell'. Though her answer was predictable, he asked whether she had any connection with Brazil. He swiftly fired another question at her: was she aware that one of the acts she'd performed in Margate had been billed as 'The sensational and daring Tassel Dance'?

She said she didn't know the dance had been advertised in that way.

'Was it sensational?'

'Not to me.'

'Was it daring?'

'No.'

'A daring dress means something on the verge of indecency, does it not?'

She denied that it did.

Beyfus followed up his question by asking her to define a daring dance.

'Something which is difficult to perform,' she replied.

Realising that Jean was being disingenuous, Hilbery interrupted the cross-examination. 'Let us talk some common sense. Does it not mean when billed in a programme like this a dance is as *near indecent as it dared to go*?'

'No.'

Beyfus then resumed the inquisition. He asked Raymond's wife whether she suffered any twinges of conscience about imposing on the public by pretending to be Brazilian.

'No. It happens every day in the theatre.'

A few minutes later she was replaced in the witness box by her husband. Fearnley-Whittingstall invited him to describe the telephone call to George Clegg on 4 July the previous year.

Raymond said Dickie Arnold had told Clegg that his wife would be replacing the missing showgirl, but she'd be wearing a bikini. Then Raymond added that he and Jean had both spoken to Clegg and made it clear to him that she *wouldn't* be appearing in the nude.

Beyfus commenced his cross-examination of Jean's husband with an ostensibly innocuous question. He enquired whether Raymond had once been labelled by a newspaper as 'the King of the Keyhole Shows'.

Raymond said he had.

'Is that to suggest peeping through a keyhole?'

'I myself would say this was meant to say "King of the *Glamour* Shows".'

Asked if he had forty nudes on his payroll, Raymond said he couldn't *find* that many nudes.

With a note of feigned distaste that camouflaged a penchant for chorus girls, Beyfus commented that all Raymond's shows seemed to be put together on the basis that 'Gentlemen Prefer Nudes'.

Ignoring the provocation, Raymond gave a matter-of-fact reply. He merely stated that he regarded himself as a specialist in nude shows.

'You take particular care to see all the nudes you produce are refined, respectable and modest?'

'Yes.'

The judge chose that moment to intervene. 'If they are recognised as respectable, modest and refined, is it not rather a compliment for a woman to be classed as a nude?'

'No.'

'In the face of your views and the way you earn your living,' Beyfus said, 'do you still suggest it was a dreadful attack on your wife?'

'I suggest it was a *disgraceful* attack.'


When Paul and Jean Raymond left the court, they had every reason to be satisfied with their performances in the witness box. After an overnight adjournment, the hearing resumed on Tuesday, 2 July 1957, by which time it had engendered a succession of amusing newspaper stories. For Raymond but not his wife, this free advertising may have partially offset the associated stress.

Opening the defence case, Beyfus told the jury that Mrs Raymond's libel action was motivated either by the desire for 'a little easy money which was not subject to tax, or publicity, or a combination of the two.' Beyfus then called George Clegg, his only witness.

Clegg said he'd had conversations with Dickie Arnold as well as the Raymonds regarding Jean's appearance in the show.

'On that day,' Beyfus asked, 'did any one of them say to you that she was going to wear or had worn a bikini?'

'No, there was not the slightest indication that she was going on stage in anything other than what the missing girl had worn.'

Fearnley-Whittingstall's ensuing cross-examination failed to call into question the reliability of the witness.

It was now time for Beyfus to make his concluding speech to the jury, a speech in which he ridiculed the notion that 'this lady, a director of her husband's company which specialised in nudes, a lady who derived her income from that company, should ask the jury for damages in respect of a statement that she had posed as a nude'. Beyfus ended by saying, 'If the plaintiff was entitled to damages, a packet of pins was worth more than enough to compensate her.'

There was just sufficient time for Fearnley-Whittingstall to deliver his closing argument before the judge adjourned the hearing for the day. Besides drawing attention to the absence of any evidence that the offending story was published with Mrs Raymond's permission, his speech dismissed the allegation that the case had been prompted by a desire to make money. 'The plaintiff's husband had rung up the news desk and asked for a retraction or correction,' he reminded the jury. 'That was all he asked, but he did not get it.'

☆

For what was likely to be the final morning of the trial, Raymond accompanied his wife to the High Court. She wore a dark, fitted suit with a pale brooch on its lapel, her fashionable narrow-brimmed hat tipped back on her head to reveal a demure, girlish fringe, the calculated understatement of this chic ensemble indicative of a desire to appear precisely the sort of fragile, refined woman who would be offended by the story in the *Daily Sketch*.

Proceedings began with Hilbery summing up the evidence for the benefit of the jury. He said the first question they had to decide was whether the words in their natural meaning were defamatory of the plaintiff, whether they tended to lower her in the estimation of right-thinking people. The judge also highlighted two other pertinent questions. Was a bikini sufficient to preserve a woman's modesty? And was a woman who wore nothing except a G-string being immodest? In a flippant aside, Hilbery added, 'Why it is called a G-string, I have no idea. All I know about a G-string is that it is the lowest note on a violin.'

His summing-up was completed just before noon, leaving the jury to ponder its verdict, the element of suspense reduced by the glaring contempt with which he'd reviewed Jean's case. At 1.25 p.m. the jurors, who had probably spent more time eating lunch than debating the evidence, filed back into their seats and revealed their decision. They declared that the words printed in the *Daily Sketch* had not been defamatory of the plaintiff either as a woman or a choreographer.

Hilbery dismissed the libel action and ordered Jean to pay the costs incurred by Associated Newspapers, these amounting to around £1,500. Along with her husband, she left the court soon afterwards. Confronted by a gaggle of reporters from the national newspapers, she mustered a rueful smile. When the reporters pressed her to comment on the verdict, she said, 'That's how life goes I'd rather face a thousand lions than go through that again.'

Raymond couldn't escape without being buttonholed by the press, too. He was asked if he'd be inviting Mr Justice Hilbery to a show, so the judge could see a model wearing a G-string.

'Free tickets for the judge?' Raymond snorted. 'No comment.'

As if the previous question wasn't cheeky enough, Raymond was also asked whether he'd be covering his wife's legal costs. 'I don't know how much money she has, but *she* will have to pay,' he answered, clearly unconcerned about purveying an image of himself as a wealthy skinflint.

But Jean didn't have to worry about the money she'd been ordered to pay. In an unpublicised gesture of gallantry, Lord Rothermere – owner of Associated Newspapers – waived his company's right to it.

# 13  A ROOM WITH A REVUE

**R**AYMOND STILL HADN'T SECURED premises for his club, but there was no disputing the obvious part of London for it. That was Soho, an area replete with favourable associations. First of all, it had been the heart of London's clubland for many decades. While it hosted none of the traditional brand of gentlemen's clubs, Soho *did* offer clubs catering for most tastes, age groups, income brackets, classes, races and sexual preferences. You could drink, dance and watch cabaret shows at supper clubs. You could, if you were a homosexual, spend the evening in a club patronised by people who shared your sexual tastes which, in the case of male homosexuals, rendered you open to prosecution. You could go to a drinking club – typically housed in a basement ripe with the sour tang of unwashed socks and unfulfilled ambitions – where alcohol was available outside the restrictive lunchtime and evening licensing hours under which pubs laboured. You could, if you were gullible, end up in a so-called 'clip-joint', an unlicensed club where a hostess would talk you into buying her glass after glass of unpalatable, exorbitantly priced fruit cocktails, all on the doomed assumption that sex was the ultimate destination. You could play the voguish card game chemin de fer – 'chemmy' – in an illegal gambling club. Or you could listen to music in one of the jazz or rock 'n' roll clubs which had sprung up over the past few years.

Another factor that made Soho such an obvious location for Raymond's venture was its perennial association with sex. More specifically, its densely populated, mile-square network of streets, alleys and squares, sometimes known as 'the Black Mile', was synonymous with the commercial exploitation of sex, with sexual transgression. Like many other parts of the West End, its pavements were patrolled by prostitutes, gold ankle-bracelets and toy poodles on leads signifying their trade. Often they'd solicit passing men with brash yet polite stock phrases: 'Short time, dearie?' or 'Would you like a good time, sir?' Other prostitutes attempted to entice passers-by from open windows. And touts wandered the streets on the lookout for suitable targets to smooth-talk into clip-joints or dingy rooms where blue movies with titles such as *Beauties in Bondage, Julia Learns the Ropes* and *Captive Blonde Girl* were screened. An additional source of voyeuristic pleasure was provided by the Visual Arts Club and other photographic studios where amateur photographers could take pictures of nude models. Voyeurs also had the option of attending illegal strip-clubs, among them Vicki's Studio on Old Compton Street, which advertised in the windows of local newsagents. Discreet little bookshops, meanwhile, conducted a booming trade in softcore pornography: 8mm films, books, magazines and photosets that were euphemistically known as 'art studies'. Representative of this trade were the peculiarly British 'panty-flasher' magazines such as *Carnival, Bamboo* and *Breezy*; the text-based fetish journal *Fads and Fancies*; plus the pin-up magazines *Can-Can, Paris Vision* and *Mam'selle*, featuring models whose photos had been heavily airbrushed below the waist.

As a potential location for Raymond's club, Soho was made even more fertile by its Continental ambience, by its sizeable Italian, French and Jewish communities who had their own bakers, butchers, restaurants and delicatessens. Given the connotations acquired by the word 'French', connotations that Raymond and his like had been exploiting for years, the sound of spoken French must – at least on a subliminal level – have nourished Soho's erotic associations.

For the would-be owner of a club seeking to emulate the atmosphere of the Folies Bergère, all this was ideal. Soho had, in any event, a long history of accommodating the illicit and the marginal, of providing a

# Fourth Floor

PRICE      SIXPENCE

SOHO
–
foriegn
spoke
here

broad

## End of the Year Issue

*Cartoon by novelist-in-the-making, Len Deighton, featured on the cover of a 1952 St Martin's School of Art and Design student magazine. Deighton was studying at St Martin's, based on the fourth and fifth floors of a Charing Cross Road building which backed onto Soho*

haven for radicals and dissenters, of hosting novelty theatre shows and exhibitions, often containing a lubricious component, often promoted by obsessive impresarios. Yet well-meaning people warned Raymond off setting up his club in that section of town. 'Whatever you do,' he recalled them telling him, 'don't go near Soho. It's an appalling place, and you won't last two seconds there because of the gangs.'

☆

He had to wait until the closing weeks of 1957 before he found suitable premises for his club. Heedless of all the warnings, he selected somewhere in the middle of Soho. Until recently his chosen location had been occupied by the Doric Ballrooms, a series of function rooms used for wedding receptions. Except for its ground-floor foyer, it was on the first and second floors of two buildings that straddled Walker's Court, an alley running between Brewer and Berwick Streets. The two sections of the former Doric Ballrooms were linked by an enclosed footbridge, the windows of which overlooked parallel rows of small businesses characteristic of Soho at that time. There was a butcher's, a restaurant, a lampshade shop, and a bookshop plying a surreptitious trade in pornography. There was also Isow's, a pricey Jewish restaurant with a famous clientele that included boxers, singers, film producers and visiting Hollywood stars, as well as home-grown celebrities such as George Formby and Tommy Trinder. Beneath the restaurant was a basement nightspot called Jack of Clubs, equally prone to inducing anorexia of the wallet.

Both the restaurant and the nightclub lent the address unexpected glamour. Their owner, Jack Isow, was Raymond's prospective landlord. A tubby, jovial man in his late fifties, Isow – born Joseph Isowitski – had a jowly profile, a bald head, a strong Polish accent and a history of unashamed hucksterism even longer than Raymond's. Unlike Raymond's, though, his activities on the black market had, ten years earlier, landed him in jail. He nevertheless owned the freeholds to a swathe of Soho property. With this, he operated a remunerative sideline in renting premises for clubs, one year's money in advance. Frequently, the clubs folded after only a few weeks, enabling Isow to pocket the rent and find another tenant.

Raymond was, once again, the recipient of advice that he chose to ignore. When he revealed that he was thinking of renting the former Doric Ballrooms, he was told that he'd 'be mad to start a club *upstairs*' – advice which failed to take into account the runaway success of the Gargoyle Club during the 1940s.

Confident that he'd be able to negotiate a satisfactory lease, Raymond went ahead with the legal necessity of recruiting a committee to supervise the running of his club. Under the chairmanship of his wife, the committee held its first meeting on New Year's Day, 1958. Just over a fortnight later Raymond signed an ambitious twenty-one-year lease on the Walker's Court premises. He agreed to pay Isow £5,000 per year rent, due in nine instalments. Possibly because Isow didn't expect this club to last any longer than the other clubs set up by his tenants, there was no provision for a periodic rent review – an omission that would have a significant bearing on Raymond's future.

As well as budgeting for the rent, Raymond had to cover all the normal running expenses, plus the refurbishment costs which, he claimed, were between £125,000 and £140,000, immense figures probably inflated in order to convey just how opulent the club would be. Even the ample war chest he'd accumulated courtesy of the ample chests flaunted in his touring shows wasn't enough to cover the investment required. He appears to have met the shortfall by remortgaging his house and selling his Jaguar car. Whatever the true extent of his investment, the club represented an audacious wager on his commercial instincts.

Then as now, nightclubs were a risky proposition, harbouring the possibility of large losses and even larger rewards. For the type of club Raymond had in mind, the rewards were still greater. Profits could be made from membership fees as well as the traditional sources of nightclub revenue, namely ticket sales and bar takings. The previous year, for example, Churchill's Club had, in the space of only eight months, recorded takings of almost £48,000 from drinks sales alone.

Once his tenancy had been secured, Raymond was able to go through the formality of popping round to Marlborough Street Magistrates' Court and paying the five-shilling fee necessary to register the premises as 'The Raymond Theatre Revuebar Club'. He could then knuckle down to the task of applying for planning permission for a huge neon sign on the Brewer Street side of the building; remodelling the club's interior;

hiring front-of-house and backstage staff; auditioning performers and a three-piece house band.

Another item on his 'to do' list was the task of moving the club's entrance from the junction with Brewer Street to a position midway along Walker's Court. This would prove an inspired, psychologically astute decision. For strip-clubs, not having an entrance on a main street was a potent advantage in those days. Reassured that the odds on being spotted by a passing friend or acquaintance had been minimised, the more sexually repressed punters would therefore be prepared to queue outside. Alternatively, they could wait for a quiet moment to dart through the entrance.

Raymond gave himself only seven weeks to prepare the Revuebar for its anticipated launch on Monday, 7 April. His self-imposed deadline was made even more ambitious by the need to combine it with the responsibilities of operating a scaled-down version of his touring revue business from his Chandos Place offices. Many of the stalwarts of these shows who'd worked onstage and behind the scenes were given jobs at the new club. Jean's friend Jan Harding, pencilled in for the role of meeter-and-greeter, was among them.

Before the building work on the interior of the Revuebar had made much headway, Raymond had already rented a rehearsal room and set up auditions for prospective strippers and showgirls. But these had to be postponed because a sudden cold snap, causing blizzards across the country, had made the draughty rehearsal room too chilly. When the weather improved sufficiently to allow auditions to proceed, more than three hundred candidates battled for the available jobs. A further eighty-two women, attracted by £2,000 in prize money, tried out for the amateur striptease competition Raymond had been advertising.

Taking time off from his stressful schedule, he granted interviews to reporters from three national newspapers, their interest presumably kindled by press releases about the club. 'I'm here to give the public what it wants,' he told the *Empire News*. 'The show I shall be putting on will be a striptease show but done in such a way that nobody could possibly take any exception to it.' He added that he wanted the club to be 'a place where a man can take his wife'.

Raymond also found himself fielding questions from the press about *French Postcards*, one of his touring revues. To create interest in the show, he'd arranged for anyone who bought a ticket to be given a photographic postcard of a nude. For each of the show's six nights, a different image was handed out. 'The photographs are very good art studies of nudes in classy poses,' he said.

It was a gimmick that doubled takings at the Aldershot Hippodrome, though it sparked protests from social workers, magistrates and clergymen. These intensified when the show moved to Doncaster, where the wife of a local vicar criticised it for being 'a shocking commentary on public taste'.

The time that Raymond had lately been spending with reporters yielded a spate of handy press coverage, not least a lip-smacking article in the *People* about the amateur striptease competition. 'Stay dressed, girls. Let Mr Raymond be the one to catch a cold with this silly and scandalous stunt,' the headline appealed. Raymond could hardly have wished for a more effective advertisement than the accompanying story, juxtaposed with a photo of two nubile entrants.

In parallel to the campaign to obtain news coverage, orchestrated by Connor Walsh, Raymond promoted the club by taking adverts in newspapers and in *What's On in London*, a magazine that should, on account of its acreage of adverts for strip-joints, have been renamed *Where* Nothing's *On in London*. Raymond also arranged to have flyers distributed round the capital, promising such delights as '20 Glamorous Stripettes'. In addition he struck deals with the Stock Exchange and 870 ticket agencies across the country, from where people could obtain membership.

All this was supplemented by an innovative scheme that involved sending letters to businesses in other cities, those letters accompanied by stacks of 'Introduction Cards'. The owner of the business just had to write his or her details on a card, then hand it to someone who might be interested in joining the Revuebar. If that person ended up taking out membership, Raymond paid three shillings and sixpence commission.

Successful though this scheme was, it resulted in one Brighton resident complaining to the local police – a development that would have undesirable ramifications. The Brighton police alerted Superintendent Charles Strath, who ran the Clubs Office, the organisation within the Metropolitan Police responsible for monitoring West End clubs and enforcing the often ambiguous licensing laws that applied to them. A cheerless Scot with a reputation for pursuing perceived lawbreakers with incorruptible zeal, Strath was capable of putting the Revuebar out of business.

Work on the interior of the club hadn't been proceeding as smoothly as its advance marketing campaign. Since the refurbishment programme was behind schedule, Raymond had no choice but to push back the launch date to Monday, 21 April. Still, he made use of the protracted build-up – all too appropriate for a strip-club – by carrying out more interviews with the press. Evading the facts as skilfully as any politician, he portrayed the Revuebar as the West End's first venue for '*true* striptease', setting in motion a process of Chinese whispers that spanned fifty years. Falsehood morphing into perceived truth, journalists and social historians would ultimately proclaim the Revuebar as Britain's first strip-club.

With only two weeks until the club's launch, the interior was still a mess. Tools were lying around the place, the freshly delivered furniture hadn't yet been unwrapped and the carpenters were still at work. Their hammer blows provided a cacophonous counterpoint to the piano and castanets used for the Spanish-themed dance number being rehearsed by the club's showgirls. Right from the start Raymond's wife had taken the role of choreographer, her know-how deployed in shepherding the performers through complex routines more reminiscent of a Broadway show than a Soho nightclub.

Fortunately work on the ground-floor foyer, entered from Walker's Court, had been completed by then, enabling it to function as a box office. There, prospective customers could pay their ten shillings and sixpence membership fee and buy tickets for specific performances of *Paul Raymond's Sensational Folies Revue*. Foreign tourists, wanting to see a show, were offered discount Overseas Membership. Once someone had enrolled as a member, that person could take a guest to the Revuebar.

Irrespective of all the effort lavished on the club, Raymond was still concerned that it wouldn't pull in enough punters. Maybe the competition was too intense. Three other strip-clubs, admittedly none of them as swish as the Revuebar, were already in business. And news began to circulate that a fourth competitor – the Casino de Paris on Denman Street – was being launched on the same night as the Revuebar. But all this competition didn't appear to have much effect. Queues of curious passers-by, as well as other people lured by the recent publicity and advertising, became a common sight in Walker's Court.

No sooner had the box office opened than Superintendent Strath placed the Revuebar under what was termed 'casual observation'. Several plainclothes officers, including Strath himself, mingled with the crowd that flowed through Walker's Court. Three of those officers also queued for membership forms and filled these out using false names. Testing to see whether they could provoke a breach of the law, which required members of clubs to be proposed and seconded by existing members, they left the 'proposed by' and 'seconded by' spaces blank. One of the undercover officers described how, when he reached the front of the queue, he pointed out to the man and woman behind the desk that he hadn't completed these sections of the membership form. He claimed the man had told him, 'That's alright. Madam here will introduce you.' The woman had, he said, then signed as the proposer and the man had acted as the seconder.

During the box office's opening week, more than a thousand people from all over the country became members, generating well in excess of £10,000 in fees. Raymond observed that many of them asked 'specifically that their membership cards when available should not be sent to their homes'. In a crafty manoeuvre that played on his customers' fears, the enrolment forms coaxed applicants into having their annual fee forwarded automatically by their banks. Through sheer inertia and reluctance to hold an embarrassing conversation with the staff at whichever banks they used, a high proportion of the club's recruits were likely to remain members.

Early in the afternoon on the Thursday before the club's launch, Superintendent Strath and his second-in-command paid a visit to the Revuebar. Approached from either Berwick or Brewer Streets, its signage made it hard to ignore. A neon arrow, visible from Berwick Street, pointed towards its main entrance. London County Council had rejected Raymond's planning application for the gigantic sign he'd originally conceived, but he'd still been able to install a large illuminated advert overlooking Brewer Street. It promised 'Folies Striptease', 'Fabulous Girls', 'London's only real challenge to Paris'.

When the two policemen from West End Central arrived at the Revuebar, they were met by Raymond, together with 'Big George' Richardson, the paid club secretary. Several years Raymond's senior, Richardson was a tall former actor who had a handlebar moustache, oily hair and, where strangers were concerned, an arrogance that masked his innate gentleness. He and his boss treated the officers to a guided tour. Raymond's freshly completed refurbishment plans had created by far the most luxurious of the city's strip-clubs.

Jutting out from the black marble façade, there was now a canopy with recessed spotlights reflected by the glass swing-doors that led into the reception area. Adjacent to the box office was a miniature fountain and a sweeping staircase, covered in springy crimson carpet. Posters for the amateur striptease competition and photos of nude women were displayed on the staircase to the first floor. It linked the foyer with the cloakroom and the cavernous, expensively kitted-out lounge bar. Around this were distributed seven settees and numerous chairs, upholstered in red plush; more than two dozen small round tables; an upright piano; and a hulking television, intended for screening major sporting events. The room was dominated by a thirty-feet-long bar, lit with red bulbs which, depending on your mood, gave it either a comforting or a hellish glow.

Almost opposite the cloakroom was a set of double doors, opening on to what Superintendent Strath regarded as a 'sumptuously furnished' corridor. This led Raymond and the three other men over the bridge across Walker's Court. Punctuating the corridor were more double doors and then a pair of heavy curtains, beyond which was the theatre. Unlike a conventional theatre, the seating was arranged round eight tiered rows of circular dining tables, each seating four people. Above them hung an impressive chandelier which, Raymond said, had cost £1,000. Apparently relishing his role as tour-guide, Raymond told the detectives that the auditorium could accommodate 'a maximum of 300 persons', though membership had reached 1,400.

For all his urbanity and seeming openness Raymond failed to quell Strath's suspicions about the club. Next day the superintendent applied for permission to carry out an 'inside observation' of the place 'with a view to proceedings for striking this club off the register on the grounds that it is not conducted in good faith'.

His application granted, Strath made arrangements for his team of plainclothes detectives to infiltrate the audience on the club's opening night.

# 14 G-STING

THE FIRST PUBLIC PERFORMANCE in the Revuebar's theatre began at 2.30 p.m. on Monday, 21 April 1958. Among the audience was a plainclothes officer sent there by Superintendent Strath, all expenses paid. To comply with the law, which demanded that food had to be served with any alcoholic drinks sold outside normal lunchtime and evening licensing hours, each table carried a complimentary plate of sandwiches – a common ruse employed by club-owners. White-jacketed waiters scurried to and from the bar at the back of the theatre, replenishing those drinks.

Inevitably the sense of expectation – described as 'electric' by one witness – must have been magnified by the drum-roll that prefaced the show's debut act, billed in the programme as 'Ted and Renée Lastair'. When the drumming faded, the house band segued into an intriguing, slow-tempo theme and the ruched curtains parted, revealing two lifesize gold statues of a slender but muscular man and a busty woman, both naked, both glittering under a pink spotlight. The performers – Ted and Renée Haskell – had achieved the effect by painting themselves gold, their genitals hidden beneath a G-string in Renée's case and a gold lamé jockstrap in Ted's case.

Little by little, these statues appeared to come to life. Flaunting Ted's skills as a ballet dancer who had shared the same stage as Anton Dolin and Alicia Markova, they were soon executing a precisely choreographed, acrobatic dance to music from *The High and the Mighty* and *The Glass Mountain*.

*Front of house/publicity photo of Lorraine Burnett, a one-time Windmill girl who performed at the Revuebar*

'We never did anything rude or vulgar,' Renée remembered. 'A very classic act we were.'

Perhaps sensing that Superintendent Strath's earlier visit hadn't placated the authorities, Raymond and his staff half expected the show to be halted by a police raiding party, heavy boots clomping across the stage. But the opening performance was completed as planned. So too was the second show, which began at 6.30 p.m., its audience including a group of invited journalists and yet another undercover police officer.

Two more detectives headed for the Revuebar later that evening. By 8 p.m. the foyer was so crowded that the club's doorman, dressed in a blue pseudo-military uniform with a peaked cap and epaulettes, had to assist the box-office staff.

After they'd each downed a couple of drinks, the detectives made their way into the theatre. Too late to catch Ted and Renée Haskell's act, they took their seats near the stage where the compère, whose patter one of the detectives described as 'suggestive but by no means obscene', introduced a succession of artistes. There were topless, G-stringed women who danced and posed, nipples concealed for the sake of propriety beneath flesh-colour sticking plasters. There was a male juggler, plus a balancing act performed by a skimpily dressed man and woman. Then there was 'a striptease quiz' which involved semi-naked performers posing in a tableau at the rear of the stage. Customers had to guess the song, film or show embodied by the tableau. Four girls, standing near the front of the stage, removed an article of clothing every time there was a correct answer. Eventually the girls were wearing only their panties, the next correct answer providing the cue for them to walk to the back of the stage. As they removed their panties, the lights dimmed and the curtains closed. Whoever answered that final question correctly was awarded a plaster statuette of a nude woman, parodying the famous trophies distributed at the Oscar ceremony.

A moment later the curtains swept aside, ready for the amateur striptease competition. Its four contestants stripped clumsily down to their G-strings. Points were awarded by the compère depending on the volume of applause they provoked.

The amateur striptease competition rounded off the first half of the show. Superintendent Strath's two spies then joined the customers pouring into the lounge bar during the intermission. Positioned at the top of the main staircase down to the foyer, Raymond cast a proprietorial gaze over the thirsty horde. He must have been pleased with the way things were going. By the time the Revuebar closed at 11.10 p.m. that night, its combined takings from sales of tickets, drinks and programmes, and cloakroom fees, were over £500.

On the basis of the reports submitted by the team of undercover detectives, Superintendent Strath became convinced Raymond was flouting the licensing laws by serving alcohol to non-members. Now the superintendent resorted to the agent provocateur tactics that had brought about the closure of other central London clubs.

The day after the launch of the Revuebar, Strath sent a couple of officers over to Walker's Court. Flashing their membership cards, they went up to the lounge bar. Before ordering drinks, one of the detectives baited his trap by explaining to the barman that he wasn't a member. If the detectives were to be believed, the barman still served them, inadvertently leaving Raymond vulnerable to his unsmiling foe at West End Central.

Oblivious to what had just happened and, maybe, to the continued presence of undercover detectives, Raymond must have felt he had every reason to celebrate the club's first few days. Though the box-office takings hadn't sustained the level set on the opening night, they were still excellent over the remainder of the week. And they were bound to benefit from an alluringly censorious piece in that weekend's edition of the *People*.

Its slouch-hatted crime columnist, Arthur Helliwell, described an afternoon tour of the five Soho strip-clubs. 'Not since my old friend Pete Herman, the ex-bantamweight champion of the world, took me to see Lili St Cyr, the American striptease queen, taking a public bath in New York eight years ago, have I been as shocked and staggered as I was in London last week...' he wrote. 'Why, even the dives in the Pigalle and the tough honky-tonks along Manhattan's notorious 52nd Street wait until after dark before they put on their show. But London bests them all for naughtiness... Raymond's show is undoubtedly the most lavish of them all, but is marred by a disgraceful amateur striptease open to any girl over sixteen-years-of-age. "I have never put on an indecent show in my life," Raymond told me. "In fact, I won't engage any girl with a bigger than thirty-six inch bust because I wouldn't like to embarrass my customers." But Mr Raymond's show *did* embarrass me. For, quite frankly, I found the spectacle of a London landlady, a young mother and a former female wrestler undressing in public in the middle of the afternoon a little too much to stomach.'

Sunday's show provided the solitary blemish on an otherwise highly encouraging week. In place of the usual striptease extravaganza,

Raymond staged *Call Us Mister!*, a separate revue with an all-male cast, its title borrowed from the booklet issued to demobbed servicemen immediately after the war. Choreographed as usual by his wife, it featured cheeky renditions of 'Love For Sale' and 'Salad Days', sung by men in drag. It also incorporated drag striptease, a phenomenon born in New York during the closing years of the 1920s. For her variation on this, Jean came up with a skit on the amateur striptease competition, only on this occasion the performer was a cross-dressing middle-aged man. When he peeled off his final layer of tarty clothing, he exposed a pair of false breasts. Demonstrating impressive powers of perception, Superintendent Strath reported that the show possessed 'a distinct flavour of homosexuality'.

*Call Us Mister!* represented a daring attempt to exploit what would later be termed the gay audience: daring because this secretive constituency hadn't yet been emancipated by the repeal of legislation declaring sex between consenting men illegal. By staging the show, Raymond must have known he risked further antagonising Strath and his colleagues. Like many forerunners of successful phenomena, however, *Call Us Mister!* was a pitiful failure, bringing in few customers. Worse was to come.

Strath had already started to make arrangements for a raid on the Revuebar. Wary of the reputation of the officers at West End Central for tipping off club-owners, he released information only on a need-to-know basis. Even during briefings for raids, he'd keep the name of the targeted club secret, merely instructing his subordinates to 'Watch, and follow me'. He'd then marshal them in a crocodile through the streets.

The raid on the Revuebar was scheduled for the evening of Friday, 2 May. As the troop of twenty-four plainclothes officers and eight women police constables, headed by the superintendent, snaked through Soho, Raymond was presiding over another successful evening at the club. It now boasted almost eight thousand members, sixty of whom were boozing in the lounge bar during the run-up to the main evening performance. Little did he realise that three of those drinkers were undercover detectives.

At about 8 p.m. the raiding party arrived at the box office. Bypassing the queue, Strath went up to the box office manager, identified himself and flourished a search warrant. Strath and the other officers then rushed up to the lounge bar. There, Strath again identified himself before arranging for his colleagues to take the customers' details. A second group of detectives, meanwhile, marched into the theatre. Some of them stormed the stage, where two young girls were naked apart from G-strings. As that was happening, a detachment of women police constables barged into the dressing rooms, startling not only the loitering contestants in the amateur striptease competition but also the topless Renée Haskell who, in an unexpected flush of modesty, grabbed her poodle and used it to shield her breasts.

Hearing that a raid was in progress, Raymond – who appears to have been in his second-floor office – strode through the turmoil and into the theatre. With George Richardson alongside him, he went up to Strath. In a measured tone, emanating calmness under pressure, he said, 'Good evening, Superintendent. There's nothing wrong, is there?'

'I have entered these premises with other officers on authority of a search warrant under the Licensing Act, 1953,' Strath said. He added, 'You *are* Mr Raymond, are you not? And this *is* Mr Richardson, the secretary?'

Both Raymond and his sidekick replied, 'Yes.'

The exchange was recorded by a woman police constable, there to document all such conversations in shorthand.

Strath showed Raymond his search warrant and recited the official caution. 'Do you wish to say anything in answer to the charge? You are not obliged to say anything unless you wish to do so, but whatever you say will be taken down in writing and may be given in evidence.'

Raymond didn't respond. Nor did Richardson.

Addressing both Raymond and Richardson, Strath said, 'Observation has been kept inside this club on a number of dates since 16th April 1958, and prior to your opening on 21st April 1958 persons were seen to come to the reception of this club, complete nomination forms and at the same time purchase tickets for future performances. These persons were accepted to provisional membership on payment of a 10/6d fee without being introduced or seconded by anybody.' Strath went on to state that a large number of patrons were served alcohol with little or no challenge as to membership.

'That is not true,' Raymond replied. 'The barmen have very strict instructions to serve full members only. I sacked one the other week because of that.'

Strath noted approvingly that patrons were, on more recent nights, requested to produce pink membership cards before being served. But he qualified his approval by going on to say, 'From the police observations and advertising literature in my possession, it appears that a large number of your patrons are *not* bona fide members, in that application for membership is only a formality and few, if any, of the persons seeking membership are proposed or seconded.'

'I have no comment,' Raymond answered.

Somewhat ominously, he and Richardson were then asked to accompany Strath. The superintendent ushered them downstairs, where they witnessed the box office manager and another employee being grilled about the provision of membership cards and drinks. Raymond tried without success to put an end to the questioning by saying to the box office manager, 'I advise you not to make any comment until you have seen your solicitor.'

About five minutes later Strath guided Raymond and Richardson back to the lounge bar, where a detective introduced them to two customers. Like the master of ceremonies at some grand reception, the detective announced, 'Mr John MacKenzie-Clarke, holder of the blue provisional card, and Mr John Bull, his guest.' Without commenting on the guest's implausibly patriotic name, he added, 'Mr MacKenzie-Clarke has been served with a gin and orange for himself and a gin and tonic for his guest.'

'That's a lie,' Raymond protested. 'Show me the waiter who served you.'

MacKenzie-Clarke looked round the bar and replied, 'I can't see him now.'

'When did you join the club?' Strath asked.

'Yesterday.'

'Did the waiter who served you ask for production of your membership card?'

'No.'

'Were you proposed or seconded?'

'No, I wrote in.'

Raymond summoned the head barman and said to him, 'These men don't know who served them. What is the rule?'

'No person is allowed a drink unless he is in possession of a pink membership card, countersigned with his signature,' the head barman said.

To emphasise the hopelessness of Raymond's predicament, Strath summoned a couple more detectives who, with robotic attention to detail, listed specific breaches of the laws on licensing and club membership. The ordeal culminated in the superintendent saying to Raymond and Richardson, 'You have seen and heard what has taken place tonight. Non-members and overseas members have been served with intoxicants and the majority of the persons present claiming membership are not bona fide members of the club. Is your theatre licensed for public music and dancing?'

Since London County Council still refused to grant these licences to strip-clubs, Strath knew what Raymond was going to say.

'We are not licensed for public music and dancing,' Raymond conceded.

'Each of you will be reported for selling intoxicating liquor without authority of a Justices' Licence and for permitting unlicensed public music and dancing.'

The only reply Raymond could muster was, 'We do not agree.'

Strath turned to Richardson and said, 'You will be reported to show cause why this club should not be struck off the register on the grounds that it is not being conducted in good faith.'

Neither Raymond nor Richardson responded.

It was 9.15 p.m. by the time Strath left the Revuebar. His colleagues had already preceded him, lugging box after box of the club's paperwork, plus samples of the nude photos displayed at reception. As soon as the police had departed, Raymond put into practice that old theatrical maxim about how the show must go on – and, in this case, the clothes must come off.

# 15 TREASURE CHESTS

**D**ESPITE WHAT SUPERINTENDENT Strath had said, weeks passed without the anticipated court summonses. Raymond was left to concentrate on running the Revuebar as well as the remnants of his touring revue business. In an effort to appease Strath, he ordered the staff at his club to enforce the laws on membership. Yet that didn't deter Raymond's would-be nemesis from submitting a report to the Metropolitan Police Solicitor's Department urging legal action against the Revuebar.

Late that summer Raymond and Richardson received summonses to appear at Marlborough Street Magistrates' Court on thirteen charges. In preparation, Raymond hired Gilbert Beyfus and another barrister to represent himself and Richardson. Beyfus's victorious performance during Jean's libel action had obviously impressed him.

Just after lunch on Tuesday, 23 September 1958, the hearing began with Raymond pleading 'not guilty' to the charges. The prosecution then outlined their case and called two of Strath's undercover detectives as witnesses. During cross-examination they were compelled to concede that the Revuebar was 'extremely well run'. Scenting an opportunity, Beyfus used a legal technicality to obtain an adjournment until November.

Before the case resumed, Beyfus's assistant reached a deal with the prosecution. Since the club was now strictly enforcing the laws on membership, the prosecution agreed to suspend the charges against Richardson – charges that threatened to close down the club. An agreement was also struck for Raymond to alter his plea to 'guilty' on five counts of breaking the licensing laws and three counts of using his premises for unauthorised public dancing. When Raymond next appeared in the dock, clad in a Savile Row suit, he was fined £20 for breaking the licensing laws and £10 for staging unlicensed public dancing. He was also ordered to pay the Metropolitan Police's legal costs, amounting to £52 10s. Raymond's own legal expenses were much higher – about £2,000. But he regarded this as a sound investment. Back at the Revuebar, he told a reporter from the *Daily Mail*, 'Every penny of it has been well-spent. I now have the legal okay to go ahead with my plans for this place.'

As Raymond saw it, the magistrate's judgement was tantamount to giving him permission to continue operating the Revuebar provided he obeyed the laws on club membership and the sale of alcohol.

The reporter asked him where he'd got the money to launch the club.

Euphoria at the outcome of the case possibly clouding his judgement, Raymond grinned and – in a reply guaranteed to feed rumours of gangland connections – said, 'Just say I've been around... around *plenty*.'

Raymond had certainly been around long enough to recognise the value of publicity. Surrounded by showgirls, his immaculate suit augmented by a dandyish display handkerchief, he sat in the lounge bar of his club that evening and celebrated in the company of journalists from three national newspapers that would subsequently savour his victory. A glass of champagne in hand, he smiled broadly and proposed a toast 'To striptease'.

Striptease wasn't merely the toast of the Revuebar by then. It was the toast of Soho. The conspicuous success of Raymond's club, along with the Casino de Paris, the Nell Gwynne Room and other venues, led to the creation of a new club on Great Windmill Street. Advertising itself as 'London's only non-stop strip revue', this latest downmarket addition was called the Panama Theatre Club. Soho was now in the early stages of a strip-club boom. 'The face of our town's West End is disfigured by an eczema of crude club shows known collectively as "the multitude of skins",' complained the theatre critic of *What's On in London* – the very magazine that had done so much to popularise those clubs by carrying adverts for them, adverts that lent new meaning to the term 'display advertising'.

Having secured the future of the Revuebar, Raymond was able to close down both his touring revue business and his offices on Chandos Place. By the tail-end of 1958 he was boasting to the press that his club had 36,000 members and that it was taking £5,000 a week. The true figures were much smaller, though the success of the Revuebar couldn't be questioned. Nor could Raymond's inability to extract maximum pleasure from that success. He evidently loved the power, fame and material rewards it bought him, but he admitted that he had no hobbies on which to lavish his new-found wealth. He didn't play golf. He didn't support a football team. He didn't gamble. He didn't yearn to travel round the world. And he didn't collect anything apart from money, regarded by him as life's scoring system. Work wasn't just a means to an end. It seems to have been what he most enjoyed.

In the hope of garnishing his success with an image of respectability which might deter the authorities from continuing to harass him, he started telling reporters that the Revuebar's members encompassed lawyers, judges and City gents. Again, the truth was slightly at odds with what Raymond told the press. Admittedly, the lounge bar was often dotted by men in evening dress and women in chic gowns, yet the club's clientele wasn't restricted to the professional classes whose salaries could accommodate the high prices for membership, tickets and drinks.

Every night Raymond's wife liked to sit in the auditorium, intent on checking that the performers were following her choreography. Attracted by its sheen of luxury and louche glamour, the Revuebar was also frequented by an odd range of other people. There were provincial

football fans in London for away matches. And there were gangsters –
big-timers such as Billy Hill and small-timers such as John 'Scotch
Jack' Buggy. 'The Kray twins were in the lounge-bar a lot,' remembered
Kenny Cantor, a comedian and Revuebar regular whose father had given
Raymond his first booking as a mind-reader. 'They'd send somebody
ahead of them to look round before they came in. Everyone treated them
like the Queen at the Royal Command Performance. If *they* laughed,
everyone laughed. You wanted them on your side.'

Mixing with the gangsters were celebrities from the metropolitan
showbusiness world: people as varied as Stanley Baker, Peter Sellers,
John Mills, Alma Cogan, Laurence Harvey, Michael Redgrave, Trevor
Howard, Graham Stark and the crooner Dickie Valentine, who became
a friend of Raymond's. 'All the top British stars went there. Hollywood
ones, too,' Kenny Cantor recalled. 'They knew they could have a drink
in the lounge-bar and nobody would bother them. The musicians would
get out their instruments and we'd have a sing-song round the piano. It
was fabulous fun. And very good for Paul's business because the punters
liked having these big stars drinking side by side with them.'

Few of the Revuebar's show-business customers were more glamorous
than Diana Dors, the bottle-blonde film star endowed with the type
of spectacular figure depicted on the fuselage of wartime American
bombers. Recently separated from her husband, she'd often be seen in the
lounge bar with Tommy Yeardye, her boyfriend and supposed 'business
manager'. He was a muscular, good-looking stuntman and bit-part actor
whom she'd met while he was working as Victor Mature's stunt double
on one of her movies.

Generally, these ill-assorted audiences were well behaved. For many
customers, drawing attention to themselves was the *last* thing they
wanted. Entering the club had been enough of an ordeal without courting
further potential embarrassment by wolf-whistling at the girls.

The most common trigger for raucous behaviour was provided by
the striptease quiz. Shouting and pushing occasionally broke out when a

customer gave an incorrect answer at the crucial soon-to-be-topless-or-knickerless stage.

Curiosity about Raymond and the club had reached the point where reporters often tried to obtain quotes from his employees. On the recommendation of Connor Walsh, who must have realised the risks implicit in such untramelled access, Raymond's employees were forbidden from talking to the press about their employer or their work. It was a rule that Raymond would impose for the rest of his life, during which his attitude towards journalists grew ever more ambivalent. One minute he was happy to use them to publicise his business ventures, the next he was complaining about press intrusion. Motivated by a blend of loyalty, affection and pragmatism, employees refrained from anything but occasional furtive off-the-record conversations with reporters.

Probably thanks to Walsh's PR expertise, Raymond was invited during the run-up to Christmas to appear in a short documentary about the flourishing Soho club scene. The invitation, which marked his most dramatic publicity coup so far, came from Pathé, one of the leading producers of newsreels shown in British cinemas. A film crew duly turned up at the Revuebar, where they shot night-time footage of its exterior. They also filmed the club's chorus line in action and interviewed Raymond.

Debonair in flawless evening dress, hair neatly parted and brilliantined, he sat at one of the dining tables in the theatre, an ice bucket with an uncorked bottle of champagne in front of him. Until he spoke, he could have been mistaken for an aristocratic man-about-town. 'I have a very successful club here,' he said, his delivery rendered slightly awkward and halting by the presence of the camera. 'It is a bona fide club and is run along the correct lines. We also abide by all the licensing laws. Personally, I think that some of these tiny, one-room backstreet clubs should be more controlled. They are the ones that could give the properly run, bona fide clubs a bad name.'

*Front cover of the programme for the Fabulous International Striptease Spectacular No.3, 1958. The inside pages of Revuebar programmes featured a few black and white photos of topless performers. Note the seal on the righthand side which deterred customers from flicking through the magazine before buying it*

When the film – entitled *Clubs Galore!* – was screened in cinemas during the penultimate week of December, the Revuebar sequence was introduced by a pukka-voiced narrator who said, 'High-class floor-show clubs are the vogue just now. And, being clubs, they are free of some of the regulations that apply to theatres, so the entertainment is Continental. Paris has come to London. Members can imagine they're on the other side of the Channel. All the same, some authorities don't like the idea. They want Paris kept on the French side of the water.'

It was hard to imagine a more effective and widely seen advertisement for Raymond's creation.

The deluge of attention devoted to him and the Revuebar had one unwelcome side effect. His father, who was extremely hard up, contacted him and asked for a hand out. Understandably aggrieved by what had happened decades earlier and by his father's cynicism, Raymond refused to bail him out. Besides, Raymond had enough responsibilities without acquiring a dependent father.

Early in 1959 his wife added to those when she announced that she was pregnant again. To celebrate, she and Raymond threw a party at the Revuebar.


In a bizarre bid to enhance its dubious credentials as a bastion of Establishment respectability, Raymond sought to involve the Church of England in the running of his club. Via the Actors' Church Union, an organisation set up in 1899, he proposed the appointment of a club chaplain. With their support as well as the blessing of the Bishop of London, Raymond's friend, the Reverend Edwyn Young, was assigned the role.

From around the spring of 1959 the Revuebar's new chaplain, conspicuous in his cassock, spent at least an hour a week there, though he confessed to being 'disgusted and shocked' by the sections of the show that he witnessed. Most of the time he was backstage, where he chatted with the performers about everything from their love lives to their financial problems.

It wasn't long before a Fleet Street reporter seized on the news that the Revuebar now had its own chaplain, news endowed with potential for comedy and controversy. The eventual article, which highlighted the incongruity of Young's presence, quoted him as saying, 'In time I hope that all the striptease clubs will have chaplains.'

That spring Raymond faced even greater competition for customers. Surely inspired by earlier visits to the Revuebar, Tommy Yeardye – whose romance with Diana Dors had ended in acrimony – set up his own strip-club with financial backing from a wealthy investor. Yeardye's venue, situated just off swanky Portland Place, was called the Paint Box Restaurant Club. When they weren't drinking or eating, his customers were invited to sketch near-naked, lingerie-clad models, an ingenious gimmick designed to alleviate the punters' embarrassment, though Yeardye – somewhat unconvincingly – insisted its sole purpose was 'to bring art into the average man's life'.

Endorsing the impression that a striptease boom was under way, the opening of Yeardye's place was followed by the launch of the diminutive Tropicana Theatre Club. Unlike the Paint Box, this was in Soho. There, Murray Goldstein – a young impresario-in-the-making – staged shows that featured singers and comedians, alternating with questionable routines such as 'School for Strip', the cast of which was dressed in schoolgirl uniforms. Within only a month the Tropicana's membership had passed 2,000 and the pavements outside were clotted with stage-door Johnnies.

Raymond felt threatened by these new rivals and by the Casino de Paris, which had established a reputation for staging more daring shows than the other venues. One of its presentations involved a woman stripping in front of a man while the song 'Love For Sale' was played. Such risqué routines prompted Raymond to convene a crisis meeting of his senior staff. Conveniently forgetting his previous claims about how respectable the Revuebar was, he told them, 'We must go one better.'

Urged on by Raymond, his staff discussed 'just how far they could go to outdo their rivals'. And they thought up ideas for more suggestive shows, for shows that didn't merely consist of girls taking off their clothes and posing in G-strings. Historical tableaux were proposed, often depicting slave-girls and their captors. Another idea entailed strippers venturing into the audience and inviting customers to help them remove items of clothing. What Raymond wouldn't countenance, though, were any ideas for routines that involved nuns. 'I don't like blasphemy,' he said. 'It doesn't shock me. I just don't see the need for it.'

He also tried to spice up the posters outside the Revuebar. The phrase 'audience participation' became a recurrent ingredient. So did jokey words such as 'sexational' and 'sexciting', devised in collaboration with his employees. But the club's new direction provoked the resignation of at least three outraged members of staff.

Funnily enough, just as the Revuebar was becoming more blatant in its front-of-house publicity, the pavements of Soho lost the atmosphere of brazen sexuality provided by the occupying army of prostitutes. Like a Third World guerrilla force that slips away when confronted by superior firepower, the tarts largely disappeared from the West End streets on the morning of Sunday, 16 August. That was when the Street Offences Act became law. Second convictions for soliciting, previously punishable by an insignificant fine, now carried prison sentences.

Prostitutes rapidly worked out how to dodge the law by advertising their services through cards in newsagents' windows or taped to lamp-posts or even pinned to the back of market traders' barrows. A typical, heavily coded message read, 'Gents' Hand-knitted Jumpers'. When a reporter rang the accompanying phone number, he was told, 'We have a good selection. I'm sure we will be able to suit all tastes. We have a nice redhead model, 36-24-36.' Other prostitutes touted their wares through euphemistic signs above doorbells, signs such as 'French Model Giselle'.

Soho was soon filled by a jostling, riotous mob of signage, this latest wave of advertising adding to the familiar traffic signs and shop signs, not to mention the urgent typography plastered across the façades of strip-clubs and on free-standing boards outside those clubs.

Heavily pregnant though she was, Raymond's wife – whose professional commitment remained almost as strong as her husband's – was determined to carry on producing the increasingly elaborate shows at the Revuebar. While she and her cast were rehearsing a new production during September, she began to feel such overwhelming tiredness that she went to see Dr Stanley Perchard, the Harley Street gynaecologist supervising her pregnancy. Diagnosing fatigue but unable to persuade her to relinquish her choreographic duties, Dr Perchard taught her to hypnotise herself for ten-minute intervals, enabling her to obtain extra rest whenever necessary. The technique would, he assured her, be equally useful for controlling the pain of childbirth.

So consistently profitable had the Revuebar become that Raymond could afford regular flights to the Continent, where he offered up to £1,000 a week to foreign striptease stars to appear in his shows. He was also able to splash out on an ostentatious new car – a maroon Bentley Continental that set him back £8,500. As well as acquiring this emblem of wealth, he could afford to give his wife money to buy expensive clothes. And he could initiate what became a sartorial ritual: his purchase of a dozen made-to-measure suits which he'd keep for a year before replacing them with another batch. Continuing this spending spree, he invested somewhere in the region of £4,000 in a multicoloured, thirty-feet-by-forty-feet neon sign to advertise the Revuebar. He'd just obtained planning permission for this at the third attempt.

The sign, large enough to dominate all the neighbouring signage, its orange lettering glowing in the dark like the tip of a cigarette, faced Brewer Street. Against a backdrop of flashing stars, it read, 'Paul

Raymond Presents The Fabulous International Striptease Spectacular'. Next to the show's title was a jaunty, illuminated cartoon of a showgirl with a feather headdress and a skirt that she appeared to lift in a classic can-can move. Raymond's new sign would become a Soho landmark, remembered by generations of tourists and Londoners.

Just before its unveiling, he was interviewed by a reporter from the *Daily Herald* who asked him whether he was worried about 'the anti-strip lobby' and its plans for legislative control over strip-clubs. 'Worried?' he blustered. 'Good heavens, no. Why I *welcome* the idea of controls. Controls over the strip clubs are going to come. That means the hole-in-the-wall places will be put out of business. And that will leave three or four big, properly-run clubs to which no one can object.'

Nearly three weeks after the Revuebar's new sign had been switched on for the first time, Raymond's wife was taken to Welbeck Street Nursery Home, a private maternity hospital in Marylebone. Under self-hypnosis, she gave birth to a seven-pound baby boy. She and her husband immediately named him Howard.

Within hours of the birth, Jean was already making plans to return to work the following week when she intended to start producing the next show. Raymond's growing renown ensured that the child's arrival was covered in two Fleet Street newspapers. Questioned by a reporter from the *Daily Mail*, Raymond said, 'One day my son may take over the business – but who knows what is going to happen in twenty years?'

# 16 THE WAGES OF SKIN

**H**IS RAPIDLY EXPANDING bank balance enabled Raymond to spend £10,000 on a new, larger home for his family. The house was at 5 Parkside Avenue, looking across the verdant expanses of Wimbledon Common. Pleasant though Wimbledon was, Raymond had qualms about moving there. The area, colonised by higher-echelon civil servants and City workers, had long been associated with upper-middle-class propriety. His neighbours would, he feared, so disapprove of the Revuebar that they'd ostracise him and his family.

At first he detected 'a suspicious curiosity' about 'this man who ran such a notorious show'. Once that curiosity had abated, however, he found his previous worries unfulfilled. He took tremendous pleasure in defying the preconceptions which, he assumed, his neighbours had about him. 'If they expected a fat, slimy racketeer with a cigar and some luscious blonde doll chewing gum as my wife, they must have been disappointed,' he remarked.

Apart from the nocturnal hours the Raymonds kept, their neighbours would have noticed little to distinguish them, superficially at least, from other Wimbledon residents with young families. Shown into the spacious lounge, its red carpet bouncy underfoot, visitors had to sidestep their daughter Debbie's toys and dolls, habitually strewn across the floor. Only then could they admire the expensive furnishings: the white bearskin rug, the fashionable ebonised furniture, the walnut-veneered cocktail cabinet, the low Swedish-style coffee table, the pair of grass-skirted statuettes of African dancers at either end of the mantelpiece. Through windows that faced the garden, visitors could see further evidence of the material attention lavished on Debbie. The garden was dotted with a seesaw, a swing, a slide and a playhouse.

'I think he indulged his daughter because he loved her and because it was a way of making him feel less guilty about how little time he spent with her,' one former neighbour concluded.

Raymond's work always took precedence over his family life. Like other ambitious businessmen with families, he claimed *they* were the reason why he worked so hard. It was all for their sake. He just wanted to provide them with the best of everything. He may even have believed this himself. But his true motives don't appear to have been that straightforward. Business didn't merely offer him a means of supporting his family. It offered a way of satisfying his appetite for money and status, an appetite that would prove unquenchable. And it offered him a tremor of excitement analogous to the feeling experienced by a gambler placing a bet.

With a second child to look after, it was more difficult for Jean to share her husband's immersion in the Revuebar. No longer would there be quite such a potent sense of professional collaboration between them. Around this time, Jean later reflected, the happiness began to seep out of their marriage.

Even though the Revuebar absorbed most of his time, her husband made the effort to call on a Wimbledon-based Catholic priest during the spring of 1960. Raymond had long since lost the habit of going to mass and taking confession, yet he still possessed a residual reverence for the Church of Rome. Consequently, he was keen to arrange for Howard to be baptised into the faith.

A reporter from the *Empire News* recorded the encounter between Mr Striptease and the priest. Casting an appreciative gaze over the sober cut of Raymond's suit, which suggested a burgeoning career in the City or Inns of Court, the priest enquired about his profession.

'I'm a West End club-owner,' Raymond replied.

'Not, I hope, one of those strip-clubs about which I've heard so much,' the priest said with a smile.

'I run the biggest and best of those clubs. And I have the spiritual needs of my employees very much at heart. Right now my club padre is with some of my girls who are helping in a church bazaar.'

Only a little while before his visit to the priest, Raymond also popped round to an address in Soho – 56 Old Compton Street. Murray Goldstein, former owner of the Tropicana, was converting the ground-floor and basement there into a Japanese-themed strip-joint called the Geisha Theatre Club. So much cash was being lavished on the conversion that Raymond must have been worried about the Geisha having an adverse effect on takings at the Revuebar. But Goldstein's club, which seated only eighty people, turned out to be too small to present a significant challenge.

The Geisha opened in late March, its interior decorated with bamboo and Japanese murals. Abandoning the revue format and the house bands used by the Revuebar and other clubs, it featured girls gyrating to records. Coincidentally, one of the Geisha's regular customers was Raymond's old schoolmate John Gregson, already a fast-fading film star whose credits embraced *Miracle in Soho*, a mawkish studio-bound fantasy that presented a sanitised, de-nuded version of the district.

Despite the Geisha's restricted capacity, attendances were such that Goldstein was able to recoup the initial £6,000 investment in less than three months. With profits like that, no wonder the West End had been infested by strip-clubs, all competing for the attention of passers-by, their advertising slogans ranging from the functional to the inventive, none wittier than the Winston Churchill parody, 'Never has so much been seen by so many for so little'.

By May that year, the Metropolitan Police estimated that there were about two dozen striptease venues: twelve full-time clubs, plus a further dozen or more drinking clubs and clip-joints where occasional shows were staged, the more popular strippers each evolving their own gimmicks. One girl would ease herself out of a coffin with such vampiric tardiness she should have been billed as 'Nosferatu, the Stripper'. Another would sashay on to the stage in a nurse's costume. Another would make her entrance in a tasselled cowboy outfit and startle the audience by firing caps from a toy pistol.

Since the same performers – other than those employed by Raymond – tended to freelance in several venues each day, they'd be seen hurrying from club to club, sometimes on scooters but more often walking. They were easily identifiable because of their fishnet tights, wobbly high heels, and vanity bags, chock-full of cosmetics, lingerie, records, fancy dress and assorted accessories. The other unmistakable attribute was their make-up, which had to be heavy enough to be visible beneath the ultraviolet lights favoured by most clubs. Similarly decked out women were now as familiar a sight in Soho as the touts, the prostitutes, the Tommy Steele lookalikes, the students from nearby St Martin's School of Art, the man with the barrel organ playing *Cavelleria Rusticana*, the gaggles of aproned waiters, or the gofers lugging precarious stacks of film canisters between the offices of movie companies and the numerous screening rooms.

Except for the Revuebar, all twelve of the full-time strip-clubs were fairly small. An informal survey nonetheless estimated their combined membership to be 200,000 and their average weekly gross to be about £48,000. On that basis their annual box-office receipts were around £2.5 million – more than quintuple the entire British takings for *Spartacus*, one of the biggest blockbuster movies of the early 1960s. There were even claims that the Soho strip-clubs were bringing in nearer to £5 million a year once the income from part-time venues was considered.

Such startling figures lent credence to the claim by the *Empire News* that striptease was 'the most fantastic evolution in British entertainment since the talkies'. Catching Raymond in reflective mood, the reporter behind this story quoted him as saying, 'The female form is one of God's most beautiful creations. It is something to be admired to the point of worship. It has been an artistic inspiration throughout civilised history. I have used that inspiration to make myself a fortune.'

The rapid multiplication of strip-clubs prompted doom-mongers to warn Raymond that the trade would soon reach saturation point. As yet, there was no sign of this, partly because the market spanned most of the country. Men living in the provinces would often detour into Soho when they travelled to London for the FA Cup Final, the Motor Show at Earl's Court, the Royal Tournament, trade fairs at Olympia and conferences of various types. For many companies it had become an accepted practice to take visiting businessmen to striptease venues.

'Whether you like it or not,' Raymond told a reporter, 'the strip-club is here to stay.'

Other people, notably the Labour peer Lord Stonham, were not so keen on the prospect. A welter of unflattering newspaper stories featuring strip-joints and drinking clubs inspired him to table a House of Lords motion to establishing stricter controls over them.

Late on the afternoon of Wednesday, 1 June, he stood up in the House and opened the debate. It was just drawing to a close when the early evening show at the Revuebar was scheduled to begin. Most evenings Raymond could be found there, working in his office, breezing round the club or chatting with customers in the lounge bar, where he indulged his fondness for trotting out stories that mutated in the course of successive retellings. One of these yarns concerned an aspiring stripper who had auditioned at the Revuebar. 'This girl had long legs and a generally attractive figure,' he'd say, 'but that bosom! Impossible.' He would reveal that he'd issued a tactful rejection, only to be telephoned from the outskirts of Northampton a week later by the girl's mother. The girl had tried to commit suicide by putting her head in a gas oven. At that point, Raymond would describe how he'd got in touch with a Harley Street plastic surgeon who was a member of the Revuebar. Continuing the story, Raymond would talk about speeding up the M1 motorway in his Bentley, collecting the girl and taking her to London, where he'd paid for her to have surgery. 'Today', he'd say, 'the girl has a well-balanced bust.' With the satisfied air of a conjuror who had just pulled off a baffling illusion, he'd add that she ended up on stage at the Revuebar, performing for an audience that included her future husband.

From his position in the lounge bar, a glass of champagne usually in hand, Raymond could monitor the number of customers for each show. 'When you consider I do three shows-a-day and a late night cabaret, you can work out for yourself how the cash rolls in,' he crowed. His income from the Revuebar was, he claimed, 'in the region of £2,000 a week' – more than ten times the salary of Harold Macmillan, the prime minister.

Among Raymond's regular customers was the self-styled Madame Bluebell, who recruited performers for the celebrated Lido strip-club in Paris. Her presence was, he informed the press, an endorsement of the productions he was staging. Probably via Madame Bluebell, he heard that her employer, Joseph Clerico, wanted to sell another of his famous Parisian clubs – the Bal Tabarin. Flush with the profits from the Revuebar, Raymond considered buying it, even though it wasn't a going concern, having been closed for six years.

Three days after the Lords debate, Raymond was in Paris, looking round his prospective purchase which, he said, would cost about £125,000 to renovate. Undaunted by memories of his earlier foreign business venture, the disastrous trip to Vienna, he began negotiations with Clerico, but the pair of them couldn't reach an agreement.

Even so, the journey wouldn't have been wasted because it gave him the chance to visit the Lido, the Sexy Club and other venues, from where he could poach performers for the Revuebar. His French recruits included the striptease star 'Madamoiselle Véronique', an exceptionally glamorous, blue-eyed brunette who was given a six-month contract.

Raymond later described how his counterparts in Paris reacted with incredulity to the news that the Revuebar and other strip-clubs were under such attack by the British press and police. On returning to London, he decided to use his surplus cash to buy the lease on a West

*Paul Raymond posing on stage with an unidentified performer, January 1960*

End restaurant. He chose the Celebrité, a huge but frequently half-empty cabaret venue located in a basement at the junction between New Bond and Clifford Streets. Immediately, he drafted plans to rip out the existing fittings and transform the place into what, he hoped, would be 'the most modern and comfortable spot of its kind in Europe'. His recent trip to Paris encouraged him to flirt with calling it the Bal Tabarin.

Seemingly prodded into action by the House of Lords debate, West End Central marked Raymond's return from the Continent by inaugurating a campaign against London strip-clubs. Just after midday on Saturday, 11 June, Superintendent King – Strath's equally zealous successor – led the first in a sequence of raids, carried out by sizeable squads of police. Their target was the Geisha, the owner of which found himself facing an unexpected criminal charge. This had nothing to do with licensing or the laws on running private clubs. Instead, he was charged with 'keeping a disorderly house'.

In a sly change of tactics, the police were using the Disorderly Houses Act, legislation from 1751, directed at brothels. The law's imprecise wording, which referred to 'places of publick entertainment', allowed it to be applied to Soho strip-clubs. Jail sentences could be imposed on anyone found guilty of breaching this law, though the nature of the felony remained nebulous. For at least one officer, the sight of a fully clothed dancer pressing her breasts together was enough to merit prosecution.

King's next victim was among the district's more conspicuous characters, a handsome, moustachioed Persian businessman named Freydoun 'Freddy' Irani. In his capacity as proprietor of the Tropicana and the Peeporama strip-clubs, Irani faced twin disorderly house charges.

The already high probability of Raymond's name also appearing on a police charge-sheet was increased when the Revuebar's chaplain rashly agreed to be interviewed by Michael Dale, a reporter from the *People*. Dale quizzed him about the current show, which featured a specially imported film called *The Frenchman's Dream*. With its recurrent close-ups of women's breasts being kneaded, the film would have been more fittingly titled *A Handful of Bust*.

Commenting on the show, the Reverend Young said, 'It's quite terrible, isn't it? I can hardly believe that men would pay to see that sort of thing.' Then he added, 'It would be betraying my friendship with Mr Raymond if I were to interfere with the running of the club or the type of act put on.'

His naivety resulted in a predictably critical yet salacious double-page spread, published on the final Sunday of June. In large type, it reproduced a less than timely quote from the reverend: 'What I saw frankly disgusted me.'

To gather evidence that would justify pressing charges against

Raymond, Superintendent King placed the Revuebar under observation. On Wednesday, 31 August, Detective Sergeant Albert Corry and a plainclothes colleague from the Clubs Office went there to see Edition No. 9 of *Raymond's International Striptease Spectacular*, featuring among others Melody Bubbles; 'the Fabulous Véronique'; 'the British Strip Star, Trixie Kent'; 'Bonnie Belle, the Ding-Dong Girl'; 'Les Batix: The Whip Sensation of the Century'; and 'Julie Mendez, the Snake Girl', who had made a fleeting appearance in *The Two Faces of Dr Jekyll*, a Hammer horror movie due for release that autumn.

Three thousand customers a week, many of them wearing evening dress, were attending the show. Amid the crowd gathered in the bar before each performance, it wasn't unusual to see Raymond enjoying a drink with the Reverend Young. Nor was it rare to glimpse a few famous faces: a Hollywood producer and his French movie star girlfriend, for instance.

As the scheduled start time for the next performance approached, the sell-out crowd funnelled across the footbridge into the theatre, where an atmosphere of nervous expectation tended to prevail, lone City gents rustling copies of the *Financial Times*. They were joined by Detective Sergeant Corry and his colleague, a plate of dried-up sandwiches on the table in front of them. Eventually the lights dimmed, the band struck up the overture and the show was ready to begin.

# 17 THE MEN WHO WOULD BE KING OF CLUBLAND

IN THOSE DAYS Soho was synonymous not just with striptease but also with hot air: the serpentine hiss of espresso machines, the fractious shushing of steam irons, the aromatic breath from restaurant doorways and, above all, the sound of conversation. Nowhere was the varied nature of the people who lived, worked and relaxed in that area more palpable than in the soundscape of its streets. A brisk walk across what journalists liked to call 'the Square Mile of Vice' was akin to twiddling an old-fashioned radio dial. Snatches of Italian, French, Yiddish and English – barrow-boy cockney juxtaposed with accents redolent of East European shtetls, of Caribbean islands, of gentlemen's clubs, of the movie business, of the backstreets of Naples – loomed out of the metropolitan static, only to recede with comparable rapidity. Housewives and shopkeepers exchanged pleasantries. Waiters and kitchen staff in soiled whites swapped racing tips while savouring a brief respite from the heat and noise of cramped kitchens. Provocatively dressed tarts chatted. Bookies stood on street corners taking illegal off-course bets. Arty bohemians enjoyed intense conversations in pubs, clubs and cafés. Touts attempted to entice suckers into clip-joints. Black men gathered in conspicuous, voluble groups. And teenagers, their faces just visible through the steamy windows of coffee bars, talked excitedly above palpitating rock 'n' roll playing on jukeboxes. Between these disparate factions, gossip was the common currency, disseminated – according to many a Soho veteran – with the speed of an airborne virus infecting the occupants of a crowded room.

It's hard to believe, then, that Tommy Yeardye, one of the Men Who Would Be King of Clubland, wasn't the focal point of some of this gossip during the first week of September 1960. A long interview with Yeardye had, after all, appeared in that Sunday's edition of the *People*. For once the article had nothing to do with Diana Dors or any of the other co-stars of his well-publicised love life.

Beneath the headline 'A Protection Mob Drove Me Out of Business', Yeardye told a predictably receptive journalist what had happened to him since he'd expanded into Soho. His experiences provided a sobering lesson for Raymond and other local businessmen.

The story, told by Yeardye, dated back to the previous year. Here's how it went… Two months after taking over the El Condor, a capacious nightclub on Wardour Street, he receives a phone call from a man claiming to represent an insurance company. Ignorant of the brutal etiquette of his chosen turf, Yeardye politely declares that he already has plenty of insurance.

With a smooth, matter-of-fact air, the caller replies that the insurance he and his partners are offering is *different*. He says it covers a great many things: personal accident, breakages, you name it.

Undeterred by Yeardye's rejection of his offer, the man rings again a few days later. He informs Yeardye that his firm's £50-a-week insurance policy has 'found favour' with all the other clubs in the area. The caller goes on to explain that the policy covers fights or any other kind of trouble in your club. What's more, the policy includes *non-payment of bills*, words spoken with menacing emphasis.

Yeardye responds by saying he's quite capable of looking after the club and resolving any arguments.

Ignoring what Yeardye has just told him, the caller reveals that his company has a special technique for dealing with people who fail to settle their bills. The company finds out where they live, then pays them a visit.

But Yeardye says *that* isn't the sort of thing he needs, prompting the caller to issue a stream of threats. Yeardye reacts by putting the phone down.

His next unsolicited tutorial in the way of the underworld comes when he's buttonholed at the El Condor by two heavies who attempt to intimidate him into shelling out the protection money. No lightweight himself, the young fifteen-stone, six-feet-four-inch-tall Yeardye, well-developed muscles discernible beneath even the smartest of suits, tells the strong-arm boys to clear off. Though they do as he orders them, he hasn't seen the last of these charming representatives of the insurance company.

One night when he's watching a boxing match at the Earl's Court arena, several of their colleagues attack him. They try to knock him to the ground, where he'll be more vulnerable. To protect himself from their punches and kicks, which leave him badly bruised, he grabs one of the smaller members of the gang and uses him as a shield. Effective though this is, it doesn't protect Yeardye from being lashed across the face with a bicycle chain, the impact of oily metal on cartilage breaking his nose.

After he's been discharged from hospital, he receives Phone-call Number Three. 'You were lucky that time, Mr Yeardye,' the voice on the other end says. 'Next time you might be minus an arm or leg.'

Still obstinate in his refusal to be bullied, Yeardye has to cope with a succession of stage-managed scuffles and arguments at the El Condor, all calculated to scare off his customers and reduce the club's takings. But these are only the preface to a much more serious incident which takes place towards the end of that month – November 1959.

Two men provoke a row outside the entrance to the club. While one of them holds the doorman at gunpoint, the other beats up a waiter who comes to assist. Hearing the commotion, Yeardye rushes into the street. The man who has just beaten up the waiter slashes Yeardye's cheek with a razor. Both troublemakers then run off. Bleeding profusely, Yeardye calls the police, but they arrive too late to catch either of the men.

His photogenic features now disfigured by a prominent arc of stitches, Yeardye soon has to field another phone call. A tone of mock-concern infusing the now familiar voice, the caller asks how he is. 'Nasty business, wasn't it?' the voice says. 'For fifty quid a week we can take all those troubles off your hands.'

Yet again, Yeardye refuses to pay up.

As he's leaving the El Condor the following week, a sports car accelerates down Wardour Street. He's about to cross the road when he realises that the car is heading straight towards him, so he backs away from the kerb. But it mounts the pavement, compelling him to leap out of the way. Despite his rapid reaction, the car only just misses him.

This narrow escape precipitates the usual gloating phone call. 'You must be more careful how you cross the road. You're not insured.'

Yeardye remains defiant until the following April, when Len Stevens, the club's general manager, gets into an argument with a customer over a bill. The customer demands to see the owner. But Yeardye isn't there. In his absence, the customer brandishes an iron bar and hits Stevens with it. The blow lands with such force that it fractures Stevens's jaw in two places. The customer then drops the weapon and dashes out of the club.

Cue the obligatory phone call from the protection mob.

Unable to cope any longer with the incessant threat of violence, Yeardye decided it was time to sell both the El Condor and the Paint Box. Venting his outrage, he explained to the reporter from the *People* that he'd since moved into the property business. 'You meet a much better class of person there,' he added.

# 18 STORM IN A D CUP

**B**ETWEEN MID-AUGUST and Friday, 16 September 1960, Detective Sergeant Corry and the other undercover officers continued to patronise the Revuebar. After every visit they were expected to make a typed statement describing what they'd witnessed. Detectives from the Clubs Office had a well-deserved reputation among strip-club owners for scribbling a few furtive notes on the back of a cigarette packet, then expanding these into implausibly detailed accounts of specific performances.

While the police surveillance operation was under way, the freshly modernised Celebrité Restaurant had reopened under Raymond's management. Customers could eat and drink to the accompaniment of a resident singer, backed by the fifteen-piece Miff Smith Band. There was also a late-night cabaret, featuring the chorus line from the Revuebar, which had, by then, closed for the evening. As the Celebrité wasn't a members' club, the cabaret incorporated no nudity.

By mid-September the Clubs Office had amassed sufficient information about the *International Striptease Spectacular* to carry out its second raid on the Revuebar. Questioned by Superintendent King, a sour man with a military demeanour, Raymond could say nothing to avoid the charge of keeping a disorderly house.

Seeing as the definition of 'disorderly' was so hazy, he had scant indication of how he could modify his show to prevent further breaches of the law. In the end he simply toned down the whole thing, even banning strippers from using such suggestive props as bananas and inflatable rubber rings. Once a stripper had removed her last item of

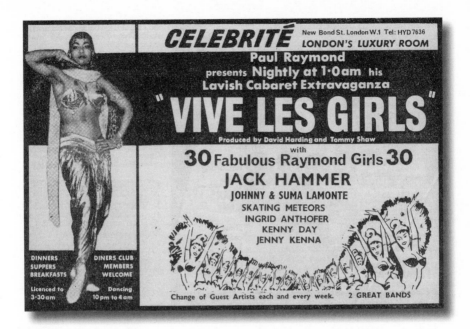

clothing, she'd have to hold a static pose until the curtains closed, whispered instructions of 'Don't move!' sometimes coming from the stage manager, who'd be lurking in the wings.

Lately the Raymonds had been encouraging their wilful, pigtailed four-year-old daughter's theatrical leanings. These had reputedly become evident when, cast as a pixie in her nursery school's pantomime, she'd refused to leave the stage. She had since been enrolled in ballet classes. Her parents had even started allowing her to watch auditions, rehearsals and shows at the Revuebar, where the strippers would give her sweets and other small gifts. Mischievous journalists treated Debbie's attendance as an excuse to ask the Raymonds whether they'd let their daughter become a stripper when she grew up.

Unruffled, Jean would reply, 'If Debbie wants to go in for that side of showbusiness, it's up to her.'

Raymond's stock response was: 'Better she should take off her clothes on a glamorously-lit stage and be proud of the body God gave her than to think the female form is something wicked that should be hidden away like a dark secret.'

Debbie's budding interest in all things theatrical seems to have strengthened the bond with her father, who liked to refer to her – with a note of formality – as 'Deborah'. No such bond, however, existed between Raymond and Darryl, his eldest child. Until then, his former girlfriend had continued to believe that he might seek custody of their pudgy-faced nine-year-old son. Only now did she relax sufficiently to allow Darryl to enter formal education. But she never talked to him about his father. Her antipathy towards Raymond had been intensified by the belief that his nude shows had contributed to the decline of variety theatre and, through that, to the end of her own stage career as 'Gaye Dawn, Telepathic Venus'.

Apparently oblivious to the psychological wreckage he'd left behind, Raymond was enmeshed in the preparations for a legal battle. Like the two other strip-club owners who had been charged with keeping a disorderly house, he faced the possibility of imprisonment as well as loss of income. Even though he gave friends and employees the impression that he relished these sort of challenges, he was in no hurry to end up fighting a test case for the application of the law, so his lawyers employed delaying tactics. They succeeded in preventing Raymond's case from reaching the courts first. That honour was taken by Murray Goldstein and his business partner who, when they appeared at Marlborough Street Magistrates' Court on the last day of October, followed their lawyer's instructions to plead 'guilty'. They were spared prison and each fined £350. This boded well for Raymond – assuming he was prepared to kowtow to authority. Yet he was too proud and obstinate to do that, especially when he was still unsure what he'd done wrong. The case had become a point of principle for him.

Ready for the inevitable trial, he shot a half-hour silent colour film, capturing three of the striptease acts featured in the offending show.

Unfortunately the other performers cited by the police were no longer available, two of them having left the country.

His preliminary court hearing was fixed for Thursday, 29 December.

Jack Isow had, by early November, helped to ratchet up the pressure under which Raymond was living. 'Paul told me what happened,' remembered Mark Fuller, who got to know him decades later. 'His landlord wanted to put up the rent on the Revuebar, but Paul said to the bloke, "Where in my lease does it say that you can put my rent up?" So the landlord checked the lease and realised Paul was absolutely right. "I'm going to have to ask you to leave," the landlord said. And Paul replied, "Where in my lease does it say you can ask me to leave if I pay my rent on time?"And the landlord said, "Well, what am I going to do? I need the money. I can't afford to let you carry on paying the same rent." And Paul said, "You could sell the freehold."'

When Isow agreed to the suggestion, Raymond was presented with a major problem. He had to ensure that Isow sold the building to *him*. If Raymond didn't buy it, there was a good chance that it'd be purchased by one of Soho's underworld bosses, who routinely acquired property in that part of town. With a gangster for a landlord, his business prospects would be severely curtailed.

Negotiations for the freehold were complicated by Raymond's relationship with Isow, which had deteriorated markedly since the launch of the Revuebar. 'Jack really didn't like Raymond,' recalled the son of Michael Klinger, one of Isow's friends. 'I don't know if it was an affectation or not, but Jack would almost spit any time Raymond's name came up.'

Tough though Raymond was as a negotiator, circumstances compelled him to agree to a steep purchase price – £14,000. Contracts were exchanged on Wednesday, 16 November. 'Jack – who was a reliable sort of man – told me a story about the day Paul bought the Revuebar,' said Rusty Humphreys, another friend of Isow's. 'When Paul went round to Jack's restaurant to finalise the deal, Jack was expecting him to hand over a cheque. Instead, Paul gave him this briefcase full of cash. Jack said it must've been buried somewhere because it was all green and mouldy. The money smelt really damp and musty. God knows where he'd been hiding it.'

Through Green Haven Piccadilly Properties, a new company he'd set up, Raymond started buying other commercial freeholds around Soho, this time not out of necessity but as an investment. 'I remember him showing me some of the buildings he purchased just after he'd bought the Revuebar,' said Miklos Matolsci, Raymond's chief electrician. 'Most of them were rented to people who ran them as clip-joints.'

Two days before Raymond was due in court, copies of the latest issue of *Today* magazine appeared in newsagents. Substantiating the celebrity status he'd so effectively cultivated, its front cover bore a photo of him, captioned 'Paul Raymond: King of the Strip Clubs'. It contained the first instalment of the three-part feature series about him, penned by the BBC radio presenter Ernest Dudley who had, besides watching an audition at the Revuebar, interviewed Raymond and several of his star strippers. So sympathetic was the initial article that it could have been written by Raymond's publicist. It portrayed him as a devout Catholic, as a dedicated family man, as someone who 'happens to believe sincerely that it is his mission in life to display beautiful female forms'.

The timing of Dudley's article was fortuitous, in that it had the potential to sway future jury members at Raymond's trial. But Raymond had little time to savour the good publicity.

That day – Tuesday, 27 December – he became entangled in a public spat. It involved Annie Banks, a voluptuous redhead, then in her early thirties, who had, under the stage name of 'Tempest Storm', become post-war America's most famous stripper. Throughout the 1950s she'd been a regular performer at the Dunes casino in Las Vegas, her stardom sealed by a photo-spread in *Playboy* and an appearance alongside Jerry Lewis and Dean Martin on coast-to-coast television. Storm, whose bump-and-grind routine had brought new flamboyance and overt sexuality to 1950s striptease, claimed not only to have had affairs with Frank Sinatra, Elvis Presley and John F. Kennedy but also to be the world's highest-paid stripper. In America she could earn as much as $10,000 a day, so Raymond had reason to congratulate himself on persuading her to appear at the Revuebar for £1,000 a week. She'd signed a seventeen-week contract, starting in the first week of January 1961.

Raymond and his wife planned to let their daughter see the show. They were soon to discover that the prospect of having a five-year-old in the audience appalled Storm.

News of the Raymonds' plans was soon leaked to both the press and the Watch Committee at London County Council. Forced to defend those plans, Jean told the *Daily Mail* that she and Raymond wanted to broaden their daughter's education.

In a statement to the press, Councillor Bernard Bagnari, chairman of the Watch Committee, said, 'We don't like to infringe on the rights of parents, but this seems extraordinary. I shall discuss the legality of this idea with the court's officers in the morning.'

Next day the Watch Committee was notified that it was powerless to intervene. Raymond, meanwhile, made his latest appearance at Marlborough Street Magistrates' Court. Wearing a pristine brown suit, he arrived there in his Bentley. With him were Connor Walsh and his legal team, led by Edward Clarke, who had helped to defend him when he'd last faced criminal charges. A packed gallery that included several other Soho strip-club owners watched Raymond enter the dock. Proceedings opened with him being charged under the name of Geoffrey Anthony Quinn. The presiding magistrate, Paul Bennett, then invited him to make a plea. Speaking on his behalf, his barrister pleaded 'not guilty' and exercised the right to withold their defence.

This left the prosecution counsel, Sebag Shaw, free to outline the case against Raymond. Shaw said that the Revuebar was well appointed and run on very good lines. 'The only complaint was the alleged obscene character of the show.'

In support of the allegation, Shaw called Superintendent King and Detective Sergeant Albert Corry as witnesses.

Corry described how, after enrolling as a member of the Revuebar, he'd attended performances on six dates.

'I can never understand why the police have to go so many times,' Bennett commented dryly.

At Shaw's prompting – 'Come on, there's no use being shy about it' – Corry described some of the acts he'd witnessed. First, he spoke about a routine entitled 'Mutiny on the High Seas'. Set on a pirate ship, it featured a man in tights whipping a completely nude woman as she lay on the stage. 'She showed signs of extreme emotion,' Corry added.

'There are dozens of emotions,' Bennett said. 'Which did she show? Fear? Anger? Excitement? Delight? Horror? Or what?'

'Satisfaction, your worship.'

Under further cross-examination by Shaw, Corry told the court about the rest of the striptease acts, performed by Bonnie Belle among others. He said she'd allowed men from the audience to fondle her breasts and ring small bells attached to her bra and G-string. 'Once when she rang the bell herself, she called out "Dinner time! Supper time!" She also sat on a chair and made suggestive movements with a tassel.'

His testimony convinced the magistrate that there was a case to answer.

On Monday, 2 January 1961 the latest issue of *Today* magazine was released, carrying the second instalment of Ernest Dudley's feature series. It acclaimed Raymond as 'a visionary… and a considerable figure in London's late night quest for kicks'. But the congratulatory tenor of the piece offered Raymond no antidote to its alarming coda. 'Next week,'

RAYMOND REVUEBAR

Brewer St. London W.1. Tel: REG 1593

Personal appearances of the worlds
greatest names in Striptease.

Series 1.                               Number 15.
(Complete Set. 25 photographs)
... ... ... ... ... ... ...

ESTELLE.

In the Galaxy of Beauty which
thrice daily shines at the Raymond
Revuebar Estelle's electrifying personality makes her one of the brightest
of the constellation.
International Stars of the Strip-Tease
firmanent are proudly presented at
the Raymond Revuebar, London's
gayest rendezvous.

ALWAYS SMOKE THE BEST

The Raymond Revuebar Cigarettes
Published by Paul Raymond.

*Both sides of one of the cigarette cards given away with the Raymond
Revuebar branded cigarettes sold at the club*

this promised, 'the plush new club – and duels with the police and
underworld.'

Later that Tuesday Raymond and his lawyers were back at
Marlborough Street Magistrates' Court, where he was committed for
trial in April. The outcome of the trial didn't worry him so much as what
he foresaw as the dismal future of striptease. Continental strippers had,
he felt, 'exhausted every twirl and twist of the tease formula. The pattern
of strip had run its gamut of virtually every possibility, short of sending
a nude through space in Sputnik.' For that reason he doubted that the
Revuebar, which now had almost 46,000 members, could sustain its
success.

Fearful that the concluding instalment of the *Today* magazine series
might prejudice his trial, as well as contradicting his repeated claims that
he'd never had any dealings with the underworld, Raymond threatened

legal action against *Today*. His tactics worked, prompting the magazine to abandon the series.

Just as Raymond had solved one problem, another took its place.

The row with Tempest Storm having been patched up, she'd begun her residency at the Revuebar on Friday, 7 January. With minor variations, the club's new star attraction had, from 1951 onwards, been performing the same routine, disrobing in time to three classic songs. These were Harold Arlen's 'Stormy Weather', Nacio Herb Brown and Arthur Freed's sultry 'Temptation', plus the Ira Gershwin/Harold Arlen torch song 'The Man That Got Away'.

As the house band played the leisurely preamble to 'Stormy Weather', she'd slink on to the stage in a long black fur coat, white gloves and a white fox-fur stole. Smiling seductively, she'd take off her coat. Underneath was a full-length black velvet dress, the front of it bisected by a top-to-bottom zip. Hips swaying to the music's woozy, somnambulant rhythm, she'd unzip her dress, revealing a white slip. Slowly she'd remove her gloves and slip. Now she was wearing only a beaded net bra, a lacy corselette and a necklace inset with chunky rhinestones, intended to glisten in the spotlights. While the band ambled towards the closing bars of their score, she'd unclip her bra and shrug off its straps. Thousands of previous performances at venues across America had left her adept at ensuring the song's melancholy climax coincided with the moment she pulled off her bra and stretched out her arms, momentarily displaying her breasts. She'd then wriggle behind the curtain. Out of sight of the customers, she'd put on a flimsy negligee. Seconds later she'd go back on stage, bow slightly and say, 'Thank you ', her voice carrying a Southern, hillbilly lilt.

Near the end of her first week at the Revuebar, Raymond received an unforeseen telegram from Storm. It had been sent prior to her boarding a plane from London to New York. The telegram detailed her reasons for breaking the contract she'd signed. Uppermost among those was probably the Raymonds' insistence on letting their daughter attend the show.

# 19 DING-DONG

REPORTERS FROM BOTH London evening newspapers as well as most of the national press were at Marlborough Street Magistrates' Court on Monday, 10 April 1961 to cover the start of Raymond's trial. Reggie Seaton, a senior magistrate with a habit of peering over his half-glasses and delivering caustic comments, had been appointed chairman of the court. One of his first decisions was to exclude women from the jury in order to avoid exposing them to what was regarded as potentially upsetting evidence.

Opening for the prosecution, Sebag Shaw argued that the productions at the Revuebar had gone a bit too far. 'Let me say at once that the law is not so prudish as to forbid any representation of the female form even though it is entirely nude. But the law *does* say there is a limit beyond which such performances should not go if, when they transgress that limit, they offend against decency and become lewd.'

Shaw called Detective Sergeant Corry to the witness box, where he was coaxed into repeating his previous testimony about the allegedly obscene acts he'd witnessed. These began with the whipping sequence in 'Mutiny on the High Seas'. And they continued with Carla Primavera, who touched parts of her naked body, made 'suggestive movements' and poured champagne over herself. After her came Bonnie Belle, Bobbye Mack and then Julie Mendez, who removed a live, six-feet-long snake from a basket and manoeuvred the writhing creature round her bare torso. Finally, there was Mademoiselle Véronique, who stripped to music 'in a very artistic fashion', draped herself across a settee, picked up a phone and embarked on a pidgin French flirtation with an imaginary man at the other end of the line.

Given the opportunity to cross-examine the witness, Raymond's barrister asked Corry what he'd meant by the word 'obscene'.

'It would arouse their feelings,' the detective replied.

'What feelings?'

'Man's instincts.'

'Have you heard of film stars like Marilyn Monroe?'

'Yes.'

'Do *they* arouse men's instincts?'

'They arouse mine.'

'Do you think *she* is obscene on the films?'

'Generally speaking, no. But sometimes yes – a little.'


There were prominent stories about the trial in most of next morning's newspapers. When proceedings resumed, two of Corry's colleagues entered the witness box. The first of them described both Bonnie Belle's act and a short film that had been screened. It was about a myopic man whose optician gives him a pair of glasses that enable him to see through women's clothes.

The second witness referred to a routine starring three chimpanzees who 'acted with perfect decorum'. He also told the court how Julie Mendez had put the snake's head in her mouth, prompting someone in the audience to exclaim, 'How revolting can these acts get?'

Cross-examined by Edward Clarke, the detective was asked whether he considered any of the acts to have been artistic and well staged.

'I thought the chimpanzees were very good.'

Most of the court session was, however, taken up by two legal submissions from Clarke. Heard in the absence of the jury, these cited case law in a bid to get the charge against Raymond dropped on the grounds that the prosecution had offered insufficient details or evidence of the offence. But Seaton rejected both submissions.

Shortly after the trial restarted on the morning of Wednesday, 12 April, Raymond's case suffered a setback. Clarke had been hoping Seaton would allow the jury to see the film Raymond had made, featuring several of the offending striptease acts. Seaton declared it inadmissible as evidence, though, because the footage hadn't been shot during the period mentioned by the police witnesses.

Addressing the jury as 'men of the world', Clarke delivered his opening speech for the defence. He said the Revuebar didn't comply with the definition of a disorderly house. It was, instead, 'something that supplies a need for respectable people'.

Clarke followed up by summoning Raymond to the witness box. Asked about the membership of his club, he replied. 'There are very few well-known names who have not been there.' If he'd been running an obscene show, he said, the well-known people who brought their wives and girlfriends wouldn't have patronised it. He added that police officers were among the members and that some of *them* had complimented him on the show. 'One police station, which I can name, holds parties at the Revuebar.'

When his barrister questioned him about the perceived obscenity of some of the acts, he denied any of them were indecent. He said it was a high-class show in a high-class club. 'If I saw an act and thought it obscene, I would not book it.'

Clarke enquired whether he regarded the whipping act as obscene.

Raymond said he'd seen it three times a night for the first two weeks. The routine was, he explained, typical of whipping acts. These didn't involve the girl getting struck by the whip. 'In no way whatever do I think the act was obscene or conducive to sexual perversion.'

During cross-examination by Shaw, who referred to 'flagellation', Raymond lost his temper. He made the less than persuasive assertion that it was 'absolute rubbish' to suggest people came to the Revuebar for sexual excitement. And he used the same dismissive phrase to describe the police allegations.

His place in the witness box was taken by Mrs Olive Self, a glamorous thirty-year-old blonde who possessed the looks and figure of a showgirl but was, in fact, a housewife from Kent. She testified that she and her husband had been to the club five times in the last two years, and that they wouldn't have wanted to see a show containing sexual perversion.

Shaw questioned her about one of the performances she'd seen. It incorporated a competition in which the audience had to guess the identity of six girls posed behind a screen, only their naked breasts visible through a picture frame.

'I see nothing wrong with that,' she answered.

'Would you be prepared to let someone identify you by showing your breasts?'

'If I were talented and in showbusiness, I would.'

'If they asked for volunteers, would you?'

'No, I'm just not that type.'


Next into the witness box was Raymond's wife, dressed in a smart yellow outfit. She must have been dreading what she knew from previous experience might be a humiliating ordeal. At the prompting of the defence barrister, she explained that she'd been choreographing shows at the Revuebar and theatres all over the country for the past nine years. 'It would not be worth my while to put on anything obscene. We have too much to lose,' she said. 'We get royal blood, viscounts, parties of women, and I'm sure they would not come to see the show if there was anything indecent.'

Returning to the line of questioning he'd used on Mrs Self, Shaw asked, 'Would *you* be willing to show your breasts to see if the audience could identify you?'

'Yes, because I do not see anything wrong with it.' Her attitude

*Paul and Jean Raymond pictured after one of their sessions in court, April 1961*

towards onstage nudity had obviously undergone a transformation since her last court appearance when she'd been infuriated by the idea of people mistaking her for a nude in one of her husband's shows. As an afterthought, she added, 'It was a giggle and certainly not vulgar.'

She was then quizzed about Carla Primavera's act.

If there had been anything very bad in it, she replied, 'we would have asked her to cut it out'.

When the focus of Shaw's interrogation switched to Bonnie Belle's routine, Jean said, 'I don't think anyone would get any sexual satisfaction out of ringing a bell.' She insisted that Bonnie avoided physical contact with members of the audience.

'But it would have been easy enough for a dirty-minded person to touch her?'

'We do not have dirty-minded people in the club.'

Shaw pointed out that Detective Sergeant Corry had got into the Revuebar under a false name, so how did she know that *he* didn't have a dirty mind?

Glancing round the court, Jean found Corry sitting behind her. She eyed him before saying, 'I'm beginning to think he *has* a dirty mind. But if Bonnie Belle saw him in the audience, she would leave him alone. I can imagine what his face must have been like if everything he saw was so revolting.'

Once Raymond's wife had stepped down, his barrister called a parade of other witnesses. There was Harvey Riscoe, a theatrical agent who'd watched the show eight times but had 'never seen anything sexually offensive'. There were Ted and Renée Haskell, who said their performances contained 'nothing indecent'. There was the balloon dancer Valerie Salussolia, who was adamant that she'd 'never taken part in any scene which was sexually perverted or obscene'. And there was the lithe, twenty-two-year-old, Yorkshire-born Julie Mendez, her black hair styled in a beehive. She was wearing high heels and a fur coat, worn over a clingy, knee-length dress that showed off her figure. With her, she had a tall basket containing two of her four snakes. Both of these were pythons: eight-foot long José and six-feet-long Lulu. She said she'd been doing her snake act for nearly four years, during which she'd appeared in clubs, cabarets, provincial theatres and even at the Savoy Hotel. In describing her act, she pulled out her costume. It comprised a black G-string, an orange bolero top and a matching dress, edged with imitation diamonds, their tinkling audible across the court.

Seaton asked her to hold up the G-string.

'Hold it up,' Clarke reiterated. 'My Lord wants to see it.'

'*Everybody* wants to see it,' Seaton added.

She obliged by displaying the G-string. Then she proceeded to explain how carefully her snakes had to be treated and how she had to reassure them by stroking them. 'There is no word of truth when they say I have done anything indecent with a snake.'

Taking his turn to cross-examine her, Shaw asked whether the allegation that she'd put a snake's head in her mouth was true.

'It is one of the highlights,' she replied. 'It is quite a feat. You can hear a pin drop when I am working.'

After the last of the witnesses had finished giving evidence, there was just enough time left that afternoon for Clarke to deliver his ninety-minute concluding speech to the jury.

Often incorporating skittish headlines – 'Strip Girl Julie Takes Her Snake To Court' – as well as photos of Julie Mendez and her fellow artistes, the gleeful press coverage of the case had led to even better attendances at Raymond's club. He took advantage of this by arranging for an extra forty-eight seats to be squeezed into the auditorium. All three performances that evening sold out.

Arriving at court next day, Raymond must have known that the trial would soon be over. The session kicked off with Shaw's closing argument for the prosecution. His speech was followed by Chairman Reggie Seaton's summing up of the case. Seaton finished by saying, 'You may feel it was a nasty, unpleasant show which you would not attend, but that is not the charge here. You have got to be satisfied looking at this matter without prejudice one way or the other and, as judges of fact, that the evidence has satisfied you, beyond reasonable doubt, that what was going on in these premises was obscene, lewd, lascivious, debauching and wholly disgusting. If you come to the conclusion that any one of these acts fell into this category, then you should convict.'

At that point the jury retired to discuss their decision. Raymond was left hanging around for only ninety-two minutes before they filed back into the courtroom and handed their verdict to Seaton.

Raymond was found guilty of keeping a disorderly house.

Before going ahead with sentencing, Seaton asked Superintendent King for his opinion of the defendant.

Except for two minor business matters, King replied, Raymond was of excellent character.

Seaton went on to enquire about the current situation at the Revuebar.

King said that the tone of entertainment had been 'considerably modified', though 'one could still find fault with certain acts'.

All that remained now was for Seaton to deliver the sentence. 'I am quite satisfied that you went into this with your eyes open at your establishment,' he told Raymond. 'Your establishment and others have been vying with each other to see what degree of disgustingness they can introduce to attract members from all classes who are only too ready out of curiosity or lust to see the filth portrayed in this establishment. This, I think, is the fourth or fifth case I have had, and this is by far and away the worst. Part of my duty is to keep London reasonably clean. Your show can only be characterised as filthy, disgusting and beastly. If you show pornography like that, then you will have to pay the penalty for it. I regard your case as one of the group, because they were all raided about the same time. I said some time ago if anyone else offended they would go to prison, and I want it to be clearly understood that if there are any more of these filthy and disgusting performances, then to prison the people will go – and for quite some time.'

The chairman imposed a fine of £5,000 and £25 costs, easily the heaviest penalty applied to a strip-club owner since the clampdown started. Unless Raymond paid within one month, he'd face a year's imprisonment.

In addition to the fine and costs, Raymond had run up a £525 legal bill. Expensive though his point of principle had proved, the outlay was negligible when set against the Revuebar's £250,000 annual turnover and the substantial publicity derived from the trial.

Breaking off from rehearsals for Edition No. 11 of *Raymond's International Striptease Spectacular*, Jean was waiting for her husband when he walked out of the courtroom. A mink coat draped round her shoulders, she rushed over and kissed him.

With characteristic defiance, he told the press, 'The show goes on tonight. I'm not finished.'

He and Jean then hurried back to the Revuebar to reassure their worried staff that the club wouldn't be forced to close.

# 20 IMPRESARIO LOTHARIO

A WEEK AFTER RAYMOND had been sentenced, his lawyers lodged an appeal against the verdict. They claimed there had been no evidence that the Revuebar had fitted the legal definition of 'a disorderly house'. And they argued that Seaton had issued insufficiently precise guidelines to the jury about what constituted the offence of 'keeping a disorderly house'.

Raymond's appeal coincided with an unsuccessful attempt in the House of Commons to ban strip-clubs. His lawyers' submission wasn't scrutinised by the Court of Criminal Appeal until Monday, 19 June 1961. The submission ended up being debated in tandem with an appeal by Sammy Bloom, a West End strip-club owner who'd been convicted on identical charges. Such was the complexity of the case that the hearing lasted until Friday of that week, by which time Raymond's legal costs had risen to £11,000.

He was in court to witness the triumvirate of presiding judges dismiss both his and Bloom's appeals. 'If the evidence of the police officers was reliable,' one of the judges commented on his case, 'the indecency involved was beyond question serious and, in some respects, revolting.'

Trade at the Celebrité couldn't compete with the Revuebar, yet it remained gratifyingly brisk. 'Because the rear entrance faced the back of West End Central police station, there'd always be a lot of detectives in there,' said Bob Amiss, a stagehand at both the Revuebar and Celebrité.

*The Fabulous Raymond Girls dance troupe performing at the Revuebar,*
*1962–65*

'There were plenty of showbiz regulars, too, including the actor Harry H. Corbett.'

So positive had Raymond's experience been with the Celebrité that he resolved to expand his business again. During mid-August he made another costly acquisition. Despite the cash he'd lost through the recent court case, he was still able to pay £100,000 for a failing Mayfair restaurant called the Riviera. He talked about spending between £70,000 and £90,000 turning the place – located at 17a Hanover Square – into a ritzy Parisian-style cabaret venue which he decided to call the Bal Tabarin. His plans encompassed an ambitious policy of booking only big-name performers to headline the shows there. Soon he'd signed up two popular American singers, Buddy Greco and Billy Daniels, and he was in negotiations with a third – Mel Tormé. For what was then a colossal salary of £1,500 a week, he also had Diana Dors under contract. Capitalising on her fame as an actress and denizen of the gossip columns, Dors had launched a lucrative parallel career as a cabaret artiste, appearing at such prestigious venues as the Flamingo Hotel in Las Vegas.

While Raymond was busy with his new project, the Clubs Office carried on monitoring the West End strip-joints. On Friday, 17 November, Detective Sergeant Derek Caiels was sent to the Revuebar. There, he attended a show featuring an 'Arabian Nights' striptease by Trixie Kent, not to mention three uncontentious song-and-dance numbers performed by Dilys Watling, daughter of the British film star Jack Watling. Caiels then filed a report stating, 'Though not nearly so obscene as was the case during the observation of September 1960… the show is, in my view, still indecent.'

His report was submitted to the Metropolitan Police Solicitor's Department along with a request for permission to conduct further surveillance in the hope of bringing another disorderly house charge. Permission granted, Caiels and several undercover colleagues returned to the Revuebar. In the lounge bar before the show, they selflessly maintained their cover by drinking beer, chatting up women and buying them champagne cocktails.

Caiels later submitted an interminable report on what he'd seen, his account written in PC Plod style. 'One woman danced while the singer sang, "The Lady Is A Tramp",' he wrote. 'She stripped to her pants and brassiere. She finally removed those and exposed her pubic hair… The next act consisted of a man and a woman dancing. The woman stripped to her pants and bra which she finally removed and exposed her pubic hairs. The male of this couple then announced that he and his partner would next present their interpretation in mime of the record, "John and Marcia". This is a monologue in which the part of both the male and female are spoken and consist solely of the words "John" and "Marcia" and by the intonation of the words there is suggested an amorous interlude. The presentation of John and Marcia commenced with the man fully clothed and the woman wearing a flimsy nylon covering over her panties and bra. The woman spoke first the word "John" and looked invitingly at her partner and removed her nylon covering. The male replied "Marcia" and she again looked invitingly at him and offered the clip of her bra to him. This he released and they embraced. The man fondled the woman's buttocks and the female voice sighed, "John, John, John"…'

Superintendent King's successor at the Clubs Office felt that the report justified another three onerous days' surveillance on the Revuebar. But these failed to provide what the police sought. In early December, the Metropolitan Police Solicitor's Department concluded that the shows at the Revuebar didn't qualify the club as a disorderly house. Unwilling to abandon their quest to prosecute Raymond again, the Clubs Office nevertheless maintained sporadic surveillance on it.

Raymond had, by then, struck up a minor business relationship with John Mason, one of his Walker's Court neighbours. Widely known as 'Big Head', Mason was a heavily built man with a disproportionately large head, his hair worn in a convict-style crew cut. He'd already served a spell in prison, for which he'd earned the alternative nickname of 'Carpet' – cockney slang for a three-month sentence. Since his release in 1958, Mason had established a chain of pornographic bookshops across Soho, a district associated with the trade as far back as 1857, when Holywell Street – 'Booksellers' Row' – had formed its focal point. Mason's smut outlets included the Court Bookshop, close to the entrance to the Revuebar. He struck a deal with Raymond, who agreed to carry adverts for his bookshop in the glossy, pocket-sized programme sold at each show.

Most such shops had signs outside offering the euphemistic combination of 'Books and Magazines'. Inside, usually greeted by a reverential hush seldom experienced beyond the precincts of the Centre Court at Wimbledon during a tense moment in the men's singles final, customers could browse through innocuous pulp paperbacks and American pin-up magazines. Those customers were, in the main, besuited office workers, leading the manager of one of these bookshops to describe it as 'A business run by businessmen for businessmen'.

The bulk of a dirty bookshop's stock usually consisted of more explicit pornography, hidden behind a partition or in an adjoining room, marked 'Private'. Access to this inner sanctum was controlled by the typically thuggish shopkeeper, who'd sometimes solicit likely purchasers with the time-honoured line, 'Something stronger, sir…?'

Mason had become London's leading purveyor of what was then a scarce and therefore valuable commodity – hardcore pornography. In most respects, the quality of the printing and photographic reproduction aside, the hardcore material marketed by him differed little from today's equivalent. He'd negotiated exclusive rights to sell home-made magazines produced by Ron Davey, previously a binman for Hammersmith Borough Council. Known in the trade as 'MDs', short for 'Millionaire Dustman', the publications were no more than stapled-together sheafs of crudely printed photos and pornographic tales, their text concocted by Soho's reservoir of hard-up literary talent. Davey's *Playtime* series comprised eight such stories, illustrated with photos of penetration and ejaculation. Mason paid £3–£4 for each magazine, then sold them for £25. It wasn't uncommon for him to shift 300 issues over a single weekend.

His dominance of this trade had been achieved not only through his commercial acumen but also his police contacts. He was paying £300–£400 a month to members of the Obscene Publications Squad, a unit whose autonomous role within the Metropolitan Police had enabled corruption to become endemic. In return for these monthly pay-offs, Mason was allowed to run his business almost unhindered. He even received tips-offs from the OPS whenever they were, for purely cosmetic reasons, forced to raid any of his shops.

When the notoriously violent South London gang headed by Charlie and Eddie Richardson approached one of Mason's bookshop managers and

demanded protection money, the manager asked Mason what he should do. Backed by the OPS, Mason felt confident enough to say to the manager, 'Tell them to go fuck themselves. I've got all the protection I need.'

Building work on the Bal Tabarin had been completed by the end of December. As well as having refitted kitchens, Raymond's latest acquisition now had seating for 150 diners, their tables arranged on a series of terraces that faced the semicircular stage where the house band would sit. Justifying its billing as 'a new luxury Niterie', he'd installed a white marble dance floor and a gold mosaic ceiling. To differentiate the Bal Tabarin from rival cabaret venues, he'd arranged for the hostesses to wear bunny costumes (an idea copied from the recently founded Playboy Club in Chicago), high heels and fishnet tights segueing into strapless, low-cut sequinned swimsuits with white powder-puff tails, the whole absurd get-up embellished by elasticated bow ties and tall, sparkly rabbit-like ears pinned to their hair.

As planned, Raymond's chic new venue opened on Monday, 1 January 1962. The cabaret was provided by Diana Dors and her husband, Dickie Dawson, a comedian with a quickfire, transatlantic style. Fresh from topping the bill at the London Palladium, they were beginning a five-week stint at the Bal Tabarin. Dawson's act served as the warm-up routine for his wife. He liked to reel off wisecracks – 'Who booked this audience?' – interspersed by impressions of movie stars, his repertoire embracing James Cagney, Robert Mitchum and Jerry Lewis. He'd also tell corny jokes, one of which involved him mimicking a tannoy announcer at a railway station: 'The train now approaching Platforms 5, 6 and 7 is coming in sideways.'

Eventually, Diana Dors sauntered onto the stage, wearing a gold-brocade-embellished black velvet dress with a plunging neckline, its waist cinched with a diamante belt that failed to distract from her swollen stomach, evidence of the early phase of pregnancy. In a self-deprecating gag about her diminutive dress, she spoke to the audience, which included the singer Alma Cogan, who was sitting next to the up-and-coming young lyricist Lionel Bart. 'What d'you think? It's one of Alma Cogan's tea cosies.'

Cogan, known for her flamboyant taste, demonstrated she was a good sport by loosing a burst of uproarious laughter.

Onstage, Dors and her husband had a bantering relationship straight out of a Hollywood screwball comedy. Reprising the classic Marx Brothers' routine, he'd say something rude to her, then she'd look aggrieved and reply, 'I didn't come here to be insulted.'

'Oh, really?' he'd respond. 'Where d'you *usually* go?'

The preliminary sparring out of the way, Dors performed her standard nine-song set, which typically incorporated droll quips about Hollywood – 'At Gary Cooper's birthday party, there were so many candles on the cake three people collapsed from the heat.' For the show's climax she and Dawson sang a hammy duet of Cole Porter's 'Let's Do It'.

☆

Relentless ambition wasn't a trait shared by Raymond and his wife whom, he later realised, 'was happy to have a few quid and a nice home'. Unlike Jean, he was never satisfied with what he had. He always wanted more.

At the turn of that year he transplanted his family from Parkside Avenue to a much grander house at 8 Drax Avenue, towards the southern tip of Wimbledon Common. Their latest home, which set him back £25,000, was a fourteen-room, dormer-windowed, neo-Georgian mansion with a first-floor veranda, a gated car-parking area at the front and a garden at the back. The house had a view of the exclusive Royal Wimbledon Golf Club, from where the thwock of balls being driven down the fairway was audible.

In recent Revuebar programmes, Raymond had taken to using the self-congratulatory blurb at the front to present his home life as a model of suburban stability, of tranquil Sundays at home with his family. Following the move to Drax Avenue, though, he felt his marriage began to go into a slow decline which even his daughter sensed. 'From an early age,' she admitted, 'I was aware that my parents weren't happy together.'

Raymond liked to attribute this welling discontent to the lack of shared ambition, to fundamental incompatibility, yet the immediate source of their problems was less subtle. He'd embarked on a string of affairs, sometimes dating waitresses from the Revuebar. 'You'd never hear any gossip about him, so he must've been very discreet,' remembered Marjorie Davies, one of the Fabulous Raymond Girls dance troupe who worked at the Revuebar, the Bal Tabarin and the Celebrité.

Whenever Raymond's wife rumbled his infidelities, he'd placate her with extravagant gifts of diamond jewellery, mutual resentment gathering momentum like an electrical fire fizzing and sputtering in some neglected corner of a large building. Besides adding to the contents of her already brimming jewellery box, Raymond's compulsive infidelities must have contributed to the increased frequency and bitterness of the rows between him and Jean. 'I distinctly recall this Sunday when I went round to see them, and they started arguing in front of us,' one of their friends remembered. 'They never used to do that. I got the impression they tried not to argue in front of other people, their kids in particular. Not this time, though. It was almost as if we weren't there. Afterwards, Paul – normally so understated – was really embarrassed.'

Bit by bit, he and Jean began to develop separate social lives, providing short-term consolation and long-term sustenance for the growing sense of disconnectedness. While Raymond's social life continued to revolve around his two restaurants and the lounge bar of his club, his wife's expanded in other directions. 'Jean often used to come into the dressing room,' Marjorie Davies said. 'She'd talk to my friend Maggie more than anyone because she was very friendly with her. But we'd always be listening. She'd tell Maggie where she'd been and who she'd met. Quite often she'd turn up with these famous men such as Buddy Greco and Michael Rennie. They might've been boyfriends. Jean would bring them backstage to meet us.

'One day she came into the rehearsals and said we were going to dance the twist. She said, "I've brought someone to show you how to do it. He's an expert at it, and he'll be here in a minute." And in walks Oliver Reed. He spent two or three days teaching us the twist. But we didn't see him again after that. Jean must've dropped him and found someone else.'

# 21 THE BOTTOM LINE

RAYMOND'S MARRIAGE wasn't the sole aspect of his life that hadn't been progressing with the same well-sprung smoothness with which his Bentley glided over even the most potholed roads. Things weren't going well at the Bal Tabarin either. Even the presence of Diana Dors, her fame nurtured by the *News of the World*'s serialisation of her scandalous ghost-written memoirs, wasn't bringing in the sell-out crowds necessary to cover the substantial outgoings. The sight of regular queues outside Winston's, the nearby cabaret-restaurant which attracted celebrity customers as diverse as Bing Crosby, Nat King Cole, George Raft and Liberace, must have compounded his frustration.

In spite of the Bal Tabarin's wobbly start, Raymond remained committed to the concept of running a sophisticated cabaret venue, a concept into which he'd already poured so much cash, effort and credibility. Attired in spotless evening dress, he'd be at his new venue most evenings, greeting incoming customers and strolling from table to table, where he hobnobbed with the diners. 'I used to go in there maybe once or twice a week with all the chaps,' remembered former gangster Gerry Parker. 'Because we'd put a few quid about, he'd always come over and have a chat. There were plenty of film people at the Bal Tabarin. Plenty of villains as well. I used to go with Johnny Nash. I remember seeing the Kray twins there a few times, too. I also saw Charlie and Eddie Richardson there.'

As with most nightclubs at that time, the hostesses employed by Raymond were expected to flirt with unaccompanied male customers.

Officially at least, he discouraged the bunny girls from letting flirtation evolve into prostitution. Yet the hostesses performed an identical function to the hostesses in the dingy Soho clip-joints Raymond professed to despise. The bunnies were there to flatter male customers and wheedle them into spending more than they'd planned. 'If a man asked you to join him for a drink, you were supposed to say you'd like some champagne,' one former hostess at the Bal Tabarin recalled. 'A bottle of bubbly would then be brought to your table in an ice bucket. Very elegant, though it was only cheap stuff. The customers paid through the nose for it.'

Financial risk-taking was something on which Raymond seemed to thrive. With the Bal Tabarin, he was risking his money and his business record. With the Revuebar, however, the stakes were even higher.

Only four days after the Bal Tabarin had opened, rival strip-club owner Sammy Bloom was sentenced to three years' imprisonment and fined £3,000 for keeping a disorderly house. In passing judgement, the presiding magistrate said, 'People must understand that it is my duty and the duty of other judges to stamp out clubs like this and people like you who are behind them.'

The implications for Raymond were worryingly clear. If the show at the Revuebar strayed across the line separating the acceptable from the *un*acceptable, he'd be joining Bloom in Maidstone Prison. The trouble was, the authorities remained incapable of defining the precise borderline between legality and illegality. In common with his fellow strip-club owners, Raymond was vulnerable to the whims of the Clubs Office, the Metropolitan Police Solicitor's Department and, ultimately, the judiciary. His shows had to maintain a tricky balance between two contradictory requirements: the need to titillate his customers and to avoid presenting the police with an opportunity to issue another summons.

Alert for any slip-ups, the Clubs Office continued to send undercover detectives to the Revuebar. For the time being, though, Raymond wasn't giving them any excuse to press charges. Exposing a tinge of disappointment, the new head of the Clubs Office concluded, 'To decent-minded people, the present show is in bad taste, but something more is necessary to warrant proceedings.'

For the six dancers, six showgirls and two soubrettes – solo singers – on Raymond's payroll, each new show at the Revuebar, the Bal Tabarin or the Celebrité required around three weeks of rehearsals, supervised by Jean. 'These were a bit of a bind, because we had to rehearse in the afternoons even though we'd only finished work at 2 a.m. that morning,' Marjorie Davies reminisced. 'We'd practise about one number a day. Dress rehearsals were held at the Revuebar on Sundays, then we'd open the new show on Monday night.'

Amid preparations for the next edition of *Raymond's Striptease Spectacular*, Raymond emulated his wife by introducing the dancers to a famous visitor, in this instance a strapping man with a New Jersey accent. 'Girls, this is Mr Spillane,' Davies remembered Raymond saying.

His guest was the bestselling crime novelist Mickey Spillane, who had risen to prominence more than a decade earlier with *I, the Jury*, the first in a series of books starring Mike Hammer, nominally a detective but really more of a vigilante, prone to sadistic violence. Spillane had, since then, cultivated a tough-guy persona evocative of his hard-boiled, womanising hero. All very handy because he was poised to make his film-acting debut, playing Mike Hammer in a British adaptation of his latest novel, *The Girl Hunters*.

He'd arranged to visit the Revuebar because he was looking for a suitably striking girl to take a small role in the movie. Though the dancers posed and paraded for him, none of them landed the part. Raymond did, however, benefit from the visit. By way of thanks, Spillane

*Marjorie Davies, one of the Fabulous Raymond Girls, preparing to go on stage at the Revuebar, 1962–65*

supplied him with a quote that would be used again and again. The Revuebar employed 'the sexiest girls I've seen', Spillane declared, Mike Hammer's reputation as an Olympic cocksman adding lustre to the endorsement.

'We counted ourselves lucky to be at the Revuebar,' Marjorie Davies said. 'It was a nice place to work, and Raymond was a generous employer. If you were in the theatre in those days, you couldn't afford to take time off when you came down with an illness, because you'd find yourself out of a job. Well, it wasn't like that for us. Another good thing was that the dancers were paid the same amount as the chorus-girls in the top West End theatres.

'Backstage, things were all very businesslike. I was once asked to understudy for one of the solo singers. I remember Bill Dennis, the stage director, coming up to me and saying, "Mr Raymond wants to know if you'd be prepared to take your top off? Of course you'd get a couple of pounds more in your salary." And I said, "No, I couldn't possibly. What if my mum and dad went past and saw the pictures?" I was still allowed to understudy.

'It was all quite matter-of-fact at that time. We'd bring sandwiches into work and make ourselves cups of coffee and bowls of soup in between the shows. On Tuesdays we'd race through the early evening performance, so we could get back to the dressing rooms to catch the beginning of the next episode of *Route 66* on television.'

Less than a week after Buddy Greco had started a month-long residency at the Bal Tabarin, Raymond briefly relinquished his duties as the venue's affable, dinner-jacketed host. In a break from his routine, he travelled to Newcastle, where, on Thursday, 8 February 1962, he'd been invited to take part in a fifteen-minute children's television show. Recorded in the studios of Tyne Tees Television, the programme – *Youth Puts the Question* – featured ten youngsters asking him about striptease.

*Star artiste Ingrid Anthofer (centre left) and an unidentified performer pose in front of the chorus-line at the Revuebar, 1962–65*

Later that day Raymond received a phone call informing him that Tyne Tees Television had decided to cut the programme from its schedule to avoid complaints from parents. 'I can't understand why the programme was dropped,' he subsequently told a reporter. 'There were no illustrations.'

Convinced that the programme would improve the seedy image of striptease, he offered to pay 'any reasonable price' for it, his plan being to screen it at cinemas. But Tyne Tees Television refused his offer.

Possibly because of the massive losses he was suffering at the Bal Tabarin, Raymond looked around for a means of enhancing the profits from the Revuebar. Though he'd never had any interest in what might be called recreational gambling, he decided that the solution was to introduce gaming facilities in the lounge bar, an option made feasible by the 1960 Betting and Gaming Act.

Since the advent of this legislation, London had become one of the world's gambling capitals, even attracting charter flights full of Americans. Gambling had, moreover, become associated with the fashionable and often louche aristocrats who used smart new casinos such as Crockford's and the Clermont Club. To suit the Revuebar's sophisticated image, Raymond wanted to offer games of chemin de fer and roulette, games redolent of Riviera casinos. Both games also appealed to Raymond because they were so lucrative, providing the house with an inherent mathematical advantage. In chemmy, where the bets could escalate rapidly, the house took a 5 per cent commission from every winning hand. In roulette, all bets were forfeited to the house whenever the ball landed on 'o'.

Under the complex terms of the Betting and Gaming Act, however, most lawyers felt that the inclusion of the 'o' on roulette wheels rendered the game illegal. As a way of circumventing this obstacle, an alternative version of roulette – without the 'o' – had been devised. The alternative game, profits from which were made by charging players a fee for each session, was called 'Legalite'.

At the beginning of March, Raymond hired a Legalite table. He and his staff lugged it over to the far end of the lounge bar, where it was positioned alongside a traditional kidney-shaped chemin de fer table. These gave him the excuse to advertise a 'Gambling Casino' at the Revuebar.

From the second Saturday of that month, customers were often to be seen crowding round the gaming tables, the comfortable surroundings and availability of food and drink encouraging them to linger. Every twenty minutes the croupier at the Legalite table called out, 'A fresh session commencing now, gentlemen.' Before setting the timer that was built into the table, he collected a ten-shilling fee from each player. When the timer rang, the croupier wrapped up the current game. There followed a brief pause, then the croupier announced the next session.

Soon after the installation of the Legalite table, Raymond had to contend with an irritating but, in hindsight, fortuitous development at the Bal Tabarin. A mere eight days into a £2,000-a-week contract, the singer Billy Daniels revealed that he'd developed laryngitis and would be returning to America to recuperate before an engagement in Las Vegas. His unexpected departure gave Raymond a chance to staunch the losses still being incurred at the Bal Tabarin.

Realising that his policy of signing big-name performers hadn't worked, he renegotiated the deals he'd struck with two other famous American vocalists, Mel Tormé and Rose Murphy, who agreed to cancel their engagements at his club. In their place he reduced costs by booking lesser-known singers. The first of these was Donna London, a blonde former Canadian beauty queen, hired for a tenth of what Raymond had been paying Daniels. While she and the Revuebar's chorus line rehearsed the replacement show, scheduled to open in the final week of March, Raymond reached a decision to shut down the Bal Tabarin.

Annoyed by the public's failure to support his cherished venue, the imminent closure of which hadn't yet been revealed, Raymond gave a tetchy interview to the *Daily Sketch*. However frustrated he was by the setbacks he endured, that frustration never spilled over into blaming Jean or his employees for his own mistakes.

Raymond's admission to the *Daily Sketch* that he'd lost sizeable amounts of money on the Bal Tabarin provoked an approach from a wealthy consortium under the leadership of John Aspinall, the charming but unscrupulous owner of the Clermont Club. On the assumption that Raymond's recent losses had left him vulnerable, they offered to buy the Revuebar. Raymond replied that he wouldn't consider selling because the club was far too successful.

Aspinall contacted him again a few days later with another bid from the consortium. This second bid was for the Celebrité, but Raymond rebuffed that offer as well.

He received a third bid from the consortium around the beginning of April. Now they were interested in acquiring the Bal Tabarin, which they planned to turn into a casino.

Had he not already lost about £120,000 on the venture, which showed no sign of becoming profitable, he wouldn't have been tempted to part with it. The consortium was offering in the region of £100,000. Raymond regarded the bid as 'too good to refuse'. By Saturday, 7 April he and Aspinall had shaken hands on the deal.

Enabling the impatient members of the consortium to push ahead with their plans, Raymond arranged for apologetic dismissal letters to be handed to the staff at the Bal Tabarin after they finished work that night. As if there was nothing out of the ordinary, he was there during the run-up to closing time, chatting with Donna London's manager and discussing changes to her repertoire for the following week. In a display of uncharacteristic cowardice, he had, however, disappeared by 4 a.m. when the last of the customers left and the dismissal notices were handed out, leaving the waiters, doormen and other employees to gather in shocked huddles.

Several hours later he gave a gloating interview to the press about the excellent deal he'd struck. 'People have been saying that this was the sort of sophisticated night restaurant the West End wanted,' he added sourly. 'I'm afraid they've been kidding themselves. The West End doesn't want it.'

But the public weren't, as things turned out, the only people who were kidding themselves. Within about a week, the deal with Aspinall's group had collapsed and an estate agent's sign had gone up outside the Bal Tabarin.

# 22 MISLEADING LADIES

T HE INTRODUCTION OF GAMBLING at the Revuebar precipitated
a spell of police surveillance during mid-April 1962. Raymond
soon discovered that the Clubs Office envisaged launching
another prosecution against him, not for running a disorderly house
but for allowing 'unlawful gaming' in the club. Whether Legalite was
permissible under the Betting and Gaming Act hadn't, after all, yet
been tested in the courts. When Raymond returned from a foreign
trip, probably spent talent-spotting performers, he prepared for the
anticipated summons by taking legal advice. His solicitor informed him
there was nothing unlawful about Legalite.

Raymond didn't have long to wait before the police visited him at
the Revuebar. Just after 9 p.m. on Friday, 27 April he was told that Chief
Inspector Bill MacKinnon and a group of other detectives were waiting
in the lounge bar. Together with George Richardson, Raymond went over
to MacKinnon, who asked them to accompany him to the Legalite table.

A few customers were grouped round it as the male croupier said,
'Place your bets, please.'

Once the customers had laid their sixpenny coins on the green
baize, the croupier's female assistant spun the wheel. After three games
had been played, MacKinnon turned to Raymond and said, 'Who is
responsible for having this game installed on the premises?'

'I am responsible.'

'You are taking full responsibility for gaming on the premises?'

'Yes, I take full responsibility.'

MacKinnon and another officer continued the interview in Raymond's office, which was adorned by family photos. At length MacKinnon said he'd been advised that Legalite was unlawful under Section 16 of the 1960 Betting and Gaming Act. Next, he issued Raymond with a formal caution.

So famous had both Raymond and the Revuebar become that these latest charges made front-page news in the *Daily Mirror*. But the resultant court appearance didn't take place until Thursday, 5 July when, yet again, he found himself in the dock at Marlborough Street Magistrates' Court, faced by the legal expertise of Sebag Shaw.

In contradiction of the advice Raymond had been given about Legalite, he was found guilty, fined £10 and ordered to pay £10 10s costs. Not satisfied with nailing him on this relatively minor charge, the Clubs Office resumed undercover operations at the Revuebar, where they hoped to gather evidence for a second disorderly house prosecution. Their efforts were, however, to no avail. 'None of the acts could be regarded as indecent or offending against the law,' concluded the ensuing report.


Earlier that summer Frank Fraser had been released from the prison where he'd been serving a sentence for the attack on Jack Spot. Fraser had promptly gone into business with Eddie Richardson. Bankrolled by Billy Hill, they ran a company called Atlantic Machines, which installed fruit machines in clubs and pubs, initially concentrating on the West End. 'Our reputation carried a lot of weight,' Fraser recalled. 'We'd approach someone and say, "Would you like to have our machines?" They'd already know who you were and ninety-nine times out of a hundred, they'd say, "Yes." We put a couple of machines into the Revuebar, though Raymond didn't need any persuading because we'd always got on well.'

Both machines were positioned in the lounge bar. Each game cost only sixpence, yet machines in busy venues like the Revuebar could swallow as much as £200 a month. The takings from Raymond's two machines were split 50/50 between him and his new partners.

'He seemed happy to be involved with us because we made him a lot of cash,' Fraser added. 'And he knew that he had our backing if anyone asked him for protection money. Also, if he sensed someone was going to cause trouble, he could drop our names into the conversation.

'We ended up doing a lot of other business with Raymond. He'd buy any crooked gear we had: jewellery as well as spirits, tobacco, cigarettes, stuff he could sell through the bar. He'd sell the jewellery to the brasses who used to go to the Revuebar. The place was packed with them. They were run by one of the Maltese mobs, though Raymond must've got a rake-off.

'Me and Eddie Richardson became good pals of his. We supplied him every week or so. Here's the drill: we'd ring up and say, "How're the machines going?" He'd say, "Good" or whatever, then he'd invite us over for a drink or a meal at the Revuebar. Then we'd show him the stuff. Course, he couldn't drive a hard bargain like he normally did. Not with us. He was sensible enough not to try.'

For most people seeking to extract protection money, casual references to friends such as Fraser and Richardson would have been enough to scare them off. But Raymond had the misfortune to be targeted by someone they couldn't intimidate. That someone was the self-styled 'Uncle Harry': Detective Sergeant Harry 'Tanky' Challenor, a broad-shouldered forty-year-old former war hero and amateur boxer from Staffordshire, who had a flat-nosed profile, a bullying manner and a disconcerting habit of addressing people as 'me old darling'. Recently posted to the West End, where he'd become a ubiquitous presence, pacing the streets, lurking in doorways or sitting in pubs with drinking buddies who included Ron 'The Dustman' Davey, Challenor regarded policing Soho as being 'like trying to swim against a tide of sewage'. So frustrated was he by the legal niceties – 'I feel as if my hands are tied behind my back' – he'd taken to obtaining convictions by planting evidence on people, often innocent men with criminal records. To his colleagues, he was a tough gangbuster who 'did not use kid glove methods'. To many of the people who lived on the fringes of the underworld, he was a despised figure. His reputation among them wasn't helped by the way he'd slid from one form of corruption to another. Now he wasn't just fabricating evidence: he was extorting cash from Soho club-owners, generally between £50 and £100 a time.

'Raymond often talked to us about the trouble he was having with Challenor, who was taking money off him,' Fraser recalled. 'Raymond knew we could protect him from anyone else, but *not* from a bent copper like Challenor.'

Pitted against the swaggering bulk of 'Uncle Harry', Raymond had three choices, none of them appetising.

He could refuse to pay, a surefire route to a black eye, a couple of broken ribs or even a jail sentence. As someone with a criminal conviction against his name, he was vulnerable to having evidence planted on him. He'd have been dragged off to West End Central, then locked in an interview room, where he'd have been presented with a weapon and told, 'That's yours. Sign for it.'

His second option was to complain to Challenor's superior officers, but there wasn't much point in that. Other people had tried it, their complaints dismissed as malicious attempts to discredit a conscientious officer.

Of the three choices available to Raymond, pulling out his wallet and peeling off a thin sheaf of banknotes was the simplest and least objectionable.


During mid-September the Clubs Office's interest in the Revuebar was revived by a letter sent to Scotland Yard. The letter, which criticised the show at Raymond's club, came from the general secretary of the Public

*The Fabulous Raymond Girls take part in an elaborate dance sequence at the Revuebar, 1962–65*

Morality Council, an organisation dominated by senior Church of England clergymen, the Archbishop of Canterbury among them.

In the last week of October, the Clubs Office deployed three undercover officers to the Revuebar. Between them, they submitted a couple of reports on what they'd seen. Neither of these deemed the latest instalment of *Raymond's International Striptease Spectacular*, featuring Ryta Himalaya and her appropriately mountainous breasts, worthy of legal action. 'The show could fairly be described as lavish and spectacular and although the principal artistes each finished their act by removing their G-string or fig-leaf and thus showing their pubic hair, there was nothing that could be described as obscene or suggestive,' the first report stated. 'In each case there was no movement while the woman was completely naked. And she was only exposed for a few seconds prior to the lights being extinguished.'

Dogged in their pursuit of Raymond, the Clubs Office nonetheless kept the Revuebar under observation, generating yet more reports. By early November, though, the surveillance had to be suspended because Raymond had discovered the identity of the plainclothes detectives. Substitute officers had to be recruited before the operation could resume.

The chances of obtaining a conviction against Raymond under the Disorderly Houses Act remained slim, so the Clubs Office searched for another way of hauling him back into court. Consideration was given to pressing further illegal gaming charges, but that would have been similarly futile because Raymond and his lawyers had found a loophole which enabled Legalite to be played in the Revuebar without contravening the law. Instead, the Clubs Office sought to employ the licensing laws to prosecute him. These specified that drinks could be sold outside normal pub opening hours only on condition they were accompanied by 'substantial refreshment'. As the latest observation report pointed out, a single plate of four curling fish-paste sandwiches between four people hardly fulfilled that requirement.

But one of the senior officers at West End Central vetoed any legal action against Raymond. By initiating another prosecution, the officer feared they might be accused of victimising him, given that the Establishment Club – the comedy club on Greek Street, run by Peter Cook and others – had only received a warning for committing much more serious contraventions of the licensing laws. Raymond should, the officer recommended, be 'told of the irregularities and strictly warned as to his responsibilities'.

Raymond still hadn't found a buyer for the Bal Tabarin, so he decided he might as well reopen the premises. If he was to find a profitable use for them, he obviously had to try something different. Rather than present conventional cabaret there, he devised a plan to copy the transvestite floor show staged at the Paris Carrousel, a venue he'd visited during a trip to France. When he unveiled the concept, only a fortnight before the Bal Tabarin was due to open its doors again, he didn't mention the show's likely appeal to the gay audience. Instead, he preferred to tell the press that he was aiming for a husband-and-wife clientele.

As envisaged, he relaunched the Bal Tabarin on Monday, 19 November. Diners were treated to a one-hour show which, in a nod to its Gallic origins, was called *Carrousel*. It had eight misleading ladies, glamorous transvestites clad in tall feathered headdresses, sparkly fishtail evening gowns and long white gloves, their voices indistinguishable from women's as they sang and told jokes laden with innuendo. They also danced and performed a spoof fashion parade, culminating in one of them mincing onto the small stage in a bridal dress.

Exactly three months after the relaunch, Raymond was at work when he received a disturbing phone call from his wife. She told him that there'd just been a robbery at their house. Before going out with some friends that evening, she'd been supervising bath-time for their children – six-year-old Debbie and two-year-old Howard. Above the noise of the kids' laughter and the water gushing into the bath, she hadn't heard a gang of burglars climb onto the first-floor veranda and break into the master bedroom. Until she had started getting ready to go out, she'd remained unaware of what had happened. That was when she'd discovered that the burglars had stolen half a dozen of her wigs, six of her husband's suits, her wedding ring and four of her furs – a full-length sable coat, plus three mink stoles.

Interest in anything associated with Raymond was such that two national newspaper reporters covered the story. Through the journalist sent by the *Daily Mail*, his wife issued an appeal to the burglars, which revealed just how committed she remained to her marriage. 'Please return that little ring,' she implored. 'It matters more to me than all the rest.'

☆

Attendances at the Bal Tabarin were still disappointing. Sometimes the twice-daily shows were watched by as few as twenty customers.

Ditching the transvestite cabaret concept, Raymond contemplated offering the diners an altogether different form of entertainment. No doubt inspired by the success of the National Sporting Club which staged professional boxing in top West End hotels, he applied to the British Boxing Board of Control for a promoter's licence. Though he was interviewed by the board's Southern Area Council, his scheme came to nothing and he fell back on getting Jean to produce conventional cabaret shows at the Bal Tabarin.

Cheekily milking the burgeoning fame of the popular American girlie magazine *Playboy* and the associated Playboy Clubs, which used a pair of bunny's ears as their logo, he started advertising the struggling venue as the Bal Tabarin/Playboy Club. In the regular adverts carried by *What's On in London*, he also tried to entice prospective customers with references to 'the Fabulous Playboy Bunnies' who were there to serve them, drink with them and dance with them.

Such cynical exploitation of the Playboy trademark risked legal action. One thing was for certain: if the Playboy company ever resorted to that, Raymond wouldn't be charged under his baptismal name because he'd just altered it by deed-poll. Within less than two months of doing this, the name 'Paul Raymond' appeared on a court summons. But the summons wasn't from Hugh Hefner, founder of the Playboy empire. It was, instead, from the Metropolitan Police, who charged him with a couple of minor infringements of the gaming law. When the case reached Marlborough Street Magistrates' Court in mid-June, he experienced something novel – the jury found him not guilty.

# 23 TANKY PANKY

**M**ORE GOOD NEWS was brewing, though the relevance of what happened wouldn't be apparent to Raymond for several months.

Outside Claridges Hotel on the second Thursday of July 1963, a demonstration was being staged against the Greek government, represented by the visiting king and queen of Greece. The demonstrators were held back by a cordon of police officers. When a young protester named Donald Rooum attempted to unfurl a banner, it was snatched by four plainclothes officers, among them Harry 'Tanky' Challenor. Rooum later recounted the following conversation with Challenor:

'Can I have my banner back?'

'Can you have your *what* back?'

'My banner.'

'You're fucking nicked, my old beauty.'

Grabbing him by the collar, Challenor shoved him in the direction of a police van.

'Please, officer, I'm coming quietly.'

'Don't say "please" to me, my old darling. I've got a heart of stone.'

Rooum was taken out of the van at West End Central and forced upstairs by Challenor, who kept clouting him. At one point Challenor knocked him over. Rooum was then frogmarched into an interview cell. Locking the door behind them, Challenor said, 'Boo the Queen, would you?'

'No, not at all.'

From his pocket, Challenor produced a broken brick, wrapped in newspaper. 'There you are, my old beauty. Carrying an offensive weapon. You can get two years for that.'

Later on, Challenor hauled three other young demonstrators back to West End Central, where he told them to pile their belongings on the desk in front of them. Placing a piece of broken brick on the first two piles, he said, 'A present from your Uncle Harry.' As he dropped another chunk of brick onto the last of the three piles, Challenor cheerily commented, 'The biggest piece for the biggest boy...'

The trial of Donald Rooum and the other three demonstrators arrested by Challenor began on Friday, 19 July. Long after the court had adjourned for the day, Raymond was putting in his usual late-night stint at the Revuebar. He didn't leave until 4 a.m. Instead of going straight home, he appears to have enjoyed a clandestine tryst with a girlfriend. Afterwards, he climbed into his Bentley and, even though he'd been drinking heavily, set off for home. Around 9 a.m. he drove past Putney Hill, just to the north of Wimbledon Common. His wayward driving attracted the attention of a detective in a police car. The detective tailed the Bentley as it headed along Parkside, skirting the eastern side of the common. Raymond was so drunk that the car kept lurching across the white lines before drifting back into the proper lane. Soon he was driving down the middle of the road. As he approached the junction with Castle Close, he almost toppled into the passenger seat. He jerked upright at the last moment, but he couldn't prevent his Bentley from scraping an oncoming vehicle, which had to swerve onto the pavement to avoid a head-on collision.

Pursued by both the police car and the car he'd just hit, Raymond accelerated away without stopping. In a vain effort to lose his pursuers, he took a left-hand turning off Parkside, leading him on to a suburban side street. Here, he was pulled over by the police car. He had trouble keeping his eyes open as the detective questioned him. With drunken truculence, Raymond refused to give his name.

The owner of the damaged car had, in the meantime, caught up with them.

Asked by the detective whether there was anything wrong with him, Raymond said, 'No.' Then he added, 'You're not a policeman. I'm going.'

Before Raymond could restart his Bentley, the detective tried to grab the ignition key. While an arm-wrestling contest ensued, the detective told the driver of the other car to get help. Too sozzled to resist for long, Raymond had his car keys yanked from his grasp by the detective.

When a second policeman arrived, Raymond had the chutzpah to gesture towards the detective and say, 'This man has assaulted me.' But his accusation didn't prevent him from being carted off to Wimbledon Police Station. He told the inspector on duty that he wanted to charge the detective with assault. 'It is the way he took the keys from me,' he explained. '*That* is what I object to.'

At the police station he was examined by Dr Sidney Lewis. Raymond said to the doctor that he'd had 'four or five whiskies', but he refused to specify where he'd been since leaving the Revuebar.

Lewis reached the obvious conclusion that Raymond's abilities had been impaired by alcohol.

Raymond was now ready to be charged. In the course of completing the accompanying paperwork, one of the policemen asked Raymond to give his age. Always touchy about that, Raymond wouldn't oblige. Despite the incomplete paperwork, he was charged with four offences: dangerous driving, failing to stop after an accident, driving without due care, and driving while unfit through drink. Probably because there was minimal chance of success, he later dropped his threat to launch a counter-charge against the detective who had arrested him.

First thing the following week he appeared at Wimbledon Magistrates' Court where he pleaded 'not guilty' to all four charges. He was then released on £50 bail and slated to return in the autumn. Well before that could happen, the trial of Donald Rooum and the others had shuffled towards a conclusion. Owing to forensic evidence which proved that

Rooum couldn't have hidden the broken brick in his jacket pocket, he was acquitted, though one of his fellow defendants wasn't so fortunate.

By drawing attention to the untrustworthiness of the prosecution evidence, the verdict marked the beginning of Challenor's fall from grace. In early September, just short of a month after Rooum had been freed, his ruthless adversary was declared unfit for duty as a result of a nervous breakdown, conveniently removing him from court scrutiny. Nevertheless, he continued to be seen around the West End, so Raymond wasn't yet spared the prospect of further visits from good old Uncle Harry.

Challenor's vision of Soho as a Hieronymus Bosch nightmare had, by that stage, been fortified by the recent proliferation of strip-clubs. Paradoxically, this had gathered pace since the laws governing them had been tightened.

Under the 1961 Licensing Act, owners of drinking clubs or strip-clubs couldn't renew their licences or obtain new ones without police approval, itself contingent on the results of background checks on the proprietors. When the legislation came into force, there were nearly four hundred registered clubs, mostly one-room drinking clubs. About a quarter of these folded because the owners couldn't obtain licences, often owing to their clubs being located in basements with no emergency exits. An unforeseen consequence of the new legislation was that the freshly vacant premises tended to become strip-joints. Legally speaking, these venues – which accommodated between 60 and 100 customers, sometimes seated on nothing more comfortable than bentwood chairs – weren't clubs, yet that didn't stop their owners from charging *membership* as well as entrance fees. The owners could expect to earn around £1,000 a week in box-office takings.

Would-be club-owners with unsavoury backgrounds also got round the new regulations by employing 'frontmen' who would pass the police checks and obtain licences. Among the principal beneficiaries of this latest phase of the Soho strip-club boom were two of London's most feared

*Advertisement printed in the 13 December 1963 issue of* What's On in London

gangland bosses: Bernie Silver and 'Big Frank' Mifsud, who had forged an unlikely alliance. Silver was a working-class East Ender with a taste for fine restaurants and flashy clothes. Mifsud, on the other hand, was a giant, muscular, quietly spoken Maltese who wore perpetually crumpled clothes. Together they'd formed what they called the 'Syndicate', which controlled as many as twenty-four Soho strip-clubs, including the Striperama on Greek Street. Through a chain of frontmen, they also ran clip-joints, brothels and mucky bookshops.

With occasional exceptions, the Syndicate was able to operate with impunity thanks to its corrupt links to senior Scotland Yard detectives. On the pretence that Mifsud and Silver were valuable police informants, those detectives protected them, blocking investigations and feeding information back to them.

The spread of strip-clubs wasn't the only respect in which Soho had changed lately. Along with Chelsea, it had, by the closing months of 1963, established itself as one of the twin centres of what the press was calling 'Swinging London', an alluring generalisation which obscured the fact that London didn't swing for many people.

Carnaby Street, just a short walk from the Revuebar, had been the cradle of the entire phenomenon. Hitherto an urban backwater, lined with ordinary shops, it had, since 1960, become the teenage Savile Row, dominated by so-called 'boutiques'. Now its pavements were aflutter with fashionably dressed young people, beneficiaries of London's comparatively high salaries which granted them unprecedented spending power. In order to service this new market, Soho businessmen had followed the Parisian example by setting up 'discotheques', notably the ultra-trendy Ad Lib Club, where the capital's bright young things could dance to music played by a dinner-jacketed DJ, as well as sneaking glances at Ringo Starr, David Bailey, Mick Jagger and other famous customers. Already there were signs that this youth-oriented form of nightclubbing would sweep aside supper-and-cabaret clubs such as the Bal Tabarin and the Celebrité. Perhaps the most high-profile casualty was the El Condor, which had, under the ownership of the slum landlord Peter Rachman, become La Discothèque.

Almost three months after his meandering drive through Wimbledon, Raymond stood trial in Kingston-upon-Thames. Invited to explain his actions, he said he'd been 'completely and utterly dog-tired' on the morning of his arrest, having worked even longer hours than usual. To avoid any embarrassing questions about where he'd gone after leaving the Revuebar, he changed his story. His normal working day, he told the court, finished at 5 a.m., but he'd been occupied until 8.30 a.m. on that occasion.

With the help of his lawyer, Raymond was able to mount a case so persuasive that the jury acquitted him of drink-driving. He was, however, found guilty of the other charges, for which he ended up being fined £50, ordered to pay £42 legal costs and disqualified from driving for three months.

Unable to pilot his Bentley, he employed a chauffeur whose crisply uniformed presence became a familiar sight at the Revuebar, Celebrité and Bal Tabarin. Most evenings Raymond's newest employee would be seen manoeuvring the Bentley into a space between the other expensive cars – Jaguars, Rolls-Royces, Jensens, Lotuses – which tended to be parked along the stretch of Brewer Street close to the junction with Walker's Court, their paintwork reflecting the flashing neon sign above. Many of those cars must have been owned by the wealthy businessmen and celebrities who frequented the Revuebar, Isow's and similarly fashionable clubs and restaurants.

Frank Sinatra, Judy Garland, Stewart Granger, Peter Finch, William Holden and the television presenter Dan Farson were among the famous faces glimpsed as they entered Raymond's club. Isow's – the Jewish restaurant directly below the Revuebar's auditorium – continued to attract an equally well-known clientele, its customers including Jack Hawkins, Orson Welles, Elizabeth Taylor, Burt Lancaster and Walt Disney. A younger crowd, meanwhile, competed for tables at 'the Trat' – the nearby Trattoria Terrazza, haunt of actors, photographers, models and pop musicians.

Try as he might, Raymond couldn't endow the Bal Tabarin with that sort of enviable cachet. He couldn't even turn it into a viable business. Among the West End's club-owners and restaurateurs, it had acquired a reputation as a white elephant. Raymond made no secret of his willingness to part with the place if someone came up with a reasonable offer.

Around the end of that year he received just such an offer. It originated from an unlikely source – Danny La Rue. Long since established as the star attraction at Winston's, La Rue had been hoping to be awarded a partnership in the business. When the anticipated recognition didn't materialise, he began to rethink his future. Backed by a millionaire customer from Winston's, La Rue opened negotiations with Raymond. A well-concealed streak of altruism surfacing, Raymond tried to put him off several times during the ensuing month. Much as Raymond wanted to sell the Bal Tabarin, he didn't want to see La Rue, who appeared naively unaware of the difficulties inherent in running a West End venue, make what he feared would be a catastrophic mistake. His motives were, La Rue thought, complicated by an element of vanity: if *he* couldn't turn the place into a money-spinner, then nobody else could. Refusing to be deterred by Raymond's crises of conscience, La Rue pushed ahead with the deal, which was finally completed in early 1964.

Humiliating though the failure of his Mayfair venture had been, Raymond could feel proud of the continuing success of the Revuebar and, to a lesser extent, the Celebrité. In January the latest edition of *Raymond's International Striptease Spectacular* opened at his Walker's Court club, where the lounge bar had been rechristened 'The Playboy Room' and staffed by bunny girls who, one customer noted approvingly, were 'good at social niceties'. As an additional enticement, Raymond started organising professional wrestling bouts there every Thursday or

Friday evening. Starring Mick McManus and other big-name performers, these profitably exploited the popularity of wrestling – or at least a pantomime version of the sport – on television.

Beneficial publicity for the Revuebar was soon provided by an inventive collaboration with a shoestring outfit called Delmore Film Productions. The company made a fifty-five-minute film featuring not only the Revuebar's bunny girls but also one of the main acts from Raymond's latest show: Ingrid Anthofer, a svelte blonde, variously billed as being from anywhere from Vienna to Chicago. Screened as a so-called 'programme filler' in cinemas across Britain, the film was titled *It's All Over Town*. It starred Lance Percival and Willie Rushton, stalwarts of the hit satirical television show *That Was The Week That Was*. Percival was cast as a stagehand who falls asleep after he's finished work and dreams he's on the razzle with a friend, played by Rushton. Together they embark on a nocturnal tour of London's clubland or, rather, an appropriately dreamlike studio evocation of it. Rubbing shoulders with Patricia Hayes and Ivor Cutler, both in non-speaking roles, the two friends listen to performances by The Hollies, Frankie Vaughan, Acker Bilk and the Springfields – a fresh-faced trio fronted by the young Dusty Springfield.

Between these musical numbers, the two would-be Lotharios gaze admiringly at Raymond's employees. First, there are the bum-wiggling bunny girls, who are seen dancing the twist in an imaginary West End club. Then there's a virtuoso routine by Ingrid Anthofer, who performs a mischievous send-up of striptease. It begins with her lying naked on a bearskin rug, spread across a lazily revolving stage, decked out to resemble someone's living room. Dancing in time to swooning music, she demonstrates what might be called sleight of body, wriggling languorously into her clothes, this reverse stripshow performed without exposing her breasts or genitals. As the music fades at the end of her routine, she's wearing a black sheath dress, long black gloves, matching high heels and a fur coat.

# 24 UNDRESSED TO THRILL

**N**EARLY ELEVEN YEARS had passed since Hugh Hefner had launched *Playboy* magazine in America. Over that period his publication, distinguished by innovative graphic design and high-powered literary contributors such as John Steinbeck, Jack Kerouac and P. G. Wodehouse, had become immensely popular there. Its availability on this side of the Atlantic was, however, limited to pricey imported editions which its British distributors censored by placing stickers on the cover and even tearing out specific pages.

The success of Hefner's magazine, which was generating $2.4 million in annual sales, had inspired a flurry of American imitations such as *Mate!, Satan* and the delightfully titled *Gay Blade*, the word 'gay' having not yet acquired homosexual connotations. *Playboy*'s success also inspired Connor Walsh to approach Raymond with a business proposition. Walsh asked Raymond whether he'd be interested in funding a British equivalent. For the man known as 'Mr Striptease', this seemed an obvious move, *so* obvious it was surprising he hadn't thought of it already.

Walsh's proposed magazine would, of course, require ample investment. If *Playboy* was anything to go by, though, the risks were worthwhile because the potential profit margins on each copy were enviable.

Back in 1964, Walsh's proposal wasn't as straightforward as it now seems. It wasn't simply a matter of weighing risk against reward. Any publisher attempting to replicate *Playboy* in Britain required considerable nerve, which explains why numerous potential investors had already turned Walsh down. By printing photographs of naked women, however anodyne, the publisher could find himself being prosecuted for contravening the 1964 Obscene Publications Act, the imprecise wording of which left it open to interpretation. As the old joke goes, pornography is in the groin of the beholder. Publishers of anything vulnerable to accusations of obscenity were at the mercy of the notorious Obscene Publications Squad, the branch of the police responsible for enforcing the Act.

Never someone who shied away from a confrontation with authority, Raymond agreed to finance Walsh's magazine, his belief in his own commercial discrimination undented by the losses at the Bal Tabarin. Assigned the role of managing editor, Walsh then set about recruiting staff. He assembled a nine-strong editorial and design team whose work would be supplemented by freelancers. It included experienced journalists such as Bill Sinclair, Ted Simon and John Sandilands, plus the future agony aunt Irma Kurtz. They were squeezed into a cramped and rather dilapidated office at 2 Salisbury Square, not far from Fleet Street. Happy to let Walsh get on with the practicalities of launching the magazine, Raymond paid him and his staff only occasional visits. 'He never appeared very comfortable there,' Irma Kurtz remembered. 'Being a tall man, he always looked too big for our little offices.'

His involvement with the magazine wasn't limited to signing cheques and exercising benign supervision. He also supplied many of the models. The connection between the magazine and Raymond's other businesses didn't end there. He and his editorial staff came up with ways of using it to promote both the Revuebar and the Celebrité.

For the launch issue Jo Brooker – the magazine's nineteen-year-old editorial assistant – devised the imaginative concept of a feature series that provided an edited transcript of a discussion between two well-known people from different walks of life. The venue for the first such dialogue was the Celebrité, where she brought together an unlikely pair of writers for a conversation about espionage. They were Len Deighton, young author of the bestselling Cold War spy thriller *The Ipcress File*, and Malcolm Muggeridge, journalist, broadcaster and one-time editor of the weekly magazine *Punch*. Formerly a committed Marxist, Muggeridge had been a hard-drinking libertine who had once indulged in a threesome with Kingsley Amis and George Orwell's widow. Since then, he'd affected a dramatic transformation, embracing ascetic Christianity and becoming a vocal critic of sexual liberation and materialism. Strangely enough, Raymond had already met Muggeridge, who had been a customer at the Revuebar. Raymond had, on that occasion, been impressed by his sardonic wit.

The debut issue was scheduled for release during the closing months of that year. In a larky allusion to *Queen*, the women's magazine, it was going to be called *King*. Like *Playboy*, it aimed to reach an affluent mainstream audience far removed from the market enjoyed by *Kamera* and other British softcore pornographic magazines, sold furtively through Soho bookshops and seedy newsagents. Provided everything went according to plan, *King* would be available from W. H. Smith's and other chain stores. To achieve that goal, Walsh and his colleagues strove to give the magazine the aura of sophistication projected by *Playboy*. The nudes would be no more sexualised than classical statuary, their pubic hair discreetly concealed. The accompanying features and fiction would be classy. The contributors would be drawn from the ranks of famous writers, their involvement signifying the magazine's seriousness. The layout and typography would be refreshingly arty. And the entire concoction would be infused with a flavour of hedonistic consumerism.

Its name changed to 'Danny La Rue's' and its decor altered, the walls now sheathed in black velvet, the Bal Tabarin reopened during late March with revues written by Ronnie Corbett and Barry Cryer. It rapidly attracted a devoted following that included Princess Margaret, Peter Sellers and Richard Harris. Far from being bitter and envious, Raymond voiced his pleasure at the transformation his friend had wrought. He was soon a regular at what became known as 'Danny's', where the shows were dominated by comic sketches, many of them topical. Gentle satire was offered through La Rue's role as the Tory Hostess, aka 'The Hory Tostess'.

'Life's much better under the Tories and I should know,' the Tostess would proclaim. 'Harold Wilson's worried about a swing to the right. I told him to change his tailor immediately.'

As Raymond made his chauffeur-driven way round the night-time streets of the West End, one person who could no longer be glimpsed striding along the pavements was Harry Challenor. He and three police colleagues were being tried at the Old Bailey on charges of perverting the course of justice. But Challenor's involvement was cut short by supposed ill-health, culminating in him being declared insane and unfit to stand trial.

He hadn't long been incarcerated in a psychiatric hospital when his old Soho territory became the subject of another parliamentary debate. The focal point wasn't police corruption. It was, instead, ill-fated legislation seeking to eradicate the clip-joints from Soho.

Whenever Raymond sauntered down its streets, he'd often bump into people he knew. They included Paul Lincoln, still combining co-ownership of the nearby 2i's with a wrestling promotion business. 'We'd run into each other a heck of a lot and always stop for a chat,' Lincoln recalled. 'I had a wrestler on my books at that time called Society Boy. He looked a lot like me. His gimmick was that he went into the ring dressed like a City gent, wearing a bowler hat and a suit and carrying an umbrella. Well, one day he told me he was walking through Wimbledon when Paul, mistaking him for me, pulled up in his Bentley and offered him a lift into town. Society Boy took up the offer and got into the car. Paul must've realised there'd been a mistake but he was too stylish to admit it.

'That was around the time I had a minor falling out with Paul. I wasn't very happy because he poached my star wrestler, a Hungarian called Baron von Heczy. Genuine aristocrat. Really debonair bloke.

'"You bastard," I said to Paul when we next ran into each other. "You're undermining my business." Paul just laughed.

'Anyway, I soon resolved my differences with both Paul and the Baron. For his act, the Baron would dress up in a Nazi uniform and enter the ring with a cheetah on a lead. He trained the cheetah to appear in Paul's other shows and pull the clothes off a stripper. While the Baron was working at the Revuebar, he kept the cheetah on the roof. Every Sunday afternoon, we'd go over there, collect the cheetah and take it for a walk in Hyde Park.'

# 25 THE SIN CROWD

**A** RECENT ADDITION to the oft-replenished ranks of West End strip-clubs was at 5 Walker's Court, only yards from the Revuebar. But Raymond doesn't appear to have felt threatened by it, probably because it was far smaller and less luxurious than his long-established venue. In any case, it presented a different form of nude entertainment, specialising in so-called 'posing shows', the curtains opening and closing every couple of minutes to reveal one of a rota of nudes striking a different would-be seductive pose.

This new club, the unimaginatively named Walker's Court, hadn't been open long before a friendship developed between Raymond and the vivacious married couple who ran it. Like him, they had good reason to celebrate Harry Challenor's downfall, having been victims of Uncle Harry's extortion racket.

Raymond's freshly acquired friends were Jimmy and Rusty Humphreys who, in common with so many of Soho's residents and traders, already knew him by sight. 'I'd seen him walking along the street. He cut quite an impressive figure,' recalled Rusty, a quick-witted and strikingly attractive redhead who had worked for Jimmy as a stripper before their marriage the previous May.

Freed just over two years earlier from the latest of several prison sentences, Jimmy was a handsome, softly spoken Bermondsey boy with a snappy dress sense and an ambition to duplicate Raymond's success. Since coming out of jail, he'd been operating a couple of other small Soho strip-clubs, first on Old Compton Street, then on Macclesfield Street.

Soon Raymond had introduced Jean to the Humphreys and the four of them were socialising together. 'We'd go out with Paul and Jean at least once a week,' Rusty said. 'Sometimes we went to a restaurant or saw a show together, but mostly we'd go up to the Revuebar. We never went in to see his show. There was no reason for us to see it: we'd seen more than enough naked bodies, so we'd just sit with Paul and Jean in the lounge bar. My husband got on really well with Paul.'

Early in September 1964 Raymond and Jimmy Humphreys would have had plenty to talk about. The Humphreys' club had just been damaged by an arson attack, carried out by a gang wanting protection money. This attack, which put the club out of action for a few days, was followed by a series of threatening phone calls warning Jimmy that the place would be firebombed again unless he saw reason. Rather than pay up, Jimmy contacted the police, acquired some guard dogs, and installed steel shutters to protect the doors and windows overnight.

Other dramatic news reached Raymond three weeks later. The news, which had been percolating through the West End, was that the Windmill Theatre was closing down. Maybe because of its association with Home Front heroism during the Second World War, the Windmill remained such a cherished part of British culture that *Panorama*, BBC Television's prestigious current affairs programme, was marking the occasion by broadcasting from backstage on the closing night.

Sheila Van Damm, who had taken over the management of the theatre from her father, blamed its demise on clubs such as Raymond's. She said they made the Windmill seem 'too respectable'.

In spite of the fact that he'd never been a fan of its famous shows, Raymond felt obliged to write her a sympathetic letter, offering to employ all of the girls who worked there. But the altruism of the gesture was diminished by him blabbing about it to a reporter from the *Daily Mirror*.

More good publicity came his way soon afterwards. Tying-in with the general election on Tuesday, 13 October, that night's show at the

*Four days before a bout at the Royal Albert Hall during March 1965, American middleweight title contender, Rubin 'Hurricane' Carter, pretends to spar with a Raymond bunny girl. Veteran lightweight Joe Brown, due to appear on the same bill, stands behind them. Carter's subsequent conviction for a triple murder inspired both Bob Dylan's song, 'Hurricane' and the 1999 movie,* The Hurricane, *starring Denzil Washington*

Revuebar incorporated an amusing gimmick which caught the attention of the press. At 9.30 p.m. five girls stood at the side of the stage wearing nothing more than a smile and a ribbon in their hair. The ribbons were colour coded – blue for the Conservatives, pink for Labour, yellow for the Liberals, red for the Communists, and white for independent MPs. As the final tally of votes in each parliamentary seat was announced, the girl representing the winning party picked up a chiffon scarf of the appropriate colour and tied it round herself. Raymond had had trouble finding a girl prepared to represent the Communists, not because of any anti-Communist bias among strippers but because everyone knew that the girl with the red ribbon in her hair would, most likely, end up spending the whole time naked and shivering.

After that night's performances of *Raymond's International Striptease Spectacular* had finished, the five beribboned girls were still lined up across the stage. By closing time one of them was swathed in pink chiffon, indicating the arrival of a Labour government. Raymond wouldn't have shared the mood of jubilation evident across large swathes of Britain, his sexual radicalism, his flouting of convention, his questioning of the status quo conflicting with his political conservatism, his abiding reverence for the Catholic Church and respect for the Royal Family, respect that even extended to watching the Queen's speech on television every Christmas.

The electoral upheaval coincided with preparations for the launch of *King*. Tame though the magazine was, even by the standards of the early 1960s, each of its photos had to negotiate a stringent vetting process. Initially, they were taken to a lawyer who would try to ensure they didn't contravene the Obscene Publications Act. 'It was my job to show them to a bowler-hatted gentleman named Mr Watkin-Powell,' remembered Jo Brooker. 'He'd gaze at the transparencies on a light-box and look for any crevices that shouldn't be seen.'

Even after the pictures had been okayed, they still had to pass another round of vetting. 'In those days, if you couldn't get your magazine into W. H. Smith's, you might as well forget it,' Bill Sinclair explained. 'The people at Smith's were always very worried about magazines that had any nudity in them, so we were absolutely forbidden to feature even the slightest hint of pubic hair. That was what they were most worried about. They appointed a lawyer who came to our office with a magnifying-glass and examined every photo. Until he'd given the magazine the OK, Smith's wouldn't agree to stock it.'

In about late October, two events were held to celebrate the release of the winter 1964 issue of *King*. There was a boozy party in Connor Walsh's Bayswater flat, attended by the television presenter David Frost and other luminaries from the London media world. Also there was a more formal press launch at the Celebrité, where Raymond posed for photographs, a group of grinning bunny girls peering over his shoulder as he sat leafing contentedly through the magazine.

Just beyond the contents page was an introduction ghost-written for Raymond by Walsh. Copying *Playboy*, which had, in turn, copied a rival American magazine called *Nugget*, the subsequent pin-up photos were interspersed with literary alibi material: not just the conversation between Malcolm Muggeridge and Len Deighton, but also a short story by Keith Waterhouse and an extract from *Candy*, the American writer Terry Southern's racy new novel. Another of the contributors was Colin MacInnes, author of *Absolute Beginners*, who had written a feature on Christine Keeler, one of the prostitutes at the centre of the scandal that had recently forced the resignation of John Profumo, Secretary of State for War in the now deposed Conservative government.

MacInnes's article appeared in tandem with specially commissioned pictures of Keeler taken by Brian Duffy, one of the most famous British photographers of that period. 'Someone had left the Keeler transparencies on a desk in our office and spilt tea over them,' recalled Sinclair. 'They stuck together, but we were determined not to waste them, so we printed them as they were. There's one shot where you can see Keeler's head superimposed over her chest. People thought it was deliberate. There was even a piece in the magazine *Encounter*, praising us for our tasteful shots of her.'

Tasteful or otherwise, *King*'s debut issue, partly because of the involvement of so many celebrities, created a lot of controversy. As the magazine's publisher, it's inconceivable that Raymond didn't attract the attention of the Obscene Publications Squad. Anyone who produced what was regarded as pornography could expect a visit from its officers.

Nicknamed 'the Dirty Squad', the OPS earned its alternative title because of the dirty books that were its stock-in-trade, because of its moral grubbiness and because of the corruption that permeated its hierarchy. Raymond's erstwhile neighbour John Mason was just one of numerous smut-peddlers making regular monthly payments to the squad. Fail to stump up whatever the OPS demanded and you'd find your entire stock confiscated.

The widespread availability of Raymond's magazine helped it to register promising sales figures despite its seven shillings and sixpence cover price – slightly more than a one-day ticket to watch the Test match at Lord's that summer. With its stylish graphics, its line-up of rising young literary stars and its attitude of comparative sexual openness, it was part of the wave of early 1960s dissident creativity – manifested in fashion, painting, music, photography, film-making and writing – that so effectively challenged the old order.

Raymond was so pleased with the way things were going that he treated the magazine's staff, along with their partners, to a night at the Revuebar, where they were joined by his wife and eight-year-old daughter. After dinner in the lounge bar, they moved into the theatre to see the show. 'For me, the highlight was a brilliant performance by the trumpeter Eddie Calvert,' Bill Sinclair said. 'I also remember there were a couple of glamorous dancers on roller-skates. They kept hurling each other across the stage.'


When he wasn't at the Revuebar, Raymond was often sitting in some other West End nightspot with his friend Billy Smart, son of the recently deceased circus owner of that name. Almost ten years Raymond's junior, Smart ran the touring circus with his two brothers as well as starring in the popular BBC Television programme *Billy Smart's Circus*, which featured his troupe of performing elephants. So inspired was Raymond by his friend's shows that he was soon toying with the idea of putting together his own circus, specifically aimed at children.

Away from the big top, Smart was a boozy and ebullient womaniser who regularly featured in the gossip columns, linked to Jayne Mansfield, Diana Dors, Shirley Bassey and other glamorous female stars. On nights when they weren't chasing women together, they were often to be found in the Artistes & Repertoire Club at 142 Charing Cross Road. Otherwise known as 'the A & R', it was a disreputable yet atypically light and airy ground-floor club, the walls of which were papered with signed photos of famous musicians. Though the A & R had been set up as a meeting place for people in the music industry, its membership also encompassed actors and criminals. Other regulars were the singer Dorothy Squires, the comedian Harry Secombe, the borstal-boy-turned-writer Frank Norman, plus the film star and gangland hanger-on Stanley Baker. Frequently, Baker was accompanied by his friend 'Italian Albert' Dimes, Billy Hill's former right-hand man, said to be connected to Angelo Bruno of the Philadelphia mafia. While the A & R's clientele chatted, musicians would sometimes play the piano, lending the place an ambience out of keeping with mid-1960s London.

Most days Raymond didn't get home until 5 a.m., a routine that accounted for his embalmed pallor, described in the trade as 'a nightclub tan'. His noctural working life meant that he saw relatively little of either Debbie or Howard, both of whom he'd insisted on sending to Catholic schools. Like many a brother and sister, they often bickered when they were at home together, Debbie's seniority giving her the advantage. During these squabbles, Howard remembered his sister donning high-heeled shoes and treading on his hands.

As a friend of their father's said, 'Raymond's tough, business persona faded when he was with his children, though it was clear from quite early on that he was closer to Debbie than Howard. In their presence he became this rather soft father. He knew they both liked animals, so he'd bring home the cheetah which was appearing at the Revuebar.'

His paternal softness towards Howard and Debbie didn't extend to hugging or kissing them much, this apparent detachment reflecting his own upbringing. If he'd been a more tactile, more open parent, he might also have revealed that they had a half-brother, yet he insisted on concealing Darryl's existence from them even after the monthly maintenance payments to Noreen O'Horan had alerted Jean to the truth.

Before setting off to work on Saturdays, Raymond would take Debbie and Howard shopping. He'd give them both a small amount of spending money, but Debbie – who addressed him as 'Pa' – would insist on him buying her the most expensive toys. Unless she got her way, she'd throw tantrums that led him to conclude 'she was impossible to control'. He found emotional outbursts so embarrassing that he'd buy her whatever she wanted in order to pacify her. Fittingly, he arranged for her to appear as an extra in *The Great St Trinian's Train Robbery*, the fourth in the popular series of comedy films, based on Ronald Searle's books about a ramshackle, anarchic girls' school, populated by mutinous, hockey-stick-wielding little monsters.

Raymond's routine didn't just keep him away from his children. It meant that he had, as he admitted with impish pride, 'few friends in the daylight world'. The Reverend Edwyn Young was part of the select band of chums who straddled both milieux. Even so, Raymond no longer saw him on a regular basis, not since his recent appointment as rector to a parish church in Liverpool, which had led him to resign the chaplaincy of the Revuebar. Perhaps this was just as well because Young wouldn't have approved of Raymond's latest plan for the club.

By November he was poised to provide saucy entertainment in the lounge bar as well as the theatre. In the centre of what was still known as the Playboy Room, he installed a transparent-sided, six-foot-deep, fourteen-foot-by-fourteen-foot swimming pool, lit by yellow bulbs that gave it a honeyed glow. Working in quarter-hour shifts, a G-stringed but otherwise naked girl – advertised as 'The Girl in the Golden Fish Tank' – swam round in the pool while customers drank, smoked, talked and gaped at her.

As with so many of his gimmicks, Raymond appears to have purloined the concept. As far back as 1949, 'Divena the Aqua Tease' had been performing a similar underwater routine in America. Had Raymond been superstitious, the fate of Divena's swimming pool might have deterred him from installing the Golden Fish Tank. When Divena appeared at the Casino Royale in New Orleans, a jealous rival – Kitty West, aka 'Evangeline the Oyster Girl' – had shattered the pool with an axe.

For Olivia Newton-John and Pat Carroll, a young female song-and-dance duo from Australia who had been performing at the Celebrité as 'Pat and Olivia', the sight of the Girl in the Golden Fish Tank yielded their first inkling that they might not be in an ordinary cabaret club. 'We thought this was kind of strange, but thought nothing of it, being young and naive,' Newton-John recollected.

Under the misapprehension that they were willing to combine their usual act with striptease, George Richardson had booked them to appear at the Revuebar, its Brewer Street stage door offering them no indication of the type of shows presented there. Reminiscing about the reaction of the club's audience, Carroll said, 'I don't think they liked us at all. We were very cute and innocent. We were too young and we had too many clothes on.'

Once the song-and-dance duo had finished, Raymond went backstage to speak to them. 'He came in, gave me £40 and said, "Thank you very much, but you don't need to come back. I don't think it's going to work out for you here",' recalled Newton-John, who would go on to star opposite John Travolta in the hit movie *Grease* (1978).

Unless the water in the Golden Fish Tank was cleaned regularly, the Revuebar's customers would have felt as if they were looking at the naked swimmer through eyes turned hazy with cataracts. That's why Raymond instructed Miklos Matolsci to put chlorine in it every other day. First, he'd dissolve the chlorine in a bucket. Then he'd decant the contents of the bucket into the pool and check the acidity of the water.

'I was off work for a few days, so someone else had to do all that,' Matolsci remembered. 'But he didn't do it properly. Instead of mixing the chlorine in the bucket, he threw handfuls of it into the water and it floated straight to the bottom, where the circulating pump couldn't reach it and make it dissolve.'

The consequences could have been fatal for thirty-year-old Jean Francine who, on the evening of Friday, 16 April 1965, began her next stint as the Girl in the Golden Fish Tank. Ninety customers in the lounge bar, mostly businessmen, watched as redheaded Francine plunged into the pool. When she began to flounder, most of the audience assumed it was part of her performance. In fact, she'd blacked out, probably because, just as she had dived into the water, she'd inhaled chlorine gas produced by a chemical reaction between the undiluted chlorine and whatever cleaning solution had been used to wipe down the sides of the pool. Moments after Francine's blackout, a man shouted, 'She's in trouble... She's drowning!'

Raymond, who happened to be in the lounge bar with Eddie Calvert, took off his coat and clambered into the pool. He was soon joined by Calvert, a dapper fellow Lancastrian several years older than him. For the next two minutes they struggled to haul Francine to the surface and drag her out. They then laid her next to the pool, alive but unconscious. Her husband, who had been in the audience, gave her mouth-to-mouth resuscitation until a doctor arrived.

Recuperating in her Earl's Court flat, Francine expressed her determination to continue her role as one of the Girls in the Golden Fish Tank. But the incident must have alarmed Raymond because, not long afterwards, he replaced the girls with some aquatic plants and 150 goldfish. Naked ones, of course.

Another act that went dangerously wrong was billed as 'Miss Snake Hips'. It starred a blonde who performed a swaying, nude dance with a nine-foot-long boa constrictor draped round her shoulder. On her opening night at the Revuebar, the snake suddenly coiled itself around her and started squeezing. Raymond had to sprint out of the theatre and into Isow's, where he found the former heavyweight boxer-turned-doorman Nosher Powell, who came to the rescue of the crimson-faced Miss Snake Hips.

After this, Raymond became wary of hiring strippers using snakes as part of their act. One exception was Shirl Andress – her stage name a rather laboured joke – who performed with a large rubber snake which she'd manipulate in a way that made it appear to be alive. 'She'd get it to move in a peculiarly realistic way,' Pamela Green recalled. 'It'd slide round her shoulders and up between her legs. She'd approach men in the audience, dance round them and say, "Would you like to hold it?" The men would be absolutely petrified.'

Green and George Harrison Marks, her boyfriend and business partner, had gone to the Revuebar on a scouting mission. They were hoping to find girls suitable to model for *Kamera*, the popular nudie magazine they ran from a studio on Gerrard Street. A former art student with the flawless beauty of a young Brigitte Bardot, Green designed the sets and also posed for *Kamera*. Through her appearances there and her starring role in the hit 1961 nudist film *Naked – as Nature Intended*, she'd become Britain's most famous nude pin-up. 'Raymond approached me when we were at the Revuebar,' she remembered. 'He said, "Would you like to appear in my show?" And I said, "What would I do?" He replied, "You could appear with Shirl Andress. She does an act with a piano." But I turned him down. I said, "Knowing what she does with the snake, what the hell does she do with the *piano*…?"'

The near-fatal incidents featuring Jean Francine and Miss Snake Hips didn't deter Raymond from staging other novelty acts at the Revuebar. In his relentless quest to prevent the show from feeling stale and to distinguish it from its rivals, he visited Wally Lucken, an ageing animal trainer who had worked in most branches of show business. Surrounded by a menagerie that included a whippet, a gorilla and a white mare named Beauty, Lucken lived in a caravan behind the Wee-Waif pub near the village of Twyford in Buckinghamshire. He was a shambling, ruddy-cheeked character with wavy hair, a mellifluous voice and loquacious manner, casually dispensing references to previous assignments such as teaching a lion to wear a pair of spectacles.

Can a horse be trained to remove the clothes from a stripper? That was what Raymond wanted to know.

For an appropriate fee, Lucken arranged to train Beauty. He did it by sewing sugar lumps into the lining of a bra and a pair of knickers. As Beauty nibbled the sugar lumps, she pulled off the clothing. Soon she'd been so conditioned that she would remove a bra and knickers without the sweetener. Well prepared for her latest theatrical engagement, she was driven to the Revuebar each day and kept in a nearby garage between shows, her nightclub debut pre-dating the famous appearance of the white horse at New York's Studio 54 by the best part of a decade.

'We'd bring the horse in through the main entrance to the Revuebar,' Miklos Matolsci said. 'To get her into the theatre, we'd walk her up the staircase, through the lounge bar and across the bridge. Somebody had to follow us with a bucket. I don't think the horse was one of Raymond's better ideas. We had to lead her across a ramp to get her onstage. The ceiling in the theatre wasn't all that high, so there wasn't much headroom

*Beauty and the Bust: Adele Warren and Wally Lucken's horse, Beauty*

for the naked woman who sat on the horse. I reckon we'd have been better off with a naked dwarf on a pony.'

In February 1965 the third issue of *King* – now a monthly rather than a quarterly – reached the shops. Like previous editions, it featured a starry line-up of contributors, including the playwright Noël Coward and the film director Otto Preminger, paired in that issue's heated instalment of 'The Conversation'. Sales of *King* hadn't, however, met Raymond's expectations, so he announced that he was withdrawing his support. 'The magazine wasn't making a great deal of money,' Jo Brooker recalled, 'and he wanted a better return on his investment.'

The sense that *King* was too upmarket, too literary, for him also contributed to his decision. It had taken him into a market he didn't understand, a market that had little in common with the populist entertainment that had made him wealthy.

'He looked at it and said, "This isn't for me. This isn't my kind of thing",' Connor Walsh remembered. Deprived of Raymond's backing, the magazine nevertheless managed to continue, attracting a group of investors, one of whom was the film director Bryan Forbes.

Around then, Raymond got in touch with a Channel Islands-based organisation which advertised in the national newspapers. For an exorbitant £300 fee, sometimes reduced or waived if the applicant couldn't afford it, the organisation offered twelve-day courses that claimed to cure stammering. Patients were offered their money back if the therapy failed.

Mild though his speech impediment was, Raymond was obviously troubled by it, otherwise he wouldn't have enrolled in the course and travelled to Jersey. His destination was the Seagull, a single-storey, concrete-rendered 1930s folly. Owing to its resemblance to a beached ship, the likeness accentuated by its sharp prow, its mast, its windows shaped like portholes, and its deck that doubled as a roof, it had long been known by locals as 'the Barge Aground'. It was positioned next to the beach at St Ouen's Bay near St Helier, the attractiveness of its setting enhanced by a landscaped garden dotted with rockeries. In this improbable location, far removed from his normal habitat, Raymond would have joined a disparate group of about eight fellow stammerers, ranging from infancy to old age, some of them so badly afflicted that their eyes closed, their faces flushed and their heads convulsed with the effort of speaking.

They were tutored by Bill Kerr, a retired sergeant-major in his early fifties who had taken a degree in philosophy and English literature. He was a craggy-faced man with a burly physique, a harsh Glaswegian accent and a personality of such force that he could swiftly induce a state of quivering, sweaty-browed anxiety among his pupils. Kerr, who held no medical qualifications, had developed a brutal but effective therapy based on the assumption that stammerers were victims of an irrational fear of speech, caused by a sense of their own weakness. By forcing them to uncover the reserves of strength which, he believed, everyone possessed, he aimed to solve what often amounted to a debilitating problem.

Each day at the Seagull began at 7 a.m. – about the time Raymond usually went to bed. The first morning started with Kerr videotaping everyone as they introduced themselves. For many of Raymond's classmates, just saying their names would have been a laborious process. In contrast, Raymond's stammer retained its mysterious tendency to disappear whenever he spoke in front of groups of people.

As soon as the protracted preliminaries were over, Kerr ordered the whole class to sit upright and, one by one, purse their lips tightly and say their names, nodding their heads with each syllable. 'I said, "My na-me is Jon-a-than Sm-ith…"' recalled another of Kerr's pupils. 'It's excruciatingly slow, but it's very difficult to stammer if you do that. Your brain begins to think, "If I can do it at this speed, I might be able to do it when I'm speaking faster." Anyone who made a mistake would get screamed at or hit. I got a whack round the back of the neck one day. Somebody else got hit in the stomach.'

Once everyone in the class had taken their turn to speak, Kerr would randomly select a pupil who was then expected to purse his or her lips and, syllable by syllable, nodding each time, talk until he told that person to stop. Whenever his patients failed to follow his instructions, he'd bellow at them, 'Repeat, repeat again what you said – properly!'

With an hour's break for lunch, the classes carried on until 7 p.m., after which Kerr's pupils went back to a hostel. 'You had to order your dinner without stammering,' Jon Smith said. 'One bloke had a bowl of soup poured over his head because he stammered.'

Day after day Kerr worked his way round the class, forcing everyone to practise talking, the pace of their speech gradually increasing. 'The whole thing was astonishing,' Smith remembered. 'By the end of the second week of the course, we were all talking without stammering. During that second week, we were taught certain helpful techniques. Right until the end of the course, Kerr was obnoxious, but he cried when it was over and we were all cured. Before we left, he presented us each with a copy of the videotape he'd shot on the first day of the therapy. We only needed to look at that to see how effective the course had been.

'To prevent us from slipping into bad habits and stammering again, we were instructed to phone him every Sunday for the next year. After about nine months I started slipping back – because you *do* get careless. So I phoned him one Sunday and he said to me, "You're stammering again! You're going to ruin my life's work. I'm coming to London." And there was I, in London, shitting myself. The next day he phoned and said, "I'm at the Regent Palace Hotel. I want you here now." I got screamed at and he put me right in about half an hour.'

Unlike so many of the other people who made the pilgrimage to the Seagull, Raymond was still stammering when he returned to his nocturnal routine on the mainland.

# 26 STRIP SPECIAL

RAYMOND HAD BEEN using bunny girls in his venues and exploiting Hugh Hefner's Playboy brand for the last three and a half years. Sooner or later Hefner was bound to take legal action. That moment arrived in the second week of July 1965.

Uneasy about the adverse effect Raymond's bunny girls might have on the Playboy Club due to open in London, Hefner issued a writ against Raymond. It sought to prevent him from dressing female employees in bunny costumes and advertising them as 'bunnies'. The apparent weakness of Raymond's position didn't stop him from reaching a settlement with Hefner which allowed him to continue kitting out his employees like that.

He soon faced another legal obstacle – an obstacle no more difficult to overcome. In the months approaching the fifteenth birthday of the son he'd never met, Noreen O'Horan applied to extend his maintenance payments for another three years. Raymond responded with a letter to the court agreeing to her request and asking them to name an acceptable figure.

Ever since the early days of the Revuebar, Raymond had incorporated occasional short films into the show. Now the films, placing considerable emphasis on female nudity, were a regular facet of the programme. In a humorous reference to 'Cinerama', the spectacular curved-screen system used in a few big-city cinemas, Raymond took to advertising his 'Sin-erama', which presented *Coldfingers* and similar celluloid treats.

During February 1966 he also held screenings at the Celebrité. The films viewed there weren't sex films, though. They were films of obscure American horse races, shown on what Raymond promoted as 'Race Nite'. Customers would draw tickets for each of the runners, then watch the race. A bottle of champagne was presented to the holder of the winning ticket.

'It goes to prove that, although sex might be here to stay, our Anglo-Saxon heritage will always put more important matters first,' Raymond declared breezily.

He had plenty to be cheerful about. His businesses were raking in so much money he could afford to spend £1,000 on the personalised number-plate 'PR 11', which he fitted to his Bentley. When the press picked up on the story, he offered £1,500 to anyone who'd sell him the 'SEX 1' number-plate.

As Raymond was chauffeured round Soho, the area was being afflicted by a serious outbreak of violence. One night in late April, two youths set fire to a nameless hostess club above a radio shop on Lisle Street. A customer, trapped in an upstairs lavatory, died in the blaze. Less than a month later another man was killed when the Gigi Club on Frith Street was burnt out.

Afraid that football fans visiting London for that summer's World Cup might get caught up in more violence and fall victim to Soho's thieves and con men, the Metropolitan Police staged a very successful offensive against crime in the area. By the end of the tournament, only one of the numerous clip-joints was still trading. And even that wasn't open on a regular basis.

Within a few months the arson attacks had resumed, but the Revuebar remained unscathed. Despite the intermittent violence, Raymond felt buoyant enough about the club's future to turn down a purchase offer of £250,000.

The spate of attacks on Soho clubs yielded an unforeseen by-product during mid-December. In the interests of checking that strip-clubs had proper fire exits, Greater London Council – the organisation that had replaced London County Council – repealed its previous ban on granting them Public Music and Dancing Licences. For the West End's striptease scene, this was a significant step towards legitimisation. From now on, licensed strip-clubs would no longer have to go through the charade of paying monthly fines for breaching the regulations.

As part of the council's change of policy, the decision was also taken to lift the ban on striptease being performed anywhere other than private clubs. Venues were invited to apply for licences to host public strip-shows.

By relaxing its rules on London's strip-venues, the council contributed to the sense that Britain was, to use a catchphrase of the period, becoming 'a permissive society': an impression reinforced by the sight of so many miniskirted women and by the pornographic bookshops scattered across Soho. Among supporters and opponents alike, this gradual liberalisation of British sexual attitudes tended to provoke clichéd responses. For those in favour, their stance not yet tempered by feminist criticism about male exploitation of women, the process demonstrated that Britain was shaking off its legacy of Victorian hypocrisy and acquiring new-found maturity. For their conservative opponents, the term 'permissive society' was spoken with grimacing distaste, the merest reference to it prefacing forecasts of moral and cultural decline. But these irreconcilable groups hadn't, by the end of 1966, yet coalesced into warring factions. When they *did*, Raymond would find himself in one of the forward trenches.

Before that, however, he witnessed one of the stranger manifestations of permissiveness. In June 1967 he was approached by the divisional commercial manager of British Rail's Southern Region, who suggested they collaborate on a 'Strip Special'. Mercifully, the proposal *didn't* involve disrobing ticket collectors. Customers would, instead, be able to

*A Wild West-themed dance routine at the Revuebar, c.1966*

buy joint, discounted train and Revuebar tickets. Though Raymond was keen on the idea, it was vetoed by Southern Region's top brass.

The mere suggestion of such a scheme by a senior British Rail manager was indicative of just how relatively mainstream striptease had become. Even Raymond's fierce, perpetually black-clad mother, who had retired to the Sussex seaside town of Worthing, was no longer ashamed to tell her friends what he did for a living.

Like previous rule-changes aimed at strip-clubs, Greater London Council's new-found willingness to issue them with Public Music and Dancing Licences had unintended results. Some of the clubs that had been refused licences on health and safety grounds stayed in business by pretending to carry out the required building work. Others became box offices for clubs that *had* managed to obtain licences, those box offices often comprising nothing more elaborate than a Maltese bruiser sitting at a trestle table.

Attracted by the garish, neon-lit window displays and loud music which gave the impression that a show was under way, customers would buy tickets from these box offices, only to be informed that the show was being staged elsewhere. The poor punters would then have to wait until another of the club's employees guided them there. Gradually expanding flocks of impatient men would be shepherded from box office to box office before being taken to a genuine strip-joint.

One of the clubs that turned into a box office was Walker's Court, the venue run by Jimmy and Rusty Humphreys. They used the profits from it to buy and refurbish a large building on the corner of Berwick and D'Arblay Streets, where they planned to open the Queen's Club, an upmarket joint in direct competition with the Revuebar.

To launch their new venture, the Humphreys decided to throw an extravagant party, the invitations for which mimicked banknotes, Rusty's portrait replacing that of the Queen. So realistic were the notes that a plainclothes woman detective on surveillance duty in the West End was conned into accepting one as legitimate currency. Under threat of prosecution by the Bank of England, the Humphreys had to withdraw their invitations. Nevertheless their launch party was packed, Jimmy's underworld pals heavily represented among the crowd, which included the Raymonds.

Though Raymond retained his slim waistline and fastidious dress sense, he no longer cut such an impressive figure. Nowadays his hand-tailored suits looked a bit old fashioned, and his hair had continued its retreat. In order to hide the bald patch that offended his vanity, he favoured a hairstyle that had, courtesy of the Manchester United and England footballer, become known as 'a Bobby Charlton'. Long strands from the side of his skull were laid across the bald spot and doused with sufficient hairspray to hold them in place – a precarious, carefully engineered arrangement that left him wary of rain and gusts of wind.

At the Humphreys' launch party he'd have discovered that the Queen's Club offered a newer brand of striptease than the Revuebar, its style more indebted to discotheques than cabaret or theatre. Dispensing with the house band, Rusty choreographed dance routines in time to booming pop records, the drumbeat counterpointing the quickening pulse of the club's customers. Despite the challenge that the Queen's represented to the Revuebar, Paul and Jean Raymond remained friends with the Humphreys. Rightly as things turned out, Raymond must have felt that there were enough customers for *both* clubs.

Raymond's daughter, who had recently celebrated her eleventh birthday, was studying at the Ursuline Convent School in Wimbledon. The fathers of her schoolfriends often asked Raymond for complimentary tickets to the Revuebar. Along with several of those friends, Debbie had developed the fixation with horses that provided the common denominator between so many girls of her age and class. Raymond's inclination towards appeasement conspiring with both her self-confessed skill at 'playing her father' and his instinctive desire to make her happy, she soon acquired a horse which she rode with obsessive enthusiasm. At weekends her mother would get up at dawn and take her to showjumping competitions in the Home Counties, a world divorced from the worlds in which Jean and Paul Raymond had grown up. Accustomed to mixing with well-heeled families, Debbie was mortified by Jean's references to her own comparatively impoverished background.

By caving in to Debbie's every demand, Raymond only encouraged her to keep exercising her power over him. Before long she was pestering him to let her go to boarding school. Not just *any* boarding school but one of the most expensive in the country – Cheltenham Ladies' College where, she'd discovered, she would be allowed to take her horse. Raymond agreed to send her there, even though he'd never heard of the place and people told him that he 'must be mad to allow a person of that age to choose her own school'.


The new school year at Cheltenham had just started when Raymond made a rare Monday morning appearance at the Revuebar. Normally he didn't roll up until later in the day, but Monday, 18 September was no ordinary day. What made it so different was that the Revuebar had, at short notice, been hired as a location for a television film. Raymond was astute enough to realise that the consequent disruption would be offset by the free publicity that the film would provide.

Ready for when shooting commenced, a raggle-taggle crowd associated with the production, most of them in their twenties, had already gathered in the theatre. They'd been joined by the Bonzo Dog Doo-Dah Band, a then obscure pop group booked to appear in the film. The joint managers of the band had insisted on them getting heavy-fringed Brian Jones-style haircuts for the occasion. Vivian Stanshall, the Bonzos' lead singer, described these as 'outrageous pooftah jobs'. To make matters worse, when they'd unloaded the instruments, amplifiers and other equipment from their van that morning, an opportunist thief had stolen their drum-kit. A replacement had since been borrowed and the ensuing panic quelled.

Stanshall and Co were now waiting for the arrival of the film's stars, who were travelling on a coach that had begun its circuitous journey from London to Cornwall and back to the capital seven days earlier. Along with an ever-expanding cortège that created traffic jams wherever it went, the coach was currently threading a route through the streets of Soho. Numerous shopkeepers and pedestrians turned to stare at the passing vehicle, the appearance of which could scarcely have been more conspicuous. Painted mauve and decorated with cartoonish psychedelic imagery, it had the words 'MAGICAL MYSTERY TOUR' written down the sides in swollen letters. The passengers included John Lennon, Paul

McCartney, George Harrison and Ringo Starr, four of the world's most fêted people at that time, their celebrity consolidated by the recent release of *Sgt. Pepper's Lonely Hearts Club Band*, the Beatles' ninth album in a few frenetic years.

Soon Lennon, Harrison and several other men were being filmed as they trooped down the red-walled corridor that led into the Revuebar's main auditorium. Shooting was directed by an unlikely trio, McCartney and Starr assisted by Bernard Knowles, a veteran television director whose credits were sprinkled with episodes of such famous 1950s series as *The Adventures of Robin Hood* and *Fabian of the Yard*.

Striptease was nothing new for the Fab Four, much of their apprentice days in Hamburg having been spent providing backing music to marathon strip-shows. At their request Raymond had arranged for Jan Carson, one of the Revuebar's current headliners, to perform an act which they intended to film. Under normal circumstances her routine would have been prefaced by the house band. This time, however, the music was provided by the Bonzo Dog Doo-Dah Band.

To the accompaniment of two guitarists, a drummer and a saxophone player, the gangling, ginger-haired Stanshall, sporting a modish Zapata moustache, loped onto the stage, arms pumping in slow motion as he mimed a sprint towards the microphone stand. He was wearing an open-necked shirt and gold lamé suit, from the breast pocket of which a voluminous display handkerchief cascaded. In a fruity send-up of Elvis Presley's mannered vocal style, he proceeded to sing the opening lines of his group's song, 'Death Cab For Cutie'.

Prearranged whistling from the audience signalled the slinkily self-confident emergence of Jan Carson in a matching silver sequinned skirt and blouse that twinkled in the spotlights. She had shoulder-length auburn hair, heavy mascara and false eyelashes that drew attention to her dark eyes. Clutching the ends of a luminous pink feather boa which she tugged coquettishly across the back of her neck, she danced in time to the music.

*Just before the filming of the Revuebar sequence in* Magical Mystery Tour, *the Beatles watch Jan Carson take part in what was known in the striptease business as 'an undress rehearsal'*

Without the usual protracted preamble that puts the *tease* into striptease, she peeled off her blouse to reveal a scarlet bra. Briefly, she started synchronising her movements with those of the crooning Stanshall. Turning away from the audience, she removed her bra, then pirouetted round, breasts bared. Stanshall posed with her as the curtain glided down on the most famous show in the Revuebar's existence.

Before the Magical Mystery Tour headed off to its next stop, an old RAF base near Maidstone, Raymond had his photo taken with the Beatles, who lined up across the stage. Making no concessions to the hippy era, he was wearing a well-cut black suit, a white shirt and a dark tie. He and the band were joined by Carson, naked apart from a pair of black briefs and high-heeled shoes, her feather boa coiled round her bust.

Like the Beatles, she had the practised nonchalance of someone who was used to being ogled. In contrast Raymond appeared gauche, beaming proudly over the shoulder of John Lennon.

*Magical Mystery Tour* received its first television screenings on Boxing Day 1967 and then ten days later, a black box emblazoned with the word 'CENSORED' was superimposed over Jan Carson's naked breasts. These would otherwise have led to the broadcast being cancelled.

Trading on television's squeamishness about striptease, Britain's low-budget film industry had already produced a short-lived cycle of dramas and documentaries set in and around London strip-clubs. Prominent among the feature films was the Jayne Mansfield vehicle *Too Hot to Handle* (1960), lip-lickingly billed as an exposé of 'sexy, sordid Soho, England's greatest shame'. Other dramas in the cycle comprised *Undercover Girl* (1958), *The Small World of Sammy Lee* (1962), *Jungle Street* (1961) and *The Strip Tease Murder* (1963), as well as *Beat Girl* (1960), in which Christopher Lee played a strip-club owner whose debonair dress sense was surely modelled on the Revuebar's founder.

Along with exploitation documentaries such as *Soho Striptease* (1961) and *Caroussela* (1965), both of which had trouble negotiating the censorship process, the striptease films gave provincial audiences a piquant taste of London sleaze. In all likelihood drawing on downmarket newspaper coverage of court cases involving Raymond and his fellow striptease barons, most of the feature films also propagated a potent stereotype of strip-club owners. That stereotype depicted them as silver-tongued metropolitan bogeymen, latter-day incarnations of the White Slaver, predatory spivs whose synthetic bonhomie and sleek suits failed to camouflage their true nature.

# 27 YES, WE HAVE NO PYJAMAS

IN LATE JANUARY 1968 Raymond stumbled across an unlikely pretext for another publicity stunt. An avid fan of the Oxford and Cambridge University Boat Race, staged on the Thames each year, he was surprised to discover there was no trophy for the winning crew. Through a reporter from the *Daily Mail*, he offered to donate a two-and-a-half-foot-tall, solid-gold statue. 'But it won't be shaped like a naked girl or anything like that,' he assured the university authorities, who saved him a great deal of money by failing to take advantage of his proposal.

More important matters soon claimed Raymond's attention. He and his wife quarrelled about the content of the shows at the Revuebar. Until now these had always incorporated the dance numbers that were Jean's speciality. Raymond had, however, come to the conclusion that the dancing should be axed, leaving extra space for striptease – more *explicit* striptease, performed to records rather than live music. Recalling their disagreement, Jean said, 'He told me I was Victorian and didn't move with the times. I am not a prude, but the simulated sex seemed so unnecessary.'

Since Raymond wasn't willing to compromise, she decided to stop producing the shows at both the Celebrité and the Revuebar, curtailing a working relationship that had endured for over a decade and a half. As Raymond later recognised, this was a pivotal moment in their crumbling marriage. By excluding herself from his work, which was so central to his existence, she bowed out of a large part of his life and made it easier for him to have affairs with some of the nubile women who sashayed across his eyeline. According to Jean, he tried to assuage his guilt by offering to set her up with a young gigolo: 'He said, "I've phoned a little boy for you. I thought you might enjoy it." I just went barmy. Paul had to cancel the arrangement.'

His repeated infidelities fuelling Jean's accumulated dissatisfaction, that September she insisted on him moving out of their Drax Avenue home. 'Once I had time to think, I realised we just didn't have a thing in common anymore,' Jean reflected.

Despite being a lapsed Catholic and an errant husband, Raymond retained his belief in marriage as a lifelong bond, so he was desperate for a reconciliation with his wife. After he discovered that she'd submitted a divorce petition, he went on a drunken spree that concluded in the early hours when he drove the wrong way up Chelsea Embankment. Stopped by the police and asked to use a breathalyser, he sucked on the mouthpiece instead of blowing through it. He was then taken back to the local police station for a blood test. It revealed that he had two and a half times the permitted level of alcohol in his blood-stream.

For the second time in just over five years, he found himself on drink-driving charges. His protestations of innocence couldn't prevent him from being given a £50 fine – inconsequential for someone of his wealth – and a one-year driving ban.


Still estranged from Jean, whose divorce action he'd chosen not to contest, Raymond plotted a fresh direction for his business. He wanted to diversify from clubs and restaurants into theatre management. By November he'd embarked on negotiations to acquire premises in Mayfair where he could establish a 220-seat theatre/restaurant which he planned to call 'Downstage'. Twice each night a sixty-minute play would be performed there, the curtain rising only once the tables had been cleared. He envisaged staging comedies and other light drama, none of which would feature sex. He'd even earmarked the first play that would be produced there, but the deal fell apart.

The sense of disappointment was counterbalanced by progress on another front. Weeks of anguished phone calls, of nagging his wife to reconsider her divorce petition, paid off when she agreed to give him another chance and let him move back into the marital home. 'The main reason why she took him back was because of Debbie and Howard,' recalled a friend of hers. 'She didn't want them to have to grow up without him being around. I don't think she seriously expected him to change, so it can't have surprised her that his good intentions lasted about five minutes.'

His domestic crisis resolved, Raymond was able to resume the strange routine that had, for him, become normal life. Nights at the Revuebar and the Celebrité were seasoned by extramarital relationships and recruiting trips to Vienna, Paris and Hamburg, accompanied by Miklos Matolsci, who was expected to pick up new techniques for lighting the performers at the Revuebar.

Frequent press interviews provided another ingredient of Raymond's current regime. For journalists he was an attractive subject, combining fame, humour, controversy and a willingness to speak with often puckish candour. The more interviews he gave, the more journalists wanted to talk to him. Asked by a reporter from the London *Evening News* about the Revuebar, he said, 'There are always those who think there is more to it than what they see. They seem convinced I have a room and some girls tucked away. It's nonsense, of course. I grow tired denying the rumour. Now I tell 'em, "If you can find any secret attractions, you're having better luck than I am."'

During the second week of January 1969 Raymond appeared on the ITV discussion programme *For the Record*. He talked about Soho, as well as his attitude towards sin and the commercial exploitation of sex which, he felt, had to face *some* restrictions. 'In Hamburg, things have got so way out that I find it revolting,' he'd remarked a few days earlier.

One such restriction had been removed the previous autumn when the Theatres Act had been introduced. From that moment, neither the

PAUL RAYMOND'S
*Raymond Revuebar* LONDON ENGLAND

Programme 2/6

*Front cover of a 1967 Revuebar
programme, showing the venue's
star stripper, Carole Ryva*

Revuebar nor any of the other Soho strip-joints had to operate as private clubs. Customers could now walk up to the box office and buy tickets without the inconvenience of having to fill out a membership form, then wait forty-eight hours before being allowed to see a show.

By abolishing the Lord Chamberlain's role as censor, the Theatres Act had other, more widely publicised ramifications. The foremost of these was a proliferation of nudity on West End stages. Only a day after the Act became law, the musical *Hair* – the entire cast of which appeared naked – began its profitable run at the Shaftesbury Theatre. For the Revuebar and other strip-joints, the advent of nudity in mainstream theatres presented them with a challenge. If men could leer at naked women in ordinary theatres, why should those men go to the greater expense of using strip-joints?

Raymond was quick to see the possibilities opened up by West End stage nudity. Intent on mining those, he bought a short lease on the

Whitehall Theatre in late July. It was a venue associated not only with popular farces but also with Phyllis Dixey's *Peek-a-Boo Show*, a wartime nude revue that competed with the performances at the Windmill. Raymond had leased the Whitehall with the objective of blending the traditions of both farce and nude revue. This would be done by staging *Pyjama Tops*, an English version of *Moumou*, a French farce replete with nudity. He readily acknowledged the inadequacies of the play yet had faith in its ability to sell tickets and entertain audiences.

When Raymond advertised for supporting actors and actresses to appear in *Pyjama Tops*, the need to undress being a prerequisite for most roles, he was contacted by Peter Plouviez, assistant general secretary of Equity, the actors' union. Plouviez insisted that an Equity official should be present at auditions. Though Raymond was unaccustomed to this form of interference, he agreed.

Squeezing the audition and rehearsal process into less than two months, he was ready to open the production on the evening of Monday, 22 September. He invited Jimmy and Rusty Humphreys to join him and Jean at the first night. Many of the faces of the people in

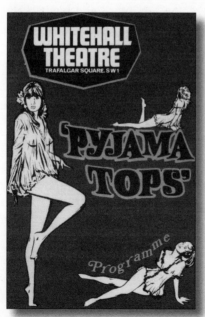

the audience wore expressions of delight, but the critics were, with only a single exception, hostile to the play, set around a transparent-sided swimming pool into which nude actresses periodically plunged. The *Evening Standard*'s drama critic wrote that 'it is a long time since dialogue so witless, characters so silly and a plot so pointless has eked its way across the West End'. His equally disdainful counterpart on *The Times* bemoaned 'this strip-club invasion of the legitimate stage'.

Such vehement criticism, contributing to possibly the worst panning received by a West End play in twenty years, didn't stop *Pyjama Tops* from becoming a hit. With the glee of the vindicated, Raymond said, 'What the critics failed to realise was that while it may not be the greatest play ever written, it is a good night's relaxed entertainment. People come up to me and say they have not had such a good escapist night for years.'

As well as boosting his already large bank balance, the success of *Pyjama Tops* carried Raymond into the mainstream of the entertainment world, provided him with a fresh formula to exploit and led him to rethink his commercial priorities. His gainful return to the theatrical world underlined the comparative failure of his excursion into the restaurant business. Presented with a £75,000 offer for the Celebrité, he accepted it. Now he was free to concentrate on the business he knew best.

The popularity of *Pyjama Tops* wasn't entirely positive for the Raymond family. Its adverse repercussions were soon felt by Howard, who attended a Catholic school in Wimbledon. Instructed by one of the teachers to produce an essay on what his father did for a living, he wrote that his dad had staged a show called *Pyjama Tops*. Raymond was then summoned by the head priest who enquired whether he was *the* Paul Raymond. When Raymond admitted that he was, the head priest asked him to transfer Howard to a different school.

His attitude towards priests apparently resistant to this collision with unchristian prejudice, Raymond sent his younger son to another Roman Catholic school: Shiplake College, a boarding establishment in the pukka Oxfordshire town of Henley-on-Thames. Even though Howard was living away from home, Raymond was still capable of causing inadvertent problems for him. At the annual school sports day, Raymond – whose dated sartorial style had begun to assimilate the gaudy informality of the era – embarrassed him by turning up wearing a flamboyant shirt and using a silk scarf in lieu of a belt.

☆

Raymond's recruiting trips for the Revuebar weren't confined to continental Europe. Like the manager of a wealthy football club, forever poised to snaffle talented players from rivals, he also liked to cast an appraising eye over the performers at other Soho strip-clubs. One of those was Maxim's Revue Bar on Frith Street. Run by Murray Goldstein who used to own the Geisha, it was the nearest thing Raymond's Walker's Court operation had to a direct competitor, spawning long queues that stretched from its Frith Street entrance on to busy Shaftesbury Avenue.

Atypically for Soho, Maxim's had an interior that lived up to the sophistication of its name. At the back was a plush bar with a small restaurant, staffed by hostesses as well as waitresses. Beyond that was a forty-five-seat auditorium which had an artfully lit wide-angle stage, visible from the bar. During the afternoons, the place was mostly patronised by office workers. From around 8.30 p.m., however, a different, well-heeled professional and sometimes aristocratic clientele descended on Maxim's in such numbers that the waitresses had trouble circulating round the tables. Raymond wouldn't have looked out of place among the club's sleek, champagne-quaffing customers.

He'd come to watch Diana Woodward, Goldstein's lissom girlfriend and star stripper, who appeared under the stage name of 'Malaika', Swahili for 'angel'. She performed a stylised routine that began with the interior of the club blacked out, the doomy preface to Bach's 'Toccata and Fugue' frequently obscured by firecracker applause. As that subsided, the curtains opened. Through a massive sheet of billowing gauze, intended to create a dreamlike effect, the lights revealed a coffin licked by tendrils of dry ice.

To a taped soundtrack extending from Afro-Cuban dance music to Mussorgsky's 'A Night on the Bare Mountain', Malaika worked her way through an act that incorporated belly-dancing, fire-eating and striptease. The denouement involved her pretending to be crushed by a large boa constrictor which looped itself round her naked body.

Taken by the cod exoticism of her act, which resembled a scene from a Hammer horror movie, Raymond invited Goldstein and Woodward to his office at the Revuebar to discuss the possibility of her performing there. But he failed to persuade her to sign a contract.

Over the past three years there had been a marked acceleration in the speed at which Raymond's Soho stamping-ground was changing. Among those changes was the emergence of so-called minicabs, vying with traditional taxis for business from customers using both the Revuebar and Isow's. 'This caused a lot of tension,' Miklos Matolsci said. 'One night about twenty minicab drivers were surrounded by licensed cabbies. Raymond – who was a very courageous man – waded into the middle of them and broke up what could've turned into a brawl. He told them they all had a right to earn a living.'

None of the changes wrought on Soho proved more conspicuous than the sustained incursion of what would one day be dubbed 'the sex industry'. Some of the old retailers and workshops, which had helped to lend the area its unique atmosphere, were being forced out by greedy landlords who imposed steep rent rises, safe in the knowledge that they could lease their premises to the owners of strip-joints and pornographic bookshops.

More strip-clubs, supplemented by box offices for those clubs, had continued to spring up lately. And a parallel expansion had taken place in the number of Soho's pornographic bookshops. By the end of the 1960s, more than fifty of them punctuated the neighbourhood, regular payments to the OPS ensuring that they could trade with impunity. Their window displays consisted of titillatingly titled books, plus magazines adorned by photos of cupped breasts, upthrust backsides, protuberant nipples, heaving buttocks, fishnet-sheathed legs, expressions of bogus ecstasy, limbs so entwined that their ownership was no easier to disentangle than the limbs themselves.

Many of the functionally titled hardcore publications available from these shops – *Intercourse in Colour, Lesbian Orgy* and *Weekend*

*Sex* – had been smuggled into the country from Denmark and Sweden, often concealed in consignments of vegetables or Danish bacon, the latter sometimes infusing the paper with a briny scent. Thanks to the recent removal of virtually all sexual censorship in those countries, Scandinavia had supplanted France as the perceived home of sexual waywardness. Deregulation in Sweden and Denmark had, along with the reduced cost of colour printing, also helped to transform pornography, once the preserve of decadent upper-class connoisseurs, into an absurdly profitable mass-market enterprise. Raymond's friend Jimmy Humphreys was among the recipients of those profits. For the right to open the first in what would become a chain of Soho smut shops, he'd just struck a costly deal with three of the area's power brokers: the gangster Bernie Silver, Detective Superintendent 'Wicked Bill' Moody – who ran the OPS – and Moody's colleague, Commander Wally Virgo.

Residents and aficionados of Soho had taken to lamenting the area's consequent sleaziness. They mourned the vanished golden age when drinking clubs had occupied the cellars now colonised by strip-joints, when gambling clubs offered the transgressive frisson currently provided by dirty bookshops, when writers and artists thronged the pubs, when shop windows displayed salami and garlic sausages rather than nudie magazines and gleaming, sinister-looking dildos. What the nostalgists failed to realise was that previous generations had been stung by this same feeling of postlapsarian loss. As far back as 1927, Alec Waugh had remarked on the 'wistful romance about the word, once so magical, "Soho".'

There was even a hand-me-down quality about the nature of the changes inflicted on the district. A similar sex industry invasion had occurred in the late nineteenth century, brothels and clip-joints multiplying at the expense of Soho's existing residents. 'Our respectable workers are in many cases being driven out of house and home to make room for the traders in vice who can afford to pay exorbitant rents,' lamented a delegate at a conference held in 1895.

☆

People had warned Raymond that the arrival of the permissive society would affect ticket sales at the Revuebar by making it feel out of date. It remained very successful, however, as the 1960s made way for the new decade.

Two things that *had* changed by January 1970 were the nature of the shows staged there and the type of audiences who watched them. In the past, people from all over Britain had made pilgrimages to the club, but its cross-country magnetism had been diminished by the availability of strip-shows in most towns and cities, darkened pubs providing the characteristic venue. Its status as a voguish hangout had, at the same time, been eroded. These days you were less likely to encounter a film star in its lounge bar than an unfashionably Brylcreemed young man with a rural accent and a shifty expression.

Through the growth in London's tourist trade, made possible by cut-price flights, Raymond was able to fill the shortfall by promoting the Revuebar abroad. Japanese, German, Italian and Spanish tourists now comprised 75 per cent of the club's audience. According to European travel agents, the Revuebar was, alongside Big Ben and the Tower of London, one of the principal attractions that lured foreign visitors to London.

Those customers, who paid as much as 55 shillings for a front-row seat, were still treated to a luxurious experience, the seemingly endless *International Festival of Striptease* striking a sharp contrast with the rudimentary shows staged in most of Soho's strip-joints. Several of the current routines, contributing to a two-hour show that also featured a conjuror and an ice-skating act, took place against specially filmed Cinemascope back-projections of Buckingham Palace and other famous London sights. Invariably the performers – meticulously coiffed, coltish blondes with firm breasts and sequinned skin – ended up sprawled across a couch or bed, miming vigorous sex. Had Raymond staged anything like that in the early 1960s, he'd have found himself in a prison cell.

Detectives from West End Central were among the Revuebar's visitors. 'Raymond was in Scotland Yard's good books,' one of those detectives recalled. 'Everyone spoke highly of him. They didn't even bother tapping his phone calls, which they did with a lot of the porn merchants. The general feeling was that he was a good bloke. We'd stop off there on a regular basis. He'd be sitting at the bar. Never very welcoming. Always complaining about something. We'd try to pick up useful information and contacts from him, but he wouldn't give us anything.'

In no hurry to return to his far-from-happy home, Raymond would often go on club crawls after the evening's final show had finished. One of his favourite haunts was an old-fashioned hostess club in Knightsbridge, owned by an elderly couple who, in defiance of the high-ceilinged chill, liked to dress as if they were on a golf course in Miami. Another of his regular stop-offs was the Blue Angel on Berkeley Street, Mayfair: a club mainly patronised by debutantes and Guards officers.

On the night when the cherubic-faced *Sunday Times* journalist Philip Norman interviewed Raymond for a profile in the paper's trendy colour supplement, the pair of them ended up in the Blue Angel. There, Raymond – who plundered his repertoire of anecdotes – ordered their sixth bottle of champagne, this one costing £7 10s. His normal courtesy to women swept away by all the alcohol he'd consumed, Raymond proffered two £5 notes to the large-breasted barmaid and said, 'Call it ten if you let us see them.' The girl refused, leading him to say, 'Call it ten anyway.'

Earlier on, just for a laugh, Raymond had taken Norman to a rival, Maltese-operated strip-joint with hoardings outside advertising '18 Lovely Girls'. 'The smell of feet is practically a killer fog,' Norman wrote. 'You stand and try to catch a glimpse through a funnel of elbows or a forest of pimply necks; for the customers are not old men; they are youths in the braces, cropped heads and Tuf boots that are the costermongers' new uniform. Somewhere out of sight a girl was taking a maddening time to remove the brassiere of a bathing suit. "Gawd," Raymond mourned, "look at her great stomach." The cellar was airless with remarks: "Get 'em off"...'

Next to fetid basement dives like this, the Revuebar exuded the grandeur and decorum of the Royal Opera House.

# 28 THE NAKED AND THE BED

GALVANISED BY THE PROFITS he was making from *Pyjama Tops*, Raymond entered into negotiations to acquire another West End theatre. By mid-January 1970 he'd signed a twenty-one-year lease on the Royalty Theatre, which propped up an unattractive 1960s office block near the London School of Economics. It had the added disadvantage of being exiled from the heart of theatreland. For several years before Raymond took it over, the Royalty had been operating as a cinema. Despite all this, he announced to the press that he'd be launching a £75,000-budgeted drag show there in the spring. Shrugging off the failure of his two earlier excursions into that brassy genre, neither of which had proved the anticipated success with the gay market, he went on to say, 'I think it is a very fair risk.'

When he cast the show, entitled *Birds of a Feather*, Raymond offered the job of compèring it to an unknown forty-six-year-old female-impersonator-turned-comedian. Raymond had spotted him the previous year, fulfilling the same function in a revue at the Theatre Royal Stratford East. The beneficiary of this bold casting decision was William White, later to achieve fame under his stage name – Larry Grayson. An alumnus of the working-men's club circuit, Grayson had developed an extravagantly camp theatrical persona that harked back to the music-hall artistes of yesteryear. One hand on his hip, the other hanging limp wristed, he'd flounce round the stage, lips puckering every so often in exaggerated disapproval as he delivered a gossipy monologue.

In *Birds of a Feather*, Grayson was required to preside over a tired medley of showbiz impersonations, classic songs, dance numbers, striptease parodies and vaudeville gags, performed by the glamorous Ricky Renée and a troupe of equally plausible cross-dressers who swished about the stage in billowing cloaks and spangled G-strings. The show received its press preview on Friday, 3 April. Though the critics lauded Grayson's contribution, they were scarcely more upbeat about the rest of it than they had been about *Pyjama Tops*. *Birds of a Feather* was, the critic from *The Times* pronounced, 'as flashily characterless as candyfloss'.

Raymond must have hoped that the critics were once again out of step with the audience. But the press turned out to be exasperatingly in touch with the preferences of theatregoers, numerous empty seats greeting the cast each time the curtain rose.

There was still a possibility that good word-of-mouth might redeem the situation. Attendances, however, remained so poor that Raymond sustained an overall deficit of £5,000–£10,000 in the show's first seventeen days. Such swingeing losses led him to cancel the production, an enduring friendship with its compère being the only positive thing to emerge from this fiasco.

As a replacement for *Birds of a Feather*, Raymond financed a production of *The Bed*, a sex comedy directed by Victor Spinetti. Like *Pyjama Tops*, it mixed farce with titillation. Set in a womanising batchelor's flat, it centred around a large bed that folded into the wall by remote control. 'I did a lot of electrical work on that bed,' Miklos Matolsci remembered.

'I used to dread Raymond asking me to do things like that. I had endless trouble making the bed do what he wanted it to do. He left me to get on with it myself, but as soon as there were problems I got a kick in the pants which was fair enough.'

The play opened at the Royalty Theatre in mid-June, attracting reviews that were only a slight improvement on the derisive criticism aimed at its predecessor. Yet there was sufficient female nudity – highlighted by the *Evening News*'s description of it as 'the bosoms and buttocks show' – to bring in audiences.

Cleverly promoting both *The Bed* and *Pyjama Tops* as theatrical aphrodisiacs, Raymond said to a reporter from the *Daily Mirror*, 'I think any husband and wife who goes to see my plays will find them sexually stimulating and it's probably true to say they will have sexual intercourse when they get home.' Hurried trips back to Wimbledon for marital high-jinks weren't part of Raymond's schedule, though. According to his wife, their sex life had long since fizzled out. Other aspects of their marriage weren't going well either. During early July Raymond moved out of their house on Drax Avenue and into a £21-a-night hotel suite which he admitted to finding 'more comfortable than home at the moment'.

With atypical understatement, his wife recalled, 'It would be fair to say there was a certain amount of *atmosphere* when he left.'

So well had they concealed the tension between them, however, the collapse of their marriage took Howard by surprise. Never having seen them rowing, he'd always assumed they were living in a state of blissful wedlock.

For all the antagonism that had developed between Raymond and his wife, Jean was keen to salvage their marriage. 'In many ways she was a strong and very independent woman,' one of her friends said. 'But at that time she just couldn't bear the idea of splitting up permanently. I got the impression she hated being with him and, probably because they'd been together so long, she hated being without him.'

☆

Soon after Raymond's departure, his wife rang the police to report a threatening phone call she'd received. She said the call, made from a phone box by an anonymous man, had come at 2 a.m. that morning. The caller had, she reported, told her, 'Your days are numbered. Watch it. Mr Richardson knows about it.'

She then got in touch with George Richardson, who still worked at the Revuebar. Just as the caller had said, Richardson was likely to have been aware of the threat against Jean because George Flowers, the club's box office manager, had already taken a similar message.

Flowers had reported the incident to Raymond. Along with Jean, Flowers gave a statement to the police. Their testimony prompted detectives to maintain casual observation on the Drax Avenue house at irregular intervals, but this failed to secure an arrest.

No more than a week after the initial threats, another menacing call came through to the Revuebar. At 1 a.m. Jan Harding, who was on the reception desk, picked up the phone and heard a man with a cockney accent say, 'It won't be long. She's only got a few more days.'

'Who d'you mean?' Harding replied.

'The guvnor's wife. Richardson knows all about it.'

Then the caller rang off.

# 29 PORN AGAIN

THREE OR FOUR WEEKS after he'd left Jean, Raymond was sitting in his first-floor office at the Whitehall Theatre when his secretary sent up a twenty-five-year-old named Julia Harrison, who had answered an advert for a small, non-speaking part as a swimmer in *Pyjama Tops*. She turned out to be a bright, attractive, high-cheekboned woman with a voice redolent of colonial garden parties. From across his ostentatiously large desk, Raymond fired a string of perfunctory questions at her. Was she an Equity member? Had she done nude work previously? Before taking her down to the stage for an audition, he informed her that the job paid £30 for a trial period covering eight shows.

At the audition Raymond, his tone as matter-of-fact as if he'd been asking her the time, instructed Harrison to take off her clothes. She was then invited to swim across the glass-sided pool that formed the show's focal point. Her audition ended with Raymond giving her the job.

On Monday, 3 August 1970 she and the other members of the new cast of *Pyjama Tops* started rehearsals. Since she had landed the role, the nude element of her part had mysteriously increased. Uncomfortable about spending such a lot of time naked onstage, she went to see Raymond and complained about it. He persuaded her to continue until the end of her trial contract.

Lest her unclothed presence on the West End stage discomfit her father who was a vicar, she appeared under the stage name of 'Amber St George'. Raymond was so smitten by her that he invited her and the rest of the cast to the Revuebar for a celebratory drink after they'd finished their first night in front of an audience. The group had shrunk to only three people – Raymond, Harrison and another swimmer – by the time they moved to Churchill's Club. Too tired to stay any longer, Harrison left, but forgot her handbag. When she arrived at the Whitehall Theatre the next day, Raymond presented her with the missing bag.

He waited until the following Saturday before making his move. As she exited her dressing room, he was waiting outside, clutching a bottle of champagne. He and Harrison, who hadn't long split up with an American doctor she'd been dating, were swiftly established as a couple. At this juncture, though, Raymond doesn't seem to have taken their romance very seriously. He gave every indication that he regarded it as no more than a brief interlude before he returned to Drax Avenue. Harrison didn't think the relationship would last either. Her expectations were shared by many of the people who knew Raymond. To them, she was just the latest in a succession of pretty young girlfriends with head-turning contours, the twenty-year age gap diverting attention from the many things they had in common, not least a dry, self-deprecating sense of humour and a background of religiosity and middle-class respectability against which they'd both rebelled. Born in a Norfolk rectory, Harrison had been brought up there and in Cornwall, where her father had preached and her mother had taught in a convent. She'd left school with two A-levels, then drifted through a sequence of jobs ranging from nannying for Sean Connery and Diane Cilento to working as a bunny girl at the Playboy Club on Park Lane.

In late August Raymond went on holiday with her to Jamaica, where he liked to stay in the Round Hill Hotel, a collection of mansions – mostly with their own servants and swimming pools – located on the hillside that overlooks Montego Bay. Before setting off, he contacted his wife, just to let her know he'd be going away. He also decided to close down the production of *The Bed* and replace it with a much more controversial show. That show, which had been selling out at the Roundhouse in north London since July, was the oddly titled *Oh! Calcutta!* Bemused Indian tourists had reputedly assumed it would be about the problems afflicting one of their country's most overcrowded cities. The title was, instead, a clever-clever pun on the French phrase '*Quel cul t'as*', meaning 'Oh, what an arse you have!'

Conceived by the critic and provocateur Kenneth Tynan, the show had debuted in New York the previous summer, where it became a vast box-office hit despite some terrible reviews. Tynan's erstwhile partner, the writer Elaine Dundy, said it had been inspired by visits to the Crazy Horse Saloon in Paris, which happened to be one of Raymond's favourite Continental strip-joints. *Oh! Calcutta!* featured music and dance, as well as sketches by John Lennon, Joe Orton, Jules Feiffer, Sam Shepard and others, boasting nudity, rape, flagellation, fetishism and simulated sex. At one time its producer, Michael White, had even considered incorporating a striptease performance by Gypsy de Rio, an acrobatic peeler who plied her trade at the Sunset Strip in Soho.

The show's deliberately scabrous contents probed the limits of the new theatrical freedom initiated by the removal of censorship. Tynan must have been delighted by the harrumphing reaction he'd stirred up. When his show had opened at the government-subsidised Roundhouse, it triggered complaints about 'state handouts for filth'. It led the Archbishop of Canterbury to call on Christians to mobilise against obscenity. It inspired a prominent former Labour MP to write to the Home Office, describing the play as 'so pornographic that it is impossible to describe… without being pornographic'. And it so incensed one member of the Greater London Council that he complained to the police. Had the Attorney-General in the freshly elected Conservative government not been wary of becoming embroiled in a politically damaging row with the liberal press, the show would have been prosecuted for obscenity.

By a strange irony, the moralising advocates of censorship were among the prime beneficiaries of *Oh! Calcutta!* Prior to its arrival, Britain seemed to be drifting towards a Danish scenario where there would, with certain exceptions, be no censorship. Impressed by the

Danish experience, the Arts Council had, only a year earlier, delivered a well-received report which recommended the abolition of the obscenity laws. After the launch of *Oh! Calcutta!*, however, there were the first manifestations of a ferocious popular backlash.

Probably aware that the show had been rejected by the management of every other West End theatre and that tickets had been changing hands for as much as £50, Raymond demanded its producer fork out a rental fee of £3,000 a week for using the Royalty Theatre. Though Raymond's demands were far more scandalous than any of the show's sketches, Michael White accepted his terms and made arrangements for *Oh! Calcutta!* to open on Wednesday, 30 September.

'I will make more money out of that show than any other individual,' Raymond predicted. 'I believe it will be a big hit. One of the biggest. It's a show of our time. You can probably see more at my Revuebar, but *Oh! Calcutta!* has broken down lots of prejudice. And it's great entertainment.'


At the hotel in the West Indies where he and his girlfriend were staying, Raymond bumped into an old pal from his variety days – Archie Lewis. Recalling the encounter, Harrison wrote, 'Archie turned almost white with shock, then pleasure. He and Raymond had not seen each other for years.' Formerly the vocalist for Geraldo and His Orchestra, the hugely popular British dance band, Lewis turned out to have moved back to his native Jamaica, where he earned a living by singing in the top hotels. He had a rich baritone voice suited to the sugary numbers he liked to perform: songs such as 'Hear My Song, Violetta'.

But Raymond's reacquaintance with Lewis was cut short by news of a fire at the Drax Avenue house where Jean and their children were still living. Anxious about the safety of his family, he flew back to London, leaving Harrison to enjoy a few more days in the Caribbean. Jean and the kids hadn't, however, been harmed. With an untroubled conscience,

Raymond was free to head over to New York on a business trip during early September.

Away from his stamina-sapping routine and the attritional conflict of his marriage, he had a chance to contemplate his future. After twelve years in the nightclub business, he wondered whether he should bail out of it. 'Being the owner of a nightclub is only good when you see Humphrey Bogart doing it on the screen,' he confessed. 'In real-life it's a bind. Drunks who won't pay their bills, that sort of thing.'

On his return from America, he was interviewed by a reporter from the *Daily Mirror* which was carrying out an 'enquiry into the disturbing growth of pornography in entertainment'. Leaning back in his office chair, a glass of champagne in hand, Raymond said, 'If it weren't true that people like nude shows I wouldn't be where I am at present. I believe that nudity is an important part of entertainment. I'm not here to prove anything or to push back moral boundaries. I'm in the business to entertain – and nudes entertain. They always have and they always will.'


Aside from sending a postcard to Howard from New York, Raymond hadn't been in touch with his family since the fire at their house. Even though his wife had grown to despise him, she resented the prospect of him leaving her for someone else. Jealousy distilling into obsession, she drove to the Whitehall Theatre where she waited until Julia Harrison emerged from the stage door and headed home. For at least three consecutive nights she followed Harrison's car. Jean also took to making mute phone calls to her in the middle of the night, phone calls which, Raymond insisted, had nothing to do with his wife. He was proved wrong when Jean eventually changed tactics, the silence replaced by acerbic remarks, not about Harrison but about Raymond – about how often he'd been unfaithful to her, how she'd never divorce him.

As her obsession deepened, Jean's stalking grew more systematic. She and a female friend regularly sat in her car outside the mews house where Harrison lived. Whenever Raymond took Harrison to dinner, Jean would be spying on them. Next day Jean would phone Harrison and treat her to an account of exactly what they'd eaten, just to prove she'd been watching.

Like a crook who fears she's being tailed by detectives, Harrison was forced to develop ruses for shaking off her pursuer. If she'd arranged to meet Raymond after work, she wouldn't take the most direct route from the Whitehall Theatre to their rendezvous. She'd dash across Trafalgar Square, then veer towards Charing Cross, where she'd use the underground station. In the minutes Jean spent driving round the square, Harrison would have lost her. Insistent though Jean's tactics were, Raymond remained unsympathetic towards Harrison. His stance was, if you get entangled with a married man, this is precisely what you should expect.

While Jean was stalking Raymond's girlfriend, she also contacted the police to tell them that she'd received further threatening phone calls, each of them from an anonymous man who informed her that the time was getting closer. On Friday, 22 September, Jean rang the police to report yet another call. Her report provoked a visit from an officer who stayed with her for a couple of hours. Possibly because she'd leaked the story herself, she was interviewed that Saturday by a reporter from the *People*. Through the reporter, she did her best to exert emotional pressure on Raymond by plaintively referring to how she hadn't seen him for a month.

Four days after the resultant newspaper story, depicting Jean as a solitary and vulnerable woman, *Oh! Calcutta!* opened at the Royalty Theatre, leading one critic to call it 'the Permissive Theatre of the Seventies'. The show was an even greater hit than previously at the Roundhouse.

Jean's efforts to affect a reconciliation with Raymond – who took the threats against her 'very seriously indeed' – soon yielded results. He agreed to give their marriage another try, but his wife wouldn't let him return unless he promised to sack his girlfriend from the cast of *Pyjama Tops.*

One rainy Saturday night, he broke the news to Harrison that he was going back to Jean and that he had to fire her from the show. But the reconciliation lasted only a couple of weeks. Separated again from Jean, he mended his relationship with Harrison and reinstated her in the cast of *Pyjama Tops*, the resumption of their romance offering Jean an excuse to carry on stalking her rival.

If Jean was hoping to drive Raymond and Harrison apart, she was misguided. The relentless pressure exerted by Jean moulded what might, as Harrison later conceded, have been a transient relationship into a more durable form. Raymond and his girlfriend were now united in adversity. Jean should have known her husband well enough to realise that, unlike most people, he *relished* difficult situations. To him, they were a test of character to be tackled rather than sidestepped. It was in those circumstances, Harrison had noticed, that he seemed most alive.

London was experiencing a chilly preview of the looming winter when Raymond was presented with a fresh problem. On Tuesday, 17 November he received an ultimatum from the cast of *Oh! Calcutta!* They gave him until that Thursday to ensure the theatre was better heated. Failure to comply with their demand would result in them wearing clothes throughout the nude scenes, which accounted for a third of the show.

Not the type of person to backpedal when confronted, Raymond reacted angrily to the threat. 'If they carry it out,' he said, 'I'll bring down the curtain and give everyone their money back. Wearing clothes in the nude scenes would destroy the very essence of the show. I would rather close it and put in another show. The Royalty is one of the most up to date theatres in the country. The heating is more than adequate.'

But he must have come to the conclusion that there was nothing to be gained by antagonising the cast. Before the show started the following night, the underfloor heating was cranked up and all the spotlights were turned on. This kept the cast warm yet left the audience feeling uncomfortably hot. 'It was like the tropics in there,' one woman in the stalls complained.

Having placated the actors, Raymond faced a more worrying threat. Not long before Christmas, George Flowers reported being on duty at the Revuebar between about 12.30 a.m. and 1 a.m. when he'd received a phone call from a man with a cockney accent. Flowers remembered the man saying, 'Tell your guvnor Jean Raymond has only a few days to live' – or something to that effect. 'I said, "Who's the guvnor?",' Flowers continued. 'And he said, "You fucking well know."'

At Raymond's behest, Flowers phoned Wimbledon Police Station and later made a statement.


Raymond's dispute with the cast of *Oh! Calcutta!* aside, the theatrical part of his business was thriving. Not only were there packed houses at the Royalty, but *Pyjama Tops* was still pulling in large audiences, encouraging him to make plans to consolidate that side of the PRO (Paul Raymond Organisation). In late January 1971, he began by lavishing £340,000 on the freehold of the Whitehall Theatre. He spent a further £150,000 on refurbishing the building, a process that included the creation of a small but opulent office for himself, the corridor outside of which was lined with old posters for his variety productions. Advertising shows at venues such as the Empire Theatre, West Hartlepool, these offered a tangible reminder of the progress he'd made within show business.

The Whitehall Theatre wasn't Raymond's sole acquisition. Asked about his previous foray into magazine publishing, he had not long ago said to Philip Norman, 'Now I don't need the aggravation.' By that January, though, he'd decided to have another stab at the business. For around £12,000 he bought the once popular magazine *Men Only*.

Founded in 1935, it had a tradition of mixing blokeish articles about sport and travel with adventure stories, humorous items and coy pin-ups – originally drawings but latterly photographs. The magazine's circulation had dwindled to 35,000 despite it being relaunched in the mid-1960s.

He was soon making plans to revamp *Men Only* again. On this occasion the overhaul would be more radical. To institute his plans, he appointed as editor a gap-toothed, frizzy-haired young journalist named Tony Power, based in offices at Melbourne House in Aldwych. With his fashionable beard and penchant for white suits, open-necked shirts and tinted aviator-style glasses, Power looked less like a journalist than a member of the Bee Gees. The age difference between him and Raymond didn't prevent the two of them from becoming friends. 'They liked each other and they amused each other and they laughed with each other and they got drunk together and they loved each other's company. And it was a great relationship,' recalled one of Raymond's other employees.

Under Power's regime, *Men Only* would be transformed into a monthly magazine devoid of *King*'s upmarket literary sheen, the limits of its writerly ambition delineated by the florid, self-parodic prose of its photo captions. Pouting, vacuous Melanie from Manchester, the zenith of whose leisure activities comprised a throaty coupling on the back seat of her boyfriend's Ford Capri, was destined to be transformed by one of Raymond's minions into Kirsten from Oslo, who spent her weekends hiking round the fjords, where the doleful sounds of Mahler drifted through the crepuscular corridors of her mind.

Power came up with the inspired idea for a series of articles in which a woman travelled round Europe 'road-testing' men's sexual performances with all the thoroughness of a motoring correspondent briefed to evaluate a car's design, reliability and after-sales service. Treating the whole thing as the ribald joke Power had intended, Harrison – who was still working as a swimmer in *Pyjama Tops* – volunteered to write the series, though she insisted on using a pseudonym.

Alongside Harrison's lurid column, entitled 'European Report by

Fiona Richmond', Power introduced more plentiful and revealing softcore pin-ups. Often these used performers from the Revuebar, coaxed into modelling for what, in the skin trade, were termed 'crotch shots', photographic retouching and clenched-thigh poses conniving to prevent the viewer from seeing anything behind the dense pubic veil.

*Men Only*'s new editor broadened the revamp by dropping the articles about sport, travel and adventure that had hitherto accompanied the pin-ups. In their place, he commissioned pieces about cars and clothes, pieces that targeted a different audience, namely affluent young men. This shift of emphasis proved a masterstroke, enabling the magazine's staff to sell advertising space to drinks and cigarette companies which tended to possess huge promotional budgets.

His separation from Jean seemingly permanent, Raymond showed his commitment to his new relationship by moving with Harrison into a rented house on Walton Street, not far from the Victoria & Albert Museum – an amenity wasted on him. He didn't want her to have to support herself, yet she disliked the idea of being a kept woman, so she accepted only £20 a week for housekeeping. Her self-sufficiency earned his admiration and, presumably, convinced him that she wasn't a gold-digger. In between cooking, shopping and cleaning, she paid her way by writing her column for *Men Only* and appearing in *Pyjama Tops*. She was, however, the beneficiary of an extravagant gift from him. He presented her with an E-type Jaguar sports car, which rapidly became one of the sights of the West End, its lemon-yellow paintwork and 'FU2' personalised number-plate making it hard to ignore.

Even though she and Raymond had demonstrated that their relationship was no mere casual fling, Jean continued to stalk her. After seeing Harrison kiss a female visitor goodbye, Jean phoned Raymond and told him that he was living with a lesbian.

Such bitterness must have contributed to his daughter's initial, sour attitude towards Harrison. 'I used to get jealous about all his young lady friends,' Debbie confessed. 'But then he turned round and said: "Debbie, it's got nothing to do with you."'


About an hour and a half after midnight one morning in early February, the Revuebar received an anonymous phone call saying that a bomb, timed to explode in fifteen minutes, had been planted at the Raymonds' house. The police were immediately notified. They called Jean, told her about the tip-off and asked her to let them in when they arrived. Within a few minutes officers were searching her home, but they found nothing.

Raymond was, meanwhile, drawing up short-lived plans to sell £3.5 million-worth of shares in the Paul Raymond Organisation. Exactly a week after he'd announced his intention to float the company on the London Stock Exchange, Jean had another visit from the police. At around 3 p.m. on Saturday, 27 February, they pulled up outside her house. The squad car had been sent from Wimbledon police station where they'd had a call from one of the newspapers which had been informed that 'Paul Raymond's house is going up'. Again, the police searched the place yet failed to find any explosive devices.

The stepping up of the harassment campaign against Jean coincided with an intensification of *her* harassment of Raymond's girlfriend. Jean often rang Harrison at home. Certain that the best way of dealing with Jean was to ignore the calls, Harrison took to putting the receiver down as soon as she heard Jean's voice. This so infuriated Jean that she rolled up at the Whitehall Theatre one evening and started banging on the door of Harrison's dressing room. Until that moment, Harrison had never met her. When Harrison opened the door, Jean grabbed her arm and treated her to an angry tirade, witnessed by several other members of the cast of *Pyjama Tops*. One of the girls who shared Harrison's dressing room helped her wriggle free from Jean's grasp. Harrison and her colleague then forced the door shut while Jean leant against it.

# 30 MR STRIPTEASE V. LORD PORN

ROWING HOSTILITY TOWARDS the permissive society, especially from evangelical Christian groups, had coalesced into multiple campaigns that challenged the long-term viability of Raymond's business. Newsagents displaying pornographic magazines on their top shelves faced protests; picket lines were organised around London cinemas screening softcore films; and the Society of Conservative Lawyers published a hostile report on the effects of pornography.

Of all the campaigns being waged during the opening months of 1971, the most famous was the National Viewers' and Listeners' Association, previously Clean Up TV. It had been co-founded by the ageing Shropshire secondary school teacher Mary Whitehouse, horn-rim-spectacled scourge of permissiveness, who accused the BBC of peddling 'the propaganda of disbelief, doubt and dirt'. In a perverse twist of fate, Raymond inadvertently supplied her most prominent and vocal ally. The birthplace of this alliance was the Royalty Theatre.

Curious to find out whether *Oh! Calcutta!* merited such a vexed response, the sixty-five-year-old Labour peer Frank Pakenham, better known as Lord Longford, went with his son-in-law to see the show. Throughout its long tenure in the West End, *Oh! Calcutta!* can't have attracted such an improbable customer as Longford, high-minded Catholic convert and liberal prison reformer. For one thing he would have been perfectly cast as a country vicar in an emollient Sunday night television drama, his bald head flanked by tufts of hair, his eyebrowless eyes blinking behind wire-rimmed glasses, his expression wavering between severity and benificence. Even his opinions, doctrinal rectitude blended with sequestered innocence, could have been mistaken for those of a vicar from some cosy rural parish. He believed that extramarital sex was sinful. He also admitted to being shocked by dirty jokes and avoiding House of Lords debates on obscenity lest they upset him.

The idealistic, self-publicising peer's immediate reaction to *Oh! Calcutta!* was predictable. By the interval he'd seen enough to catapult him out of the theatre. But his stomping indignation didn't end there. 'I think until then I had averted my eyes and hoped to run my course without having to face this issue,' he told a reporter several weeks later. 'I thought I could shirk it. But we are on a very slippery course in this matter. It is like bullying at school, when you always assumed that the headmaster would do something about it. Then suddenly you realised that the headmaster had opted out, and was just sitting there with a genial smile on his face intending to do nothing. People in authority say that there is nothing they can do because public opinion is so much on the side of the permissiveness. But some moral order has got to be restored. Some firm ground must be placed under people's feet again. It certainly will not be done by moral ranting or by old people demanding a return to the old standards. But those who are against pornography and want to stem this tide must put their heads together and work out a coherent policy of resistance.'

A brave, energetic and resolute – though often risibly naive – campaigner for unpopular causes, Longford had just found a new crusade to which he could dedicate himself. With the diligence and intensity he'd applied to previous quests, among them his campaign for the rehabilitation of ex-convicts, he began a preliminary investigation into the spread of what he regarded as pornography, be it magazines or strip-clubs.

In early April he asked a Home Office official whether they could use the law to prevent unsavoury club-owners from exploiting strippers. Eleven

244 | PAUL WILLETTS

days after the official replied with a letter giving scant encouragement, Longford tabled a House of Lords debate 'on the problems and incipient menace of pornography in Great Britain'. The motion was scheduled for Wednesday, 21 April. To prepare for the debate, he visited a sex shop, watched a succession of blue films, and arranged with his friend Philip Howard, a cub reporter on *The Times*, to cover his research trip to a couple of Soho strip-joints.

Carrying briefcases and wearing raincoats, Longford and his friend spent part of the day before the debate sampling the opposite ends of the striptease spectrum. In the downmarket Paris By Night, a murky cellar no larger than a railway carriage, they joined half a dozen silent customers staring at a girl as she stripped down to nothing but knee-high boots and a wristwatch. That lunchtime they tried the Revuebar, too. At Raymond's insistence it was no longer advertising 'striptease'. He'd replaced the term with 'erotic entertainment', his freshly minted euphemism born out of a sense that striptease sounded old fashioned.

From the Revuebar's box office, at which they bought their tickets, Longford and Howard went up to the lounge bar where the cloakroom attendant insisted on relieving them of their coats and charging for the privilege. Each of them equipped with a pricey pint of beer, they took their seats in the theatre. There, they witnessed a slim young woman shrug her way out of her clothes in time to a Beatles record.

'Philip, does this rouse you?' Longford asked his friend in a loud whisper. 'It has no effect on me. But I am an older man than you.'

Feeling awkward because he was within earshot of the stripper as well as a nearby bouncer, Howard gave a mumbled, non-committal reply. He and Longford soon made their getaway. As they sat in a restaurant afterwards, a couple of strangers walked up to Longford and congratulated him on the stand he was taking. Since tabling his parliamentary motion, he'd also received a vast number of letters, 200 of them arriving in a single day, most of them, he claimed, expressing support. Emboldened by the sense that he was articulating the majority opinion, he was already planning to use the House of Lords motion to launch an inquiry into pornography in Britain.

At 2.46 p.m. the next day he initiated the debate by saying, 'My Lords, I rise to move the motion standing in my name. I am seeking to open up for discussion this afternoon the whole field of pornography in Britain: books, magazines, advertisements of all kinds, the theatre, films, television, exhibitions, communications through the press, and anything else which the more sophisticated members of the House may be aware of...'

At the Revuebar, only a mile from Parliament, Raymond also vented his opinions. His audience was a journalist from the *Daily Mirror*, which was running a feature on the ideal attributes for various jobs. In discussing what makes a popular stripper, Raymond cited the Revuebar's current star, a leggy peroxide blonde whose portrait, resplendent in a bra and G-string, a furled whip in one hand, was taken by the fashionable photographer David Bailey. 'Serena has everything we look for in our business,' Raymond said. 'Nowadays we have as many women in the audience as men and they're very critical. A man can be blinded by a girl's appeal to him, but a woman will always say: "Her behind's too big" or "She's a bit past it, isn't she?" There's a great shortage of girls at the moment – the right kind of girl, that is. For striptease it's not enough to take your clothes off. My kind of girl has to have a great act going. And she has to project real eroticism on a high artistic level. Most of my girls are foreign – English girls don't seem to have the knack. And German girls are a bit crudish. French and Italians are good. Serena, though, is just about perfect. Actually she *is* English but she's lived in France for years.'

While Raymond pondered the question of what makes a successful stripper, his employees were preparing to launch *Men Only*, a magazine that would add to what Lord Longford condemned as the 'flow of filth'.

By electing to publish photos more explicit than those of its softcore rivals, Raymond guaranteed that the build-up to the launch of its first issue was strewn with obstacles. Though the presence of well-known advertisers conferred an aura of normality on it, several newspapers, among them the *News of the World*, declined to carry adverts for *Men Only*. The magazine's commercial prospects were dealt an even heftier blow by the refusal of W. H. Smith's to stock it.

Bewilderment was Raymond's standard response to the criticism levelled against his chosen type of entertainment. 'I have a conscience like everyone else, but I don't see anything wrong in what I do,' he announced. 'I would feel much less easy with myself if I sold cigarettes and booze because they are actually commodities that harm people.'

But his rational, man-of-the-world argument possessed the type of serious design flaw which had sent the *Titanic* diving towards the seabed. Raymond had somehow let the fact that he *did* sell booze and cigarettes at both the Revuebar and the Whitehall Theatre slip his mind.

So annoyed was Raymond by the censorious attitude of W. H. Smith's that he took out a full-page advert in the newsagents' trade journal, claiming to 'need W. H. Smith's like a hole in the head'. He could afford to thumb his nose at the company only because John Menzies, Britain's other leading chain of newsagents, had been persuaded to stock *Men Only*. Besides selling the magazine, Menzies had agreed to distribute it to around twenty thousand independent newsagents, through which pornography would be swept from the torpid, muddy shallows into the central current of British life.

Unable to secure government backing for his planned enquiry, Lord Longford had to organise it himself. Funded by a grant from a sympathetic charitable trust, he invited a deliberately wide range of people to join his committee. Raymond's friend Danny La Rue was among those who turned down the invitation. But Longford had soon recruited more than fifty people. They were an incongruous bunch, his long-standing friend Malcolm Muggeridge drafted into it alongside the former Attorney-General, the pathologist Sir Francis Camps, the Archibishop of York, the ex-chairman of the Trades Union Congress, the writers Kingsley Amis and Elizabeth Jane Howard, the showbiz personalities Jimmy Savile and Cliff Richard.

Supposedly, the committee would approach its subject with no preconceived ideas, yet any pretence at objectivity had been kiboshed by its founding premise – that pornography was a problem in need of a solution. Longford's assumption was shared by the Society of Conservative Lawyers, which put together its own committee to consider the statutory definition of obscenity, and by the National Council of Women of Great Britain, which convened a conference about 'Liberty and Licence'. Speaking at the conference, held on Monday 10 May, Longford stated, 'I have a closed mind on the threat of pornography but an open mind on how to diminish that threat.'

During the question-and-answer session that followed, a member of the audience asked, 'How can we stop pornography once and for all?'

Longford replied that he had no immediate answer. He added that he hoped his committee would come up with a solution in around a year's time.

To mark the launch of his new magazine, which he called 'a breakthrough in honesty and frankness', Raymond arranged a party at the Revuebar, beginning at 11 a.m. on Tuesday, 25 May. The previous night he offered the nine waitresses who worked there an extra £4, plus 50 pence lunch money in return for serving drinks to his guests. But the waitresses turned down his offer because they didn't finish work until 3 a.m. They told him that 'it would be impossible for them to look sexy after so little sleep'.

Unsympathetic towards them, he said, 'Turn up, or you're fired.'

When the waitresses failed to show up for the press launch, Raymond sacked them. Along with several friends and senior employees, he acted as a stand-in waiter until replacements could be recruited. His drink-dispensing services failed to coax a favourable response from the national newspapers, which branded *Men Only* 'a dirty magazine' and 'the kind of thing that gives nudity a bad name'. In sales terms, though, the magazine got off to an extremely successful start, a single branch of John Menzies on Paddington Station selling 2,000 copies.

Each morning Lord Longford would, if he was in London, go for a cooked breakfast in the Bow Tie, a greasy-spoon café just down the street from the public baths in pre-gentrification Chelsea, his choice of eaterie perfect for a self-appointed champion of the people. Its other customers were donkey-jacketed workmen, scarfing bubble-and-squeak, eggs, bacon, chips and fried bread. Gazing down at them from the wall was a calendar emblazoned with photos of nude women, among them a blonde on a pink bed. When Longford entered, the staff would flip the calendar so it faced the wall – a gesture which, he considered, 'jolly decent of them'.

Seated at a Formica-topped table laden with sauce bottles, he'd fortify himself for the other forms of sauce he'd have to confront that day. His new-found fame was something he relished. He was particularly pleased when an urchin buttonholed him in the street and said, ''Ere, aren't you the chap what wants to stop the strip-clubs?'

As part of the preparatory work for his report, he started collecting copies of *Men Only* and other porn magazines, which quickly accumulated in the old suitcase he carried around. He even had it with him one afternoon when he went in search of Mowbray's, a religious bookshop not far from Broadcasting House, headquarters of the BBC. Making his way along Wigmore Street, he kept putting the suitcase down while he asked passers-by for directions.

Two plainclothes policemen were watching him with deepening suspicion. Suddenly one of them tapped him on the shoulder. Unimpressed by his account of what he was doing, the policemen insisted on examining the contents of the suitcase. A crowd of pedestrians converged on the flustered aristocrat. They were soon peering at his exposed jumble of socks, shirts, pyjamas and skin magazines.

Salvation, albeit of an earthbound variety, arrived in the form of someone in the crowd who said, 'Isn't that Lord Longford?' Alerted to the misunderstanding, the policemen apologised, then bundled him into a cab.

# 31 FILTHY LUCRE

EXCEPT FOR during the school holidays when her children returned from boarding school, Jean Raymond was living alone in the house she and her husband had once shared. Lending credence to the previous threats against her, she reported another minor fire there on Saturday, 3 July 1971. The incident was treated by the fire brigade as suspected arson.

Around 9.50 p.m. the following Tuesday, she went round locking the windows and doors before going upstairs and getting ready for bed. Apart from her two dogs, she was alone in the house. Since she was expecting a call from America at 10 p.m. or thereabouts, she listened for the sound of her bedside telephone. When the call didn't come, she decided there was no point waiting any longer, so she took a couple of sleeping tablets.

Just after 4 a.m. she was woken by one of her dogs barking. Still half asleep, she heard banging and splintering noises coming from downstairs. As she became more alert, she realised that her bedroom was full of smoke. Venturing on to the landing, she found the smoke equally dense there. Unable to see where she was going when she tried to head downstairs, she went back to her bedroom and phoned the police and fire brigade. She also rang a friend, who helped to quell her mounting panic. Once she'd put the receiver down, she opened the bedroom window and screamed for help, but none of her neighbours responded.

She had to wait about fifteen minutes before two fire engines pulled up in front of the house, from where very little smoke had so far leaked. The firemen rescued Jean, who had to be carried through the open bedroom window and down a ladder. While she sat on a low garden wall, at least two of the firemen walked round the house in an attempt to pinpoint the source of the smoke. Through a glazed door that led on to the patio between the house and garage, they spotted a shattered pane of glass and a small fire in the lounge. One of the firemen broke a pane in the adjoining bay window, thrust a hose through it and extinguished the flames.

Positive that the danger had been averted, the senior officer, Alan Tarrant, inspected the house. All of the damage was around the bay window, but Tarrant couldn't work out how the fire had started. The combination of the mysterious broken French window and the recent case of apparent arson prompted him to record the fire as 'being of doubtful origin'.

In the subsequent statement Jean gave to the police, she wrote, 'When I went to bed… the windows and doors were secured and locked and the panes of glass in the window and the door were intact… I'm satisfied in my own mind that the fire in the lounge was *not* accidental.' The police, who made the obvious link between this latest fire and the previous threats, reached the same conclusion.

Doorstepped by Noel Botham, an amiable young journalist sent to cover what had happened, Jean blamed her husband for starting the blaze. Even if Botham had believed her, Jean's evidence-free allegations couldn't be repeated in print for fear of provoking a libel action.

Out of concern for her safety, Raymond arrived at the Drax Avenue house just after Botham had interviewed her. 'Raymond and I chatted and got on incredibly well,' Botham recalled. 'He invited me for a drink in town. From then on, we met regularly and became good friends. He was a reserved sort of person. Never really open. I don't think he had a full-blooded relationship with anyone.'

Three weeks before the fire, the newspapers had reported on the birth of the Responsible Society, another group lobbying against permissiveness. Set up by Dr S. E. Ellison, a member of staff at Middlesex County

Hospital, the group's most prominent member was the novelist Pamela Hansford Johnson. Through extensive leafleting, it aimed to combat the 'commercial sex-exploiters' and draw attention to 'the commercialisation and trivialisation of sex'. As Britain's foremost sexual profiteer, Raymond must have been one of the people they blamed for what Ellison called 'destructive and demoralising trends'.

The Responsible Society's concerns were given a more strident tone by Peter and Janet Hill, a Baptist missionary couple who, in mid-July 1971, announced the Nationwide Festival of Light, a demonstration in support of 'love and family life' and against 'pornography and moral pollution'. The event, scheduled for late September, already had the backing of Lord Longford, Mary Whitehouse, Malcolm Muggeridge, Cliff Richard and the actress Dora Bryan. It was due to begin with 200 beacons being lit all over the country, intended to 'alert Britain to the dangers of moral pollution which is now eroding the moral fibre of this once great nation'. Two days after that, there would be a rally in Trafalgar Square, followed by a five-hour gospel music concert in Hyde Park. The overambitious organisers of the Festival of Light predicted that 100,000 people from across Britain would attend this display of moral indignation.

Early that August, Longford – now widely known as 'Lord Porn' – took more practical measures against the smut merchants. In search of reliable, hitherto elusive information about pornography in Britain, information that could be used to strengthen his campaign, he commissioned David de Boinod Associates, a London-based market and social research company, to conduct a study of the business. Longford wanted the company's report to span public attitudes to it, details about the leading producers and distributors, and an analysis of the entire range of printed pornography.

David de Boinod, boss of the company, began by contacting the Home Office to request off-the-record interviews with police officers working in London, Birmingham and Manchester. Exhibiting an awareness of just how compromised the police were, a Home Office official wrote in an internal memo that the report's 'terms of reference appear to be very wide and to be likely to put the police to a good deal of difficulty and embarrassment if they try to assist them'. A decision was therefore taken by the Home Office 'that no help or encouragement should be given to de Boinod'.

Stymied by officialdom, de Boinod tried to strike a clandestine deal with the government. In exchange for their cooperation, he offered to let the Home Office censor the report before he showed it to Longford. But even this didn't sway the Whitehall bureaucrats.

Early in the research process, de Boinod's firm carried out interviews with Raymond and other publishers of pornography. Their products were categorised by de Boinod under five gradations, ranging from 'mildly risqué/imitation porn/titillation' to 'super hard'. Alongside *Playboy*, *Men Only* registered the lowest reading on his patent smutometer. De Boinod observed that 'most people' regarded Raymond's magazine as 'erotica' rather than genuine pornography of the kind epitomised by publications such as *Fuck around the Clock* and *42 Inches Plus!*, the front-cover caption for which he gleefully transcribed. 'Man is the hunter – and his prey is WOMAN,' it proclaimed. 'The game is always the same – BIG GAME.'

As well as commissioning de Boinod's study, Longford hired Major Matt Oliver, a former commando-turned-private-detective who had previously helped him stop a wrongly convicted man from being hanged. Soon to be dubbed 'Lord Porn's private eye', Oliver was briefed to investigate the activities of the top Soho pornographers and their rumoured corrupt links to the police.

Longford and other anti-pornography campaigners were given a substantial fillip by the outcome of the longest obscenity trial in British history. On Thursday, 5 August, the judge handed down harsh sentences to the three editors of *Oz*, a hippy magazine deemed to have breached the 1961 Obscene Publications Act. Stung by accusations that the police were picking on so-called underground magazines yet doing little to clamp down on the activities of Soho pornographers, Home Secretary Reginald Maudling demanded an explanation from Detective Chief Inspector George Fenwick, recently appointed head of the OPS.

In a confidential report, dated Friday, 13 August, Fenton claimed the OPS was targeting underground magazines only because they were aimed at children. And he disputed that pornography was on sale in Soho or anywhere else in London. Even if it *was*, he explained, the wording of the 1961 Obscene Publications Act rendered the police unable to take action against pornographers.

This was an explanation which, in the diplomatic words of the Home Office, 'left a good deal to be desired'. The inadequacy of Fenton's report was highlighted by the publication on Sunday, 15 August of 'Filthy Rich', an article in the *Observer* which examined the British porn industry. Its author, Raymond Palmer, identified thirty West End shops selling pornography, the takings from which were estimated at a minimum of £3 million a year. Naturally, Palmer posed the question, how could this be happening? His answer possessed disturbing simplicity – 'sweeteners to the police'.

While Matt Oliver was loitering in the Soho pubs where Jimmy Humphreys and the other kings of the porn trade flaunted their friendships with senior police officers, Longford and five other members of his committee headed off to Copenhagen, accompanied by a troop of reporters. There, Longford and his 'Special Study Group' intended to spend two days talking to Danish sociologists, criminologists and other experts about the impact of their country's decision to make hardcore pornography legally available to everyone over the age of sixteen.

Before boarding his plane, Longford spoke to Mary Whitehouse, poised to fly to Rome for an audience with the Pope. Whitehouse, who regarded *Men Only* and similar publications as being 'weapons of revolution', planned to present the Pontiff with copies of two of the recently banned underground magazines. 'Mary,' Longford said to her, 'you are off to heaven while I am going to hell.'

For Longford and his allies, Raymond's business represented a menace to family life, but Raymond was already formulating vague plans to turn the PRO into a family enterprise. He revealed that he wanted Howard to join the firm once he'd grown up. Somewhat ruefully Raymond was, however, left to observe, 'At the moment the boy's only inclination appears to be in having a dog's home.'

Devoted as Raymond was to his daughter, she too was a source of minor disappointment. By the beginning of October, Debbie – now a flighty, rebellious fifteen-year-old with a faint stammer and a lopsided perma-smile – had been expelled from Cheltenham Ladies' College, where she'd been caught smoking and drinking.

Back at Drax Avenue with her mother, Debbie could indulge her precocious appetite for holding parties. She could also pursue her embryonic theatrical ambitions by enrolling at the Corona Stage Academy in Hammersmith, a £900-a-term theatre school where her contemporaries included the future film star Ray Winstone. Her father would have preferred her to stay at school, pass more exams and go on to study accountancy or, perhaps, law at university, yet he didn't try to block her showbiz aspirations. He liked to think of himself as the type of parent who wouldn't try to force his children 'to do something career-wise against their will'.

Rationalising his disinclination to impose his authority on Debbie, he concluded that she was part of an untamable generation. 'Most girls nowadays want their own way younger,' he mused. 'They won't take instruction.'

His daughter's return to live in Wimbledon plunged her into the middle of the slow-burning crisis involving the anonymous phone calls. At about 1.10 a.m. on Saturday, 2 October, the latest of these came through to the Revuebar. Raymond was still there, probably perched on a bar stool in the lounge. The call consisted of a death threat against Jean *and* Debbie. The recent arson attacks encouraging him to take it even more seriously, Raymond phoned Wimbledon Police Station. He not only reported the call but also asked the police to check that his wife and daughter were safe.

In spite of all the booze he'd soaked up that night, he was so concerned about Jean and Debbie that he got into his Rolls-Royce and set off on the familiar route from Soho to Drax Avenue. His erratic driving through Battersea led to him being stopped by the police. When he failed a breathalyser test, he was taken back to the local police station for a blood sample. Cooperative at first, he extended his arm so the doctor could insert a syringe, but the medic missed his vein. By now losing patience and presumably desperate to get to Drax Avenue, Raymond refused to let the hapless doctor try again. The police then charged him with drink-driving, dangerous driving and failing to provide a blood sample. Weighed against the lives of Jean and their children, this was a trifling inconvenience.

He soon discovered that the death threat hadn't been carried out. The police nonetheless reverted to their old routine of making random checks on Jean's home.

Late in November, Matt Oliver handed his report on the porn business to Longford who spent that Sunday studying it. The report, no copies of which appear to have survived, listed the seven leading British pornographers. In common with Jimmy Humphreys, Raymond merited a place in this not-so-magnificent seven. 'I am told that a police tariff operates in the West End whereby certain police officers between them receive from the pornographic "kings" a sum in the region of £1,000 a week,' Oliver wrote. 'The money is paid by the "bucks" or managers of the shops either in the shop, in a club or in a pub.' Oliver went on to elaborate on those dealings between pornographers and policemen. 'From what I saw with my own eyes and from what I heard from reliable informants, the police connived at and condoned the activities of those trading in all types of pornography. I also formed the opinion that some policemen were corrupt.'

Distressed by the notion of such endemic sleaze, Longford showed the report to his committee, but they decided it strayed beyond their remit. Along with at least one other concerned member of the committee, Longford visited Scotland Yard, where he had a meeting with London's most senior policeman, Sir John Waldron, Commissioner of the Metropolitan Police. They were joined by Commander Wally Virgo of the OPS. He assured Longford that there was no truth whatsoever in the allegations contained in Oliver's report. Sceptical about these assurances, Longford realised that he wouldn't get anywhere by complaining to the authorities, so he encouraged Oliver to show the report to the *Sunday People*, which had run a Soho porn exposé earlier that year. Its editor, whose paper had a history of combining scandal-mongering with salacious explorations of the seamy side of life, was so impressed by the report that he employed Oliver as a temporary member of staff and sent him in pursuit of conclusive evidence.

Twelve days had passed without incident since the latest death threats against Raymond's wife and daughter. That changed on the night of Thursday, 14 October, when Jean walked out of her front door and across the drive. Parked on it was the car Raymond had bought her: a white Aston Martin, previously used in the James Bond movie *Goldfinger*. She discovered that all four of its tyres had been slashed.

Next day she had the tyres replaced, allowing her to use the car in the evening. She'd arranged to visit a friend, then pop into Guy's Hospital, where Jan Harding's wife, Joan, was recovering from an acute illness.

Jean had also promised to stop off and see Jan's sister-in-law, Margaret Hillier, who was staying with him in Clapham.

No sooner had Jean steered her car out of the drive and on to Drax Avenue than she noticed that its brakes weren't working as well as normal. But she didn't think this was serious enough to justify taking the car to a garage and postponing her arrangements.

Meanwhile Jan Harding was on duty behind the reception desk at the Revuebar, fretting about his wife. When the phone rang at 7 p.m., he must have wondered whether the call was from the hospital or from Margaret. Instead, it was from the same unidentified man with the cockney accent who had spoken to him the previous July and made threats against Jean. The man's message was similarly menacing this time: 'She's gone out now in the car, but she won't get back...'

# 32 TONIGHT'S THE NIGHT

CONCERNED ABOUT THE SAFETY of Raymond's wife, Jan Harding rang Margaret Hillier and asked whether Jean had arrived yet. Margaret said, 'No.'

Jan instructed her to tell Jean to ring him immediately she got there.

A nervous wait ensued, during which Jean dropped round to see her friend before going on to Guy's Hospital. Uncertain whether there really *was* a problem with her brakes, Jean asked her friend to test them. Her friend doesn't appear to have detected anything wrong, so Jean continued her drive through London.

Later that evening Jean turned up at the Hardings' house near the northern tip of Clapham Common. Jan's sister-in-law had, by then, forgotten what he'd told her. She remembered only when Jean was leaving.

'I've got to be going now,' Jean said. 'I must be careful with the car, as the brakes feel peculiar.'

Instantly, Margaret replied, 'Please phone Jan at the club.'

Jean said it seemed silly phoning him at the club. After all, what could *he* do?

Margaret told her to ring him anyway.

When Jean spoke to Jan, he insisted on her leaving the car at his place and taking a minicab home. He didn't, however, mention the threatening phone call.

Only after Jean had put the receiver down did Margaret explain to her that Jan had received a call saying that she'd gone out and wouldn't be coming back.

Though Jean must have known that the problem with her brakes was connected to the phone call, she refused to take Jan's advice. Instead, she got back into her Aston Martin and drove home. En route the brakes failed completely. She was fortunate not to have been involved in a serious accident. Her car was taken to a garage on Wimbledon High Street where a mechanic found there was no fluid in the brake cylinder.

Exactly a week later Jan Harding received another threatening phone call at the Revuebar. He wrote down what the caller had said and handed the message to Raymond. It read, 'Tell the guvnor, we're waiting for his kid to go out tonight. Tonight's the night.'

Following the call, someone set fire to Jean's car, which she'd left in the garage at her house.

The campaign against Jean and Debbie hadn't simply left Raymond with nagging fear. He also had to contend with the legal consequences of the night when he'd been stopped by the police in Battersea. During the last week of October, he appeared at South Western Magistrates' Court, where he pleaded 'not guilty' to all three charges. Reginald Mays, the prosecuting counsel, then surprised everyone in the public gallery by saying, 'Further matters have come to the notice of those instructing me, which more fully explain the circumstances of the case. It would be quite wrong for me to proceed.' He added that the case had been studied by Scotland Yard and the Director of Public Prosecutions and they were unanimous in their decision not to offer any evidence against the defendant. 'The journey was an emergency one which was vital for him to complete.'

Questioned by reporters who wanted to know why the charges had been dropped, Mays refused to elaborate because, he said, 'it would give distress to Mr Raymond to go fully into the facts'.

Raymond's mysterious acquittal precipitated a series of newspaper articles. Typical among these was a piece in the *Daily Mirror*, headlined

'Strip King of Soho in Court Riddle'. It was a riddle behind which Arthur Lewis, Labour MP for West Ham North, discerned unsavoury dealings that would reflect badly on the Conservative government. 'Justice would not appear to have been done in this case,' he declared. Besides calling for a public inquiry, he wrote to Sir Peter Rawlinson, the Attorney-General, demanding an explanation as to why the case had been shelved.

Lewis made public the contents of the Attorney-General's reply. The letter revealed that the police had accepted Raymond's explanation that he was 'in a great state of anxiety because he had heard that his wife and daughter were in danger, and he was driving to their Wimbledon home at the time'. Even though Raymond had failed a breathalyser test, the Attorney-General felt that 'it was almost certain' Raymond would be acquitted, so there was no point in pressing ahead with the case.

'It is not the police's job to decide whether a man is likely to be guilty or not,' Lewis commented to the press.

Now that Lewis had made public Raymond's concerns about the safety of his family, Raymond had to fend off enquiries from reporters. He said he wouldn't comment on this speculation.

To banish any hint of skull-duggery, the Attorney-General issued a statement reiterating his reasons for dropping the charges.

Being propelled into the centre of a political row turned out to be the least of Raymond's worries. On Tuesday, 2 November 1971, the box office clerk at the Revuebar handed him a phone message from an unidentified caller. The message read, 'We're going to get Paul Raymond's wife and the girl. Remember Mrs McKay.'

This was an allusion designed to communicate the gravity of the death threats. Returning home from work almost two years earlier, Alick McKay, deputy chairman of the *News of the World*, had found his house ransacked and his wife absent, a discarded machete hinting at the brutality of her kidnappers. Mrs McKay's disappearance was followed by phone calls from them, demanding £1 million or else they'd kill her. Failure to hand over the money resulted in her murder, though her body

– rumoured to have been fed to some pigs – was never discovered. Two Trinidadian brothers had, however, been found guilty of murdering her.

Mention of Mrs McKay pushed the police into placing Jean's house under round-the-clock guard.


That Friday Raymond received another message, not at the Revuebar but at the box office of the Whitehall Theatre. The caller said, 'You can tell the guvnor, if he's scared now, we haven't started yet.'

Cruelly heightening the tension, the caller left Raymond and his family to marinate in their own fear for the next twelve days. During that time, it was doubtful that Raymond spared more than a passing thought to his eldest child, whose twenty-first birthday signalled the end of the maintenance payments he'd been making to Noreen O'Horan.

When the messages resumed, Raymond took the unusual step of scheduling a press conference. On the evening of Saturday, 20 November, he told the assembled reporters, 'I appeal to this man to telephone me and tell me why he does it. There seems to be no sense in it – yet it has been going on too long for the man to be just a crank.' Raymond then outlined the sequence of events that had begun the summer before last. 'I suppose some people might think that I am behind the calls because of our separation, but I certainly could not make them because my voice would be recognised however I tried to disguise it. Some people might even think it was Jean trying to get at me, but that is impossible. The calls are from a man. You could not hire anybody to make calls like that because then you would be open to blackmail. There is just no logical reason.' He went on to say, 'If somebody is trying to get at me, why should he threaten Jean? It may be somebody who is opposed to my form of entertainment, but Jean has nothing to do with that. She used to arrange dances for me, but she has not done that for about seven years.'

Raymond had to wait until Thursday, 25 November before his appeal had the desired effect. While he was out of his office at the Revuebar, someone left a message on his answerphone. Playing back the message, he heard a slow, deliberate voice with a soft Irish accent say, 'Good evening, Mr Raymond, I speak for the IRA Movement Action Group responsible for the collection of funds needed for our cause. We have no scruples for the methods we use. We consider the cause to be greater than anyone or individuals. You have received a sample of our methods in the past. Our threats are not idle ones  If it's any consolation to you, you're not the only one. We're asking for the sum of £15,000. Failing to pay will result in the death of you and your wife. Make no mistake about it, this will be carried out. If by any chance the police are called or anyone is caught, there will be fifty more to take his place.' The voice then explained that Raymond should, provided he was willing to pay, take out an advert in the personal column of that Saturday's *Evening News*. Once he'd placed the advert, reading 'Happy Birthday, P. and J.', he'd receive further instructions. 'You can have our word: we only want payment. We keep our word. Anyone taking this message, give it personally to Mr Raymond.'

# 33 THIS IS YOUR EXECUTIONER SPEAKING

THOUGH RAYMOND'S EARLIER appeal had nudged the saga towards a conclusion, the discovery that the calls were being made by Irish Republican Army terrorists can only have deepened his anxiety. Since the so-called 'Troubles' had flared up again in Northern Ireland during 1969, the IRA's bloodthirsty methods had garnered ample media coverage. In the past few months alone there had been stories about a bomb attack in a Belfast pub, about the IRA-inspired hijacking of a plane, and about a milkman who'd been gunned down in front of a group of children.

Ignoring the instructions he'd been given in the answerphone message, Raymond passed over the tape to Detective Inspector Ray Adams, who was investigating the case.

The call from the IRA was followed by a second demand for money, contained in a letter posted to the Revuebar on the same day that the answerphone message had been left. 'We think it's time to come to the crunch,' the letter informed Raymond. 'We don't like the joint you run – living off girls.' To ensure that 'no further damage' was done to his wife and daughter, the writer ordered him to leave £500 behind the phone box outside the Robin Hood pub in the east London suburb of Barking.

When Raymond showed the letter to the police, they must have realised they were dealing with a copycat, hence the abrupt change in the amount of money being demanded. The police then set a trap for the extortionists. That Sunday evening Raymond drove his Rolls-Royce over to the location specified in the letter. A detective crouched in the back of the car while Raymond left a parcel behind the phone box. Inside the parcel was an empty container.

After Raymond had driven away, two young men picked up the package and were promptly arrested by lurking detectives. The men, identified as twenty-year-old William Lamb and his eighteen-year-old friend Michael Brittan, both denied attempting to extort money from Raymond or even having any knowledge of the threats against him and his family.

It quickly became apparent that the voice on Raymond's answerphone tape belonged to neither of the young men in custody. The assumption that they weren't connected to the message or the previous threats was reinforced by Ray Adams's investigation into their past, which revealed 'nothing to suggest either man is an IRA agent'. He concluded that they obviously read the newspapers and had attempted to cash-in on the incidents' reported in the press.


Raymond's Sunday drive to Barking coincided with the delivery of David de Boinod's report to Longford, who spent that day reading it and mulling over its findings. If the interim report, submitted five weeks before, gives any indication of these, they represented an uncontentious statement of the obvious.

Even though de Boinod felt that *Men Only* scarcely qualified as pornography, the OPS began an investigation into Raymond's role in the industry. A prosecution against him was soon 'under consideration', the possibility of legal action serving a convenient dual purpose for the OPS. Besides demonstrating that they were fulfilling their responsibilities, it offered potential leverage that could be used by them to obtain payments from Raymond.

☆

Until Monday, 6 December 1971 Raymond received no more calls from the man with the Irish accent. At 1.30 p.m. that day Raymond answered the phone and heard the familiar voice say, 'This is your executioner speaking.' The man introduced himself as 'Mr Mesh'. 'Did you get our message? We will require £15,000 for our funds. This is no idle threat. We mean business.'

Raymond lied to the man, claiming that the message hadn't reached him. Under the pretext that he needed to fetch a pencil and paper, he put the receiver down and used another phone to ring the police and try to get the call traced. Mr Mesh had, however, hung up before that could be accomplished.

Over the following weekend Raymond was twice informed that a 'Mr Wilson' had phoned him but left no message. Seeing as he had no social or business connection with anyone of that name, he assumed the calls were connected to the extortion plot.

Just after lunch on Tuesday, 14 December he answered the third call from Mr Wilson, who turned out to share Mr Mesh's voice. 'This is your executioner speaking,' the caller said to Raymond. 'You did not do as we told you. We mean business. You will have until Friday to make up your mind. It is not your wife and children we're after. It's *you*. We will do the Whitehall Theatre unless you place the notice in the *Evening News* before Friday.'

Raymond asked what the advert should say.

'Happy Birthday, Jean and Ray.' Then the man added, 'I will contact you again giving you instructions.'

Taking the advice of the police, Raymond placed the required advert in the next two days' editions of the *Evening News*.

At 2.25 p.m. that Thursday an anonymous man phoned Raymond at the Whitehall Theatre, but Raymond wasn't around. The man told Raymond's secretary that he was calling from Ireland. He also said he'd try again later, yet the call never came through.

Five days before Christmas Raymond received a mid-afternoon call from Mr Mesh, alias Mr Wilson, whose latest redundant alias was 'Mr Jackson'. 'You will not be hearing from me any more,' the man said. 'It's now in the hands of the collectors who'll be contacting you. Do not try any funny stuff. Remember André Mizelas, the Mayfair hairdresser. *He* didn't pay. They phoned you from Ireland last week to contact you but you weren't in.'

The owner of a chain of salons, Mizelas had been found shot dead at the wheel of his car, two bullets in the back of his head. But his killer had never been caught.

Following police instructions, Raymond agreed to pay whatever the IRA wanted.

'It's now out of my hands,' the man told him. 'You will be hearing from the collector.'

On that ominous note the caller put the phone down.

# 34 GREETINGS FROM PORNLAND

INCE THE RELAUNCH of *Men Only* seven months previously, the eponymous chairman of the John Menzies distribution and retail chain had announced that his shops would no longer stock the magazine because he wanted them to be 'suitable for the whole family'. Nevertheless the circulation of *Men Only* had, assisted by the continued distribution deal with John Menzies, reached around 350,000 per month, making it by far the most popular publication of its sort in Britain. It had also made Raymond's girlfriend famous, courtesy of her monthly column. This had turned her into a cross between a conventional pin-up and something new: a lithe figurehead of the permissive society, of unabashed female sexual appetite, albeit channelled through the scrofulous filter of male fantasy.

The magazine's popularity caught the attention of Lord Longford who was still preparing his report on pornography. Straight after the Christmas and New Year break, he asked Raymond and Tony Power round for a discussion about their publication. They arranged to visit Longford the following day – Tuesday, 4 January 1972. Their meeting took place at 1 Tavistock Chambers, a late Victorian building in Bloomsbury which housed Sidgwick & Jackson, the unassailably reputable publishing firm run by Longford. Raymond and Power, gold-jewellery-decked emissaries from the far-flung kingdom of Pornland, must have seemed absurdly out of place in the donnish confines of his book-lined office, scene of many a friendly chat with authors and colleagues over a glass of sherry. But the encounter between this incongruous trio doesn't appear to have been as convivial. According to Raymond, the tweedy peer accused sex shows and magazines like *Men Only* of corrupting people. 'I replied that he had seen them all and *he* hadn't been corrupted,' Raymond recalled, his version of the conversation dubiously self-aggrandising.

Unlike Bob Guccione – publisher of the rival magazine *Penthouse* – who had admitted to one of Longford's colleagues that he exploited women, Raymond and Power were, for all Raymond's talk about sexual honesty, calculatedly *dishonest* in their response to the peer's earnest enquiries. They both stressed that *Men Only*'s rapid success wasn't due to it being more explicit than its competitors. It was not, they argued, 'catering for any masturbatory or abnormal tastes'. Instead, it was offering its readers 'simple enjoyment at the sight of beautiful women.' To combat the inevitable accusations of sexism, Raymond told the credulous peer that thirty-five of the sixty-two copies of *Men Only* recently sold during a single hour had been bought by women. Raymond even echoed David de Boinod's verdict on his magazine by claiming it couldn't be categorised as pornography because it avoided sadistic or homosexual material.

Asked how he'd define two recent features, dealing with flagellation and the erotic rituals of Hells Angels, he said they were perfectly acceptable. He added that *Men Only* 'made no attempt to offer value judgements'.

Before winding up the conversation, which apparently covered 'all aspects of pornography – soft and hard – along with sex and nudity', Longford quizzed Raymond on the boom in magazines such as *Forum* and *Curious*, magazines that presented themselves as scientific studies of sexual behaviour, mostly based on readers' letters. 'The self-styled sex education publication is deluding both itself and its readers,' Raymond assured him.

Raymond's publicity-hungry host was probably responsible for the arrival of a photographer from the *Evening News*. To commemorate the unlikely encounter between Raymond and Lord Porn, the newsman took a picture of them sitting side by side.

When Raymond and Power emerged from their seventy-five-minute meeting, a reporter – also from the *Evening News* – waylaid Raymond and asked what he thought of his host.

'Lord Longford?' Raymond replied. 'He is so sincere. We got along splendidly.' Raymond gave a brief summary of the meeting, then went on to say, 'We agreed on certain points and agreed to differ on others.' Demonstrating that he shared Longford's taste for press coverage, he flourished a copy of *Men Only*. 'I told him this was not a porno magazine – just call it sexy. We were not there to ask him his views on our magazine or the various forms of entertainment I specialise in.'

Between the final weeks of December 1971 and January 1972, Raymond had missed several calls from unnamed people – members of the IRA, perhaps – who wanted to talk to him. None of those people had left a message. On Tuesday, 25 January there were three more calls, the man on the other end identifying himself as 'Mr McGrath'. Raymond wasn't, however, available to take any of these.

McGrath didn't catch him until about 2.50 p.m. next day. 'Have you got the money?' an unfamiliar voice said.

'Yes,' Raymond replied, 'I've had it since last week, waiting for your call. I'm scared out of my mind. I just want this matter finished. I can't do any work. I've just got to get it over with.'

'I hope you've got the money in old notes.'

Raymond said he had.

'I hope you're going to be sensible. If you are *not*, you know the consequences. You will not be around for a second chance.'

Doing exactly as the police had instructed him, Raymond assured McGrath that he'd cooperate.

'I will keep to my side of the bargain if you'll keep to yours,' McGrath said. He added that he'd been personally assigned to this job and wouldn't allow anything to go wrong.

Before hanging up, the extortionist told Raymond that he'd hear from him again.

That Friday McGrath rang the office, but Raymond wasn't around. McGrath said he'd call back.

Once more, there was a nerve-tweaking delay prior to the next call. Briefed on what had taken place, Ray Adams wired a miniature tape recorder to the phone line in Raymond's office at the Whitehall Theatre. Raymond was told to record any conversation he had with the IRA gang.

The next call came through at about 2.45 p.m. the following Wednesday. Raymond's secretary answered the phone. She told McGrath that Raymond wasn't there but he'd be back later.

Around 4 p.m., by which time Raymond had returned to his office, McGrath rang again. Lifting the receiver and switching on the tape recorder, Raymond said, 'Hullo.'

'Mr Raymond?'

'Mr McGrath…'

'Will you stay in your office until five o'clock this evening?'

Raymond agreed to be there at that time.

'Right, I'll contact you then.'

There was a silence that made Raymond suspect the caller had hung up. 'Hullo, Mr McGrath…' Satisfied that McGrath was still on the line, Raymond said, 'Can I mention this to you now? I thought I'd be hearing from you before this.'

'Don't worry about it.'

'I'm concerned about it.'

'Don't worry about it.'

'But I *am* worried because I've got to go away.'

Yet again, McGrath told him not to worry. 'Stay in your office until five o'clock. You'll get further instructions then.'

☆

After he'd finished talking to McGrath, Raymond must have got in touch with Adams and his team, who were on stand-by. With payment of the extortion money imminent, the police set in motion what, as one of Adams's colleagues recalled, was 'a big operation', designed to catch the IRA men.

Adams and a group of other plainclothes officers, including Detective Chief Inspector Ronald Hardy, headed over to the Whitehall Theatre, the façade of which was still emblazoned with a giant advertisement for *Pyjama Tops*. In advance of the 5 p.m. call from McGrath, Hardy coached Raymond on the best way of handling the call. Hardy told Raymond to insist that the cash be handed over that evening.

Presupposing that the IRA would order Raymond to meet them elsewhere, Adams and Hardy concealed themselves in Raymond's Rolls-Royce, parked at the back of the theatre. But there was no phone call from McGrath.

At about 6 p.m. Hardy, who wanted to find out what was happening, joined Raymond in his office. Hardy hadn't been there for more than a few minutes before the phone rang. Raymond switched on the tape recorder as he answered it. 'Yes. Hullo, Mr McGrath?'

'Mr Raymond... Mr McGrath here. Stay there till six-thirty.'

'Six-thirty.'

'And then we'll tell you where to bring it.'

'Oh, dear. Are you sure? Because I've got an appointment tonight which, you know, I don't mind... I'll, un...'

'*This* is more important than your appointment.'

'It is to me because, as I said, I'm going away this weekend.'

A second voice cut in and said, 'You know the consequences, don't you?'

'Well, I do. And this is why I'm concerned.'

'We will contact you at six-thirty sharp,' the second voice said.

'Six-thirty here,' Raymond replied. 'Alright, I'll wait here.'

# 35 MONEY WITH MENACES

**M**CGRATH DIDN'T RING at the appointed time, yet both Raymond and the police carried on waiting for the call. By 8.30 p.m. they must have started to wonder whether the IRA had decided to postpone the handover or realised that a trap was being set. Those fears were allayed about half an hour later when Adams, still hiding in the Rolls-Royce outside the Whitehall Theatre, saw a man stalk round the car and take up a position in front of the stage door. Adams could make out only his silhouette through the wintry darkness. The man remained there for several minutes, then walked away, by which point he was under police surveillance, radio messages crackling to and fro across the West End. Once the man's footsteps had receded, Adams got out of the Rolls-Royce and joined Hardy inside the theatre.

From an upstairs window with a view of Whitehall, the two detectives peered at the silver Ford Cortina parked on the far side of the road. Sitting in the driver's seat was the middle-aged man who had been loitering round the back of the theatre. Suddenly he got out of his car and went over to talk to a much younger man. The pair of them set off towards Trafalgar Square.

Leaving Hardy and the other detectives at the theatre, Adams followed the two men down Whitehall, across Northumberland Avenue and over to Charing Cross Station. Adams watched them enter the foyer and head for one of the phone boxes. Neither man ventured into the box, though. Instead, the older man stood outside it and looked around. Unaware that Adams had him under observation, he nodded towards the box. While the younger of the men made a phone call, Adams walked hurriedly back to the theatre.

About three hours after McGrath had been due to call, the phone in Raymond's office rang. Cunningly exploiting the delay, the police had told Raymond to pretend that he'd become distraught while he'd been waiting, that he'd been drinking heavily in a failed attempt to suppress his anxiety, that he was impatient to put the whole ordeal behind him.

Raymond picked up the phone and said, 'Hullo.'

Through the receiver, he could probably hear the background noises from Charing Cross Station.

'Can I speak to Mr Raymond, please?'

'Speaking.'

'This is Mr McGrath.'

'I've been waiting since half-past bloody six.'

'I must apologise.'

'Appointments, you know…' Raymond let the sentence trail off, his awkward pause dripping with the desperation he was meant to be conveying. 'I'm out of my bloody mind.'

'I must apologise,' McGrath said. 'I'm afraid our plane was delayed.'

'You know, if we make a deal, let's make a deal because I'm going away, for fuck's sake. You don't understand. I'm pissed, I'm drinking here by myself, and you're driving me mad.'

'Alright, alright.'

'Okay.'

'Be in your office.'

'Pardon.'

'Be in your office at two o'clock tomorrow.'

'Be in my office at two o'clock tomorrow?'

'Two o'clock tomorrow.'

'No, I'm sorry. I cannot do this. You see, I think this – you're trying to bluff me.' Throwing himself with gusto into the role of an emotional drunk, he added, 'Everything you've said, I've done. I've been here since half-past six and it's now bloody well ten o'clock or half-past nine. I cannot do this Mr McGrath. You're driving me mad. You don't understand what you're doing to me. If you want the money, I've got the money here now.'

'Sorry.'

'I've got the money now if you want it. For Christ's sake, you know, be a human being for my sake.'

'Just a moment...' Raymond heard McGrath have a mumbled fifteen-second discussion with someone. Then McGrath said, 'Mr Raymond?'

'Yes,' Raymond replied. 'You don't know what you're doing to me. Honestly, you don't.'

McGrath's accomplice, who must have snatched the receiver, said, 'Deliver this tomorrow.'

'No, I will not do it tomorrow, Mr McGrath. I'm out of my mind. I've got the money now. I'm pissed. I'm drinking brandy on my own, which I've done since half-past six. I was waiting for you. I've cancelled my appointments. I've work to do. I've got the money now. If you want it, it's yours. I cannot stand this, Mr McGrath. You don't know what you're doing to me. Honestly, you don't.'

The man on the other end mustered only an ambiguous 'Yeah...'

'If you want it, I don't care where we go. Tell me where to go. I can't sleep. For three months, Mr McGrath, you've been on to me. I cannot stand it anymore.'

'We've been busy,' McGrath explained.

'I'm not interested if you've been busy. What you've done to me...'

'Just a moment...' McGrath broke off and had another brief, inaudible conversation with his accomplice. 'Mr Raymond,' he continued, 'this will have to be tomorrow.'

'I will not do it tomorrow, otherwise you can stick a bomb wherever you want to,' Raymond said, seizing the initiative. 'The money, I've got.

I've got work to do. You can't understand what you've done to me. I've got the money. I don't care where you say. Tell me, bloody...' By appearing to let his train of thought fizzle out, Raymond gave the impression of being distracted and panic-stricken. 'I don't care where you say. I cannot stand another night like this, Mr McGrath. You're driving me out of my bloody mind.'

Again, Raymond could hear McGrath talking to the other IRA man. 'I've got my boss here with me...' But Raymond interrupted before McGrath could say anything else.

'Look, I can't fight you, you know. The IRA at the moment... The aggravation abroad... The police can't fight you, the forces can't fight you. What chance have I got, for Christ's sake? None whatsoever. Give me peace of mind, Mr McGrath, please.'

'You will have *permanent* peace of mind if you don't do what you are told.'

'Well, I'm not going to do it tomorrow. I can't stand this anymore. I've got the money now. Tell me where. It doesn't make any difference to me. I've had this for, what, two weeks now since you said. I've had the money in a safe. It's been in my case now since half-past six. Just please, Mr McGrath, just think what you're doing to a human person.'

'We understand this.' McGrath broke off while he had a much longer discussion with his accomplice, at the end of which he said, 'Mr Raymond?'

'Mr McGrath...'

'If you're not going to be there tomorrow, when *can* you be there?'

'I won't be there tomorrow, I've told you. I'm going away on Friday night for three weeks. I've got work to do tomorrow. I'm packed. Every appointment you've told me to do, I've kept. I can't sleep at night. I've work to do. I've had to put off appointments. I'm going abroad on Friday night. I don't care whether you blow my place up or not. I can't care less anymore. You're driving me out of my mind.'

'We're not interested in blowing your place up.'

'This is what you said – you would blow my place up. I can't fight you. I couldn't care less anymore, Mr McGrath. If you were a West End thug, okay I could fight you.'

'We will not blow your place up. We will bloody shoot you.'

'Well, you can shoot me as well, if you want to, you know. But this, I cannot stand. I have got the money now. If you don't want it, I am going to put it back in the bank. You can do whatever you want, Mr McGrath. I'm fed up with it. I admit, I'm pissed. And I cannot think straight. But when all this is said and done, please think of me as a human being.'

'Pardon.'

'I'm a human person. Your cause is right. I don't want the IRA shooting the Catholics and the Protestants because I'm a Roman Catholic myself, as you must know.'

Raymond was interrupted by an impatient bleeping. McGrath put another coin into the phone box and said, 'We'll send somebody to collect you in the next quarter of an hour. And no bloody nonsense.'

'There is no nonsense,' Raymond assured him. 'Where should I wait, Mr McGrath?'

'In your office.'

'In my office…'

'Yes,' McGrath said, just before putting the receiver down.

Ronald Hardy then detached the tape recorder from Raymond's phone line and, together with Adams, walked across to a window overlooking Whitehall. They had to wait only a few minutes until the elder of the two IRA men strode back along the street and got into his Ford Cortina. He flung the car into a U-turn and drove away.

# 36 ROOM AT THE TOP SHELF

**A**S RAYMOND WAITED in his office for the handover, Adams and Hardy stayed with him. Not long after 10 p.m. one of the theatre's front-of-house staff let Raymond know that 'a gentleman had called to collect the parcel'.

Carrying a briefcase supposedly filled with £15,000 but, in reality, stuffed with telephone directories, Raymond went down to the foyer. He was followed by Adams. In the foyer, where another plainclothes detective was loitering, the younger of the two IRA men approached Raymond. The man said he'd come to collect the parcel. Raymond handed the briefcase to him and asked for his word that the threats would stop.

'I've only been sent here to collect a parcel,' the man replied. Abruptly shifting tone, he said that he also wanted tickets for himself and his wife for next Wednesday's performance of *Pyjama Tops*.

Later admitting to being 'rather amused' by the stupidity of this request, Raymond fetched the tickets from the box office.

When the man turned to leave the foyer, the lurking detective constable stepped forward and arrested him. There was a brief struggle between them before Adams intervened and helped to overpower him. He was then taken up to Raymond's office, where Adams identified himself, cautioned the prisoner and, in Hardy's presence, set about questioning him.

'My God, I'm sorry,' the young man said.

'Who *are* you?'

'Eden Reid, sir.'

Adams asked whether 'McGrath' was his alias.

'Yes, sir. That's me.' After a momentary pause Reid said, 'I didn't want to do it.'

Reid had, by then, started to cry.

'Are you a member of the IRA?'

'Heavens, no. He told me to say that. I just wanted a job. He made me do this.' Quizzed about how many of the threatening calls had come from him, Reid replied, 'I'm sorry, sir. *I'm* McGrath. I'm not IRA. Please, believe me.'

'What's all this about, then?'

'I wanted a job but the man asked me to do this. I didn't want to hurt anyone. I was told what to say on the telephone and then tonight he made me come in and collect the parcel. I'm sorry.'

'Who's this other man?'

'Doug White. He's waiting round the corner for me to come back. I told him I didn't want to come in, but he insisted.'

'I've no way of knowing how much of what you're saying is true,' Adams said to him.

'I'm sorry, I'll tell you the truth. All of it. I didn't want to do this tonight, but he was on to me. First of all, he wanted me to make it tomorrow. Then when Mr Raymond argued, he told me to come in for it.' Bursting into tears again, Reid added, 'Did you set a trap for me?'

But Adams didn't reply. Instead, he arrested Reid for extortion. 'I'm sorry, sir,' Reid said. 'I really am.'

By midnight Doug White, a fifty-two-year-old painter and decorator, was in custody, too. He and Reid were taken to Cannon Row Police Station, where they were interrogated, the background to their plot gradually emerging.

Like White, Reid was a painter and decorator. They'd met through work. Knowing that Reid owed money to his landlady, White appears to have asked him whether he 'wanted to earn some money that was a bit dodgy'. Reid had, in the opinion of Adams, been pressurised by White into taking part in the extortion plot.

White had only one twenty-five-year-old criminal conviction – for theft – yet James Franklin, a former colleague of his, claimed that Raymond wasn't the first person from whom he'd tried to extort large sums of cash. Franklin testified that White had attempted to recruit him to take part in a plot to obtain money from Bob Guccione. White had allegedly asked him to go into Bob Guccione's Penthouse Club in Mayfair and leave a balloon in the gents' toilet with the word 'BOMB' written on it. 'Afterwards he was going to contact Guccione and tell him that the bomb could have been real and that he could now be dead,' Franklin explained.

Adams and his team had soon amassed enough incriminating statements and other evidence against White and Reid to present at Bow Street Magistrates' Court. Both men were committed for trial. In preparation for this, the Raymonds had to make separate trips to the eighth floor of Tintagel House, a modern office block on the south bank of the Thames where Adams and the rest of No. 9 Regional Crime Squad were based. Raymond and his wife gave written statements about the death threats, the sabotage of Jean's car and the repeated fires at her house, all linked to the apparent IRA extortion plot. Based on the Raymonds' statements and previous dealings with the couple, Adams rated them as 'good witnesses'.

While the legal process moved ponderously forward, other unrelated detective work was starting to yield results. Still temporarily employed by the *Sunday People*, Matt Oliver had contributed to the latest and most dramatic of the paper's exposés of the porn business, published during the last weekend of February. The story, which ran under the headline 'Police Chief And The Porn King', alleged a corrupt link between Raymond's friend Jimmy Humphreys and Commander Ken Drury, boss of the Flying Squad, the Metropolitan Police unit responsible for dealing with armed robberies and other organised crime. Humphreys had, the article revealed, taken Drury on an expenses-paid holiday to Cyprus, accompanied by their wives.

Many of Drury's colleagues tried to protect him, but Robert Mark, recently appointed Deputy Commissioner of the Metropolitan Police, ordered his suspension. Disciplinary proceedings were then initiated against Drury, who reacted by resigning from the police and selling his story to the *News of the World*. He also made the mistake of ratting on Humphreys by portraying him as a paid police informant – a label guaranteed to ruin his reputation in the underworld. Drury and Humphreys would, before long, find themselves in the middle of the biggest scandal to hit the Metropolitan Police that century.

The best part of eighteen months had slid past since Raymond's last failed reconciliation with Jean, its failure leading her to confess, 'I'm something of a man-hater now.'

Finally abandoning her destructive obsession with Raymond, she'd been spending protracted periods in America, where nobody seemed to know who Raymond was. To them, unlike their British counterparts, she was no longer just Raymond's 'ex-missus'. In America she'd embarked on a romance with Joe DiMaggio, the ageing former baseball star and husband of Marilyn Monroe. Her experience with Raymond had, however, made her reluctant to remarry.

Raymond was, meanwhile, still living with Julia Harrison. 'They had a great relationship,' Noel Botham remembered. 'She was a really nice person. Very warm, very giving, very normal.'

Harrison tried to persuade Raymond to cast her in one of the leading roles in *Pyjama Tops*. Uncertain about her suitability for this, he sought a compromise by offering her a small speaking part in a production of the play scheduled for the forthcoming holiday season at the Palace Pier Theatre in Brighton. But she still pushed for one of the starring roles, the subsequent audition earning her the part she wanted.

☆

In mid-May 1972 the Old Bailey hosted the trial of William Lamb and Michael Brittan, the first pair of men charged with attempting to extort money from Raymond. What had originally seemed a strong case against them swiftly fell apart and they were cleared of demanding £500 with menaces. Far from being extortionists, they were just unfortunate passers-by. Intrigued by the unlikely spectacle of someone famous parking his Rolls-Royce in Barking and slipping a package behind a phone box, they hadn't been able to resist retrieving the parcel, their curiosity leading them straight into a police interview room.

Whoever was really responsible for the letter telling Raymond to leave the money behind the phone box remained unidentified. One thing was beyond doubt, though: the culprit must have been a mere copycat, inspired by press coverage of the threats against Raymond and his family.

Now that the primary conspirators had been arrested, Raymond could focus all his attention on expanding the publishing and property aspects of his empire. The profits from *Men Only*, sales of which were approaching 400,000 per issue, encouraged him to launch *Club International*, another soft porn magazine suitable for distribution via newsagents. As Lord Longford observed, Raymond's new publication was 'considerably more borderline than *Men Only*'.

Suppressing his aversion to debt, Raymond meanwhile took out a bank loan so he could pay £500,000 for a house and five bungalows in Essex, which he planned to replace with thirty houses. Simultaneously, he discussed the possibility of merging several of his companies with those of the pop music and theatre impresario Larry Parnes, a flamboyant homosexual who used to manage Billy Fury, Joe Brown and Georgie Fame. Together, he and Parnes – whose notorious avarice had earned him the nickname 'Parnes, shillings and pence' – hatched a scheme to raise £6 million by floating their joint company on the stock market that September.

During periods like this, unsullied by any crises, Harrison noticed that Raymond tended to lapse into boredom. The current impression of monotonous success was reinforced by the continued popularity of his theatrical ventures. *Oh! Calcutta!* was still playing to packed houses, and *Pyjama Tops* was poised to enter its fourth year, provoking a sniffy lament from the theatre critic Irving Wardle: 'Why bother with art when the West End can be vanquished with a pair of knickers?'

Raymond's usual defence against such disdainful comments was unequivocal: 'What I have always done,' he declared, 'is to give the public what it wants, not what I think it *should* have.'

But Wardle's attitude towards Raymond's theatre productions wasn't shared by everyone at the high cultural end of the theatre. Two of the more improbable fans of *Pyjama Tops* were the playwright John Osborne and the urbane Old Etonian actor John Standing, who had just joined the cast of Osborne's latest play at the Royal Court Theatre. In between rehearsals, Standing took the author of *Look Back in Anger* to see *Pyjama Tops*. 'I thought he was going to be sick, he laughed so much,' Standing recalled. 'The joy of it was that it was completely tasteless. For no particular reason all the girls leapt into the swimming-pool in their pyjama tops. And then there was the ghastliness of all these tourists in raincoats wanking in the stalls. I knew John would love it.'

He liked it so much that he saw it twice more, even going so far as to declare, 'It's the best entertainment in London – a hundred minutes not wasted.'

Many of those minutes were dominated by Chubby Oates, the malleable-faced cockney nightclub comedian and occasional actor whom Raymond had been bold enough to install in the main role. Oates was surprised at how prim and squeamish Raymond could be. 'I was on stage and I just happened to fart, and there was a bird stood on stage with nothing on. And I glared at her as if it was her fault,' Oates remembered. 'It got a terrific laugh. The audience loved it, but Raymond got very annoyed. He sent me a memo. But the memo didn't say I'd farted. What it said was "an incident occurred..."'

☆

The ex-Labour MP Raymond Blackburn, friend and ally of Lord Longford, had recently commenced his own informal research into Soho's strip-clubs and dirty bookshops. Most of these were, he discovered, owned by five men, Jimmy Humphreys among them. Of the forty-five bookshops in the district, he visited twenty, two of them in Walker's Court. Those twenty shops all sold what Blackburn described as 'the most extreme and explicit porn... including colour photographs in full physical detail of group sex, sadistic sex, bestiality, sexual perversions and sexual acts involving violence'.

Appalled by what he found in the bookshops and by the availability through newsagents and sweet shops of glistening lines of magazines such as *Men Only* and *Club International*, Blackburn wrote a letter of complaint to Robert Mark, newly installed Commissioner of the Metropolitan Police. 'This country has been and is being flooded with obscenity and pornography as a result of the failure of the police to enforce the law and, in particular, the provisions of the Obscene Publications Act 1959,' he remarked.

Just over a month after Blackburn made his complaint, Longford's 490-page report on pornography was completed. It provided not only a survey of the phenomenon in Britain but also numerous recommendations, the most significant of these being that the law on obscenity should be revised and the punishments increased. Rather than rely on the old 'tendency to corrupt' definition of pornography, the report suggested that a publication or performance should be regarded as obscene 'if its effect, taken as a whole, is to outrage contemporary standards of decency or humanity, accepted by the public at large'. The report also urged the creation of a new offence specifically conceived to target Raymond and his ilk. This new statute would 'punish those who, for purposes of gain, induce others to take part in any obscene or indecent performance to be shown to the public, or as models for any photographs or films of a similar kind for a like purpose'.

Abundant space in the report was devoted to the type of magazines produced by Raymond. Ignoring de Boinod's conciliatory comments on his softcore output, the committee stated that '*Men Only* had outstripped its rivals by becoming more explicit and Mr Raymond's trend is made still more obvious in *Club International.*' To prevent schoolchildren from buying these publications, Kingsley Amis argued that magazines of this nature should, like movies, be classified according to their suitability for specific age groups.

By demonstrating that the trade in pornography was flourishing, the *Longford Report* lent implicit support to Blackburn's all-too-accurate contention that the police were failing to enforce the law. His letter of complaint having elicited nothing more than a detailed defence of the sterling work of the OPS, Longford's friend resorted to an obscure legal ploy. He applied to the High Court for an Order of Mandamus – an edict through which a third party could be compelled to obey or, in this case, *enforce* the law. In a shrewd manoeuvre, he directed the order at Robert Mark. Though Blackburn's application was turned down by the High Court, it conjured plenty of embarrassing publicity for the OPS. 'The plain fact is that the efforts of the police have hitherto been largely ineffective,' one of the High Court judges announced.

This wasn't an opinion echoed by Raymond when, just prior to the publication of the *Longford Report*, he spoke to a reporter from the *Daily Express*. His response shaped by self-interest, he said, 'I see no reason to worry about pornography in this country. What bad stuff there is, is well dealt with by the police.' Yet Raymond only had to visit one of his sex shop tenants to see what Blackburn defined as 'extreme pornographic material eg young lady sucking the penis of an Alsatian dog'.

The new Commissioner had, however, finally recognised the validity of Blackburn's concerns and taken action to deal with them. Being a former provincial policeman, always been made to feel an outsider within the Metropolitan Police, Robert Mark harboured an instinctive mistrust of his West End colleagues, who appeared to feel greater loyalty towards each other than to the public. Only six days after taking office, he'd stripped the OPS of its previous autonomy. By placing it under the operational and administrative control of one of his subordinates, he instantly undermined the relationship between the OPS and the Soho porn merchants. If the OPS officers could no longer guarantee immunity from large-scale raids, there wasn't any point in the pornographers making generous payments to them.

# 37 SOMETHING BLUE

**E**ARLY IN SEPTEMBER 1972 Raymond held talks over the planned stock market flotation, from which he stood to gain £3 million-worth of shares. His current good fortune contrasted sharply with what had been happening to Jimmy and Rusty Humphreys. After an unusually vicious row between the couple, Jimmy had gone off with their children, leading Rusty to pursue him with a gun. That summer she'd ended up being arrested and jailed for possession of an unlicensed firearm. Jimmy was, in the meantime, ostracised by Frank Fraser and many of his other pals, who believed Ken Drury's claim about him being a police informant. Raymond was among this exodus of erstwhile friends. 'Soon as the trouble with the police started, he didn't want anything more to do with us,' Rusty Humphreys recalled.

Within about a fortnight of the talks about the stock market flotation beginning, Raymond decided that £3 million was too low a price for surrendering his commercial independence to a potentially meddlesome board of directors. His embryonic partnership with Larry Parnes then dissolved into acrimony. 'It was probably just as well,' recalled a former employee of Raymond's. 'He was a bit of a loner, so a partnership wouldn't have suited him. Anyhow, Parnes was the last person he should've gone into business with. If they'd stayed together, they'd have driven each other crazy.'

Two days after Raymond had told the press about his decision to pull out of the deal, the *Longford Report* was, amid enormous publicity, released as a fat paperback. It generated reviews ranging from the enthusiastic to the contemptuous. In a belated attempt to dispel the aura of police acquiescence conveyed by the report, the Metropolitan Police chose the day of its publication to launch a major operation against Raymond, the pornographer featured most prominently in its pages.

He was in his office at the Whitehall Theatre when he learnt that the OPS had staged simultaneous raids on both the Aldwych headquarters of Paul Raymond Publications and Sun Printers, the Watford firm where his magazines were produced. Detectives had also intercepted two lorries delivering them to newsagents. As well as seizing photos and negatives, not to mention proofs of the next issue of *Men Only* and the next two issues of *Club International*, the OPS had impounded 160 tonnes of Raymond's magazines: 175,000 finished copies of the October issue of *Men Only*, along with a further 139,580 partially printed copies. This represented the biggest cache of pornography so far seized in Britain.

When the OPS questioned him about the confiscated material, Raymond explained that before any edition of either *Men Only* or *Club International* was printed, his solicitors liaised with lawyers representing Sun Printers, a process intended to ensure that the contents didn't breach the law. The OPS nevertheless left Raymond waiting to find out whether he'd face prosecution or recover the lost magazines.

Owing to the scale and topicality of the raids, they merited front-page stories in the *Daily Express* and the *Daily Mirror*. 'I cannot understand why anyone should object to quality publications such as mine,' he was quoted as saying. 'They are well-produced and intended for adults and no one else.'

Fearful of the penalties that might be imposed, Sun Printers refused to carry on producing Raymond's magazines. So well publicised were the seizures that no other British printing firm was prepared to handle the contract either, lucrative though it was, *Men Only*'s print-run having expanded to 430,000 copies a month. Unless Raymond wanted to mothball the business, he had no choice but to farm out the printing to a foreign firm.

Interviewed the following week by a reporter from the *Evening News*, he complained, 'The law isn't clearly defined. It's so much a matter of opinion. You can show something to one person and he will say, "That's rather tame." Yet another person will say, "That is rather obscene and disgusting." You can even go to three or four firms of solicitors for something to be vetted and you get a different reply from each.' He added, 'Strangely enough, I wouldn't like to see all restrictions lifted. One has to draw the line somewhere – but the problem is where it is drawn and who draws it.'

What he neglected to mention was that softcore magazines like *Men Only* and *Playboy* had been vying with each other to produce more daring photos. Inevitably, such competition narrowed the safety margin for publishers.

The extensive press coverage of the raids and the *Longford Report* encouraged London Weekend Television to ask Raymond's girlfriend to appear on the inaugural edition of the current affairs programme *Weekend World* to talk about her role as a columnist for *Men Only*. Though she was still busy starring in the Brighton production of *Pyjama Tops*, she accepted the invitation. Now a peroxide blonde, widely known as 'Fiona Richmond' in tribute to her journalistic alter ego, she appeared at the end of the twenty-minute programme, broadcast on Sunday, 1 October. She reduced her interviewer to embarrassed giggles when she told him about her fictitious working schedule of sleeping with a different man each month and writing a consumer report on the experience.

Raymond can't have been surprised to receive a summons to appear at Watford Magistrates' Court in mid-December. During the month before his visit there, the pressure on him – both in his professional and personal life – mounted.

First, his seventy-eight-year-old mother suffered a fatal heart attack in her home at Worthing. Nine days after that emotional blow Jean, who had spent most of the past year in America, filed a divorce petition which

Raymond decided not to contest. The document cited Fiona Richmond as the other woman. She was annoyed at being assigned this label because *she* hadn't been responsible for the breakdown of the Raymonds' marriage. Her lover had, after all, been living apart from his wife when the affair had ignited.

Laced with intriguing references to Richmond, press stories about the divorce petition abounded. These had one positive consequence, boosting audiences at the Whitehall Theatre where, having proved herself in Brighton, she'd taken a leading role in *Pyjama Tops*.

During early December, the unwelcome developments in Raymond's personal life were supplemented by the discovery that customs officials, who were under instructions to stop incoming consignments of *Men Only*, had impounded 323,480 copies of the bumper Christmas edition. It featured photos of a woman masturbating, photos explicit enough to bring an extra blush to Santa's cheeks. Printed in Holland, the magazines had just been shipped in eight containers from Scheveningen to the Norfolk port of Great Yarmouth, where they were under constant guard. Raymond was now in danger of forfeiting a total of more than half a million magazines and, with it, a vast profit. Even though the 1952 Customs and Excise Act, which governed the importation of goods, was less favourable to publishers than the 1964 Obscene Publications Act, Raymond's lawyers were optimistic about the chances of compelling the authorities to release the expropriated porn.

On the following Monday, Raymond had to appear as a prosecution witness at the trial of Doug White and Eden Reid, who denied charges of trying to extort money from him. White faced an additional charge of doing the same to Bob Guccione.

Guided by the prosecuting counsel, Raymond recounted the story of the eighteen-month campaign against him. 'I was in fear for the lives of my wife and children,' he told the court.

Two days into the trial, proceedings were adjourned so that Raymond could attend the hearing at Watford Magistrates' Court, held to determine whether the confiscated magazines should be forfeited. At stake was a huge sum of money: the magazines had cost Raymond £70,000 to produce and possessed a retail value of £180,000, plus the related advertising revenue.

He was accompanied to Watford not only by Tony Power but also by Fiona Richmond, whose appearance was guaranteed to catch the eyes of reporters and members of the public. She wore her bleached hair loose, its tips brushing the shoulders of her fur jacket, her well-sculpted legs exposed by a dark miniskirt. With her at his side, Raymond sat in the public gallery that afternoon, head bowed attentively as he listened to the opposing lawyers present their cases to a panel of three ageing magistrates under the chairmanship of a balding retiree who used to work for the Gas Board.

Brian Leary, representing the Director of Public Prosecutions, began by describing the police raid on Sun Printers and the material subsequently impounded, material that included a nude photo competition and an article entitled 'Lesbianism in Prison – A Firsthand Account'. He also suggested that the magazines in question conformed to the legal definition of obscenity, in that they'd deprave and corrupt their readers.

Raymond's case was presented by the barrister Edward Gardner, who admitted that *Men Only* was clearly preoccupied by sex. Gardner said that the descriptions of sexual passion didn't make the offending issue obscene. It was as well to remember, he commented, that the legal definition of obscenity was based on a court ruling from 1868, a period when people referred to men's legs as 'their understandings'. He explained that readers of *Men Only* were ordinary, healthy-minded and responsible adult men who could be relied on to keep a sense of proportion. They purchased the magazine to enjoy 'excitement of the senses'.

Once Raymond's barrister had finished his speech, there was a brief break while the magistrates deliberated. About three hours after the hearing had opened, the chairman of the court delivered their verdict. 'We concede that an adult male is entitled to gentle excitement of the senses and this may be generally acceptable but by no possible stretch of the imagination can it be said that the material in their publications is restricted to gentle excitement. In our considered view, we have no hesitation in saying that they *do* corrupt and deprave. We order that the publications be forfeited.'

Smiling defiantly as he left the courtroom, Raymond told waiting newshounds, 'We shall be lodging an appeal. We feel it is a very wrongful decision which strikes at the very roots of free publishing and civil liberties. As for future issues, we don't know exactly what the magistrates object to, so we will print the magazine as we think the law will allow it to be produced.'

Richmond also paused to talk to the press. 'I think it is absolutely disgusting that three elderly magistrates should decide what five million readers of *Men Only* should read,' she said. 'I thought they would be against us from the start of this case because *Men Only* is a magazine written and produced by young people and they are old people who don't understand what we are trying to say.'

Poised to drive Raymond and Co. back to London, his chauffeur had parked his Rolls-Royce nearby. Everybody in Raymond's circle knew the car by its personalised number-plate, 'PR11', nomenclature that made it sound more like a tax form than a deluxe vehicle. At last freeing himself from the milling reporters, Raymond got into the seat next to his chauffeur while Power and Richmond sat in the back. Moments later PR11 glided away from the court.

# 38 THE RAYMOND FOLLIES

B Y LODGING AN IMMEDIATE APPEAL against the magistrates' ruling, Raymond earned a stay of execution for the confiscated magazines, which would otherwise have been incinerated. Had the seizure taken place before the appointment of the new Commissioner of the Metropolitan Police, Raymond wouldn't in all probability have needed to resort to further legal action. That was because pornographers and bookshop owners often used to be given the opportunity to buy back their merchandise from the OPS. A typical scenario involved George Fenwick, until recently head of the unit, loaning a CID tie to one of Soho's most prominent smut-peddlers, then taking him to the storeroom at Holborn Police Station. From there, he was invited to select which of the pornucopia of looted magazines he wanted to purchase. The entrepreneurial dealings of the OPS were lent an element of farce when John Mason, Raymond's old business associate, bought back a consignment of his mucky mags, left them in his car and went off to slake his powerful thirst, only to find that they had, in his absence, been pinched, suspicion instantly falling on those cheeky chappies from the Dirty Squad.

There was also an unexpectedly comical element to the trial of Doug White and Eden Reid, which resumed the day after Raymond's fruitless excursion to Watford. Groping for a plausible explanation for his actions, Reid contradicted the alleged confessions he'd made to the police. All of a sudden he claimed ignorance of the extortion plot. He said he'd been told that the briefcase, which he'd picked up on White's behalf, contained the plans to a building where White had landed a decorating contract.

The plans had, Reid added, been accidentally left in the briefcase at Mr Raymond's office.

Adjourned for the weekend, the trial didn't reach a conclusion until the following Monday, when the jury found White and Reid guilty of trying to extort money from Raymond. White was, however, acquitted of the charge relating to Bob Guccione. Noting the callous way they'd attempted to exploit for their own gain, 'the appalling violence of which there is so much in the world today', the judge dispensed sentences of five and three years respectively to White and Reid.

That evening a reporter asked Raymond to comment on the outcome of the case. 'The police did a marvellous job,' he replied. 'Now we can relax and live a normal life.'

Not that many people would have regarded Raymond's life as being *normal*.


Even though Raymond was living happily with Fiona Richmond, the equilibrium of their relationship threatened by only the occasional row, he didn't want a divorce. 'He couldn't understand why his current separation from Jean couldn't be like all the previous break-ups, each of which had culminated in a reconciliation,' one of his friends recalled.

Divorce would lend a dismaying air of permanence to the arrangement. Another thing that troubled him was the likely cost of a divorce.

On the eve of the climactic hearing at the Family Division of the High Court on Friday, 2 March 1973, he had, his wife claimed, phoned her and pleaded unsuccessfully with her to withdraw her petition. He wasn't in court the next day to witness what was no more than a legal formality – the granting of a decree nisi. The judge also awarded Jean custody of Howard, whom Noel Botham described at that age as 'a sweet kid'. Now seventeen years old, Debbie was disregarded in the judgement because she'd already left home. With Raymond's support, she had just moved to Las Vegas, where she'd got a job as a showgirl. Of late, her ambitions had shifted from acting to singing, the trip to America representing a tentative step towards achieving her goal of becoming the type of performer who'd headline at one of the Las Vegas casinos.

Smartly dressed as usual, Jean – who was wearing a pale, belted dress with long sleeves and a short hemline – reacted to the judge's pronouncement of the decree nisi by performing an excited, schoolgirlish jig, then throwing her arms round her solicitor and planting a kiss on him. As she left the court, she was pounced on by reporters. She told them she felt like kissing the judge. 'This is a good day,' she added. 'It is like chucking away your crutches.'

Asked whether she intended to remarry, she replied, 'Don't dampen my day. I'm perfectly happy as it is. I've got my kids and that's enough for me.'

She later changed into a chic emerald-green velvet trouser-suit and, in a gesture surely calculated to annoy Raymond, spent the evening sipping celebratory glasses of champagne with three friends at Isow's, only yards from the Revuebar.

The Raymonds' divorce coincided with Howard's expulsion from Shiplake College where he'd been caught bunking off school. Raymond was furious with him – not for missing those pricey lessons but for *getting caught*. After his expulsion Howard moved back to Drax Avenue. Each weekend he'd head off to stay with his father, a tense stand-off concurrently developing between his parents.

Jean's solicitors were impatient to begin haggling over what was bound to be a sizeable divorce settlement. According to her, Raymond delayed the process by failing to turn up to successive court hearings, tabled to determine a mutually acceptable figure. Raymond expressed bemusement that Jean, who hadn't previously appeared to share his acquisitive drive, was demanding £250,000.

In her account of what happened, he tried to get her to accept a lower figure by complaining about being short of cash. Such complaints may have possessed fleeting validity because he had, around then, suffered his most serious commercial setback in recent years, plummeting property prices having scuppered his hefty investment in the planned Essex housing development. This had left him with a considerable debt and interest payments so heavy that he vowed never to take out a loan again.

He was, however, still turning an impressive profit from the Royalty Theatre, where *Oh! Calcutta!* continued to bring in large audiences. The sense that those audiences could have been even larger breeding dissatisfaction with the show, he gave its producer notice to quit. Raymond aggravated this already questionable decision with his choice of replacement show. Veering away from the type of production that had made him so much money, he committed to substituting Tynan's revue with *The Water Babies*, a winsome musical which, though it sounded like an underage prequel to *Pyjama Tops*, was based on Charles Kingsley's classic Victorian fairy tale. Due to open in late July, the production starred the faded singing star Jessie Matthews, then in her mid-sixties, her dubiously titled yet saccharine opening number, 'I Like To Cuddle Little Babies', setting the tone of a show that seemed to offer employment to every precocious dancing tot in London.

A couple of days before the press preview of *The Water Babies*, Raymond appeared on *These Young People*, a BBC Television programme, talking about the type of stage shows more readily associated with him. The programme formed part of a five-part series, each weekly instalment of which starred a different eighteen-to-twenty-five-year-old quizzing a celebrity guest. That week's interviewer was a young man with a staid dress sense, a pompous manner and a scrape-over hairdo even less plausible than Raymond's. Accused of using the theatre to peddle filth, Raymond lost his characteristic sangfroid, a peevish expression descending over his features. 'I *beg* your pardon,' he retorted, forefinger waving at his interviewer like a windscreen wiper on its fastest setting. 'The sight of a nude man or woman on stage is *not* filth.' As he spoke, his eyes scanned the audience with all the wariness of a market stallholder on the lookout for pilferers.

The decision to drop *Oh! Calcutta!* proved a costly mistake. What had previously been a crowded auditorium was now half empty for most performances. Within days he was already contemplating its imminent closure and making plans for a new show there.

In some respects a return to the old formula, in others a fresh departure, its planned successor was a big-budget revue called *The Royalty Folies*. Perhaps inspired by seeing Debbie perform in America, Raymond envisaged it as a mixture of a sumptuous Las Vegas floor show and a saucy Parisian cabaret. It would, like the show at the Revuebar, be aimed at tourists and out-of-towners. With luck, he reasoned, it might run for as long as four decades, periodically revitalised by changing the cast, choreography and sets. While preparations were being made for the new show, Raymond lured *Oh! Calcutta!* back to his now vacant theatre for the remainder of that year.

He was enduring no such problems with his publishing business, the continued prominence of *Men Only* and *Club International* catching the attention of Martin Amis, Britain's leading young novelist. Amis responded by writing a forthright survey of the softcore magazine market for the *New Statesman*, a tone of mock stoicism joining forces with a semi-Germanic pseudonym to facilitate his frolicsome candour. That pseudonym was 'Bruno Holbrook' which Amis had, coincidentally, used two months earlier for another self-incriminating article, its subject none other than Soho strip-clubs, the Revuebar excluded on the pragmatic grounds of high ticket prices. Bestowing on Raymond's publications grudging admiration, the diminutive author of *The Rachel Papers* wrote, 'Instead of being implicit recommendations of the priestly life, like their tawdry counterparts, these magazines actually *sex you up*.'

☆

From the start of 1974, the preparatory work for *The Royalty Folies* intensified. Its budget soon escalated from £250,000 to £300,000, making it a contender for the title of the most expensive theatre production hitherto staged in Britain. An appreciable percentage of that exorbitant budget went on an artificial ice rink that had to be imported from America and on the fur coats worn by forty showgirls. Raymond even had to acquire a hydraulic lift capable of moving two huge, water-filled tanks, occupied by a pair of dolphins which were taught to remove Miss Nude International's bikini. Deploying the same principle used to train Wally Lucken's white horse, this was done by repeatedly hooking a piece of fish on to the girl's bra strap.

Raymond's commitment to the show wasn't just financial. He helped to devise the acts and hire the cast, all of whom had to appear naked on stage. In a gesture of unashamed nepotism, he gave Debbie – just back from Las Vegas – one of the plum singing and dancing roles. There were, however, two conspicuous snags, the most glaring of these being that her voice, pleasant and tuneful though it was, had neither the character nor the strength to sustain a West End show. Even if she *had* been able to sing like Judy Garland, there remained another seemingly insurmountable problem. Lifelong exposure to what her father liked to call 'nude entertainment' had given her a nonchalant attitude towards public nudity, yet she wasn't prepared to go on stage in the nude herself. 'It's not right for me,' she insisted.

And what wasn't right for Debbie wasn't right for her father. Laying himself open to ridicule, Raymond arranged for his daughter to be the sole performer in *The Royalty Folies* who kept her clothes on, *her* modesty preserved while other people's naked daughters cavorted round the stage. When a reporter picked up on this double-standard, this apparent contradiction of his decade-old claims that he'd be happy to let Debbie become a stripper, he came out with a sharp, twinkly-eyed riposte. 'Pure coincidence,' he said. 'Somebody had to keep their clothes on. Debbie bravely volunteered.'

☆

On her return to London, Debbie – hair dyed blonde and modishly tousled – had moved into the exotic three-bedroom penthouse flat her father and Fiona Richmond had recently acquired. Debbie's boisterous presence gave Raymond a soupçon of the family life he appeared to have forsaken. 'Letting Debbie move in with him and Fiona seemed a recipe for trouble,' one of their friends recalled, 'yet the three of them got on fantastically well. There always seemed to be a lot of laughter, a lot of fun, a lot of in-jokes.'

Under Raymond's lax parental regime, which differed from Jean's stricter approach, Debbie was free to copy his nocturnal way of life and indulge her impetuosity as well as her unquenchable thirst for nightclubs, parties, men and Jack Daniel's whisky. Among her circle, sometimes supplemented by her adoring 'Pa', she acquired a reputation for being generous, extravagant and unruly.

Fitzhardinge House, a 1960s block on the corner of Baker Street and Portman Square, provided the otherworldly setting for Raymond's louche ménage. Routinely compared to a film set, the sort of place designed for the megalomaniac villain in a James Bond movie, their seventh-floor flat was entered via a private lift which carried them from the communal foyer and underground car park below. Visitors to the flat – large enough to include accommodation for a live-in housekeeper – were always struck by the thirty-foot-long lounge, scene of many lavish parties, its chill prickle of air-conditioning offering what was something of a novelty in those days. But the air-conditioning was the least unusual aspect of the room's blousy opulence. It had a ceiling encrusted with chunkily menacing mirrored pyramids that reflected a jagged, Futurist's eye vision of the room below: the thick blue carpets, the white leather upholstery, the ultra-modern television projection screen, the sliding blue wall panels, the adjoining patio, bordered on three sides by the penthouse.

Ex-Beatle Ringo Starr and his girlfriend Robin Cruickshank, partners in a design firm called ROR, had been hired by Raymond to design the patio, now usable throughout the year. Above an illuminated fountain, the submerged lights from which could pulsate in time to music, there was an enormous glass and aluminium domed roof that retracted like the cover of a missile silo when a button was pressed. One Sunday morning Baker Street had had to be closed to traffic while a crane lifted the structure into position.

Even more electrical gadgetry was in evidence in the bedroom shared by Raymond and his girlfriend. Reclining on the seven-foot-by-seven-foot bed, less a king-size bed than a *kingdom* in its own right, they were within reach of a control panel that looked as if it belonged on an airliner. One of the buttons switched the lights on and off. Another drew the leopard-print curtains, which matched the walls. Another opened and closed the wardrobe door. Another summoned the housekeeper, who kept all three of the flat's residents supplied with freshly laundered clothes and food from Harrods, Selfridges and equally expensive shops. Another caused the panel at the foot of the bed to slide back, revealing a huge television. And yet another operated the mirrored canopy above the bed. Press that button and the canopy – forthright token of virility and kinkiness – made way for a concealed sunray lamp, regular use of which had given Raymond a fashionable tan, his skin grilled to the colour of caramel.

So satisfied was Raymond with ROR's work on his penthouse that he commissioned them to redesign the interior of the boat he'd just bought. He and Richmond had seen it at the Boat Show and placed an order immediately. The vessel, which cost £50,000, was a powerful forty-eight-foot-long flat-bottomed river and coastal cruiser. It had an interior which he hated, its walls and floors sheathed in turquoise plastic. At Ringo Starr's suggestion the plastic made way for a blue carpet, featuring a different coloured stripe in each cabin.

Richmond talked her boyfriend into naming the boat 'Get 'em 'orf' in Latin. Her mother, who worked as a teacher at a convent school, ended up persuading the nuns to provide a translation: '*Veste Demite*'.

☆

Debbie Raymond was six weeks away from taking her first curtain call at the Royalty Theatre when the High Court convened to determine the fate of all those thousands of copies of the Christmas issue of *Men Only*, seized at Great Yarmouth. The case, which began on Tuesday, 5 February 1974, centred on the question of whether the jury of nine men and three women regarded the magazine as indecent. If so, its seizure and destruction were justified. After two days of legal argument, the judge delivered his summing-up, during which he couldn't resist commenting on the 'charming' pictures of 'the very attractive girl' on page 19. He warned the jury to take into account that *Men Only* 'was obviously not the Bible, a medical textbook or *Tiger Tim's Weekly*'. Duly warned, the jury concluded that the magazine *was* indecent, their verdict leading Raymond to defend himself with the line that would become his aggrieved mantra: 'I'm not a pornographer. I'm an entertainer.'

The court case set Raymond back around £200,000, yet he was still able to afford two hulking theatrical investments that month. Encouraged by the £800,000 profit he'd earned from *Pyjama Tops*, now in its fifth year, he paid £340,000 to extend his lease on the Whitehall Theatre by sixty years. He also bought another West End theatre, an acquisition that made him London's biggest independent theatre operator and garnered him an appreciative profile in the *Sunday Telegraph*.

His latest purchase was the Windmill Theatre, which had, for the previous nine years, been a cinema. He paid about £100,000 for the 114-year lease on it, part owned by the film producer Tony Tenser. Raymond felt that its enduring association with nudity would make it a surefire success as a venue for his type of entertainment. When a journalist enquired what sort of shows he'd be staging there, he said, 'Tits, bums and a few laughs. That's what people like. That's what *I* like.'

Budgeting for a total cost of £150,000, he began the refurbishment of the building, within which he created a tiny cinema as well as offices that could be used as the headquarters of the PRO. These were reached via an unmarked doorway on neighbouring Archer Street, only a few yards from the downmarket Charlie Chester Casino & Niterie, which contributed to the street's sordid ambience. Raymond was old enough to remember the days when dozens of unemployed musicians had gathered here on Monday afternoons in the hope of being recruited by the nightclub owners who treated it as an informal job centre.

Through the door to Raymond's new headquarters was an undersized foyer. To get to his office, Raymond had to take an even more cramped, shagpile-carpeted lift to the third-floor reception area, the walls of which were decorated with framed posters from his days as a promoter of nude revues. Beyond the reception area lay his surprisingly small, unostentatious office, where a large desk took up the majority of the floor space. Around it, a perpetual, heavy odour of cigarette smoke hung. Other than a few showbiz mementoes and an ornate mirror with the 'PR' logo incorporated into its metalwork frame, there were no embellishments. It was clearly an office for working in, not for impressing visitors.

Raymond envisaged using the Windmill's freshly created cinema to host a film club. Since 1960, when the Compton, a mini-cinema on Old Compton Street, had opened, interspersing art-house with tart-house, gaudy little film clubs had popped up all round Soho, their members-only status permitting them to reap handsome returns by screening soft porn movies deemed too spicy for conventional cinemas. The Compton had been set up by Tony Tenser in collaboration with Michael Klinger, former co-owner of the Nell Gwynne Club. A fifty-three-year-old East Ender who had produced films ranging from Roman Polanski's *The Tenant* to *Naked – as Nature Intended*, Tenser had known Raymond for several years. As soon as he heard about Raymond's plans, he offered to run the film club for him. Raymond agreed to Tenser's proposal and made him a partner in what would be known as the Windmill Cinema Club.

☆

Nudity had, by March 1974, infiltrated not just cinemas, theatres, pubs, clubs and the top shelves of newsagents but also other public spaces. The well-documented unisex craze for streaking, imported from America, ensured that wobbling breasts, goose-pimpled thighs and jiggling testicles were now occasionally exposed at sporting venues and even on suburban streets. Feigning outrage at the thought that his potential customers could eyeball naked girls for free, Raymond complained to a reporter about 'those damned amateurs'.

But *The Royalty Folies*, scheduled to open on Monday, 25 March, faced a far more serious threat than mere streakers. During the run-up to its launch, there had been a spate of weekend power cuts in central London, caused by a miners' strike. These had disrupted *Pyjama Tops* and other West End theatre shows, diminishing income by as much as 30 per cent in some venues. Fortunately for Raymond, the crisis had receded before the first night of *The Royalty Folies*, in which he'd made a prodigious financial and emotional commitment, the latter magnified by his daughter's participation.

True to his initial idea, the show blended a slick interpretation of Parisian sauciness and Las Vegas pizzazz, 'extravagant' and 'spectacular' being the words that commonly made cameo appearances in its acreage of pre-publicity. Both epithets were well merited. The show involved singers sashaying in front of a high-kicking chorus line; showgirls executing complex dance numbers in a shimmer of feathers and sequins; half-naked women suspended in giant bird-cages; skaters gliding and pirouetting round the ice rink; nudes making air-borne entrances through purpose-built trapdoors, nicknamed 'tart-traps' by the

stagehands; and dolphins assisting Miss Nude International to perform her underwater striptease. Yet *The Royalty Folies* failed to pull in the anticipated crowds, possibly because it possessed neither the arty chic of *Oh! Calcutta!* nor the bawdy humour of *Pyjama Tops*.

Week after week it accumulated losses that were enough to make even Raymond flinch. Loath to abandon his pet project, he persevered with the show in the misguided hope that it might gradually acquire box-office momentum. Three months into what he'd once forseen as a run destined to rival the record-breaking longevity of *The Mousetrap*, he finally succumbed to commercial logic and closed the show, its losses amounting to £410,000. Anyone with less self-belief than Raymond – and that encompassed most of the population – would have questioned his continued involvement in such a capricious business.

The closure of *The Royalty Folies* was doubly disappointing for Raymond because it had not only left him with a depleted bank account but it had also failed to advance Debbie's nascent showbusiness career. His money could buy her most things, but it *couldn't* buy her the international singing stardom she craved.

## 39 LET'S GET LAID

O N WORKING DAYS Raymond would sometimes go for a post-prandial drink at Gerry's, a traditional basement drinking club, founded by Gerry Campion, the actor famous for playing the beachball-stomached schoolboy in the 1950s television series, *Billy Bunter of Greyfriars School*. Unfairly nicknamed 'the Losers' Lounge', Gerry's was at that time located on Shaftesbury Avenue, close to the Windmill Theatre. 'Raymond just turned up one day,' recalled Michael Dillon, who worked behind the bar. 'He was so well known around Soho that his face was his membership card.'

Entered via a precipitous staircase, the club provided a claustrophobic haven for bibulous journalists, actors and theatrical agents. Within its dusky, theatrical-memorabilia-lined confines, you could routinely encounter a crowd that included the actors Ronald Fraser, Michael Elphick and John le Mesurier, as well as the writers Keith Waterhouse, Willis Hall, Jeffrey Bernard and Frank Norman. But Raymond seldom mixed, preferring to drink a few glasses of the house red wine in the company of whichever senior member of staff or business contact had accompanied him to this convivial cave.

'I once asked him about his stammer,' Dillon said. 'I was curious about it because I used to have one as a child. He replied, "I wouldn't want to lose it because it gives me time to think." I wish I'd come up with that.' Dillon added, 'I also remember telling him a story about how this bloke had approached me as I was walking down Shaftesbury Avenue. I assumed the bloke was a member of Gerry's, so I smiled at him and he smiled at me. "I know *you*," the bloke went. "You're that Raymond

Revuebar chap..." When Raymond heard this, he said to me, "If you're mistaken for me, you have my *deepest* sympathy."'

The summer of 1974 marked the end of Fiona Richmond's marathon stint in *Pyjama Tops*, during which she'd also found time to record a very popular LP of songs written by Anthony Newley. Each track was interspersed by orgasmic groaning and brief reminiscences in the style of her *Men Only* column.

After she'd left the cast of *Pyjama Tops*, she took several weeks' holiday. Whenever she wasn't in a show, she and Raymond tended to seize the opportunity to go abroad, often to Europe, where they'd visit obscure old nightclubs, scouting for striptease and novelty acts suitable for the Revuebar.

Raymond and his girlfriend were still getting on so well that friends and acquaintances speculated on whether he'd propose marriage to her. But he admitted that he couldn't see any point in marrying again, a feeling no doubt buttressed by the memory of the divorce settlement with Jean. 'Once the ring is on, people change,' he remarked. 'You start taking each other for granted.'

Earlier that year he'd hired Victor Spinetti to write and direct a sex comedy with a role suitable for Richmond. The show had to be ready for September's relaunch of the Windmill Theatre. Spinetti obliged by creating *Let's Get Laid*, a string of comic sketches about two innocents who find themselves flat-sitting for a James Bond-type figure, visited by an array of leggy girlfriends.

With its modest £20,000 budget, *Let's Get Laid* represented a retreat from the high-risk strategy of *The Royalty Folies*. As a way of saving money, Spinetti decided to kit out the girlfriends in the extravagant costumes, strings of pearls, diamond chokers and feather boas acquired for the drag artistes in *Birds of a Feather*. Naturally, Richmond was cast as one of the girlfriends. The central roles were assigned to John Inman and Jack Haig, talented comic actors who went on to star in the hit BBC television sitcoms *Are You Being Served?* and *'Allo, 'Allo!*. Inman – whose mincing onstage persona rivalled Larry Grayson's for camp flamboyance – liked to claim he'd told his mother that *Let's Get Laid* was a play about life on a poultry farm.

To promote the production, Raymond and his girlfriend staged a memorable publicity stunt. Naked apart from a straight blonde wig that reached down to her waist, a Mexican-bandit-style gunbelt, red thigh-length boots and a large straw hat, Richmond climbed onto a chestnut horse waiting outside the Windmill Theatre. Faced by a gaggle of photographers and at least one television news crew, the horse was led on to Shaftesbury Avenue. They were also followed by Raymond, together with a growing throng of curious onlookers that threatened to congeal around them. At Piccadilly Circus a combination of the crowd and the sight of a famous woman in the nude – a woman instantly recognisable from posters, billboards, magazines and interviews – stopped the traffic. Raymond had, by then, instructed his chauffeur to phone the police, who unwittingly contributed to the stunt. As Richmond clip-clopped slowly past Swan & Edgar's, the gigantic department store at the meeting point of Piccadilly and Regent Street, a police inspector marched up to her and told her to get off the horse. In a tone of mock-bewilderment, Raymond demanded to know what she was doing wrong.

Swathed in a silver and black dressing gown, Richmond was soon escorted away by the police. A few hours after that, she was at Bow Street Magistrates' Court, where she pleaded guilty to a charge that earned her a £20 fine.

The resultant publicity helped to ensure good ticket sales for *Let's Get Laid*. But the backstage component of the Windmill Theatre's revamp, initiated months earlier, still hadn't been completed when the show premiered on Monday, 2 September. The dressing rooms didn't even have glass in the windows.

On the first night, the comedian Ernie Wise as well as the film star

Elizabeth Taylor were in the audience. Afterwards, Taylor wanted to meet Raymond and the cast, so Spinetti took her backstage. 'When Fiona opened her dressing-room door, she was wearing nothing but a merkin (that's a pubic wig),' recalled Spinetti. 'Elizabeth didn't bat an eyelid. "Darling, you're so slim, if you were on the pill it would show."'

Raymond's flourishing career had yielded bountiful advantages for his daughter – material, educational and otherwise. It also had a corrosive influence familiar to many children of rich and successful people. On the one hand it lent her existence a potentially demotivating sense of freedom. And on the other hand it exerted insidious psychological pressure to live up to Raymond's achievements, to prove to other people that she wasn't merely the pampered daughter of a multimillionaire.

Lately Debbie, who liked to emphasise her showbiz credentials by telling stories about how she'd watched strip-shows from her pushchair, had been filling in as stage manager, usherette and barmaid in Raymond's theatres, jobs that fed her deluded belief that she was following her father's advice 'to work up the hard way'. Obstinately pursuing her ambition to become a singer, she picked up a booking – which Raymond had probably lined up for her – as a cabaret artiste at the Showboat Restaurant on the Strand. She was due to begin in early November. Both her parents were already planning to be there for the opening night, though Jean admitted they were unlikely to share a table.

On the Monday before Debbie embarked on her cabaret booking, her parents had to appear at the Family Division of the High Court, where they were due to wrap up the still-unresolved financial terms of their divorce. Sporting a sandy beard, Raymond didn't exchange a word with Jean that morning as they stood only a few yards apart in the corridor outside the court, seldom intervening while their haggling lawyers endeavoured to reach an out-of-court settlement. At length a confidential agreement was negotiated. As Jean walked out of the court, she patted her ex-husband on the shoulder and said, 'Bye, bye, Paul...'

In an adroit move surely calculated to turn the inevitable publicity to his advantage, Raymond revealed to the reporters who'd been following the case that he'd paid his ex-wife £250,000: £160,000 in cash, the remainder in the form of the house on Drax Avenue, valued at £90,000. On top of the settlement Raymond claimed to have accrued a legal bill of about £16,000. 'I hope we are still friends,' he added without much sincerity. 'I am very happy about the settlement.'

He left court in a red Rolls-Royce. Already making arrangements to rejoin Joe DiMaggio in America, Jean meanwhile departed in a battered second-hand car. Interviewed at home that afternoon by a journalist from the *Daily Mirror*, she said, 'I'm numb with joy at the amount and numb with relief that it's all over. I asked for a certain figure right at the start and I was determined to get it. Some people will think I've been too hard – but I deserve every penny. I worked damned hard to help Paul make his business the success it is.'

Next morning their divorce was covered by several of the national newspapers, including the *Daily Mirror*, which tagged it with the irresistible headline 'Stripped of £250,000'. The settlement made Jean one of Britain's wealthiest divorcées.

'I will not be selling the Rolls or anything to help pay for it,' Raymond told a *Sunday Mirror* reporter. With a boastful swagger, he added, 'It will make no difference to me or my companies. I can afford to pay that sort of money.'

Raymond also expressed relief that his divorce had at last been resolved. Nonetheless, he still had to deal with the familial wreckage that had been left behind. The chances of establishing a healthy father–son relationship with Howard were reduced by Howard's decision to accompany Jean to Miami, where she'd bought a house. Matters weren't helped by Howard's recent discovery that Raymond had fathered an illegitimate son or the fact that Raymond wasn't on speaking terms with

Jean, the antipathy between them lingering despite mutual protestations of friendship made via the press.

One aspect of Raymond's vanished family life did, however, survive. His relationship with Debbie was still intact, the bond between them simultaneously strengthened and compromised by her financial dependence on him. 'Paul was always in a position of power over her,' recalled the man who would become her first husband. 'You could tell he enjoyed the fact that she relied on him. She knew that, if she wanted anything, she could always get it from her pa. I think it made her feel bloody useless.'

When she told him that she'd like to move out of Fitzhardinge House into a place of her own, he covered the cost of her flat – a plush two-floor penthouse, located in Shakespeare Tower, part of the upmarket Barbican housing development. From the west-facing windows of her new home, she could see the domed roofs of Smithfield Meat Market, the Gothic tower of the Prudential Building and, beyond that, the streets of Soho, their tightly interlocking pattern liable to be veiled by the slightest atmospheric haze.

What with his divorce and the failure of *The Royalty Folies*, it had been an expensive year for Raymond, yet he'd still had enough surplus cash to exploit the sharply declining West End property prices that marked the nadir of the early 1970s economic crisis. Displaying remarkable foresight, he didn't just invest in undervalued properties. He invested in undervalued properties located within an undervalued district. That district was Soho which, by 1974, had become not only disreputable but also squalid: a malodorous enclave of run-down buildings, rancid hallways, peeling flyposters, urine-soaked alleys, refuse-spewing dustbins and recumbent, grubbily shrouded figures on park benches, stale perspiration and cheap booze scenting their slipstream.

Clad in a voluminous fur coat, he'd turn up at property auctions and, whenever he spotted a bargain, he'd pounce, never letting sentiment or the competitive instinct lure him into paying more than he planned. Most investors calculated the cost of refurbishing a building, then based the rent on a preconceived profit margin, whereas Raymond reversed conventional practice. He'd begin by working out how much potential tenants could afford to pay. Once he'd arrived at this figure, he gave himself no elbow room.

He was similarly intransigent in his attitude towards borrowing money to fund property acquisitions. His painful experience with the loans he'd taken out for the failed Essex housing development had taught him to avoid credit, relying instead on the cash reaped from his other businesses.

Each time the property arm of the PRO acquired a freehold, massive rent increases would – not always with Raymond's approval – be imposed on the sitting tenants as soon as their lease expired or the next rent review came round. Traditional businesses often found it hard to cope with such steep rises, forcing them to close down or relocate, their premises taken over by the sex merchants whose vast profits could cover the new rents.

The acquisition of the freeholds of building after building in Soho would eventually be recognised as a masterstroke. Raymond was perceptive enough to identify these purchases as an investment carrying minimal risk. If Soho shook off its grubby reputation or if Westminster City Council went ahead with its controversial plans to allow most of the area to be bulldozed and redeveloped, he'd be the owner of numerous valuable central London sites. Even if Soho remained unchanged, he'd still be able to collect inflated rents from the shady businessmen who ran the local dirty bookshops, clip-joints and sex shops.

While stealthily parlaying the fortune he'd made from breasts and buttocks into bricks and mortar, he continued to look for ways of funding more property purchases. The British market for softcore magazines such as *Men Only* and *Club International* offered negligible scope for expansion, but there were significant opportunities in America. Raymond entrusted Tony Power, who had become one of his closest friends, with the responsibility for launching his magazines there during January 1975. As an incentive, Power was promised 10 per cent of the profits from them. He went ahead and created magazines so sexually explicit that they'd have been illegal in Britain, the success of these American editions soon engorging Power's pay cheque – never less than £30,000 a month.

Armed with an ample supply of cocaine, Power and some of Raymond's other young employees would join Raymond after work most nights for marathon drinking sessions in the West End. These would begin with Raymond arriving in his chauffeur-driven Rolls-Royce which would shuttle them from one theatre bar to the next, frequently subsidised by their boss.

'Watching Raymond with Tony was like watching a really close father–son relationship – the sort of relationship Raymond never seemed to have with Howard,' remembered a former participant in their epic bar crawls. 'They'd be talking and laughing and generally having a great time. Those evenings would whizz past in a blur of cigarettes, hard liquor, glamorous women and coke, though I don't recall Raymond being into drugs at that stage.'


Changes to Raymond's business weren't, in the first half of 1975, restricted to publishing. Early that May falling ticket sales led him to close *Pyjama Tops* which, over the past five and a half years, had been seen by more than a million people. He replaced it with another sex comedy – the spicily titled *Snatch 69: The Confessions of a Sex Star*. But this couldn't replicate even a fraction of the success of its predecessor.

Always alert to commercial opportunities, Raymond chose that summer to make his first excursion into the movie business. Unsurprisingly, following the example set by several of Soho's other pornbrokers, he targeted the sexploitation end of movie-making. This was the only thriving facet of the British film industry at that time, the sleazy sensibility of Soho film clubs having recently seeped into the mainstream, where high-street cinemagoers could choose between movies such as *Mistress Pamela, How to Succeed with Sex* and the sci-fi spoof *Flesh Gordon*, promoted as starring 'Chesty 73-32-36 Morgan and Her Deadly Weapons'.

Raymond started by bankrolling *Exposé*, a bloodthirsty soft porn thriller garnished with lesbian sex scenes. Funding was provided only on condition that one of the lead roles was given to Richmond who had, the previous year, made her movie debut as a stripper in the Barry Humphries comedy *Barry McKenzie Holds His Own*.

Directed by James Kenelm Clarke, an experienced BBC documentary-maker, *Exposé* would achieve notoriety during the early 1980s as the sole British contribution to the list of so-called 'video nasties' banned by the Director of Public Prosecutions. The film was shot on location just outside Chelmsford that summer, Richmond appearing opposite the appropriately demented-looking German actor Udo Kier, best known for his role in *Dogville*, Lars von Trier's 2003 feature. She played the girlfriend of a pulp novelist who, while working in the seclusion of a rented country cottage, was tormented not only by nightmares and gory hallucinations but also by his manipulative, knife-wielding secretary.

Some of the film's atmosphere of sexual jealousy and violence would, in a bizarre development, be replayed in reality later that summer. Taking a break from her frantic schedule which had expanded to include writing *Fiona*, a volume of soft porn confessions that exploited her outrageous *Men Only* persona, Richmond drove her E-type Jaguar down to the Riviera, where she was due to spend three months living on Raymond's boat. Raymond joined her soon afterwards.

He combined the holiday with a talent-spotting mission to a nightclub in Toulouse where he saw The Climax, a four-person nude cabaret troupe which he signed for a year's residency at the Revuebar. The troupe featured a handsome and charming young Corsican former ballet dancer named Gérard Simi, who would go on to become his choreographer.

When Raymond's holiday ended and he left the Riviera, Richmond began an affair with a man she'd met at a party: Tony Douthwaite, the bearded forty-three-year-old skipper of *Ann V*, a luxury yacht moored in St Tropez. The yacht was owned by someone Raymond knew – Jim Gregory, chairman of Queen's Park Rangers Football Club.

One night towards the end of August Richmond's Mediterranean idyll came to an abrupt end. In a jealous rage that carried echoes of *Exposé*'s violent conclusion, Douthwaite's much younger fiancée, who worked as a cook on board *Ann V*, stabbed him in the stomach with a carving knife. The wound was so severe that it necessitated a five-hour emergency operation, after which Richmond paid for him to convalesce in a private hospital.

Raymond flew down to the Riviera as soon as he heard what had happened. Disclosing a gentle side of his personality that he kept well hidden, he admitted to being very concerned about Douthwaite, whom he must have met earlier in the summer. Raymond stayed long enough to discover that his girlfriend had fallen in love with the wounded man. After parting with her at Nice airport, where she gave Raymond a fond goodbye kiss, he flew to Italy on business, leaving her to mull over the question of whether they had any future as a couple.

Though she went back to Raymond, the romantic side of their relationship – but not their friendship – was already on the wane, neither of them making any secret of the fact that they were sexually involved with other people. In Raymond's case he wanted to invite those other people into bed with himself and Richmond who, for all the self-declared sexual liberation of her *Men Only* column, found the prospect unedifying. Fittingly, his next theatre production, due to open at the Whitehall in late January 1976, was called *Come into My Bed*.

For the time being Raymond and Richmond were still a couple – one of Britain's foremost celebrity pairings, their names and pictures embellishing the national newspapers. As they walked into the dining room of the Hilton Hotel on Park Lane where they often spent their evenings, the house band would stop playing and strike up a jaunty rendition of what became Richmond's signature tune – 'The Stripper'. And when she and Raymond took a flight to Los Angeles, they were greeted at the airport by a mob of photographers. Cold-shouldering the film star Gregory Peck and the Osmonds pop group, who were all on the same flight, the paparazzi concentrated on getting shots of Britain's King and Queen of Porn.

The bitterness that had prevailed between Raymond and his ex-wife, who made a habit of returning to Britain from Miami three or four times each year, had ended at last. Whenever she was back in London, she'd get together with Raymond for a drink and also meet Debbie, now involved in an argument-punctuated relationship with Paul Musetti, a young Italian-American racing driver.

On Jean's next visit in early January 1976, she and Raymond organised another drink. Recalling their encounter, Raymond said, 'We were talking about the success of my magazine *Club International* in the States. Then she said, "*My* body is just as good as these young girls', and I'm twice their age." I said, "It certainly *was* the last time I saw it." So I said I would take some nude pictures of her and she agreed.'

He paid her a fee that was four or five times what he normally gave his models. The photo session took place at the house on Drax Avenue, where he posed his ex-wife sitting naked astride a stuffed tiger, its mouth open in a silent growl, expressive of all the hostility she'd once felt towards him.

Roughly six weeks after their photo session, the results of which formed a *Men Only* centrefold, the Soho porn industry faced a dramatic shake-up. Encouraged by the *Longford Report*, along with Raymond Blackburn's allegations and recent newspaper stories about police corruption, Robert Mark had authorised an investigation of the Soho sex industry. This inquiry was being run by an outsider, recruited because he was likely to be immune to any attempts by the West End police to compromise his work. It culminated in the arrest of Ken Drury, Wally Virgo, Bill Moody and nine other police officers. Their seniority guaranteed a major scandal, fated to have an indirect bearing on the property side of Raymond's business.

In the final week of February, Raymond gave up his lease on the Royalty Theatre which had, since the closure of *Oh! Calcutta!*, been a financial drain. Nevertheless, he remained committed to his bare-breasted type of theatre. Besides staging *Come into My Bed* at the Whitehall, he was preparing to put on a fresh show at the Windmill, a show bearing the spectacularly ill-chosen title of *Rip-off*. Produced by the team from the Revuebar, it comprised a jumble of disconnected modern dance sequences. Their elaborate settings encompassed a men's prison, the wheel of a storm-lashed ship and a mysterious temple, wreathed in dry ice, all contriving to offer a pretext for nudity and simulated sex, 'The Song of the Volga Boatman' at one point providing the rhythm for a foursome involving a girl who had – for unexplained reasons – just strayed into a men's prison. All of which stoked the rancour felt by Irving Wardle, theatre critic of *The Times*, who decried 'the Tamburlaine-like advance of the Paul Raymond Organisation' which, he argued, represented West End theatre at 'its lowest point'.

The opening night of *Rip-off* was still several months away when *Exposé* commenced its West End run, its publicity justifiably proclaiming Richmond 'Britain's No. 1 Sex Symbol'. To dispel any impression that Raymond had backed the film purely as a means of advancing his girlfriend's career, its credits made no reference to Raymond's contribution to the film: a contribution that would ordinarily have earned him billing as executive producer. Richmond's celebrity status enhancing its box-office appeal, *Exposé* went on to enjoy a lucrative tour of the seedy Classic cinema chain, which specialised in softcore sex films.

Back in her more accustomed role as a columnist for *Men Only*, Richmond was sent to interview Malcolm Allison, the flamboyant, cigar-smoking, white-fedora-wearing manager of Crystal Palace Football Club. 'Big Mal', as he was known, was a perfect interviewee, sharing his fellow manager Brian Clough's reputation for smart one-liners, impulsive behaviour and stirring up vainglorious controversy.

With a photographer in tow, the fur-coated Richmond and her tracksuited, fashionably sideburned interviewee were chauffeured to the club's training ground in Raymond's Rolls-Royce. The players, including Terry Venables and Peter Taylor, both of whom went on to manage the England team, were in the final stages of their daily practice session. Once they'd finished, they headed for a communal bath. Richmond and their manager followed them into the changing rooms. Apparently anxious to demonstrate that his nickname owed nothing to his weight or height, Big Mal accepted Richmond's invitation to strip off and join her and the players in the bath, a moment captured by the hovering snapper. 'I was out of the bath like lightning when I saw the photographer lurking round,' Terry Venables recalled. 'Malcolm later told me he had never seen me move so fast on a football field.'

Leaked to the tabloid press, the pictures whipped up what must, for Raymond and his partner, have been a gratifying hullabaloo. Richmond's shared bath with Big Mal and the Crystal Palace team became the subject of newspaper debate, even prompting a long piece in the *Sunday Times* by the chat-show host Michael Parkinson. The debate extended to the Crystal Palace directors and the bigwigs at the Football Association who failed to see the funny side of the incident. Big Mal found himself contesting an FA charge of 'bringing the game into disrepute', a charge that led to a brief touchline ban and played a role in his sacking a few weeks later.

Richmond was at the hub of another risible spat the following month.

Across the façade of the Whitehall Theatre a giant picture of her advertised *Come into My Bed*, her gargantuan, semi-clad form dominating the street. When the hoarding was taken down in late June, Raymond's company faced a rare accusation – of bowing to authority. They were accused of removing the photographic panels to avoid causing offence to the Queen and the French president, who were due to drive past that Tuesday. In fact, the panels had been removed because Richmond had left the cast. 'We wouldn't take them down for the Queen,' a spokesman responded defiantly. 'She must have driven past them dozens of times and nobody's complained.'

More than twenty-five years had elapsed since the birth of Raymond's eldest son. During that time Darryl had, like his father, changed his name, his chosen moniker being Derry, a name reflective of his mother's Irish heritage. Except for the monthly maintenance payments – which, by Derry's calculations, amounted to a paltry £3,100 – Raymond had played no part in his upbringing. So far, the two of them hadn't even enjoyed the briefest of meetings.

Despite the resentment Noreen still felt towards her one-time boyfriend, Derry yearned to forge a relationship with his father, who had become a glamorous figure in his mind, that glamour nourished by absence and the stream of publicity Raymond attracted. Himself a would-be entrepreneur, Derry fantasised about being invited to help his father run the family business. Though no such invitation had been forthcoming, the estrangement between the two of them was about to end.

Back in London after a business trip abroad, most likely one of his regular scouting missions, Raymond found a note from Derry waiting for him at his office. The note was written on stationery from a cheap hotel in Bayswater where Derry, who'd travelled down to London on a work-related trip, had been staying. Via the note, Raymond discovered that Derry had phoned his office while he'd been away. Obviously intrigued, Raymond wrote Derry a friendly letter three or four weeks later. Besides informing his son that he'd welcome the chance to meet, Raymond's letter provided the address and phone number of his Portland Square home. The letter also invited Derry to get in touch the next time he was in London.

Raymond ended up asking Derry round to his penthouse one morning while Richmond was out. He must have been curious to see what his son was like. The young man waiting outside bore a closer resemblance to Noreen O'Horan than to him. Plump faced with a button-nose and stubby eyebrows, angled like Tower Bridge in the process of opening, Derry had a soft Mancunian accent and a gentle, articulate manner. Derry remembered Raymond's relaxed charm soothing his nerves. Over coffee the two of them chatted, their conversation flowing effortlessly through lunch, prepared by Raymond's housekeeper. 'He portrayed her as a battleaxe,' Derry recalled. 'He had a dessert he wasn't very keen on. He said, "For God's sake, I daren't send this back. It'll cause a row", so he crushed it up onto his plate on his fork and, in the particular area we sat in, part of the roof slid back and he flicked the dessert on his spoon out of the roof so that she'd never notice.'

Derry was still there at around 5 p.m. when Richmond got home. Accepting an invitation to stay to dinner, he continued talking to Raymond – about Noreen O'Horan, about what he was doing with his life. He didn't leave until 8.30 p.m., the foundations ostensibly laid for an agreeable relationship with Raymond.

But neither of them consolidated the encounter with a phone call, a letter or even a postcard. 'If I had the guts and wasn't totally terrified of rejection,' Derry admitted, 'I would pick up the phone and ask him, "How about a coffee?"'

Each passing week added to the sense of awkwardness that flooded into the widening gap between them. For Raymond, that sense of awkwardness may have been compounded by the suspicion that Derry possessed an ulterior financial motive for getting in touch, extreme wealth providing fertile ground for the associated distrust that compounded his native wariness. Soon the opportunity had gone, leaving father and son estranged once more.

# 40 A CAPTAIN OF SKINDUSTRY

S O PROFITABLE HAD Raymond's first tentative venture into the film business been that he went on to provide uncredited backing for two more low-budget movies, shot in rapid succession. His latest films, both featuring Richmond and directed by James Kenelm Clarke, were *Frankly Fiona* and *Let's Get Laid*.

Beyond its title and star, *Let's Get Laid* had no connection to the popular stage show of that name. It was, instead, a lame comedy about a case of mistaken identity revolving round a demobbed Second World War soldier who possessed a name straight out of some feeble schoolboy joke – Gordon Laid. Hamstrung by unconvincing 1940s sets and costumes, it co-starred an improbable triumvirate of British actors. There was Graham Stark, familiar from the Pink Panther films. There was Anthony Steel, 1950s matinee idol, Hollywood man-about-town and ex-husband of Anita Ekberg. Then there was Robin Askwith, the gurning, Jagger-lipped star of softcore hits such as *Confessions of a Driving Instructor* (1976), his involvement offering a pretext for the film's specious tag-line, 'Now, Britain's Sexy Superstars Get It Together'. As a concession to Richmond's fans, Kenelm Clarke shot several dream sequences which allowed her to flaunt the attributes that had made her famous.

Partially based on *Fiona*, the fancifully fictionalised, smut-injected autobiography Raymond's girlfriend had written, *Frankly Fiona* sought to duplicate the commercial success of the *Confessions* films by presenting the story as a deluxe sex comedy. The film, shot on location in France and Norfolk, blended fact with fiction, portraying her schooldays in a

*Fiona Richmond and Robin Askwith in a scene from* Let's Get Laid

Norfolk vicarage, her West End stage career and her stint as *Men Only*'s sexually insatiable columnist. Playing herself with no more conviction than she'd played other characters, she appeared alongside Anthony Steel and Graham Stark again, plus Adam West, one-time star of *Batman*, the popular 1960s American television series. This unlikely mélange of thespian talent was completed by the presence of Victor Spinetti and the character actors Harry H. Corbett and Ronald Fraser, the latter cast as Raymond's surrogate, a seedy theatrical agent who signs Richmond to appear at the Windmill Theatre. For the scenes depicting her as a pubescent seductress, Richmond wore pigtails and a school uniform, her costume heightening the absurdity of the entire enterprise, one of the main purposes of which seems to have been to advertise *Men Only* and the Revuebar, as well as the Whitehall and Windmill Theatres.

*Frankly Fiona*'s closing scene involved its star departing with her latest lover, ready to embark on another adventure. The scene would prove prophetic. In the course of promoting her freshly published book, she travelled to Southampton to appear on the Southern Television programme *Day by Day*. She was soon romantically entangled with the programme's director, James Montgomery. Still close friends with

Raymond yet unable to endure his nocturnal lifestyle or his penchant for threesomes, she ended their relationship and left him for her new boyfriend.

Raymond's reaction to the separation was less sanguine than she might have hoped. Without warning, in November 1976 he arranged to have her sacked from her job on *Men Only*. 'We felt that after six years it was time to have a change,' he told the press. 'One can't keep doing the same thing time after time. It gets boring.' He added, 'I haven't spoken to Fiona since she heard the news. I don't know how she took it, but firing staff is never a pleasant experience.'

His comments drew a tetchy response from Richmond, who chose the pages of the *Daily Express* as a vehicle for conveying her annoyance. Had anyone else behaved like this, it's doubtful that Raymond would ever have forgiven them. Their fate would have been excommunication. Richmond was different, though. Even her criticism of him in the press was insufficient to destroy his rapport with her. 'He used to say I was his only proper friend,' Richmond later confessed.

Her departure inaugurated a period when Raymond's nightly trawls of the West End theatre bars in the company of Tony Power and the others became more excessive, his consumption expanding from alcohol and cigarettes to cocaine.

The domestic turmoil experienced by Raymond found a parallel in his daughter's life, her refusal to abandon her show-business aspirations in favour of marriage and motherhood hastening the dissolution of her relationship with Paul Musetti. In a tacit acknowledgement that her singing career might not prove the success she'd hoped, Debbie was already considering the possibility of copying her father by becoming a theatrical impresario. She didn't see herself producing nude shows, however. She envisaged specialising in drama pitched at the youth market. Though Raymond was a long way from the official retirement age, she claimed he found it comforting to know she was capable of taking over his theatre business whenever he wanted to relinquish control of it.

After Debbie had split up with her boyfriend, Fiona Richmond became the co-tenant of her penthouse in the Barbican. The two flatmates got on so well that they soon went on holiday together to New York. There, they saw and enjoyed *Women behind Bars*, a lewd, expletive-filled stage parody of 1950s Hollywood prison movies. When they returned to Britain, they set about putting on a London production of it, starring Richmond and Divine, the obese American drag artiste, soon to find cult acclaim through the films of John Waters. For a fee of £1,000 per week and a share of the box-office takings, Raymond agreed to provide a venue for the show that summer: not the Whitehall nor the Windmill but the Boulevard, a small upstairs theatre which he'd established next to the Revuebar.

Now approaching its twentieth birthday, the Revuebar had, by January 1977, long ceased to be somewhere you were likely to spot celebrities or well-heeled City gents. Like anything fashionable, it had been preordained to become *unfashionable*. In the world of Soho clubs there was nothing unusual about this arcing trajectory.

For Raymond's club, the cycle had already been completed before what promised to be the *coup de grâce* had been administered by the rise of feminism, or what was then labelled 'the Women's Liberation Movement'. In late 1970, with the publication of Germaine Greer's bestselling polemic *The Female Eunuch*, British feminism had acquired its manifesto, though the movement had taken a few years to establish itself on this side of the Atlantic. Women, Greer's book argued, should be freed from the tyranny of male stereotyping and condescension. Striptease, along with softcore pornography and other manifestations of the permissive society, no longer seemed sophisticated or amusing. Instead, it came to be regarded as degrading, seedy and exploitative, all part of the process whereby women are turned into objects of male sexual gratification.

Defending his business against feminist criticism, Raymond said of his nude employees, 'They get paid. No woman has to do it. Perhaps it's *them* that's exploiting men.'

Only by marketing the Revuebar abroad had Raymond been able to ensure that his venerable creation continued to flourish while preserving an upmarket flavour distinct from its increasingly tawdry rivals. These days the customers herded across the bridge into its auditorium were mainly besuited Japanese businessmen, the lack of any speech in the shows designed to cater for them. Bobbies walking the beat in Soho would frequently be stopped by lost Orientals, wanting directions to 'Way-mon Wevue-bar'. Once they found their way to Walker's Court, they'd have to fork out large sums to watch Raymond's cast of supple, anatomically flawless performers: pedigree girls who looked as if they were the product of some sinister selective breeding programme.

To his annoyance, he'd noticed that a lot of would-be strippers were being told by their boyfriends not to accept jobs at the Revuebar. Highlighting the hypocrisy that prevailed among so many men, he said, 'The guy is prepared to come to the show and look at other girls nude, but he doesn't like *his* girl being nude.'

Despite the Revuebar's £41,000-per-week turnover, Raymond was pessimistic about its capacity to survive much longer. When he appeared in mid-January 1977 as a guest on LBC, the London radio station, he conceded that striptease was finished. A week later the *Guardian* journalist Alex Hamilton questioned him about his surprising and ill-judged admission. The scene of their encounter was the Whitehall Theatre on the opening night of Raymond's new show which starred Warren Mitchell as Alf Garnett, the comic bigot from the popular BBC Television series *Till Death Us Do Part*. Like a beleaguered cabinet minister trying to wriggle out of a difficult situation, Raymond backtracked on his previous admission by claiming that 'when he said strip was finished he only meant that so was the circus and the gin palace and the music hall', all of which survived on a vastly reduced scale, even if they *were* sliding towards extinction.

Over at the Old Bailey that spring, Bill Moody, Wally Virgo and four junior officers faced an aggregate of twenty-seven charges arising from the investigation into Soho-based police corruption. Jimmy Humphreys appeared as the star prosecution witness. His evidence helped to secure convictions against all six defendants, though Virgo would ultimately be freed by the Court of Appeal.

While Jimmy was reinforcing his reputation in the Soho underworld as that most despised of creatures, an informer, a nark, Raymond was supervising the release of *Frankly Fiona*, which had been given a cynical new title. Using the type of deceitful marketing ploy common to so many 1970s British sexploitation films, it was now called *Hardcore* and billed as 'the frankly sensational adventures of a liberated lady'. Its emphatically *softcore* contents were, of course, doomed to disappoint its audience.

The film was due to be launched in April at the recently reopened Moulin Cinema, just up the road from the Windmill Theatre. To publicise the release of *Hardcore*, Richmond posed outside the cinema where press photographers took shots of her, bare breasted and grinning as she clutched a bunch of bananas in one hand and a jumbo cucumber in the other. But the film's misleading marketing couldn't save it from becoming a box-office failure. It was swiftly replaced at the Moulin by the future football club-owner David Sullivan's *Come Play with Me*, another British sex comedy promoted with an even more disingenuous advertising campaign.

Two weeks after that, a large poster suddenly appeared outside the Windmill Theatre. Devised by Raymond and his staff, the poster exploited recurrent news stories about the rising jobless figure. 'Don't be one of the one-and-a-half million unemployed', it read. The poster offered 'attractive boys and girls' a wage of £100 a week.

This conjured free publicity in the *Daily Mirror* as well as a lengthy queue, comprising about 150 applicants, mostly young men, some of them students, others long-term unemployed. Of those hopefuls, only a small proportion went on to the second round of auditions, for which ten applicants were given jobs as nudes in various productions of Raymond's, including the demurely titled *Penetration: An Erotic Adventure in French Pornography*, which was running at the Boulevard Theatre.

During mid-June, Ken Drury and two of his former colleagues took their places in the dock for the last of the big police corruption trials, stemming from the investigation commissioned by Lord Longford. Again, Jimmy Humphreys accepted the role of star prosecution witness. And again the parade of disquieting testimony raised but failed to address the question of how such rampant corruption could have flourished within the Metropolitan Police without the knowledge and connivance of the defendants' colleagues.

As the trial edged towards its denouement, *Women behind Bars* opened to largely unenthusiastic reviews, the best of them praising Divine's 'performance of outrageous splendour'. Reportedly costing £30,000 to produce, the show – in which Divine played the prison matron and Richmond was cast as a new inmate with a winning habit of shedding her clothes – would nevertheless run for almost five months.

Indignant at suggestions that her father had provided her stake in the production, Debbie defended her illusory financial independence by telling a journalist from the *Daily Express*: 'I've been working since I was four years old... I've earned a lot of money and invested it wisely. Daddy *did* help me there. I want to make a lot more money in my own right. As Paul Raymond's daughter I could just sit here eating chocolates and going out with terrible people who are interested in me only because of who I am. But that's not my way. I am a worker.'

Her work also extended to plugging away at her singing career. It acquired renewed impetus through a chance encounter with Jonathan Hodge, an extrovert, jocular thirty-five-year-old who composed everything from advertising jingles to film scores, the most prominent of these being the music to *Villain* (1971), the Kray twins-inspired movie starring Richard Burton and Ian McShane. What made him potentially useful to Debbie's career was that, in between composing music, he produced records, many of them released on his own label. 'I became a friend of Debbie's while she was still with Paul Musetti who lived next door to me in Tavistock Court in Bloomsbury,' Hodge remembered. 'I met her one night when there was this terrible crashing noise outside the building. I went rushing over to help and discovered she'd smashed her car into a lamp-post. You could tell she'd had a bevy or two. She wasn't badly hurt, but I took her round to University College Hospital's Accident and Emergency Department and managed to ward off the police until Raymond turned up.'

Hodge – whose tinted, round-framed glasses, luxuriant sideburns, droopy fringe and Zapata moustache accentuated his resemblance to John Lennon – was soon writing the lyrics to what would be Debbie's first record. Taking his cue from the recent popularity of several so-called 'jingles-to-singles', he fitted these whimsical lines to the melody he'd composed for a new television advert promoting the British Leyland motor company. He called the song 'You And I'. Against a disco backing, indebted to black American music, fuzzy guitars meshing with a brass section, Debbie's thin voice struggled to make the lyrics audible. The recording was released on Hodge's label, Pepper Records, her status as Raymond's daughter enabling her to obtain a smattering of coverage for it. Despite being distributed by the United Artists conglomerate and promoted by Mickie Most, one of the leading song-pluggers, it failed to register on the British Top 30 singles chart.

# 41 PLAYBOY OF THE WEST END WORLD

**A** COUPLE OF WEEKS after the launch of *Women behind Bars*, Ken Drury and one of the other officers standing trial at the Old Bailey found themselves headlining in a widely reviewed production of *Detectives behind Bars*. Under the royal prerogative of mercy, Jimmy Humphreys was then released from prison as a reward for his part in the successful prosecution of Drury, Moody and Co.

Humphreys and his wife, their reputations ruined, left London and bought a guest house in Southend. By then, they'd disposed of most of their Soho property empire, the sudden availability of so many freeholds inevitably pushing prices down. Property values had also been eroded by the downfall of the OPS which had done such a lot to reduce the risks inherent in the porn business.

With typically good timing, Raymond chose 1977 as the year for a second major round of property acquisitions. Buying an average of one freehold a week, many of these on Old Compton, Dean and Brewer Streets, he soon became the landlord of more than a hundred buildings. Each purchase, he said, gave him a 'thrill'. For him, the map of Soho began to resemble a Monopoly board. Immediately he bought any building, recalled a property developer who worked closely with him, he'd be interested in acquiring the one next door. To conceal the scope of his holdings, these purchases were made through companies in which Raymond wasn't listed as either a director or shareholder, the growing secrecy of his property dealings paradoxically coexisting with his insistent self-promotion. That secrecy would, in turn, backfire by piquing the curiosity of journalists and fortifying the image of him as someone who had things to hide.

Property wasn't his only astute acquisition that year. As the PRO expanded and diversified, he sought to alter the way it was managed, to delegate more of the day-to-day tasks. These management changes centred on the creation of the post of chief executive. He offered this to a young, pipe-smoking South African barrister named Carl Snitcher, who was employed as assistant director and legal officer of Equity, an organisation that had striven to prevent the exploitation of nude performers. The requisite incentive for Snitcher to defect was provided by a fivefold pay rise. It would prove one of Raymond's soundest investments, his new employee quickly establishing himself as a friend and faithful lieutenant whose legal expertise became invaluable.

By now duplicating her father's penchant for not only alcohol but also cocaine, Debbie attracted renewed interest from gossip columns when she started dating Jonathan Hodge, who moved into her flat in the Barbican. As someone in the music business, someone 'doing well', he fulfilled both of the requirements she'd listed as prerequisites for any potential husband. They hadn't been together for long before Raymond received a phone call from Debbie to announce that she and her boyfriend were planning to get married.

'She was desperate to tie the knot,' Hodge recalled. 'She kept going on and on and on about it. One night when we were sitting in a club called the Tatty Bogle, I eventually gave in and said, "Oh, go on then." She immediately rushed out to the nearest phone box to let Raymond know.'

Her father, who got on well with his prospective son-in-law, gave his stamp of approval to the marriage. Jean was similarly affirmative about it: so much so that she admitted to feeling extremely happy for Debbie.

Raymond and Debbie then started making elaborate arrangements for the ceremony, scheduled for Saturday, 14 January 1978.

A walnut-brown tan advertising her prosperity, Jean flew into Britain on the Sunday before the wedding. Superficially at least, prolonged separation had alleviated the tensions between mother and daughter, Debbie even venturing to describe Jean as a 'super' person.

On the day her plane touched down, Raymond drove Jean through London in his Rolls-Royce. She subsequently said how 'stunned' Raymond had been by the news that she too was planning to marry a musician. Her husband-to-be, who had given her a £20,000 engagement ring which she enjoyed showing off, was Monroe Powell, recently recruited lead singer of the Platters, a black vocal group with a fluid line-up, whose heyday as a popular rock 'n' roll act had been during the 1950s.

The new-found understanding between Jean and her volatile daughter survived only a few days. It ended when Jean had her first exposure to the abrupt mood swings precipitated by Debbie's heavy drinking and cocaine-taking. 'She called me and snapped, "You're an old cow and I don't want you at my wedding!"' Jean said.

In advance of the nuptials, though, things had been smoothed over, the outburst consigned to Jean's bulging mental scrapbook of her daughter's misdemeanours. But the truce didn't hold. Jean later described being on the phone to Monroe Powell, currently on an American tour, when Raymond and daughter had rolled up. 'They were both high as kites,' Jean added. 'She started screaming and trying to break down the doors and accused her boyfriend and me of having an affair. We'd only met half an hour earlier. The next day everything was back to normal.'

'It was all very odd,' Jonathan Hodge remembered. 'I liked Jean but, apart from anything else, she wasn't my type. I think it was an anti-mum thing rather than an anti-*me* thing. I remember Debbie complaining, "My mother can't leave anything alone…"'

Raymond spent the night before the wedding staying at the Barbican with Debbie and his future son-in-law. 'While he was with us, I had a hairdresser friend over to do my hair, so she did his, too – or, at least, she glued his comb-over into position,' Hodge said. 'We started drinking quite early on the day of the wedding. We were all pretty merry when we got to Finsbury Register Office that morning.'

Both the bride and her husband-to-be arrived there wearing all-white outfits. Hodge had donned a white bomber jacket, matching trousers, plus tennis shoes. And his bride had chosen flowing robes that made her look as if she was playing Aphrodite in some cheesy 1950s sword-and-sandal movie. By turning up in an ankle-length white mink coat, Jean provoked another row with Debbie, who felt in danger of being upstaged.

After the marriage ceremony was over, Debbie and her new husband posed for pictures outside the register office. 'In the background of one of the photos,' Hodge recalled, 'there was a double-decker bus going past. It had an advert along the side that read, "Enter a different world…" I didn't think much of it at the time, but that sign was something of a portent.'

From Islington, the group moved on to the grand setting of the chapel at the Savoy Hotel, where Raymond had arranged for the marriage to be blessed by Canon Edwyn Young. Raymond's old friend had lately achieved the unique distinction of rising from being padre of a strip-club to being Chaplain to the Queen. Once the blessing ceremony was over, the wedding party climbed into a line of pristine vintage cars which Raymond had hired. These processed from the Savoy to a hotel in Kensington for the reception, where the half-sozzled groom gave a thank-you speech, his efforts bested by a witty routine from that most practised of raconteurs, Victor Spinetti, whom Raymond had invited. Their ill-assorted audience comprised more than two hundred guests, including the squiffy-looking Canon Young, a sprinkling of porn models, the chart-topping singer Steve Harley, the television sitcom star Robin Nedwell, and Hodge's formally attired father, a banker and poet manqué whose writing had been praised by T. S. Eliot.

☆

*Debbie Raymond and Jonathan Hodge photographed at their wedding*

In the months immediately after their daughter's wedding, Jean had married her fiancé. She and Monroe Powell were now living in Las Vegas. Around June or July they travelled to London together, where Debbie had arranged for her husband to record some of the Platters' new songs. Debbie had also arranged for Jean, Monroe Powell and the rest of the band to stay with them at the Barbican. 'We had a great time,' Hodge

Raymond delivers a speech at his daughter's wedding reception

Past animosity set aside, Paul and Jean Raymond enjoy a lighthearted moment at the reception

Showing off his sartorial finery, Howard Raymond stands next to the vintage Rolls-Royce used to transport the bride and groom from the Chapel at the Savoy to the reception

Paul Raymond and Fiona Richmond at the reception

*The Reverend Edwyn
Young with two
prospective converts*

recalled. 'Raymond would sometimes join us. We'd have chilli-con-
carne-cooking competitions to find out who could make the hottest one.
It was all very silly. There were people screaming with laughter.'

But the mood of jollity was, for Jean, truncated by an incident at the
recording studios used by Pepper Records. 'While we were at the studios I
heard two girls talking about Debbie,' Jean said. 'She herself had recorded
a few songs there. To my horror I heard one of them say my daughter was
bad news and a junkie. I got straight on to Paul who twisted my words
and told Debbie that her mother was spreading it around that she was a
drug addict.

'I will never forget her phone-call to me. She swore at me, called me
all the names under the sun and said she never wanted to see me again.'

Unlike Raymond, though, Jean remained close to Howard, who had,
until recently, been living with her in Florida. There, he'd worked as a

$45-a-day bellhop and as a tennis pro, and latterly he'd been training to be a press photographer. But he lacked the unrelenting ambition that Paul and Debbie shared and which provided yet another bond between father and daughter.

'Howard was a big disappointment to Paul,' remembered Raymond's old friend Noel Botham. This sense of paternal disappointment appears to have been rooted in Howard's aversion to fulfilling his anointed role as heir to his father's business empire. Instead, Howard – a quiet, laid-back, unobtrusive young man – often talked about 'doing his own thing'. The situation can't have been helped when Howard moved back to England and, without telling his father, married Maria Labriola, an American former waitress whom he'd met in Florida.

One of seven children, brought up in an impoverished household, Howard's beautiful young bride had curly black hair and a darkish complexion, inherited from her Italian father and South American Indian mother. Her marriage to Howard took place at Chelsea Register Office that November. The ceremony gave her a taste of the poisonous rivalry between Howard and his sister, who had picked up tips from their mother in the art of upstaging the bride. Debbie 'did not say a lot, just "Does Dad know?" and smiled through gritted teeth,' Maria recalled. 'But when it was time for the photos she came barrelling down the stairs in this fur coat down to the ground and plunged in front of me, so I was buried behind this big fur coat. She had to be moved aside.'

Until Howard took her into Soho that evening and showed her round the theatres and offices owned by his father, Maria had no idea of either the nature or the extent of the Raymond fortune. All she'd previously known about her future father-in-law was that he was a businessman.

Raymond had been out of the country on the day of the wedding. He first heard about it through Debbie's husband, who'd been deputed to break the news to him. 'Paul was very pissed off with Howard for not telling him about it,' Hodge commented.

Speaking about her first encounter with Raymond, Howard's wife recollected, 'We met in the bar at the Raymond Revuebar. He had an aura of power about him and everybody, I mean *everybody*, hovered around him and seemed to idolise him. He was pleasant to my face but I soon found out he was telling everyone, "She is just a gold digger. It will be only a matter of time before she starts asking me for things."'

His suspicion about his new daughter-in-law's motives receded as she and Howard embarked on a frugal existence in a small rented flat in Maida Vale, furnished with what little they could afford. 'In the end,' she said, 'Raymond was proud that we had a nice proper existence.'

That April marked the twenty-first anniversary of the launch of the Revuebar – an occasion that called for a celebration. On Monday, 23 April 1979 Raymond obliged by hosting an extravagant party at the Inn on the Park hotel, situated at the Mayfair end of Hyde Park. Victor Spinetti was recruited to give a speech to several hundred guests, whom he jokily addressed as a 'rent-a-crowd'. They encompassed other old pals such as Diana Dors, very overweight these days but still vivacious, charming and witty; plus Canon Edwyn Young, who spent part of the evening in the company of a busty South American model. Some of the Revuebar's erstwhile performers were there as well, among them Ted Haskell and his wife Renée. So too were many of Raymond's showbiz acquaintances, few more famous than the singers Neil Sedaka and Maurice Gibb, whose triumphant careers Debbie – known to the tabloids as 'the Porn Princess' – still had hopes of emulating.

Her next bid for chart success was a song called 'Perfumed Garden', written and produced by her husband. Raymond arranged for the head photographer from Paul Raymond Publications to shoot a series of publicity shots that played on the song's Chinese allusions. It elicited another ripple of interest from the press, the *Daily Express* cooing compliantly over the way she'd harnessed 'a little bit of magic' to 'a lot of hard work', but it ended up being shelved by United Artists.

She was left to concentrate on a more successful career recording jingles for television adverts. Her employers included Pepsi-Cola, McDonald's and Mothercare. Most famously, she belted out the lyrics used to promote the Yellow Pages phone directory. Whenever she had the chance, she'd recreate her performance, dropping one shoulder, cupping her palms round imaginary headphones, then navigating her voice into a coordinate somewhere between Land's End and New York as she sang its refrain.

Influenced by his daughter, Raymond had been cultivating a youthful style, faintly ridiculous in someone approaching his fifty-ninth birthday, even someone with such an obstinately youthful waistline and way of life. He grew his hair and had it permed, his ears and collar concealed beneath shaggy, spaniel-like flaps. He dispensed with his beard in favour of the same type of Mexican moustache worn by Debbie's husband. He acquired a pair of tinted glasses. He chose more modern suits. And he took to combining them with matching open-necked shirts, his accustomed tie making way for a medallion on a long gold chain. Those weren't his only favoured accoutrements. His other preferred accessory was a striking young woman, boasting a prominent cleavage and skin that appeared to have been airbrushed to perfection. In short, he now resembled a drug-toting gangster from an American cop show – *Starsky and Hutch* perhaps, or *Kojak*. While this may have helped him blend into the West End bars and nightclubs he frequented, it projected a message that surely contributed to rumours about his links to organised crime.

Other than his devotion to his daughter, little remained of the family life in which he'd once been a peripheral participant. His feelings were reciprocated by Debbie who, whenever the opportunity arose, gave gushing interviews to the press about his sterling qualities as a father and businessman.

The closeness of the ties binding him to his daughter hadn't been frayed by her marriage. He and Debbie continued to socialise together, joined by Jonathan Hodge, who provided Raymond with genial company for marathon drinking sessions, the two of them often staying up until the early hours and knocking back as much as a bottle and a half of cognac. 'I always liked him, even if he did have a one-track mind. And I'm not talking about sex,' Hodge said. 'It was money, money, money. But he could be very generous. He kept offering me strange gifts: diamond-encrusted Cartier watches and pendants. They were the sort of thing he liked himself, but they were a little gaudy for my taste. I think of him sometimes as the Mayor of Toytown. You could hear him coming as the chains rattled.

'I remember having a conversation with him about launching an erotic magazine that men could take home and their womenfolk would be interested in: one with soft-focus photography where people could use their imaginations about what might be happening. And he said, "I don't think so, Jonathan. I'll stick with what, I know, works. There are hundreds of dirty bastards out there who like the kind of magazines I produce."

'Dinner parties were where you'd see a less endearing side to his personality. He'd start winding up Debbie and Howard. I'm not sure why he did it. I suppose it was about control, about probing their loyalty. He'd be sitting next to some new glam thing from the Revuebar and wink at us and say straight faced to Debbie, "This is going to be the new Mrs Raymond..." Debbie would look as if the roof was about to cave in.'

Returning from a business trip with Raymond that spring, Debbie announced to her bemused husband that she wanted a divorce. 'Raymond told me he was upset about Debbie's marriage breaking up,' one of Raymond's friends recalled. 'He always used to say that her biggest weakness was that she was constantly falling in love. All the same, I got the feeling she could do no wrong in his eyes. I think he made an effort to get on with whoever she was with.'

She left her husband for David Wilkie, the strapping, dark-haired, dark-moustached former swimmer, famous for winning a gold medal at the 1976 Olympics, her liaison with him meriting a snide reference in the *Daily Express*'s famous 'William Hickey' gossip column. Wilkie's healthy-living, athletic past apparently rendered him incompatible with the Raymond clan, yet his medal-winning style of swimming couldn't have been more appropriate – the breaststroke.

In an echo of what Raymond had endured years earlier, Jonathan Hodge received a threatening answerphone message soon after Debbie's departure. Hodge suspected that his soon-to-be-former father-in-law was behind it. The message had been left by two men with cockney accents who said they'd slash the tyres of his car and blow up the car with him inside. Hodge took this so seriously that he hired a couple of ex-SAS bodyguards and reported the threats to the police, who kept the answerphone tape as evidence. Somehow news of the incident reached the *Daily Mirror* which ran an article about it, bolstering the perception that Raymond had links, however indirect, with the underworld – a perception Raymond had grown accustomed to dismissing, his tone mocking and contemptuous of such an absurd idea.

The involvement of the police and the bodyguards failing to act as a deterrent, Hodge was on the receiving end of other threatening phone calls and had menacing notes left under the windscreen wipers of his car. 'I'm sure they were just copycat messages,' Hodge concluded. 'By far the creepiest part of this whole saga came when my divorce lawyer asked me to retrieve that answerphone tape from the police. But the cops told me they'd mislaid it. I'm certain Raymond was behind that. He had an amazing web of contacts.

'After the divorce came through, I met him in Morton's, a nice restaurant in Berkeley Square, mainly frequented by music people. I think Raymond must've gone there especially to talk to me. He said, "Come on over and have a drink." And I said, "Oh, fuck off, Paul, I'm annoyed with you." So he sent Charles, his chauffeur, over to have a word with me. Charles said, "Please have a drink with him. He's lonely." When I went over to Paul's table, I said, "What was all that shit with the answerphone message about?" He replied, "I thought you needed a distraction because you could've taken Debbie to the cleaners in the divorce court."

'There's always the possibility he might've been pulling my leg. It was sometimes hard to tell with Paul. I couldn't help liking him, though.'

# 42 WHEN THE KING OF PORN MET THE QUEEN OF CLEAN

THE FORMULA APPLIED to *Club International* was still very popular, its lavishly staged pin-ups seasoned with textual erotica sophisticated enough to embrace 'Vaginismus', an early short story by Ian McEwan, who would go on to win the Booker Prize. In the spring of 1979 the magazine – now retitled *Club* – stirred up ample controversy by alerting the press to the fact that it was about to publish nude photos of Jackie Onassis, President John F. Kennedy's widow. These had been taken with a telephoto lens while she was sunbathing on a privately owned Greek island.

Early that July, Raymond strove to match this publicity coup. Utilising the national newspapers as a convenient messenger, he made a slyly facetious and deliberately provocative offer to Anna Ford, the young television newsreader whose broad-cheekboned good looks had won her an ardent following. He offered her £50,000 to pose nude for *Club*. Whatever her response, he was bound to profit from the stunt. In the unlikely event that she accepted the money, *Club* would benefit from enormous amounts of free publicity and sales to match. Even if she turned him down, his magazine would still receive a useful burst of coverage.

'It was a perfectly serious offer,' Raymond told the *News of the World* when she failed to respond. 'Almost every man in Britain would like to see her with her clothes off.'

As a way of prolonging this self-propelled news story, he went ahead and upped his offer to £75,000, though the extra cash failed to persuade Anna Ford to pose for the delectation of all those dirty bastards who'd helped to make him wealthy.

Probably motivated by his relish for self-promotion and his combative streak, Raymond was in Norwich on Thursday, 2 August to take part in a debate with Mary Whitehouse, who remained one of his most resolute and strident adversaries. His magazines were, she'd recently stated, 'a violation of the most basic of human rights – privacy'.

The scene of the broadcast discussion between her and Raymond was the studios of Anglia Television, the small independent station that broadcast across East Anglia. Nattily dressed, Raymond arrived clasping a dinky black manbag. As if practising subtle oneupmanship, his owlishly bespectacled opponent carried a white handbag that dwarfed its counterpart. Like Margaret Thatcher, the new prime minister, she had a starchy dress sense, its well-pressed headmistressy formality accentuated by a hairstyle no more flexible than her outlook.

She and Raymond took their seats in front of a clamorous Labour Party-dominated audience of fifty of the city's councillors. With bulky television cameras recording every gesture, Raymond and Whitehouse began their debate, the state of Britain's pornography laws yielding an area of unexpected harmony. Both panellists agreed the laws were shambolic but differed on how those statutes should be amended. Raymond said the trouble with the porn laws was that nobody knew what was permissible and what wasn't. Clarification was necessary, he argued. The answer, he added, was a Porn Board, working on the same principle as the Gaming Board, which regulated gambling.

Raymond's suggestion met with scornful head-shaking by his opponent.

After what a *Daily Mail* reporter described with euphemistic delight as 'a frank exchange of views', the phalanx of local councillors was required to vote for the panellist whose views they endorsed. The result was nine abstentions and a 24–17 victory for Mary Whitehouse.

Though Raymond had lost this skirmish, the war was going his way. In the closing week of November, the thirteen-strong committee set up by the previous government to investigate the laws on obscenity delivered its report. Chaired by Professor Frank Williams from Cambridge University, it reached a unanimous conclusion, the tenor of which was measured and tolerant. What became known as the Williams Report recommended, with certain safeguards, liberalising the law. But the discussion about pornography continued.

Within weeks of the report's publication Raymond took part in another debate, aired by a provincial television station, the adversarial role played this time by Lord Longford. Their host was the blousy forty-nine-year-old Diana Dors who had, following a pilot programme featuring Mary Whitehouse, just been granted her own chat show by Southern Television. Sadly, the programme, entitled *Open Dors*, hasn't survived. Nor is there any other record of Raymond's encounter with Lord Porn.

During the three and a half years since Fiona Richmond's departure, a troop of photogenic young women had writhed across the mirrored ceiling of Raymond's bedroom, his dissolute charm, enduring fame, conspicuous wealth and reputation as a roué probably acting as aphrodisiacs. Part of the reason for this high turnover was that several of his girfriends had expressed a desire to have children, the mere mention of which justified him breaking off a relationship.

His latest girlfriend was Di Cochran, a party-loving twenty-year-old former public schoolgirl with fashionably short blonde hair and an ambition to become an actress, her prospects not improved by a voice that sounded as if she had too many teeth. She could easily have been a slightly more grown-up version of the friends Debbie had while she

*Paul Raymond pictured in the type of shot that became familiar to readers of tabloid newspapers, 1981*

was at Cheltenham Ladies' College. Her pukka background must have appealed to the self-confessed vein of snobbery that Raymond had inherited from his mother.

Unlike most of her predecessors, she made more than just a few guest appearances on his bedroom ceiling. To the dismay of her parents, she and Raymond were soon living together at Fitzhardinge House, their shared taste for kinky sex sealing their compatibility and earning her the nickname 'Dirty Di'. 'One night Paul and I were out late and went to Tramp nightclub,' she confessed soon after she'd moved in with him. 'We met a beautiful girl there and invited her back to the flat. We'd all had a lot of champagne. The girl started pouring perfume over both of us. Raymond just laughed. Then we moved into the bedroom. She and I had a naughty nude frolic on Paul's king-size bed. It's rather exciting when you know you really shouldn't. I'm not a lesbian. We were just having some fun. Paul had his turn as well. He's very virile. Two of us was no problem for him. He's a very gentle and considerate lover.'

Belatedly introduced to Cochran's parents, Raymond succeeded in winning over her mother, though her father – a specialist in aeronautical navigation systems – remained steadfast in his disapproval. The attitude of Cochran's father was reiterated by Fiona Richmond, poised to star in Raymond's next stage comedy at the Whitehall Theatre. When Raymond arranged for Cochran to have a small role in the new show, *Wot! No Pyjamas!*, Richmond was appalled. On the grounds that Cochran had no acting talent, Richmond threatened to withdraw from the production, her enduring status as a box-office attraction rendering this a potent ultimatum.

Ruthless enough to give the show's commercial prospects priority over Cochran's feelings, Raymond agreed to drop his girlfriend from the cast. But he clearly disagreed with Richmond about Cochran's abilities as an actress because he assigned her one of the starring roles in the immodestly titled *Paul Raymond's Erotica*, the soft porn movie he'd helped his long-time collaborator James Kenelm Clarke set up.

The movie, conceived as little more than an extended advert for the Revuebar, had a reputed budget of £1.5 million, vastly more than any comparable film. It was due to be directed by Brian Smedley-Aston, who had been the producer on all three of their previous collaborations. Unafraid to provoke well-founded accusations that it was a vanity project, Raymond cast himself in another of the lead roles and also arranged for Debbie to provide some of the music – a dated disco score. For the central role, he and Kenelm Clarke obtained the services of Brigitte Lahaie, a peroxide-blonde French hardcore porn actress. She was cast as a journalist sent to London to research a magazine feature about the Revuebar, research consisting of little else but athletic and often orgiastic sex with most of the people she met, generally before she'd had time to say more than '*Bonjour*' to them. Her conquests, destined to be intercut with a show at the Revuebar, included an aristocratic *Men Only* photographer, played with mumbling ineptitude by Cochran.

Sensibly, Raymond neither participated in Lahaie's ecstatic workouts nor shed any of his clothing. He was also prudent enough to appear in a role that the Hollywood star Errol Flynn would have branded 'NAR', No Acting Required. It was a role that Raymond had been perfecting for decades – himself.

He featured in several scenes, the first of these showing him being interviewed about the Revuebar by Lahaie. Others involved him auditioning strippers alongside Carl Snitcher, chatting with Tony Power in the PRO's offices, and dispensing champagne to a gaggle of naked girls aboard *Veste Demite* as it cruised provocatively past the Houses of Parliament. Even though no acting seemed to be required, he looked ill at ease in front of the camera, the gaucherie of his performance demonstrating just how much artifice goes into the appearance of *not* acting.


Margaret Thatcher had been elected as prime minister of a Conservative government during the spring of 1979. It was an occasion that Raymond treated as a cause for celebration. Everything about him, everything from his wardrobe to his involvement in pornography, made him an unlikely supporter of the new premier, yet he felt that her free market policies would benefit business in general and *his* business in particular.

To demonstrate his backing for her and to capitalise on a tantalising opportunity, he offered to sponsor her twenty-six-year-old son Mark, who was trying to forge a career as a motor-racing driver. On behalf of *Men Only*, Raymond proposed a £25,000 deal that would underwrite the cost of competing in a forthcoming race at Brands Hatch.

His proposal led to the prime minister's son scheduling a meeting with him for Friday, 15 February 1980. The venue was Raymond's office at the Windmill Theatre, the entrance to which was surrounded by reporters and press photographers who had, possibly thanks to a tip-off from Raymond's publicist, got wind of the meeting. Several prostitutes, meanwhile, hovered in front of the theatre, asking passers-by if they'd 'like some action'.

Dressed in a sports jacket and looking a bit sheepish, Mark Thatcher cut through the crowd and went into the theatre for his meeting with Raymond who, for public consumption at least, viewed him as 'a very sincere young man with a great respect for his mother, his father and his country'.

A little later, Raymond and the would-be recipient of his cash appeared briefly outside the Windmill. Raymond read from a short press statement they'd prepared together. He said, 'We sincerely hope that over the next few days an arrangement will be made whereby Mark Thatcher will be involved in a "Racing for Britain" team.'

Already the butt of criticism from MPs and trades unionists for accepting sponsorship from a foreign company, the Thatchers' son came under pressure that weekend. Despite Downing Street officials briefing the press that his business affairs were of no concern to the government, his mother told him not to accept Raymond's offer. By Monday the deal had been rejected, sparing the prime minister the embarrassment of being associated with Raymond.

The political wisdom of her decision, never in doubt, was swiftly validated. Confirmation took the form of an incident whereby Raymond outraged Pamela Stephenson, one of the stars of the hit television sketch show *Not the Nine O'Clock News*. Stephenson was furious that he'd sanctioned the publication in *Club* – the magazine that had lately reverted to being called *Club International* – of nude photos of her. These had been lifted from the 1977 film *Stand Up, Virgin Soldiers*, in which she'd played a small role. 'Mr Raymond printed the beastly pictures without telling me,' she complained to the *Daily Mirror*. 'It was a rip-off.'

# 43 PAUL RAYMOND KILLED MY MOTHER

S INCE RAYMOND'S FIRST major round of property acquisitions, Soho had continued its descent into moral and physical grubbiness. Already occupied by an army of sex shops, dirty bookshops, clip-joints and strip-clubs whose furtive and more often than not lone clientele could be seen cruising the streets, the district now faced further incursions from the latest progeny of the sex industry – peepshows and so-called 'nude encounter parlours'. Flourishing briefly before the police closed them down, the latter offered punters the opportunity to touch and, if they were lucky, fondle naked girls. Peepshows were, in contrast, a more widespread and resilient phenomenon, the caustic tang of bleach leaking from their doorways, these characteristically fringed with bright yellow light-box signage proclaiming 'Peepshow' or 'Live Bed Show'. Customers, their bodies vibrating to the erotic thrum of disco music, would be ushered into rickety private booths where they'd slide a couple of fifty-pence coins into a slot, prompting an eye-level, letterbox-like flap to open. Through this, they'd have a view of a naked, bored-looking girl in sunglasses writhing on a platform two or three feet ahead of them. After about thirty seconds the letterbox would snap shut and the frustrated punter, his moist reverie so rudely interrupted, would be left to fumble for his wallet.

Soho was changing in other ways, too. Over at the Nell Gwynne, Soho's oldest surviving strip-club, a boom in stand-up comedy had begun. Around 11 p.m. each Saturday night, by which time the last item of lingerie had been unpeeled, the club hosted the Comedy Store, where a disparate group of amateur comedians performed. They included Alexei Sayle, Nigel Planer, Rik Mayall and Peter Richardson, representatives of a fresh generation of young performers. When Richardson, an impresario in the making, failed to persuade the owner of the Nell Gwynne to let them stage comedy shows every night, he started hunting for another venue.

'I went round Soho, looking at strip-clubs,' he remembered. 'I'd say to the guys on the door, "Can I come in and have a look round?" And they'd say, "No, you've gotta pay." And I'd say, "But I'm interested in putting on a stage show." And they'd go, "We're not interested. Fuck off." Eventually, through Ruby Wax, I heard about the Boulevard Theatre and went round to see Carl Snitcher. I said what I wanted to do, then Carl and Paul struck a very hard bargain. Basically, they said, "We'll take all your money." Well, almost all of it.'

In 1980 the Boulevard Theatre hosted the launch of the new two-nights-a-week club, which would soon establish itself as the cradle of what the press christened 'alternative comedy'. 'On the first night Paul and I had a bit of a falling out because I'd called it the Comic Strip,' Richardson recalled. 'And he said, "I won't allow you to use the word 'strip'." He insisted on me amending the poster in the glass case outside. The "S" in "Strip" had to be covered with lots of little stars, so the club ended up looking as if it was called "the Comic Trip".'

Next to the amended lettering was a picture of a large black Second World War-era bomb descending on London, the words 'Have a nice day' chalked on its flank. As the new club shared the Revuebar's main entrance, this was on one side of the door and a poster for the Festival of Erotica was on the other. To get into the Comic Strip, its predominantly middle-class, university-educated customers also had to walk past numerous glossy photos of buxom strippers that lined the staircase, a sight capable of endowing their visit with a gratifying frisson of rebellion against liberal anti-sexist orthodoxy. 'I remember seeing the members of this left-wing collective house arguing about whether or not they should even set foot in the building,' Alexei Sayle recollected.

Raymond was in the audience for the Comic Strip's first show. 'Keith Allen came on and began this really rough-and-ready act,' Peter Richardson recalled. 'Right away he says, "I'm going to play a song now called 'Paul Raymond Killed My Mother'". And he points at Raymond and says, "See that bastard over there... You know what's really stupid: he won't allow the word 'strip' to be used outside this theatre." Then Keith just laid into him. I thought our club was finished, but Raymond came over to me later and said, "*Fantastic.* Don't worry about what that bloke said about me. I don't give a damn what anybody thinks about me." He told me he loved the show and that it'd run and run.'

His prediction about the Comic Strip's prospects was accurate. It soon became so popular that two shows had to be squeezed in each evening, and so fashionable that musicians such as David Bowie and George Harrison, film stars such as Dustin Hoffman and Jack Nicholson, writers such as Ian Hamilton and George Melly were trooping down Walker's Court and up the staircase of the Revuebar. 'Turn right for the Festival of Erotica, upstairs for the Comic Strip,' a tuxed bouncer would instruct them when they reached the lounge bar where Raymond would often be sitting. He'd frequently join them in the theatre.

A rock version of the theme music to *Crossroads*, the television soap opera synonymous with crumby sets and even crumbier storylines, heralded the arrival on stage of Alexei Sayle, the show's portly compère, who possessed the strutting gait of a seagull. Typically corseted by a shiny, multi-button suit, his convict haircut in harmony with the chin-thrusting belligerence of his demeanour, he'd launch into a chippy, Scouse-accented monologue, peppered with swear-words, the spotlights momentarily illuminating the spittle as it arced from his mouth. He'd deliver anti-Conservative asides – 'That Willie Whitelaw, half fucking bumblebee, the wanker'. And he'd lambast the audience, addressing them as 'cunts' and 'silly fuckers from Hampstead and Islington who'd been conned into paying four fucking quid in the hope of seeing something "alternative"...'

Any Japanese businessman who'd strayed into the Boulevard Theatre, expecting to ogle naked women, must have been severely disappointed.

Once Sayle, the venom of his invective leaving his face doused in sweat, had paced offstage, he was replaced by the Comic Strip's other performers, several of whom, Nigel Planer remarked, 'used to take the piss out of Raymond's funny haircut'. When the audience trooped into the lounge bar during the interval, they usually had the opportunity to savour the miraculous engineering of the famous Raymond coiffure. At the behest of Planer and the rest of the troupe, he'd been persuaded to turn off the non-stop porn videos normally screened in the vicinity of the bar.

The Comic Strip's regulars were two double-acts: Nigel Planer and Peter Richardson, plus Rik Mayall and Adrian Edmondson, who performed as 'the Dangerous Brothers' and 'Twentieth-Century Coyote'. In addition there were guest comedians, among them Chris Langham, Jennifer Saunders, Dawn French, Arnold Brown, Angus Deayton, Michael Palin and, on one occasion, even Robin Williams. 'Just as the show was about to end one night, he turned up and begged me to let him go onstage,' Peter Richardson said. 'Raymond insisted on us paying extra to keep the place open a bit longer than normal while Robin Williams did his act.'

After the show, Raymond would have a drink with Richardson and sometimes Sayle. 'Raymond was always very nice to me,' Richardson observed. 'But I think he prided himself on his reputation as a tough businessman. I'm sure he enjoyed acting the role of Mr Bastard. I remember the time when we were at the bar when Jennifer Saunders came over and blagged a cigarette off the barman. Raymond waited until she'd gone before calling the barman over and saying, "What were you doing there?" The barman said, "What's wrong?" To which Raymond said, "You gave that woman a cigarette." And the barman said, "Well, she asked me for one." And Raymond went, "But you could've sold her a *packet*..." I knew he did that just to show me he wasn't a soft touch.'

☆

That year Raymond snaffled the freeholds of most of the buildings in Walker's Court. Posing as an ally of the Soho Society, the residents' conservation and lobbying group founded eight years earlier, he claimed that these purchases had, in part, been motivated by a desire 'to keep out the Maltese' – a reference to the Maltese gangsters who still ran many of Soho's seedier clip-joints, sex shops and strip-clubs.

One of Raymond's new acquisitions was 9 Walker's Court, occupied by Kramers, a shoe shop which pre-dated the setting up of the Revuebar. In a letter to the Soho Society, he declared that there were too many sex shops in the area, so he was keen to prevent these premises going the same way. After he'd purchased the freehold on the building, he bought out the remainder of the lease, then applied to Westminster City Council for permission to turn Kramers into an amusement arcade. When his application for change of use was rejected, he leased the premises to a Maltese sex shop operator for £78,000 a year. That man was probably Charlie Grech, a smooth-talking twenty-seven-year-old with dark Mediterranean looks, who had recently taken over from Bernie Silver as kingpin of the West End sex industry.

Raymond already had strong business links to Grech, the reputation of whom was such that every Metropolitan Police officer had been banned from talking to him without reporting it to a senior colleague. Along with Silver, Grech had also been the subject of a front-page story in the *News of the World*, headlined 'Beware of This Pair'. For £3,000 a week Raymond rented premises to him on Old Compton Street, used for a tiny porn cinema called the Londoner. A further £4,000 a week from Grech had secured another of Raymond's Walker's Court shops. Grech ran a sex shop there, equipped with video booths in which customers could masturbate to the accompaniment of blue movies.

Accurate though Raymond's prediction about the popularity of the Comic Strip had been, the diminishing impact of his own activities as a theatre impresario called into question his recurrent boast about his gift for divining public taste. By the final week of January 1981, the Windmill Theatre was no longer flourishing. Nor was the Whitehall Theatre, where he'd been forced to close the production of *Wot! No Pyjamas!*, lately retitled by the backstage staff as *Wot! No Audience!*

Within the theatrical world there was a sense that he was out of touch, his preferred brand of entertainment appearing increasingly anachronistic in the new decade. Sex farces of the type he'd been producing so successfully had drifted out of fashion, perhaps because the novelty of onstage nudity had faded. Through the growing influence of feminism, there'd been an appreciable cultural shift. Plays that would, not so long ago, have been regarded as mainstream, plays that purveyed the bawdy humour of traditional seaside postcards, were now, at best, considered faintly reprehensible.

This change of mood had recently been reflected by legal action launched against Raymond by Greater London Council which objected to the posters outside the Whitehall Theatre, posters featuring photos of Fiona Richmond semi-naked. Another sign of the changing times was provided by the angrily lettered 'Sexist crap!' stickers that often tattooed the women on the adverts outside Raymond's theatres. 'We used to have to peel loads of the bloody things off every morning,' recalled one ex-Whitehall Theatre employee.

Back in the previous decade, Raymond had reacted to setbacks like the demise of *Wot! No Pyjamas!* by immediately replacing the show. Not this time, however. Unable to find a suitable production to take the place of Richmond's failed star vehicle, he mothballed his largest theatre. Formerly the source of bountiful profits, the Whitehall had become a financial liability. In the event that he couldn't find a bankable new show to stage there, he and Carl Snitcher drew up contingency plans to convert the building into what they called 'an all-day entertainment centre', featuring a restaurant, amusement arcade and facilities for cabaret. But those plans didn't have to be implemented.

Demonstrating a belated capacity to adjust to the cultural shift, Raymond agreed to stage a different type of farce at the Whitehall – farce minus the bare breasts. That show, directed by Dick Clement and written by John Wells, was *Anyone for Denis?* Based on a column Wells had created for the satirical magazine *Private Eye*, it portrayed Denis Thatcher, father of Mark and husband of Margaret, as a lovable buffoon, a prototypical Little Englander, mistrustful of Johnny Foreigner, his conversation sprinkled with offhand remarks that betrayed reflexive social and racial prejudice. It starred Wells as Denis, Angela Thorne as his wife, Joan Sanderson as their housekeeper, Nicholas Farrell as their over zealous bodyguard, and Edward Fox in two roles – as a priapic French diplomat and a booze-marinated army officer.

Even though Raymond continued to express support for the prime minister, his decision to stage a play lampooning her and her consort can't have been unrelated to him being slighted by the Thatchers. If the long queues for tickets to the Comic Strip hadn't already done so, the success of *Anyone for Denis?* – which opened at the beginning of May – emphasised the commercial possibilities of less formulaic comedy, of shows more in keeping with the tenor of their times.

During late April Raymond had put his Fitzhardinge House flat on the market for £485,000. Its fixtures and fittings were available for an extra £100,000. The estate agent entrusted with selling this unabashed temple of vulgarity tactfully described it as 'one of the most individual apartments in London'.

A buyer hadn't yet been found when Raymond and his employees, striving to promote *Anyone for Denis?*, pulled off another of their publicity coups. On Sunday, 12 July Margaret Thatcher was persuaded to attend a charity fund-raising performance of the show. Unless she wanted to endorse her reputation as a humour vacuum, she had little choice but to describe it as 'a marvellous farce'. Afterwards Raymond went to a champagne reception at Downing Street, where he was introduced to the prime minister. Recalling the encounter, he said, 'We didn't talk much, but she *did* say she thought the newspapers were out to get both of us.'

That August Raymond's estate agent sold his flat – complete with fixtures and fittings – for close to the asking price. From Portman Square, Raymond and Di Cochran moved to another penthouse. Their new home was at the top of Arlington House, a broad, ten-storey 1930s building on Arlington Street, behind the Ritz Hotel, one of Piccadilly's most famous landmarks. The building, which had once housed the newspaper tycoon Lord Beaverbrook, had a capacious foyer staffed by a regiment of flunkeys who warded off unwanted visitors and guarded the gates to its underground car park.

Ringo Starr and Robin Cruickshank's redesign of the roof terrace at Fitzhardinge House had so pleased Raymond that he employed them to revamp the entire three-bedroom flat he'd just bought. By the time he and his girlfriend took up residence there, the walls of its lobby had been sheathed in mirror-glass and its floors covered in beige marble. Mirrors had also been installed in the dining room. These reflected the gilt and silver colour scheme and the furnishings, which included potted palms, a marble backgammon table and part of Raymond's expanding troupe of nude female figurines, elegant art deco bronzes juxtaposed with expensive items of kitsch.

More mirrors were to be found in the master bedroom, the now customary mirror on the ceiling capturing the ebonised sheen of a vast, troilism-friendly bed. Like Raymond's previous bed, it had a television implanted in the footboard.

Yet more mirrors had been mounted in the bathroom, now fitted with a walk-in wardrobe and a banquette upholstered in white towelling. Even the cocktail bar in the lounge was surfaced in green and blue mirror-glass. Small though it was, the construction of the bar – stocked with Raymond's favourite Rémy Martin brandy – reputedly set him back £110,000.

Adjoining the lounge was a private rooftop terrace that had views across Green Park. Beyond that, he could see the front of Buckingham Palace. Had he been living any closer to the Queen, the King of Soho could have referred to her as a neighbour.

He'd been ensconced at Arlington House for only a few weeks before his latest cinematic offering, never likely to feature at the Royal Command Performance, was ready for its British premiere at the Rialto Cinema on Coventry Street. Relishing the opportunity for some mischief-making, he added Pamela Stephenson to the guest list. She greeted the invitation with a telegram that read, 'I am amazed that you had the gall to invite me to your nasty little flick. I bet your film stinks and I hope it sinks.'

Raymond couldn't resist teasing her by offering her £50,000 to appear in his next movie.

The offer needled her into sending him another irate telegram. It read, 'I don't want anything to do with you or your rotten money.'

Distributed by Brent Walker, the company founded by George Walker, former gangland minder, *Paul Raymond's Erotica* was released in London during the final week of August. Not the best moment to unveil a soft porn movie, the market for the genre having all but disappeared, thanks to the availability of illegal hardcore films in cinema clubs and on videotape.

Initially, Raymond's movie did well at the box office, occupying the No. 4 spot in the charts, not far behind *Raiders of the Lost Ark*. But its brief popularity must have been quashed by adverse word-of-mouth. Here was a movie that was not only unerotic but also *tedious*. As the critic from the *Daily Express* noted, the soundtrack couldn't be heard above the clatter of people getting up from their seats and hurrying towards the exits. That said, the soundtrack – already possessing a muffled, deep-sea quality – didn't require much help to achieve inaudibility.

Long before Raymond's film could recoup its costs, it had slunk out of British cinemas, leaving him to turn his attention to other business ventures. For a while that autumn he flirted with becoming a newspaper proprietor. His target was *The Times*, owned by the Australian media magnate Rupert Murdoch, who was rumoured to be placing it on the market.

'I would certainly never dream of putting nudes on page 3 of *The Times*, but I do think the paper might benefit from a certain added glamour,' he reassured a reporter who had heard about his plans.

Those intentions weren't, however, tested because the rumoured sale turned out to have no substance.

Guided by the Soho Society, a campaign promoting the need to clean up Soho was now in progress. Ever since the late nineteenth century, the area had periodically been the subject of similar attempts to drive out the sex industry. By publicly bestowing his support on the latest of these campaigns, Raymond endeavoured to dust off his image as the West End industry's Mr Respectable. Through incessant lobbying, the Soho Society hoped to force local and national government to halt the proliferation of sex businesses and also impose a licensing system – an idea pioneered illegally by Bill Moody and his colleagues. The society's concerns about the relentless expansion of the industry were given plenty of publicity by the fate of one of Brewer Street's longest-established shops: the House of Hamburger delicatessen, which was supplanted by the area's 164th sexploitation establishment.

In what amounted to the campaign's first major victory, that October the Indecent Displays Act was passed. Under the Act, which instantly transformed Soho's streets, shopkeepers faced a swingeing fine and jail sentence for presenting pornography and sex toys in their window displays. Voicing his unlikely support for the legislation, Raymond said, 'I don't think it is right that, if a man and a woman are walking down the street with their little boy or girl, they should have to see all those displays.'

With ingenuity that matched the deviousness of Raymond's stance, the sex shop owners hastily introduced screens, curtains and blanked-out windows, emblazoned by warning notices that left potential customers to speculate on the illicit delights that lay inside. As a marketing device, it could scarcely have been excelled, something that didn't go unnoticed at Paul Raymond Publications. His magazines, along with those of their competitors, were soon plastered with enticing warnings as to the sexually explicit nature of the material they contained.

A territorial struggle of a more significant nature was about to commence on the far side of the globe. When Argentine troops under the command of the country's military dictatorship seized the Falkland Islands during April 1982, Margaret Thatcher dispatched a Royal Navy flotilla to the South Atlantic to reassert British control. In a demonstration of his support for the subsequent assault on the occupying forces, Raymond arranged for 30,000 copies of *Men Only* to be sent to members of the British task force. By way of explanation for the gesture, Raymond's secretary told a journalist who rang his Archer Street offices, 'Mr Raymond was in the RAF, you know...'

Her respectful reference to Raymond's past conjured visions of him strapped into the cockpit of a Spitfire, *not* flogging tickets to dances in Market Drayton. Overlooking both his own reluctance to go into uniform and the inglorious nature of his spell in the RAF, Raymond started advocating the return of National Service.

*Anyone for Denis?* was among the unacknowledged victims of Britain's brief war against Argentina. Now that the newspapers were filled with reports of British casualties, Margaret and Denis Thatcher no longer seemed suitable subjects for gentle farce. In May 1982 the play's extended run at the Whitehall Theatre ended. Its success encouraging Raymond to continue offering more sophisticated comedy, he replaced it with another comparatively upmarket production, though the title of the new show, *Private Dick*, suggested a return to the old days of topless girls and bottomless innuendo. Promoted as 'A Celebration of the 40s Detective Movie', the show had transferred from the studio theatre at the Lyric, Hammersmith. In a send-up of *The Big Sleep* and other films based on the novels of Raymond Chandler, it starred the handsome English leading man Robert Powell as Chandler's gumshoe Philip Marlowe, hired by Chandler to recover the stolen manuscript of his latest Marlowe novel. Unusually for one of Paul Raymond's shows, *Private Dick* attracted some very favourable reviews. The show was nonetheless unable to match the impact of its predecessor.

Poor box-office takings at the Windmill Theatre had, meanwhile, persuaded Raymond to go ahead with a second major refurbishment programme at the home of *Revudeville*. Seeking to create an impression of no-expense-spared luxury, Raymond proclaimed that the building work would cost between £1 million and £1.3 million. That work consisted of turning the interior into a combined restaurant and disco, equipped with a voguish laser light-show. Unsentimental as ever where business was involved, he authorised the removal of the theatre's neon windmill sign, the rotating blades of which had been a West End landmark for so many decades. 'We want to get away from the old image completely,' Raymond insisted. 'This will be like a Berlin nightclub in the 1930s – very *Cabaret* but way beyond Liza Minnelli.'

He wanted to highlight the Windmill's transformation by renaming it, but his preferred new name, La Vie en Rose, was problematic. Since the name was already being used by a French bistro, located less than a mile away on Charlotte Place, he was sued by its owner, who alleged that the restaurant would suffer if Raymond pressed ahead with the intended renaming. The case went all the way to the High Court, where the judge ruled in favour of the bistro's proprietor. But Raymond circumvented the judgement by approaching his adversary and negotiating what he described as 'an amicable agreement' to let him use the name – a sudden turnaround presumably achieved through a substantial payment.

# 44 NON-STOP EROTIC CABARET

RAYMOND'S LATEST ADDITIONS to his Soho property roster included several purchases on Old Compton Street. Among the victims of the subsequent rent rises was an Indian restaurant that had its annual bill raised by 250 per cent. Another restaurant and a dress shop were casualties of Raymond's policy as well. Both of them soon made way for the type of businesses he publicly criticised. While the restaurant ended up being replaced by a clip-joint, two more sex businesses took over the building where the dress shop had been. That building now housed a strip-club box office, a topless bar and a studio for pornographic photography.

The returns generated by these and other property holdings contrasted with the miserable performance of La Vie en Rose, which opened in mid-November 1982. It soon chalked up large losses, lending an air of futility to Raymond's costly tussle with the owner of the Charlotte Place bistro.

Several months previously his daughter's boyfriend, David Wilkie, had moved out of the large, tastefully furnished sixteenth-century cottage in Surrey where they'd been living together. Raymond had also separated from Di Cochran. Declaring himself 'happy without a girlfriend', he started spending more time than ever in Debbie's company, the intensification of their already close relationship fostered by recent events.

The previous year, Tony Power, one of Raymond's few close friends, had grown so addicted to cocaine that he couldn't cope with his job. In a move indicative of Raymond's priorities, which valued money more highly than people, Power was sacked from the company. Without him, Raymond became increasingly dependent on his daughter as a source of after-work companionship. He and Debbie, who described herself and her father as 'great mates', invariably ended up at Tramp, London's smartest and most famous nightclub. Not the obvious place to find a father and daughter.

Observed by the paparrazi habitually camped outside the club's unremarkable Jermyn Street entrance, they'd emerge from either of his two chauffeur-driven Rolls-Royces – a Silver Spur or a Landaulette. One of the doormen would then shepherd them into this haunt of aristocrats, celebrities, young royals, big businessmen and wealthy Eurotrash. Until the familial resemblance became apparent, Debbie could have been mistaken for another of Raymond's conquests. He often used to joke that she was, with the exception of Jean, the oldest girl he'd ever been out with.

His dandified get-up confirmed his reputation as that comic stereotype of yesteryear – the oldest swinger in town. He still liked to wear a long black fur coat, draped round the shoulders of an expensive, handmade suit, the outfit accessorised these days by a gold bracelet with 'P.R.' engraved on it, plus a diamond and gold pendant, worn over his tie. As if he wasn't already noticeable enough, he sported a pencil moustache and a deep tan that lent him the appearance of some leathery Hollywood actor made up to play a Mexican in an old western. The darkness of his skin emphasised the whiteness of his teeth and the pallor of his ever more elaborate scrape-over hairdo. Now dyed blond, the colour giving it a strange acrylic sheen, it was sufficiently long at the back to form a vallance round his neck.

Such Las Vegas flamboyance, allied to his well-entrenched fame, inspired many a cartoonist, the most astringent of them being Gerald

Scarfe. In a cartoon for *Private Eye*, Scarfe portrayed Raymond with a stack of money teetering on the tip of his erection, the mighty member held aloft by a pulley.

Inside Tramp, co-owned by the schlock novelist Jackie Collins's husband, Raymond would blend into the celebrity clientele, which included Michael Douglas, Ringo Starr, Prince Andrew, George Best, Björn Borg, Michael Caine, Imran Khan, Rod Stewart, Mick Jagger and Jerry Hall. Voices raised to make themselves heard above the electronic beat of the latest pop records, Paul and Debbie Raymond, who still referred to her father as 'Pa', would down bottles of champagne and chat with the other regulars. He surprised several of them with his reticence, his willingness to listen to what other people were saying. Every so often, members of their circle would disappear into the lavatories to snort cocaine, but Raymond was too wary to let himself be spotted doing that. He would, instead, wait till he and Debbie and their closest friends had, in the early hours, decamped to nearby Arlington House, where he usually kept a bag of the drug in his wall safe. Remembering one such night, Debbie's friend Tim Knight said, 'As he hoovered up the cocaine that Debbie put out, he told me: "The family that plays together stays together!" We took cocaine all night and it was 11 a.m. before I went home.'

Debbie had arrived at the overdue conclusion that she'd never achieve stardom as a singer, so she asked her father whether he'd let her work for him. At first he told her that working together wasn't a good idea. His response was, she sensed, borne out of a suspicion that she 'wouldn't be serious about it.'

As ever, she didn't take long to pester him into changing his mind. He agreed to employ her in a junior capacity at Paul Raymond Publications for a trial period. There, she was expected to do the proofreading and subediting, which nobody else, thanks to his penny-pinching, had been

specifically employed to do. From now on, it wouldn't be uncommon for
Raymond to walk into the open-plan office where she worked and find
his daughter checking the caption that accompanied a colour photo of a
recumbent nude, breasts and neatly barbered pubic hair thrust towards
the camera.

Far from being unique, this creepy scenario had already been enacted
more than a century earlier by Henry Hayler, Britain's first known porn
baron. Based at the family home in Pimlico, he'd enlisted the help of his
wife and children to run his business which, until they were forced to flee
to Berlin in 1874, exported mass-produced photos and slides to shops and
dealers across Europe and North America.

Employing Debbie proved just as problematic as Raymond must have
feared. 'When I first came in nine-and-a-half-years ago,' Debbie later
admitted, 'I turned round and said to him, "I don't think that's right. I'm
just not going to do it." And he said, "Deborah, you *will* do it." I said, "I
fucking well will not." So he sacked me. Then he took me back the next
day, after he'd explained, "Listen, you do not do this in the office." I said,
"Yes, I'm terribly sorry. Can I come back, please?"'

If she hadn't been his daughter, there wouldn't have been any chance
of him backing down. For situations like that, his normal rule was,
'People get bolshy, they gotta go.' Bending his principles to accommodate
Debbie, he reinstated her. He'd have no regrets about his decision, though
it did, he conceded, generate friction with his other staff.

After her reprieve, Debbie made a concerted bid to win his approval
by learning the rudiments of his publishing business and by treating
him as deferentially as any other junior employee, even addressing him
as 'Mr Raymond'. At lunchtimes, however, the egalitarianism would be
held in abeyance while she joined her father for a meal at the Piccadilly
Restaurant on Great Windmill Street, a modestly priced traditional-style
trattoria where he and Debbie tended to spend the whole time talking
about work. Its owner, Claudio Musso, remembered him being 'Very
polite, very simple, not at all pretentious. Always smiling.'

Jean Raymond had recently divorced her second husband and returned to Britain, where she'd settled in Berkshire. That Christmas Debbie attempted to make up for all the differences she'd had with her mother by inviting Jean to spend the holiday with her and Raymond at her cottage in the Surrey village of Chobham.

'Once the turkey and pud were out of the way, everyone suddenly disappeared,' Jean recounted. 'I found them gathered round the kitchen table. To my horror I saw there were lines of coke spread all over it and they were all taking turns to have a snort, including Paul.' Horrified by what she'd witnessed, Jean added that she'd confronted Raymond, who had denied being addicted to cocaine and told her to leave Debbie alone.

Getting on for a quarter of a century had passed since Raymond had first leased the premises where the Revuebar was located. By early 1983 he'd acquired eight of the twelve neighbouring shops on Walker's Court. All but one of those eight shops was now a peepshow, a strip-club or a sex shop, their signage immersing passers-by in a multicoloured neon light that made them resemble tropical fish shimmering across a well-stocked aquarium.

Where Jack Isow's restaurant had once been, Raymond had opened the Pink Pussycat Club, a topless hostess bar named in homage to the Viennese strip-joint that Raymond had often visited. Its Soho equivalent was expensively kitted out with a long counter and seats upholstered in red leather. The Pink Pussycat also had a small stage on which a continuous strip-show was held. Outside there was a sign promising 'Non-stop Erotic Cabaret'.

'It was the top place of its sort in the West End,' recalled John Morrell, a Soho veteran who had been round to Archer Street and talked Raymond into hiring him as the Pink Pussycat's doorman. 'Really classy, it was. All the staff wore bow ties. It had the best-looking girls. Raymond used to drop round there quite a lot. He'd pull up in his Rolls-Royce and sweep in wearing his fur coat. I remember he'd always have a chat with the girls, who adored him. He was a very cool cat.'

But the Pink Pussycat was as ruthless and cynical an operation as the clip-joints Raymond professed to despise. Everything about it was conceived to decant the contents of its customers' wallets into Raymond's bank account. Those customers were charged a £7 entrance fee, whereupon they had to pay as much as £5 for a glass of whisky, plus a 20 per cent service charge and a £20 'hostess fee'. Each dance with a hostess cost a further £30. Whenever a customer offered to buy one of the hostesses a drink, she was obliged to ask for champagne, which set them back £48. Only after a customer had spent at least £96 could a hostess offer to have sex with him for an additional £100. Unless the hostesses prostituted themselves, they earned no more than a subsistence wage.

Just in case the police started taking an interest in the Pink Pussycat, Raymond had distanced himself from the operation by arranging for it to be fronted by Tony Engleman, a former Soho doorman and club owner. Anyone who inspected the official paperwork wouldn't find Raymond's name on the licence.

The success of the Comic Strip had earned Peter Richardson and colleagues a Channel 4 television series, which left them too busy to continue their Friday and Saturday night shows at the Boulevard Theatre. 'After we'd all decided to stop doing our shows there, Raymond asked if I'd like to lease the place for £500 a week,' Alexei Sayle said. 'But I turned down the offer.'

Even though the Comic Strip had moved out of Raymond's building, their connection to him hadn't yet been severed. During mid-January 1983 Channel 4 screened the latest instalment of their series, *The Comic Strip Presents....* The programme took the form of a pastiche investigative documentary called *Eddie Monsoon: A Life.* Exploring the shambolic past of the eponymous veteran television and radio presenter, played by Adrian Edmondson, it featured an affectionately unflattering character closely modelled on Raymond. Through an archive interview with Eddie Monsoon, viewers were introduced to Raymond's slippery alter ego, a jailbird and veteran showbiz agent with an assumed name – Tiny Townsend. 'A bastard, of course,' Eddie cheerfully declared, 'but a very *nice* bastard.'

Townsend was soon cornered by the film-maker in his lair. Like Raymond's office, it was lined with framed posters for his old shows: *Big Jobs in My Trousers*; *Cor, Blimey, What A Pair of Bazookas!*; *Jack the Ripper on Ice*; and *Lots of Sex Please, We're Swedish*. Heedless of Raymond's reputation for being litigious, Peter Richardson made the link between him and Townsend unmistakable by caricaturing his dress sense and mannerisms. There was the bouffant hairdo, the jewellery, the tinted glasses, the ubiquitous cigarette. Richardson even copied his clipped delivery, his foppish style of smoking, his penchant for underscoring his sentences with choppy semaphore.

Channel 4 and the Comic Strip team, who could have found themselves involved in a libel action, were fortunate that Raymond had the ability to laugh at himself, an ability shared by few such powerful people. Over recent years he'd demonstrated his willingness to be the butt of humour by collecting newspaper cartoons of himself. Being caricatured was, he clearly considered, a tribute to his success. Therein lay a contradiction: his pleasure in that success exposed a level of vanity which the collection strove to deny.

'I never found out what he thought of Tiny Townsend,' Richardson said, 'but I did meet him years later and he was very friendly and charming and a lot of fun.'

# 45 SUGAR AND SPICE AND ALL THINGS VICE

**U**NKNOWN TO RAYMOND, the Comic Strip's spoof investigation into his alter ego's business dealings overlapped with a real-life undercover investigation into the PRO, conducted by two student journalists, Justine Picardie and Dorothy Wade. By exploring his covert role in the aspects of the industry that he made a show of publicly criticising, they sought to challenge his self-portrait as the Soho sex industry's Mr Respectable. First, they phoned the Archer Street headquarters of the PRO and enquired about the possibility of being employed as waitresses. They were invited for an interview by Carl Snitcher. At the interview, he offered them jobs as hostesses at the Pink Pussycat.

'You'll probably earn £20 to £40 a night this way,' Snitcher informed the undercover reporters. 'That's not much, but a lot of girls take home a lot more from after-hours activities, and that's a euphemism for a lot of things.' After Picardie and Wade had visited the club and met the manageress, they went back to Snitcher's office. There, he ran through the system operated at the Pink Pussycat and made sure that they'd been told the standard price hostesses should charge for sex.

Picardie and Wade placed their story with the *Sunday Times*, which used an experienced reporter to continue digging for scandal. The reporter even contacted Fiona Richmond, who remained a close friend of Raymond's. 'I phoned PR to tell him they were hamburging me (a wonderful Grenadian expression for annoying me),' she recalled, 'and he

*Carl Snitcher*

said, "I know. What you do is ask them for lots of money, and then you and I will make up some stuff and then you can share the money you get with me.""

The *Sunday Times* reporter also confronted Raymond about the goings-on at the Pink Pussycat. Raymond's response could have been scripted for Tiny Townsend at his most brazen. 'I will go to court,' he said, 'I will swear on a stack of Bibles that the running of that club has nothing to do with me or my organisation in any shape or form.'

But he wasn't forced to perjure himself or incur the wrath of the God he'd once worshipped with such fervour. Armed with sufficient evidence to fend off any writs issued by Raymond's lawyers, the *Sunday Times* went ahead and, during the third week of April 1983, published a double-page exposé, portraying Raymond as the abominable showman.

Further testing his previous claim that he didn't care what people thought of him, less than two months later he found himself the subject of a scathing article in an obscure South African magazine called *Scope*.

The magazine alleged that his businesses were being used to 'launder money acquired from the criminal activities of the mafia'.

However tarnished his reputation, he couldn't afford to ignore such a serious accusation, so he initiated legal action. The PRO had, meanwhile, played up its superficial likeness to the family-obsessed mafia by involving not only Debbie but also Howard, who was employed to work on the property side. Gradually winning Raymond's confidence, Howard commuted to Archer Street from the rambling £250,000 house in Berkshire that Raymond had bought him and Maria.

For many years Raymond had taken pride in his own obstinate refusal to yield to encroaching old age. With his fifty-eighth birthday looming, he maintained an unremitting schedule akin to some perverse experiment in human endurance.

After only a few hours' sleep, the previous night's cocaine, booze and nicotine by then on the closing laps of a grand prix round his circulatory system, he'd wash and shave, dousing his cheeks in aftershave strong enough to leave a pungent trail. He'd dress as carefully as a film star preparing to stroll down the red carpet. He'd use sufficient hairspray to ensure that his dyed blond hair remained in place, no bald patches gatecrashing the party. He'd put on his bracelet and pendant, as well as one of his pricey new Gianni Versace jackets. And he'd take the lift down to street level where his chauffeur-driven car awaited him.

Passers-by who glimpsed him ducking into his Rolls-Royce might have been persuaded that he was younger than he was, an illusion sustained by the cosmetic surgery he'd had on his eyelids. Seen from closer up, however, he looked less like Dorian Gray than the portrait Oscar Wilde's character kept in the attic, his bloodshot eyes betraying the depredations of the night before – and the night before *that*.

He liked to be at work for 10.30 a.m, the walk from his Rolls-Royce into the Archer Street offices constituting a major component of that day's exercise. Already making inroads into his daily quota of about eighty cigarettes, he'd often find himself sharing the lift with his employees. No matter how junior they were, Raymond – who never acquired the brusque self-importance synonymous with excessive wealth – was unfailingly courteous to them. 'He always struck me as a rather sad, lonely man,' one such member of staff recalled. 'I'd stand there in the lift, thinking "You're earning about a thousand times what I'm paid, yet I'm probably a lot happier than you."'

Awaiting him in the tatty-looking offices, which hadn't been decorated since the original refurbishment, was a longish day of phone calls and meetings, broken by an extended lunch break. He'd normally go with Debbie and Carl Snitcher to the Piccadilly. His other regular destination was L'Epicure, a famously good French restaurant on nearby Frith Street, where he liked to lunch with Noel Botham. Most days he wouldn't leave work until about 7 p.m. Then he'd meet Fiona Richmond or one of his other cronies for an expensive dinner, sometimes at Langan's or L'Escargot. Often he gave the impression that the contents of his plate were secondary to those of his glass. He and his guest would get through as many as three bottles of champagne during the meal, enough to make him confess that, 'I drink far too much.' He had, however, built up such a high tolerance to alcohol he'd give no indication of being drunk.

Primed by all that bubbly, he would be ready for his usual foray into the West End's nightclubs – squiring either his daughter or Kim Tye, the twenty-four-year-old dancer from La Vie en Rose whom he'd been dating for several months. If they were with a friend, he'd later insist on giving that friend a lift home instead of taking a taxi. Well past midnight, Raymond would return to Arlington House where he'd briefly recuperate prior to the next day's indoor triathlon.

Tenacious lobbying by the campaigners striving to clean up Soho had led to the Conservative government bringing in two significant new laws that would enable both Westminster City Council and the Greater London Council to expel sex businesses from the neighbourhood. Those items of legislation were the Local Government Miscellaneous Provisions Act and the Cinematograph Amendment Act, introducing systems of licensing for Soho's sex shops and porn cinemas. Implicit within both Acts was an assumption that pornography should be treated like alcohol or tobacco, potentially dangerous substances deemed acceptable under supervision.

The porn cinemas had been the first to suffer, twenty-nine of them having already been closed down by the Greater London Council. Next in line were Soho's sixty-five sex shops. Under the new licensing system, Westminster City Council aimed to reduce this number to no more than twenty. In order to qualify for a licence, which cost £5,000, the owners had to submit a comprehensive application form and prove they were 'of good character'. Just as the council had intended, numerous sex shops were forced out of business. But the licensing system had one unexpected spin-off. Many sex shop owners, unable to comply with its strictures, circumvented the law by turning their shops into nude encounter parlours or topless hostess bars, a change that required only the purchase of a £40 late night refreshment licence.

Any surviving unlicensed sex shops now became the target of police swoops which commenced in February 1983 with a couple of raids on the Dreaming Lips sex shop, operated illegally in premises owned by Raymond. On each occasion the shop, crammed with magazines, videos and sex toys, was full of customers.

In the first prosecution initiated under the Local Government Miscellaneous Provisions Act, Raymond faced two summonses at Bow Street Magistrates' Court during early September for 'permitting the use of the premises as an unlicensed sex establishment'. Defended by a top barrister who argued that 'the lease on the shop was stringent in terms of usage, but responsibility for the matter was out of his client's hands', Raymond succeeded in ducking the charges.

Three months after his acquittal, the Soho Society's clean-up campaign scored its biggest victory so far when Westminster City Council announced that only six of the twenty-one applicants had been granted licences to run sex shops. Shrewdly allying himself with the campaign while continuing to reap ample profits from the sex industry, Raymond told the press, 'Sex shops *should* be controlled. Quite rightly. It can't go on the way it was before.' He even claimed that he'd rejected approaches from potential tenants, offering 'big rents' so they could run 'the types of establishment we do not want'.


Raymond's main company, the PRO, was heading for a profit of £700,000 at the end of 1983, most of it conjured by the publishing side of his business. Had Raymond not suffered huge losses at his two largest venues, La Vie en Rose and the recently mothballed Whitehall Theatre, those profits would have been even bigger. La Vie en Rose alone had recorded a £250,000 deficit in its first year. To rectify the situation, he'd drawn up rescue plans for both venues.

By revamping the cabaret at La Vie en Rose, Raymond hoped to make the place more attractive to nightclubbers. On New Year's Eve 1984 he staged a 'Gala Party' there, after which he closed the place for eight days while new sets were constructed and a fresh show rehearsed. Never afraid to recycle old titles, he called the production *Paris after Dark*. Its title wasn't the sole ingredient borrowed from his 1950s revues. So was the structure of the show, which featured novelty acts, guest artistes and showgirls, all of whom performed twice nightly to a growing audience.

More radical change was, in the meantime, under way at the Whitehall Theatre. Conceding defeat in his attempt to prolong its existence as the home of British farce, he converted the building into a museum dedicated to exhibiting the collection of Second World War memorabilia which he'd been amassing especially for that purpose. With the conversion of the Whitehall Theatre, Raymond now ran only a single, small theatre. That was the Boulevard, which he rented to producers of serious drama, often starring well-known performers such as Jill Bennett.

The wartime memorabilia displayed at the Whitehall Theatre made up what was hailed as the largest private collection of its kind in the country: everything from clothing coupons to half-tracked vehicles, scout cars and numerous aircraft. Peopled by waxworks of famous wartime leaders, the new museum opened in mid-February 1984. As a ploy devised to allow him to get round planning restrictions that required permission to change the use of a building, he called his museum 'The Theatre of War'.

No sooner had he opened the place than Westminster City Council, which had previously vetoed his plan to turn the Whitehall Theatre into 'an all-day entertainment centre', instigated legal action against him. Raymond had, they argued, changed the Whitehall from a theatre to an exhibition venue.

He must have been relieved that none of the newspaper coverage accompanying the launch of the Theatre of War drew attention to the irony at the heart of his project. Here was someone seeking to profit from a war to which he'd gone to such lengths to avoid making any contribution.

His museum had only been open for a week before he was involved in an unsavoury promotional stunt. On Wednesday, 22 February, wearing an uncharacteristically sober black suit and tie, he attended a sale at Phillips, the London auction house. There, he joined the bidding for a vellum scroll with a gold-embossed eagle and swastika. The scroll, signed by Adolf Hitler, had been presented in 1942 to the Stuka pilot Hans Rudel to commemorate his receipt of Nazi Germany's highest military decoration. Rudel, a veteran of more than 2,500 combat missions, had been prominent in the neo-Nazi movement until his death less than two years earlier.

Competing against Raymond was Rudel's thirty-five-year-old second wife, but she dropped out of the bidding when it reached £10,000. Raymond had to go up to £20,000 to secure his dubious purchase.

Looking slightly embarrassed, he agreed to pose for a press photo afterwards with both the vanquished widow and the scroll.

Howard's wife Maria was, by then, heavily pregnant with Raymond's first grandchild. During the run-up to the birth, due that spring, Howard started using cocaine, his consumption escalating to seven grams a day. Maria later alleged that Debbie had confessed to introducing him to the drug in the PRO's Archer Street offices. 'She told me she was absolutely sick with jealousy because Howard had become flavour of the month, the decent bloke doing everything right,' Maria said. 'And she could see how her father had changed towards him. She used to be the centre of attention, but the son who Raymond had no time for was now in the spotlight. She set out deliberately to get him hooked on coke.'

Maria gave birth to a daughter in March. She and Howard named her Cheyenne. Until Maria caught him sniffing a line of cocaine off their dining table not long after the birth, she claimed to have been oblivious to her husband's drug-taking. She threw him out of the house, urging him to sort himself out. Though Howard, who had already taken up with another woman, carried on with his relentless drug use, Raymond ignored the problem at first, presumably because he didn't regard cocaine as a problem. If *he* and Debbie could consume large amounts of the stuff and still function, why shouldn't Howard be able to do the same?

When Jean became aware of their son's drug addiction, she begged Raymond to help him. As she subsequently recalled, Raymond responded by saying, 'Don't be silly. He's alright.'

Soon enough, Raymond realised that Howard *wasn't* all right, that he could no longer do his job. Only then did Raymond confront Howard. Years of mutual resentment powering a savage row, Raymond banished him from the family business, switched off the flow of cash handouts and refused to have anything more to do with him. The row ended with Raymond having the door slammed in his face by Howard.

'Raymond was disgusted with the way Howard had turned out,' Noel
Botham recalled. 'He even went so far as to ban Howard from all his
clubs. My wife Lesley and I tried to help. One night we smuggled him into
one of his father's clubs wearing a false moustache. Raymond thought
this was very funny, but there was no reconciliation between them.'

# 46 MONTE CARLO AND BUST

THE AGGRESSIVE HETEROSEXUALITY of the products until recently displayed in the windows of so many Soho shops disguised the area's status as a long-standing haunt of male and female homosexuals. Soho's tolerance of eccentricity and aberrance had also made it an obvious province of transvestites.

From the earliest days of the Revuebar, when Raymond had staged the drag show *Call Us Mister!*, he'd sensed the potential of the male homosexual market, of what would be called 'the pink pound'. Raymond had, however, never succeeded in translating that potential into appreciable profits. The launch in 1984 of Raymond's Piano Bar, which replaced the Pink Pussycat, represented his latest attempt to achieve this elusive objective.

Illicit gay clubs had existed in Soho for decades, even while male homosexuality was still illegal, yet the Piano Bar was among the first openly gay venues to set up in the area. Staffed by leggy young drag queens in basques, high heels and stockings, it offered a hospitable atmosphere, sliding into shrieking rowdiness during the twice-nightly cabaret shows. It was soon so profitable that Raymond was bragging about it being 'a little goldmine'.

Around the beginning of 1985 Raymond began a relationship with Belinda Pearce, a dark-haired twenty-eight-year-old whom he'd met at Tramp. In everything but her svelte good looks, she wasn't his normal type of girlfriend. For a start she wasn't a showgirl, a nude model, a girl barely out of school uniform, or an actress in one of his stage shows. She was, instead, a specialist in criminal law.

Conscious that she was an outsider to the sex industry, he tried to keep her away from it. Rather than take her to the Revuebar, where he'd spent so many nights with previous girlfriends, he met her regularly for drinks at La Vie en Rose and treated her with endearing gallantry. 'He seemed bowled over by me,' she recalled.

Their romance hadn't been going for more than a few weeks before Raymond had an annoying brush with the daytime world she inhabited. During mid-February, Westminster City Council obtained a court order compelling him to close the Theatre of War. He promptly lodged an appeal against the ruling. Optimistic about the likely verdict, he predicted that the closure would only be temporary. It became permanent, however, when the original judgement was upheld.

He wasted little time in announcing that he was going to auction most of the contents of his museum on Wednesday, 5 June – the fortieth anniversary of V-E Day. Their estimated sale price was £500,000. Among the few items exempted from the auction was a canteen of Adolf Hitler's monogrammed silver cutlery, which he regarded as a good investment and which he delighted in showing visitors to his flat. Those visitors included a Jewish business associate who was dumbstruck by his otherwise attentive and affable host's insensitivity.

At the same time as arranging to dispose of the museum's contents, Raymond put the lease on the building up for sale. Just over a month after its closure, he secured a deal with a company planning to reopen it as a theatre.

That summer he completed this self-imposed round of asset-stripping by dropping his latest girlfriend without explanation. Bewildered, she left him messages and sent him flowers, but he didn't respond. She even resorted to giving an interview to the *Daily Express*, in which she issued a forlorn appeal for him to contact her. When a reporter from the newspaper invited him to comment, he said, 'I'm amazed she should talk like this. In these Women's Lib' days I'd have thought she'd have written me off as a horrible swine, but there's no accounting for taste. She really was very, very attractive, but I didn't have the world to promise to her.'

The courtroom defeat by Westminster City Council was followed that June by a particularly satisfying legal victory over the publishers of *Scope*, the South African magazine that had made the allegations about Raymond's mafia connections. Its publishers were forced to concede that the claims were false and to pay undisclosed damages.

Free from the mafia slur, he invested £2 million in commercial property, the business he admitted thinking about 'more than anything else'. His investment bought him a dozen freeholds in Frith Street and Old Compton Street. These encompassed the building that housed the celebrated Ronnie Scott's Jazz Club, though Raymond hadn't yet told the club's eponymous owner, someone he'd known for years.

'I've invested in real estate because in my view Soho is going to become very big in not many years time,' he explained with remarkable prescience. 'I think it's going to be like Covent Garden. It has to happen here. It can't go anyplace else. The West End can only come into Soho. It can't go into Whitehall. It has to come this way. Five years time, I would have thought.'

His new acquisitions pushed the value of his Soho property holdings to about £20 million, the rental income from these swelling the profits of the PRO. One facet of the company failing to contribute to those earnings was La Vie en Rose. Raymond closed this down early in 1986 and turned it into a conventional yet much more fashionable nightclub called Paramount City, which became a favourite hangout of the singer Freddie Mercury.

☆

There was always something *King Lear*-like in Raymond's relations with Debbie and Howard, in the way he'd encouraged them to compete for his approbation. Howard's banishment appeared to have settled this long-running rivalry. Over a year had gone by since Raymond had even spoken to him. In that time Rebecca Taylor – the woman Howard had been living with since separating from Maria – had given birth to a son whom they named Boston. Despite having fathered an illegitimate child himself, Raymond complained to friends about what he perceived to be his son's immoral behaviour. With her brother still so comprehensively out of favour, Debbie continued to demonstrate her value as assistant editor of *Men Only* and, in doing so, reinstated herself as their father's heir apparent.

At a party not long before the birth of Howard's daughter, Debbie had met Duncan Mackay, former keyboard player with the pop group 10cc. They'd been a couple ever since, though they weren't living together. When she'd introduced Raymond to her new boyfriend, the two men had, to her evident delight, got on extremely well.

Debbie was soon expecting her first child. After she went into labour, Tim Knight alleged, Raymond gave her a line of cocaine to ease the pain.

She and her boyfriend called their daughter Fawn. But Debbie's latest relationship proved no more durable than any of Raymond's recent romances. She and Fawn's father split up when the child was only four months old. In order to carry on working in the publishing side of her father's business, Debbie hired a live-in nanny.

Regular contact with Fawn brought out the softer side of Raymond, the ruthless businessman miraculously metamorphosing into the soppy grandad. Seeing her also strengthened the ties between him and Debbie. 'I can phone him up at four o'clock in the morning crying my eyes out over something, and he's always there to help or listen,' Debbie revealed.

The closeness between Raymond and his daughter was further

accentuated by his burgeoning faith in her abilities as an employee. Not that she lost her manifest anxiety to please him.

As a token of his trust in her, Raymond placed her in charge of the Paramount City nightclub and made her editor of *Club pour Hommes*, the new magazine with which he hoped to break into the French soft porn market. Her appointment at *Club pour Hommes* was a gamble because, though she'd spent time on the Riviera, she knew nothing about the Gallic market and couldn't even speak French. In the build-up to launching the magazine, Raymond's gamble already showed signs of gleaning rewards. He was so satisfied with her work that, during late June, he made an unambiguous public pronouncement about the succession to his throne. 'When I die,' he said, 'my daughter will get the company.'

While he was alive, however, he retained tight control over his business, checking every expense sheet and petty-cash slip. Consolidating his reputation among his employees for miserliness, he even locked away the supply of toilet rolls for the Archer Street offices. Anyone requiring a fresh roll had to sign a request form. He liked to tell people that, by keeping such close tabs on his business, he'd be unable to blame anyone but himself if something went awry.

Raymond was less sparing and rational in the way he apportioned blame for Howard's impending divorce. His judgement warped by the fermenting hostility between himself and Maria, he held her responsible for the failure of the marriage. He reacted by repossessing the BMW car she'd been given, leaving her with a long walk to the nearest shop to buy food for herself and Raymond's granddaughter. Incensed by the discovery that the BMW had been passed on to Debbie, Maria broke into Debbie's house and used the kitchen knives to puncture all of the cushions. Debbie and her father were, as Maria recalled, 'scared witless' when she confessed what she'd done.

In the second week of July, Raymond began legal proceedings that would conclude with the eviction of his penniless daughter-in-law and grandchild from their Berkshire home, which the PRO owned. Like Howard, they were banished from the kingdom, though Raymond *did* take the trouble to set up a trust fund to pay for Cheyenne's education.

Debbie was, meanwhile, cementing her status in the court of King Paul. 'She always seemed terribly anxious to please him and nervous whenever he came into our communal office which otherwise had quite a relaxed atmosphere,' remembered one of her colleagues. 'There was something a bit sad and desperate about her, desperate to please her dad, desperate to fit in. She used to wear these distressed denim suits – skirt and jacket things that looked as if she'd got them off Berwick Street Market, but they'd probably cost a packet.'

Less than a fortnight after the court action against Maria had started, Debbie repaid her father's faith in her with the successful launch of *Club pour Hommes*, which went on to claim the title of France's top-selling porn magazine. Her management of Paramount City also yielded dividends, bringing her together with the club's manager, John James, a mild-mannered working-class Cumbrian who, in February 1987, would become her long-suffering second husband.

About seven months before their marriage, her heavy drug use won her an unwanted starring role in the next melodramatic instalment of the Raymond family soap opera. Alarmed by what appear to have been inaccurate rumours that Debbie's drug-taking had expanded to include heroin, Jean reported her to the police, imploring them to lock her up. Only by removing Debbie from the source of her pharmaceuticals would she have a chance of kicking her habit, Jean reasoned.

Though the police raided Debbie's house, the plan backfired because they didn't imprison her. As if that weren't bad enough, she found out the source of the tip-off. Furious with her mother, Debbie stopped speaking to her and even prevented her from seeing Fawn. Debbie's falling out with Jean completed a symmetrical mother/daughter, father/son pattern of estrangement. Instead of attempting to heal the schism, Raymond sided with Debbie, ostracising his ex-wife.

# 47 FIND THE LADY

THE INORDINATE SUCCESS of the Piano Bar convinced Raymond to open another, much larger gay venue on that section of Brewer Street. This new venue was run by John Wright, better-known as Madame JoJo, the Piano Bar's tall, dark-haired, effusive meeter-and-greeter. Exploiting Wright's reputation and charisma, the new venue was called Madame JoJo's. Its eponymous hostess presided over the Bar-bettes, a team of pretty young men wearing lipstick, tights and high-cut leotards, named after 'Barbette', the 1920s male stripper who had appeared in *Le Sang d'un Poète*, the avant-garde film by Jean Cocteau. The Bar-bettes doubled as waitresses and performers in the venue's bitchily misogynistic cabaret, which started at midnight six days a week.

Like the Piano Bar, Madame JoJo's swiftly established itself, becoming popular with gay men and transvestites, often en route to nightclubs. Well-known regulars included the writer and musician George Melly; the artist Francis Bacon; and the memoirist and one-time broadcaster Dan Farson. After a trip to Madame JoJo's with her husband, the Plymouth-based painter Beryl Cook declared, 'I love it. It's like a theatre, and so classy... We sat in the balcony and were so surprised when a man with a wig and false breasts sat down at our table, having just seen him on stage as Ruby Venezuela playing tweetie-pie in a golden cage.

'"My God," said my husband. "It's Brian."

'He was a neighbour from Plymouth. It was lovely seeing him.'

☆

Sales of *Club International*, once so buoyant, had lately been falling at a disconcerting rate. When the magazine's editor left in 1987, Raymond replaced him with Steve Bleach, a young journalist who was assigned one of a cluster of offices on Brewer Street. Most weeks Raymond would visit him there. To reach the new editor's eyrie, immediately above the Revuebar's auditorium, Raymond had to use the stage door. 'You never knew what you'd see when you went through that door and up the staircase,' said Clive Harris, a colleague of Bleach's. 'You'd often find some attractive girl wearing no more than two sequins. I remember this girl who was using the payphone to call her mum. She was saying, "Don't worry, Mum. I'm doing very well. I've got a job in a West End show..."'

Bleach had taken over *Club International* at a good time. 'As an editor, I could do no wrong,' he recalled. 'If I didn't increase sales, I could blame the guy before. And if I revived the magazine, I could take the credit, which is what happened. Raymond was quietly complimentary. Unlike a lot of entrepreneurs, he wasn't a bully. He was gentlemanly and, for such a secretive man, surprisingly straightforward. You knew where you stood with him.

'He's among the nicest employers I've ever had, though he could have afforded to pay better wages. I thought he was immensely charming, interesting and engaging. He didn't talk about himself all the time.

'You could say he was a bit of a showman without being a *show-off*. The perfect example was when we went to a meeting with the boss of the printing company we used in Leicester. We had a big-money contract with them. They were printing over a million magazines a month. That was for the UK alone. Raymond says to the boss, "I'll pay you x amount this year, x amount the year after that and x amount the year after that..." Then he gives it the old market-trader spiel, spits on his hand and invites the printer, who isn't used to doing business like that, to shake hands on the deal. In the end this guy says, "OK" and shakes on it. Once that had happened, the deal was done. When Raymond shook on a deal, that was better than a written contract. He just wandered off and let other people write up the contract. He did this with a real twinkle in his eye. He loved striking deals. Afterwards he kept saying, "I think we got a good deal, don't you?" He wanted me to take pleasure in it. There was something quite theatrical about the way he did business. He could savour the drama of deal-making. I suppose it goes back to his days as a variety artiste and a market trader, too. Any good stallholder has to be a bit theatrical. He relished all that.'

In December 1987 Raymond made one of the most unexpected moves of his business career – unexpected because he had never shown much interest in sport. On learning that the former glam rocker Elton John, who had a 95 per cent shareholding in Watford Football Club, was seeking a buyer for it, he arranged a meeting with the singer's business manager. Their meeting led to a further discussion, held at Raymond's flat.

Elton John wanted £2 million for the club, which was clinging to its position in English football's elite division. During the period just before the creation of the Premier League and the accompanying multimillion-pound broadcasting deals with Sky Television, this was a sizeable figure for a football club. Nevertheless, Raymond remained keen to buy Watford FC, that keenness not yet crystallising into a firm offer.

His only rival was the newspaper owner Robert Maxwell, who already had a controlling stake in Oxford United, another First Division club. At a gathering of the Football League Management Committee, however, Maxwell's bid ended up being vetoed because dual ownership of clubs was against their regulations.

For sports editors wanting a light-hearted story, Raymond's possible involvement in football was ideal. The *Daily Mirror* and its tabloid competitors ran prominent pieces about his mooted acquisition of Watford FC. Headlined 'Strip Club!', the *Mirror*'s flippant story filled the entire back page. It argued that Raymond's takeover would, according to unnamed sources within the game, leave the club 'in danger of becoming the joke of soccer, ridiculed and shamed'. If Raymond took control, it facetiously speculated on him replacing Dave Bassett, the club's manager, with Danny La Rue and installing Fiona Richmond as the physiotherapist.

Raymond's bid was in danger of capsizing beneath the weight of tabloid mirth. Early in January 1988 he emphasised the seriousness of his intentions by pledging to provide Dave Bassett with a £2 million transfer fund in the event of a successful takeover. But Raymond made the error of provoking more jokes at his own expense by revealing that he planned to introduce American-style cheerleaders to entertain the crowd before the game and during the half-time break. His much-derided idea would later be unsuccessfully adopted by Sky Television in the early days of its coverage of live football.

On the evening of Sunday, 4 January 1988 he flew off with Debbie and Fawn for a holiday at his beachfront house in Antigua. Prior to his departure, he assured waiting reporters that he'd be submitting a formal bid for Watford FC the following week. 'I've always fancied owning a football team,' he told them. 'I might have preferred Chelsea but as they are not for sale I think Watford *are* a good bet. It's a family club and it's not doing so well at the moment, as we all know. I think it would fit in with my future plans for expansion.'

While Raymond was in the West Indies, deepening his perpetual tan, he missed a dramatic incident at the Revuebar, where the evening show had attracted a full house. They witnessed a black-haired, nineteen-year-old stripper strut on to the stage, clad not in a Watford FC kit but in a gridiron football outfit. Within ten minutes of starting her routine, billed as 'American Graffiti', she was naked apart from her football helmet. Overwhelmed by the sight of her body, a bearded man in the front row collapsed and died. The rest of the show had to be cancelled, forcing the staff to refund £2,000 in ticket money to the surviving customers.

Instead of having his attempt to take over Watford FC stymied by the

Football League, Raymond found it blocked by Elton John, who refused to sell the club to him. 'Paul Raymond is not a fit and proper person to buy Watford, but Robert Maxwell *is*,' the singer remarked with laughable pomposity, Maxwell's posthumous exposure as one of the biggest fraudsters of his era adding to the amusement value of the statement.

A rapid process of gentrification had begun in Soho by then, confirming just how far sighted Raymond's property investments had been. What used to be a run-down and squalid area had been transmuted into one of the capital's priciest districts, its value per square foot exceeded only by Mayfair. The unintentional groundwork for this climb upmarket had been carried out by the Soho Society. Its clean-up campaign had proved so successful that the area had become attractive to businesses unrelated to the sex industry.

During the summer of 1986, that campaign had been accelerated by the introduction of a new, tougher licensing system for so-called 'sex establishments'. Soho, as a consequence, now boasted only five sex shops; three strip-shows, the Revuebar among them; a couple of sex cinemas; plus a sprinkling of unlicensed hostess bars and peepshows, the latter offering nothing more erotic than girls working out on exercise machines. The majority of these businesses were in Walker's Court and neighbouring streets which formed the epicentre of Soho's much-diminished porn ghetto, rendered seedier than ever by the presence of card-sharps and prowling streetwalkers.

Guarded by lookouts, the card-sharps and their stooges tried to entice passers-by into games of Find the Lady. Most of the apparent streetwalkers were just as fraudulent as the kerbside card schools. Known as 'clippers', they'd go up to a likely customer and come out with some tired euphemism, a current favourite being 'Looking for business?' The girl would then talk the customer into stumping up about £50. She'd hand him a latch-key and arrange to meet him back at her flat in about ten minutes, just as soon as she'd run some fictitious errand. But the address she gave him would turn out to be an office building or maybe the National Westminster Bank on Wardour Street.

Traditional Soho sleaze was, however, in retreat, the gentrification of the area hastened by an ostensibly unrelated rule change imposed by central government. In May 1987 the planning regulations had been amended so that property could no longer be classified as being suitable only for 'light industrial use'. When leases on Soho workshops expired, landlords were free to convert these premises into vastly more profitable office accommodation. Within just over a year, 50,000 square feet of workshop space had been transformed into offices. Many of these were colonised by advertising agencies, marketing companies and magazine publishers driven out of Covent Garden by rising rents. Chic-looking clothes shops, wine bars, shoe shops and cafés sprang up to cater for the accompanying surge of well-paid, predominantly young workers, competition for space squeezing out old-fashioned shops that had contributed to the area's haphazard character.

In defiance of the forces of homogenisation, Soho nevertheless remained bracingly varied, the affluent newcomers coexisting with as wide a cross-section of humanity as you'd find anywhere in the capital. There were Chinese, Italians, French, Cypriots, Polish, Italians and Bengalis. There were craftspeople, market traders, art students, journalists, musicians, criminals and assorted chancers. There were sushi bars, amusement arcades, tailors' workshops, drinking clubs, film-editing suites and sandwich bars, not to mention the occasional grotty doorway flanked by a doorbell with signs above it, the word 'model' paired with a Christian name. For the Filofax-clutching incomers, this variety, this proximity to the roguish and disreputable, helped to make Soho as fashionable as it had been in the 1950s and 1960s, its voguishness feeding the trend towards gentrification. In its own tasteful way, gentrification was no less destructive than the garish incursions of the sex industry. A patisserie, run by the same family for three generations, could just as easily be replaced by a shop selling expensive sunglasses to overpaid young advertising executives.

Of the businesses that survived from the period when the Revuebar had first opened, none was better known than the French House pub on Dean Street, only yards from the discreet entrance to Gerry's, which Raymond still patronised. 'The French', as its regulars call it, has a tiny, atmospheric bar where most of London's bohemian set – Lucian Freud, Francis Bacon, Julian Maclaren-Ross, to name a few examples – gathered during the 1940s and 1950s. Noel Botham and his wife had just taken over the tenancy. Raymond would regularly pop in for a drink and a chat with them. Among the subjects for conversation was the idea that Botham, who maintained a parallel career as a writer, should produce the authorised biography of Paul Raymond.

Until recently an insatiable consumer of marijuana and cocaine, Howard had kicked his drug habit and moved to Manchester, where he'd found a measure of stability. 'I just woke up one morning and thought, "That's it. I've had enough." I stopped overnight,' he explained.

Howard put his redemption down to his father's cruel-to-be-kind preparedness to cast him into financial and emotional exile. 'Looking back, being cut off by my father was probably the best thing that could have happened to me…' he said. 'I had no choice but to deal with my own problems.'

Now that Howard was no longer high on cocaine, the father–son rift had, on the surface at least, been healed. *Beneath* the surface, though, their rapprochement was poisoned by the feelings of resentment and contempt that permeated Raymond's attitude towards Howard. Raymond's low opinion of Howard ended up being exposed in cruel circumstances during April 1988. That month Raymond granted an interview to a journalist from the *Daily Mirror*. The interview was scheduled to coincide with the thirtieth anniversary of the opening of the Revuebar, which another reporter hailed as 'An institution that has come to represent a valued part of the nation's cultural heritage today.'

To reinforce the image he'd been honing for so long, Raymond assured the *Daily Mirror* journalist that he ran his shows and magazines according to a strict moral code. He claimed this excluded drugs, children and animals. In what may have been nothing more than a rash digression, he also made several remarks about Howard. Venting the parental exasperation that had built up, Raymond said, 'He calls himself an estate agent but he does nothing. I pick up the bills. He was going to prove himself but so far all he has proved is that he is unable to make a few quid.'

Dubious about whether Raymond would really have said such hurtful things about him to a reporter, Howard contacted his father who admitted the quote was accurate. 'You've got to get yourself sorted out,' Howard recalled him saying. 'You've got to get off your arse.'

While conceding that his father was right, Howard was justifiably angry with Raymond for dispensing such humiliating criticism in public. That anger led him to stop speaking to his father. In a family so polarised and prone to factionalism, the dispute was bound to escalate.

Intervening on Howard's behalf, Jean used the opportunity to deliver a withering assault on Raymond via the *People* newspaper. 'I can't bear Paul's holier than thou attitude,' she said. 'That man has less morals than my cat.' With the predictable malice of an ex-wife who feels she's been wronged, she itemised his misdemeanours: his hypocrisy; his cocaine-taking; his heavy drinking; his multiple infidelities; his offer to set her up with a gigolo; his alleged failure to give her the full divorce settlement. Referring to the settlement, she said, 'I couldn't be bothered to fight him anymore because I just wanted out. I walked away with my clothes, my jewellery and £40,000 which he paid me over a period of four years.'

Loyalty surely fortified by self-interest, Debbie had soon cut off diplomatic relations not only with Jean but also with Howard. The steadfastness of her support can't have hindered her advancement within

Raymond's publishing company where she'd become his most trusted lieutenant alongside Carl Snitcher. Her influential position within the company also provided Raymond with a potent, if unconvincing, defence against feminist-inspired accusations that his magazines were demeaning to women.

In readiness for the day when he'd hand over his kingdom to her, Raymond tried to give Debbie an insight into the property side of his business. To that end, he started taking her to auctions, where she witnessed his single-minded approach to the game of real-life Monopoly. Describing one such trip to the auction rooms, she said, 'He just turned round and bid £3 million for a property and it started off at £200,000 and he's gone straight to £3 million and the whole place has gone "Uh?" and they say, "Sold." And he says, "Thank you." He just comes in and knows exactly what he wants and how much he's going to pay, and that's it. He doesn't fool around or mess around. He goes straight for it.'

As he strolled through Soho with business acquaintances, his Rolls-Royce gliding alongside, poised to provide shelter in the event of a sudden downpour, he could now nonchalantly point to the numerous buildings he'd acquired. 'I own that one and that one and that one. I just sold that one and that one…'

Never the type who bestowed trust easily, Raymond had learned not only to rely on Debbie and Carl Snitcher but also Steve Bleach, his confidence in whom had possibly been enhanced by the discovery that he too had been brought up a Catholic. 'The first time it came up in conversation,' recalled Bleach, 'Raymond said, "RC?" And I said, "Yes." And he tapped his forehead in a knowing and approving way. I think religion had a strong sentimental value to him. All those stories you'd hear about him insisting on editors removing photos of girls with crucifixes round their necks were, I'm sure, true. We had to show him a dummy copy of every issue of our magazines before they went to press.

'When I was doing my first issue of a new title called *Razzle*, we had this meeting where we were discussing what would be in it. I said, "I'm going to get six models together and it'll be like *Tiswas*, that old television programme, except it'll be naked. I'm going to have girls in kitchens, covered in stuff. I'm going to have girls dressed as teachers and nuns…" He hit the roof and said, "You will *not* have nuns!"'

'He wasn't particularly fond of the more downmarket magazines like *Razzle* and *Escort*. *Club International* was more his sort of thing. The photography was quite classy. *Escort*, which I helped to revamp, was based on reader response, on people sending in letters as well as photos. He loved the sales figures it generated but he could never warm to Shelley from a council estate in Doncaster in a lime-green basque posed on a brown Dralon sofa and pictured against flock wallpaper. I admit, it could be quite shocking wading through stacks of photos like that, not because of the nudity but because of the home furnishings.'

Periodic rows broke out between Raymond and Bleach, rows that would get so fiery that one of them sometimes put the phone down on the other, yet a friendship between them developed. 'The first time I went out with him as a friend rather than just an employee, I got hideously drunk trying to match him drink for drink,' Bleach said. 'He asked his chauffeur to drive me back to Battersea, where I was living with my girlfriend. He was capable of doing really kind things like that.

'After I got married, I'd sometimes invite him round to our flat for meals. When this started, his housekeeper warned me, "Mr Raymond is used to the very *best* quality things, you know…"'

'Over lunch or dinner he'd tell old stories and nod sagely, but he wasn't the sort of guy who'd repeat himself and expect everybody to laugh. Then again, he wasn't an after-dinner speaker. He was just good company. He'd pull a yarn out of the bag if it was apposite, often old Soho stories. Tellingly, they were always about other people, not himself.

'He'd sometimes have me over to his flat for drinks. The employer–

employee relationship would reassert itself just as I was leaving. He'd go all formal and say, "Right, thank you..."

'Every so often – and this rarely happened – he'd open up about personal things, mainly concerning Debbie. But there was always a certain amount of awkwardness involved. He once told me, "I don't mind you having a drink at lunchtime, but never let your staff see you *drunk*." His rule was that you mustn't show any sort of weakness to people you employ.'

This remote, disengaged stance enabled him to ignore his daughter's depressive tendencies and persistent heavy drug use, cocaine inevitably playing a part in what work colleagues perceived as her effervescent character. 'She was taking a lot of the stuff,' remembered another PRO staffer. 'She kept her supply in a container the size of a tennis ball – the likes of which I've never seen before or since. It must've been worth thousands of pounds.

'At the 1988 Christmas party, held at Madame JoJo's, she beckoned me into the office and asked if I wanted a line of cocaine. I felt pressured into accepting. About an hour later she came up to me and accused me of stealing her entire supply. She'd just misplaced it but, in her druggy paranoia, she was convinced I'd taken it. In many ways she was very sweet and charming, but she had a vindictive streak when she was under the influence of drink or drugs.'

# 48 HARD CASH

**H**AD IT NOT BEEN for Raymond, Soho probably wouldn't have remained so architecturally intact, few modern buildings disrupting the pattern of low-rise, mostly pre-twentieth-century streets. By amassing such a substantial proportion of the area's freeholds, then harvesting rent from their tenants instead of bulldozing the sites, he inadvertently protected those buildings at a time when Westminster City Council was prepared to sanction wholesale redevelopment.

The ongoing gentrification of Soho owed a lot to its picturesque, ramshackle architecture which contributed to an ambience found nowhere else in the West End. Thanks to the commercial pressure applied by the encroachment of both the sex industry and gentrification, Soho had, by the end of the 1980s, lost numerous long-established businesses that had helped to sustain the district's polyglot charm. Despite his own role in the transformation, Raymond continued posing as an ally of the conservationists. On hearing that Richards, a fishmonger close to the junction between Walker's Court and Brewer Street, was being replaced by a peepshow, he declared that the person responsible should be shot.

Against the odds, many of Soho's specialist shops were still trading. Whenever Raymond asked Charles Rothenstein, his suave, imperturbable chauffeur, to drive him from his Archer Street offices to the Revuebar, they passed idiosyncratic establishments such as Lina Stores, the front window of which was sandbagged with fresh bread; House Brothers, suppliers of hardware and chefs' knives; and Randall & Aubin, the French butcher's and delicatessen where you could buy home-made sausages and ham sliced from the bone on a marble counter by its elderly proprietress.

Like these quaint specialist shops, the Revuebar was beginning to feel antiquated. *Unlike* those businesses, though, it didn't feel appealingly old fashioned. It felt outmoded and seedy, any vestige of sophistication long since vanished.

'I went into the gents' toilet and, to my surprise, every urinal was a slightly different shape or a different height off the ground or, in one case, a completely different colour – yellow instead of white,' Clive Harris remembered. 'When I bumped into the Revuebar's oddjob man, I asked him why all the urinals were different. He said, "If one of them gets broken, Mr Raymond doesn't like me buying a new one. He insists on me picking up a replacement from a condemned building." Maybe that's how you become a multi-millionaire.'

All of which went some way towards explaining why a gag about this famous old venue was in circulation around then.

Q: 'Why do bouncers stand outside the Revuebar?'
A: 'To throw customers *in…*'

Raymond no longer spent much time there, but on those rare occasions when he took his place in the lounge bar, he was serenaded by tannoy announcements in half a dozen languages. Carrying on the trend that had first manifested itself more than two decades earlier, the clientele was dominated by foreign smut-hounds, mainly Japanese and South Korean businessmen. The tannoy announcements heralded slickly choreographed shows that bore little resemblance to either the shows originally staged there or to the rudimentary shows presented by its surviving competitors, the Sunset Strip and the Carnival Revue Club. Moving in time to the loud rhythm of taped music, Gérard Simi's well-rehearsed squadron of nubile girls executed complex dance routines, often ending with them striking gymnastic poses, waxed legs parted, genitalia briefly proffered for inspection by the audience.

One of Raymond's longest-running rivals in the softcore magazine market was *Mayfair*, which combined girlie shots with mainstream male-oriented features on subjects such as steam trains and classic cars. During 1990 its owner, Ken Bound, looked around for a buyer for the business. Raymond's rival porn baron, Richard Desmond, put in a bid. Hearing about this, Raymond decided to gazump Desmond, whom he loathed. Towards the end of the year, Raymond was chauffeured round to the magazine's offices near Holborn where, with theatrical brio, he left a cheque for £3.5 million on the absent owner's desk.

*Mayfair*, which had a circulation of nearly 300,000 a month, rapidly joined Paul Raymond Publications' line-up of titles. 'I first met Raymond at that year's staff Christmas party, held at the Windmill Theatre,' recalled Clive Harris, one of *Mayfair*'s freelance contributors. 'I saw Raymond standing in the corner and I thought I should introduce myself. I went and said, "Hullo, my name's Bill Shipton" – that's my *nom de porn*. "By the way, as a lifelong stand-up comedy fan, it's fantastic to be able to say that I've been onstage at the Windmill. You used to be in variety theatre, didn't you? Did you ever play the Windmill?" And he went, "No, we were never good enough." I didn't know what to say next. Then he said, "It was a damn fortunate thing that we weren't good enough. If I'd been even *slightly* talented, I'd still be doing it now, instead of which I ended up owning the theatre."

'That was a very incisive thing to say. If you were halfway decent, you'd carry on touring in the hope that one day you'd make it. I suspect what Raymond said was a well-rehearsed line.

'I found him very easy to get on with. I met him again soon afterwards when he went through the Christmas issue of *Mayfair* with me. It was twice the size of the normal issues and packed with articles about cars and so forth. Raymond maintained a vaguely disgusted expression as he looked at these. He pointed at one of them and said, "What's *this*?" And I went, "Oh, it's about historic slot machines." To which he said, "Did *you* write it?" A note of pride in my voice, I replied, "Yes." And he said, "Well, you won't be doing anything like *that* again."

'Pretty soon Raymond had dispensed with all the mainstream features. He was a tits-on-every-page man.'

Debbie's marriage to John James brought Raymond into contact with James's friend and former flatmate, Mark Fuller. 'My wife and I would often see Paul at Debbie's house in Chobham,' Fuller recollected. 'Then he started inviting us to functions and round to his flat. John was by that time working for Paul's property division. They'd just repossessed a unit on Greek Street. Knowing that I wanted to open a club, John asked whether I was interested in taking the lease on it, but I told him I didn't think I could stretch to the figure Paul had in mind. One day my mobile phone rang and, when I answered it, a voice said, "Paul Raymond here. On the subject of No. 18 Greek Street, you are offering £100,000 rent and I am asking for £150,000 and we are settling on £135,000. Thank you, goodbye..."

'So I phoned John up and said, "I've just had this most bizarre phone call from Paul." I told him the whole conversation and said, "What does it mean?" And he said, "It means you've done a deal." And I replied, "What about the paperwork?" And he said, "Oh, we'll get round to that."

'I duly signed the papers and opened a club there called Boardwalk, but I could hardly have picked a worse time because the economy was in a bit of a mess. About three months into the lease, when the newspapers were full of stories about the first Gulf War, Paul's Rolls-Royce pulled up outside the club and Charles, his chauffeur, opened the door for him. In comes Paul, clutching a little handbag. He goes up to the bar, which isn't very busy, and says, "I'd like a Rémy Martin, and I'd like you to make it a double." When he takes out a £50 note, something you didn't see very often back then, I say to him, "No, no, please let me pay." And he goes, "If you insist on buying me this drink, I shall not only drink it but I shall turn round and I shall leave." So I let him give the barman the £50 note. Of course, the barman comes back with his change. Around forty quid. Paul says, "*What* is this?" The barman replies, "That's your change, sir." To which Paul says, "Did I *ask* you for any change?" Then the barman says, "What d'you want me to do?" Paul says, "I don't want you to give me any change." As he walks away, he says to me, "Come and join me." I sit with him, and he asks me an awful lot of questions about Soho and life and business. Clearly he knows the answers to most of them, but he wants *my* answers. At the end of our conversation he gets up and orders another drink. He pulls out another £50 note and repeats his routine with the barman before returning to where we're sitting. All of a sudden Paul says to me, "In one month's time you have to pay me your rent and you aren't going to be able to afford it." I feed him a line about how I've got some events coming up, so I might be able to get the money together. And he says, "You're not listening. You are *not* going to be able to pay your rent." "I'm going to *try*," I tell him. "You're not *listening*. You *can't* pay your rent." In the end I say, "What do I do if I can't pay?" So he says, "*Don't* pay." Then he just stands up and walks out.

'Rent day comes round and I've only got five of the thirty-eight grand I owe. I phone Paul and say, "You were absolutely right. I'm really struggling. I can't pay my rent. I'm terribly sorry." And he goes, "*Why* are you phoning me? I told you before: if you can't pay your whole rent, don't pay anything."

'Anyway, business doesn't improve and, on the date that the next quarter's rent is due, I can only afford to cover part of it. I phone him again and he says, "Stop calling me. When I want your money, I will *ask*." Then he puts the phone down.

'Apparently he said to John and Debbie one day, "I see a great deal of myself in Mark and I think he'll be all right and I want to support him."

'My rent arrears soon added up to £120,000. Paul wasn't renowned for this sort of thing. He was known for playing hardball. During that recession, he was repossessing loads of property, yet he was incredibly generous to me. I was in debt to him for a long time. He'd book my club for lots of parties, and he'd go to dinner there most nights even though I know he didn't really like the place. He gave me all the support he could.'

In November 1990 Raymond celebrated his sixty-fifth birthday. At the age when the majority of British men drew their pensions, he showed little sign of relaxing. He still spent most days at the office, from where he tried to monitor every aspect of his business. And he continued to assuage his loneliness by spending most nights on the town, sometimes staying out until three or four in the morning, his chauffeur-driven Rolls-Royce invariably moored outside whichever bar, restaurant or club he patronised. Even if he was on holiday, he'd make enough phone calls to the Archer Street offices to annoy Debbie.

He hadn't changed in other respects either. His face looked a little baggier, a little more careworn, yet his waistline remained trim. His taste in flashy suits lingered. So too did his hairstyle which the writer Jonathan Meades, who often sighted him in Soho, described as a 'backcombed mega-mullet'. Raymond also retained his residual attachment to Catholicism. 'If I was knocked down in the street today,' he admitted, 'the first person I would ask for would be the Catholic priest – to give me the last rites.'

Always an asset for anyone in his business, he even retained his gift for provoking gossip about himself, gossip that had helped to create a cartoonish alter ego. 'My favourite story about him – probably apocryphal like so many of the others – was told to me by Charles, his chauffeur, who used to spend a lot of time hanging round on reception at Archer Street,' Clive Harris said. 'Charles was just how you'd expect a chauffeur to be. He had this wonderful drawling voice. Everything was terribly calm – "Of course, no problem, Mr Raymond…" He told me that he once got a phone call from Raymond who said, "Where were we last night?" Charles replied, "As you may recall, you went to such-and-such a club." "Yes, I vaguely remember that," Raymond said. Then he added, "I've just checked my bank balance and it's down by about £200,000. I didn't go gambling, did I?" And Charles went, "No, as you might recall, we were going to visit such-and-such a restaurant, and you wanted to park outside but they wouldn't let you. So we had to go to the multi-storey car park, which was the nearest available parking space. And when they said, 'Oh, that'll be five pounds', you said, 'Get me the manager', and you asked the manager for the phone number of the owner and you ended up buying the car park.'"

Colourful though his public persona remained, advancing age had precipitated all sorts of subtle changes to Raymond. 'He seemed to be becoming less flamboyant, less of a showman and more of a businessman,' Steve Bleach observed. 'Frankly, he seemed a bit disconnected from the team putting together his magazines. He couldn't really relate to our twenty-one-year-old designers who were playing techno music at two hundred decibels.'

The changes weren't restricted to his work. As he readily admitted, these days he didn't end his West End pub and club crawls by taking his latest steady girlfriend or nightclub pick-up back to his flat. 'You may laugh at this,' he told a reporter who'd asked whether he went to confession, 'but if I went I don't know what I would have to confess.'

Though he still drank heavily, he'd stopped taking cocaine. He'd quit smoking as well, the cue for that provided by a deep, catarrhal cough which was, he thought, his body's way of saying, 'Look, I can't stand any more of that smoke down there.'

He'd changed in other ways, too – not least in the bleak view of human nature he'd acquired. 'Women will let you down, and friends will let you down. You're on your own,' he confided in Steve Bleach.

Friends, family and colleagues nonetheless testified to the fact that he'd softened, that he was less abrasive and intransigent. Previously, it would have been difficult to envisage him initiating a tentative reconciliation with Howard, yet – around the middle of 1990 – Raymond had done just that by phoning him one Sunday. They had, since then, started meeting on average once a month and ringing each other once a fortnight. Howard got the impression that Raymond at last enjoyed his company.

Among Raymond's immediate family, there was a mood of compromise that even embraced Jean and Debbie. In March 1991 Jean received a call from Debbie during the middle of the night. 'Debbie said, "Mummy, I'm so sorry, will you ever forgive me?" I just burst into tears,' Jean remembered. 'We chatted from two o'clock in the morning until 5.30 a.m. She said the following weekend she'd pop in with Fawn and see me.

'Two days later on Mother's Day I got a huge bouquet of orchids from her. I was so excited about the visit I went out and bought some expensive food and cleaned the house from top to bottom. I bought Fawn a big white teddy bear and sat with it and waited for Debbie to arrive. She never turned up and I never got an explanation.'

# 49 MATERIAL GIRL

**H**IS INTEREST IN PEOPLE always dwarfed by his interest in making money, Raymond was oblivious to his daughter's spiralling problems. Besides consuming mounds of cocaine, she'd become an alcoholic, the combination making her unpredictable and at times irrational. It also exacerbated her depressive tendencies, so effectively camouflaged by her raucous vivacity.

Blind to her patent unsuitability to cope with the pressure of running his business empire, now worth about £130 million, Raymond continued grooming her for the moment he handed over control. Not that she had any idea when that would happen. She and Raymond didn't, she conceded, 'have the sort of relationship where the subject will come up', though she had her suspicions that he'd never retire.

The next step in preparing her for the eventual succession involved appointing her as editor-in-chief of his publishing company. In that role she was responsible for a roster of top-shelf magazines which had expanded to eight titles, the newcomers including *Men's World* and *Model Directory*. But she hadn't been doing the job for long before she was, to Raymond's consternation, diagnosed with breast cancer. The diagnosis necessitated a double mastectomy, her fate lent added poignancy by her involvement in a business permeated by mammary mania.

Hospitalisation giving her time to brood over her past, she phoned Howard's ex-wife and sought forgiveness for her contribution to Maria's exile from the family. Amazingly, the two women were reconciled, bitterness modulating into a burgeoning friendship which Debbie felt compelled to conceal from her father, who would have disapproved of it.

402 | PAUL WILLETTS

Once Debbie had been released from hospital, where she had undergone reconstructive surgery, she returned to work, bravely wearing the same low-cut dresses she'd always favoured and cracking defiant jokes about how she'd never had much in the way of tits. Her superficial jollity, along with doses of antidepressant medication, masked her true state of mind which warranted regular appointments with a consultant psychiatrist. He noticed that she seemed perpetually worried – 'worried about doing things properly and fulfilling her responsibilities'.

Proud of her apparent resilience, Raymond hailed her as the toughest person he'd ever encountered. That toughness seemed to be expressed in the kamikaze gusto with which she resumed the drink- and drug-filled life she'd had before the cancer diagnosis. Remembering the period after she emerged from hospital, Maria said, 'She came to me once and carried this huge mirror down the stairs and laid it on the floor. Then she wrote her name in cocaine on the mirror ready to snort it. I was upset with her and told her to clean it up.'


However wealthy Raymond became, the symbols of Establishment approval remained out of reach, his seldom expressed yearning for an OBE or, perhaps, a knighthood unfulfilled. For a man so shrewd, cynical and worldly, it was oddly naive of him even to contemplate the possibility. No politician, irrespective of their ideological hue, would have sanctioned the presence on the honours list of someone so enmeshed in the porn trade, someone bound to provoke a flurry of negative press coverage, scorn mingled with amusement. Little imagination was required to picture the consequent tabloid headlines. Next to a photo of Sir Paul Raymond emerging from Buckingham Palace, there'd be the words 'Knight of Sin'.

Had his political acumen matched his flair for business, Raymond would have tried to launder both his money and his reputation by means of conspicuous philanthropy, though he might, even then, have been impeded by his association with the sex industry. Institutions may well have been reluctant to align themselves with him. At least one organisation had already turned down a donation from him. He'd recently offered to contribute to a refurbishment appeal by Soho Parish School, a Church of England primary school located near his Archer Street offices. But the head teacher, whose pupils included children of women working in the local brothels, peepshows and strip-clubs, had rejected the offer because he regarded Raymond's money as tainted.

Instead of using charitable donations to curry favour with the political establishment and the public, Raymond kept admirably quiet about his role as an occasional benefactor, channelling his money towards causes with which he had a strong connection. One such cause was Brinsworth House, a retirement home in the south-west London suburb of Twickenham. Out of gratitude to the performers who'd played such an integral part in his success, he donated enough money for the Entertainment Artistes' Benevolent Fund, which ran Brinsworth House, to build a new wing.

Another recipient of his sporadic largesse was the Association for Stammerers. Raymond, who needed no reminder of just how distressing a speech impediment could be, funded an event to launch a book on the subject. Held at Paramount City on Tuesday 1 October 1991, the event was attended by members of the association and several celebrity supporters: the cartoonist Glen Baxter, the novelist Margaret Drabble and the screenwriter Ray Connolly. Once this varied trio had addressed the audience about their experiences of stammering, Raymond delivered his own recollections, spanning his childhood and abortive quest for a cure at Bill Kerr's clinic.

Among the individuals and organisations who contacted Raymond to request a donation was his ex-wife, who had just moved back to her home town of Tuxford, where she'd bought a two-bedroom cottage. Together with a group of old schoolfriends, Jean had set up a tap-dancing troupe called the Groovy Grannies, dedicated to raising money for charity by performing in local village halls. Her estranged daughter's illness had inspired her to devote the troupe's first year to raising money for cancer research. She revealed that when she'd asked Raymond for a donation, telling him that even £1 would secure him a mention in the programme, he'd fobbed her off by saying, 'Jean, I think what you're doing is wonderful, but one has to draw the line somewhere. There are so many charities.'

By opening the Piano Bar and then Madame JoJo's, Raymond had helped to launch a trend within a trend. In parallel with the ongoing gentrification of Soho, the Old Compton Street area had, by 1992, metamorphosed into a flourishing gay enclave. Fuelled by the disproportionate spending power of male homosexuals, their income spared from the ravages of child-rearing, numerous café-bars had appeared, side by side with shops offering anything from leatherwear to eyelash-tinting.

Male tourists wandering through Soho were now more likely to be chatted up by some meticulously coiffed cruiser than approached by a streetwalker or by touts from the sleazier strip-clubs and hostess bars. Nevertheless, in March that year, there were still sufficient touts loitering on the streets to cajole Raymond into a sincere and indignant yet deeply hypocritical tirade. 'They're giving such a terrible name to Soho,' he told a reporter. 'It's not just taking customers away from the Raymond Revuebar. These people are crooks. They're taking money and they threaten people and it's an appalling state of affairs.'

This vein of self-righteousness led Raymond to get embroiled in an undignified encounter. Late on the evening of Monday, 8 June, Raymond was, for once, not entrenched in some West End restaurant, bar or nightclub. He was, instead, sitting at home in his brightly patterned dressing gown watching *Newsnight*, the BBC current affairs programme. That evening's broadcast featured a debate on media coverage of the collapse of the Prince and Princess of Wales's marriage. The discussion involved the Bishop of St Albans, who was in the BBC studios, and the pugnacious *Sunday Times* editor Andrew Neil, who was standing on the pavement outside a restaurant. Raymond recognised the restaurant as Le Caprice, a swish eaterie nine floors beneath his flat. Neil found himself under attack from the bishop for his paper's reporting of the story which, the bishop felt, had been biased against the Royal Family.

Raymond was similarly affronted by Neil's attitude towards the monarch. 'You might expect such behaviour in Camden, but not here in SW1,' Raymond later commented.

Without even stopping to put on shoes or rearrange his intricate coiffure, Raymond ran downstairs and out of the building. The *Sunday Times* editor was still on camera when Raymond charged towards him, but the irate sixty-six-year-old was blocked by a BBC minder, employed to prevent just such incidents during outside broadcasts. Wrestling with Raymond, the minder succeeded in keeping him out of shot.

As Neil walked back into the restaurant after the interview had finished, Raymond stepped forward and lambasted him.

Nearly three months before that, Debbie had given birth to her second child, a daughter whom she and her husband named India Rose. In another exhibition of apparent mental and psychological resilience, Debbie returned to work soon after giving birth, leaving her nanny to look after Fawn and the new arrival.

Until Debbie phoned Jean in the early hours one night that summer, Jean didn't realise Debbie had had a second child. Jean recalled, 'She yelled, "You're a selfish bitch! I've just had a baby and where were you when I needed you?" Before I could reply, she slammed the phone down.'

More volatile than ever, Debbie got into a serious argument with her husband about his role within the family business. The argument culminated in John James moving out of their cottage in Chobham. 'It's not serious. I'm just making a statement,' he assured their mutual friend Mark Fuller, who had become godfather to Fawn and India.

Debbie and her husband had briefly separated once before, their reunion engineered by Fuller and his wife. But John James's confidence in this latest break-up reaching an identical conclusion was misplaced. Stomping off to Raymond's house in Antigua, Debbie began an affair with a man she met there. Her lover was the absurdly named Ainsley Tree, a thirty-year-old London-based graphic designer whose dark hair, cut in a floppy-fringed style, tended to fall across his unfashionable aviator-style glasses.

Their relationship continued when they returned to the capital. Not long after that, Debbie was the subject of an adulatory, spectacularly ill-judged feature in the magazine *BusinessAge* which predicted that she'd become Britain's first female billionaire. Debbie Raymond 'has all the confidence of someone who has really found their feet', the article purred. 'She has no hang-ups about who she is or what she is. There are no nervous breakdowns looming and her father has a safe pair of hands to leave his empire to.'

Five years had gone by since Debbie and Howard had seen each other. On Sunday, 1 November she ended the estrangement by visiting him in hospital where he was being treated for a minor stomach ailment, her own recent illness presumably encouraging her to empathise with Howard. He thought she was in 'extremely good spirits'. She brought him a bottle of wine and about £500-worth of flowers. With her by his bedside, he eventually drifted off to sleep. While he was dozing, she drank the bottle of wine she'd brought him.

The fact that Debbie was destined to be the richest woman in Britain – unless her father disinherited her – couldn't make up for her problems: the drinking, the drug-taking, the depression, the trauma of the double mastectomy and now the break-up of her marriage. Inclined to equate well-being with money, Raymond was unaware that there might be anything wrong with Debbie. After seeing her at the office, he delivered a typical misdiagnosis. He said, 'Debbie seemed absolutely fine' and 'in great form'.

At 9.45 p.m. that Wednesday she made a phone call to his flat which perpetuated this comforting illusion. He wasn't at home, so his housekeeper took the call. Debbie sounded 'happy and totally normal'. She explained to Raymond's housekeeper that she'd wanted to discuss the television programme she was watching: the latest edition of the Channel 4 documentary series *Dispatches*, which was examining fresh evidence of a link between the increased availability of pornography and the rise in sexual violence across Britain. Raymond's housekeeper told Debbie that he might be watching it elsewhere. Debbie laughed and said, 'No, Pa will be having a drink probably.'

Just as she'd assumed, Raymond was making his customary round of his favourite West End watering holes. He would have cause to look back with piercing regret about not being around to take her call.

Unusually, he didn't cross paths with her the following day. At 10 a.m. the day after that, he received a call from a stranger, bearing terrible news. The stranger, who turned out to be Ainsley Tree, said he couldn't wake her up and that she appeared to have died.

Once he'd finished speaking to Debbie's father, Tree summoned an ambulance which rushed Debbie from his flat in Belsize Park to the Royal Free Hospital in Hampstead. Still unconscious, she was pronounced dead well before Raymond could get to the hospital.

He was, as Carl Snitcher observed, 'absolutely devastated' by what had happened to Debbie, who was only a couple of months short of her thirty-seventh birthday. Since the cause of death remained unclear, the hospital arranged a post-mortem. Detectives from Hampstead CID also began an investigation. By questioning her boyfriend for three hours, they were able to discover enough about the circumstances of her death to rule out either suicide or foul play.

She'd left her children at home the previous evening, then headed over to Tree's flat. There, she had drunk vodka and snorted what the police believed to be cocaine. Whether this had killed her was, as yet, unclear because the results of the post-mortem were inconclusive, prompting the hospital to send samples from Debbie's body to a toxicology unit for further tests.

In the meantime, Raymond was driven by his chauffeur to her cottage, where he spent the day with his son-in-law and Fawn who, unlike her baby sister, was old enough to share their grief. Decades of publicity-seeking ensured that Raymond didn't just have to cope with emotional desolation. He had to contend with a column of reporters who pitched up at the cottage wanting interviews. Sobbing over a glass of brandy, he told one of them, 'I'm a tough, tough guy, but I've been crying my eyes out all day.' In a revealing aside indicative of his blinkered materialism, he added, 'Debbie had all the money in the world, a beautiful home, beautiful kids, beautiful cars. She had everything. I don't understand it.'

About a day afterwards, Raymond phoned Steve Bleach. 'It was the most heart-rending phone call I've ever had,' Bleach remembered. 'I could tell he was distraught. His voice had gone all thin and weak. He'd not only lost the person he loved most but also the only person he really trusted. Every other relationship was, for him, contaminated by the fortune he'd amassed, by the suspicion that people were only after his money.'

Articles about Debbie's death from an apparent drug overdose appeared in most of the national newspapers that weekend, the tenor of these ranging from the sympathetic to the gloatingly prurient. When Raymond's illegitimate son Derry read about the death of the half-sister he'd never met, he used the occasion to attempt to re-establish contact with Raymond by sending him a letter of condolence, but the message went unanswered, grief trumping courtesy.

# 50 DEATH DUTIES

D EBBIE'S FUNERAL TOOK PLACE on Friday, 13 November 1992 at Golders Green Crematorium. Only a handful of tearful friends and family were invited, the guests including Jean but not Ainsley Tree. Raymond had sent a wreath that read, 'It's not the same without you – your laughter, your humour, your love, your fun.'

His ex-wife was already there by the time he arrived in a black Rolls-Royce with tinted windows. Debbie's death seemed to have sapped his confidence, his air of invulnerability, all the traits that had kept old age at bay. Peering through large oblong spectacles that emphasised his weepy disbelief, he looked elderly, anxious and a little frail.

The animosity between him and Jean was undiminished. From Jean's perspective, the death of their daughter offered yet another reason to despise her ex-husband. His indulgence of Debbie had, Jean felt, made him culpable for the tragedy that had occurred.

Reminiscing later about the funeral, Jean said, 'Paul hardly even acknowledged me. He introduced me to a couple of people, just saying "This is Jean Raymond..." He couldn't even bring himself to say I was Debbie's mother. I've made up my mind that I never want to see him again.'

After a twenty-minute service, led by a Roman Catholic priest, Debbie's coffin slid out of sight, ready for her cremation.

Few friends, acquaintances or employees who encountered Raymond in the wake of Debbie's death failed to notice how much he'd been altered by it. 'Her death changed him completely,' Noel Botham confirmed.

*Paul
Raymond
arrives at his
daughter's
funeral*

Simultaneously deprived of Debbie and burdened by a sense of guilt, which he mentioned to at least one friend, the pleasure seems to have leached out of most of the things he used to enjoy: women, eating in restaurants, chatting with strangers, telling anecdotes about his past. Even the pleasure he'd taken in making money failed to emerge unscathed. Only his feelings for Debbie's children survived the effects of that terrible night in November, his devotion to Debbie reinvested in Fawn and India. 'He absolutely adored them, and they adored him,' Mark Fuller said. 'His relationship with them was very sweet. He was a generous grandfather to them, but not *too* generous.'

Doing his best to duplicate the stoicism Debbie had shown after her cancer treatment, Raymond went back to work, back to the Archer Street offices, which were haunted by her absence. Nowadays he seldom popped into the French House at lunchtimes, his plans for Noel Botham to write his biography abandoned like so many other things. Instead, he'd simply nip out for a sandwich, this abrupt change of routine matching the perfunctory nature of his remodelled life.

That transformation was nowhere more evident than in the evenings.

Less than a month earlier he was still devoting as much energy to his social life as to his business. Not any more, though. Rather than have his chauffeur ferry him from Archer Street to a succession of West End bars, clubs and restaurants, he'd ask to be driven straight home. There, his housekeeper would prepare him a solitary meal, eaten from a tray on his lap while he embarked on an evening of television, his lonely, penitent ritual guaranteed to nourish his misery.

More than likely as a means of atoning for his unwitting contribution to Debbie's death, Raymond's life now acquired a single purpose. 'He became utterly obsessed with amassing as much money as possible to bequeath to Fawn and India,' one of his employees recalled. 'Every time a deal was clinched, he'd come out with what turned into a catchphrase, "It's all for the granddaughters…"'

They became the prime beneficiaries of nineteen trusts created to minimise the tax liabilities when Raymond died. Meanwhile Howard's two children, victims of rancorous family politics, never seem to have figured in Raymond's self-redemptive plans. Such blatant favouritism lent added motivation to Jean's bitter dispute with her ex-husband.

His first big property swoop after Debbie's death appears to have been the £2.65 million purchase of a cinema and a couple of adjoining shops on the King's Road in Chelsea. These joined an imposing stock of freeholds mostly in Soho but reputedly also in Poland and other former Soviet bloc countries.

Raymond's property empire provided the basis for a cover story in the December issue of *BusinessAge*. He was placed at the top of a league table of Britain's wealthiest men, including Richard Branson, David Sainsbury and the Duke of Westminster. The magazine, which claimed that he owned 18 per cent of Soho's 87 acres, estimated his fortune at anywhere between £1.5 billion and £5 billion. Thanks to his twin policies of secrecy and concealment, however, any attempt by an outsider to precisely quantify his wealth was doomed. Whatever the true extent of the Raymond fortune, he'd have been delighted by the assertion that he'd ousted the Duke of Westminster from the No. 1 spot and could be 'closing in on the Queen's wealth'. Told by a journalist years earlier that he had just been installed as the 123rd richest man in Britain, he'd replied, 'If I'm not in the top ten, then I don't want to play.'

From beyond Raymond's Archer Street redoubt, the reaction to his pecuniary pre-eminence was scornful. While *The Times* questioned the calculations employed by *BusinessAge*, the *Sun* ran a hostile interview with Jean. 'I'm incredibly pleased for him,' she said with heavy sarcasm. 'Money is the only thing that makes him happy.'

Adding to the chorus of disdain, the *SFX College Magazine* noted, 'Some of our readers will be aware that an Old Boy has been listed as the richest man in England. Though his route to the top demonstrates the versatility of Old Xaverians, his success has not been closely followed in these pages.'

The uncertainty surrounding Debbie's death warranted an official inquest, held at St Pancras Coroner's Court on Tuesday, 26 January 1993. Raymond, Jean, Howard, Debbie's estranged husband and Howard's ex-wife Maria were among the audience. Even in their shared grief, Paul and Jean Raymond refused to declare so much as a temporary truce, the two of them pointedly ignoring each other.

Chaired by the Assistant Deputy Coroner, Dr Ian Shedden, the court heard from a series of witnesses who provided a composite picture of events leading up to Debbie's death. The central question was speedily answered. Dr Freddy Patel, a Home Office pathologist, testified that he'd found traces of an antidepressant drug in her blood. He'd also discovered 'extremely high' levels of morphine. He told the court that 120 microgrammes of morphine per litre of blood was the generally accepted lethal dose, yet Debbie's blood contained 165 microgrammes per litre.

Debbie's psychiatrist was another of the witnesses. He informed the court that he'd seen her for a routine appointment the day before her death. 'I have never considered her to be a suicide risk,' he stated. 'Having said that, I *was* concerned about her recklessness.'

For Debbie's family, the most painfully immediate testimony came from Ainsley Tree. Always uncomfortable with displays of emotion, Raymond had put on dark glasses to conceal his response to what was said. Tree described how she took cocaine about four times a week, augmented by ecstasy and other drugs. On the night of her death, Debbie's boyfriend explained, they were happy because they'd just patched up their differences after a row that had threatened to end their relationship. Arriving at his flat that night, he said, she'd drunk a bottle of vodka and snorted a line of cocaine. He added that he hadn't seen her take heroin until that night. 'She said she wanted to try it.'

Then he told the court what had happened after she'd taken the heroin. 'She sat on the end of the bed and I went to sleep. When I woke up, I tried to wake her. She would not wake up. I thought she was joking. I thought I would try to wake her by putting her under the shower. I put her under the shower and she would not wake up. I took her back to bed and tried to give her mouth-to-mouth resuscitation.'

Concluding the inquest, Dr Shedden delivered a verdict on the evidence presented that day. 'Debbie Raymond was a young woman who had very much to live for,' he said. 'She had marital problems and she was very deeply attached to her children and had formed an important relationship with a man. Although she had suffered from depression, there was no evidence to suggest that it had led her to take her own life.' He ended by saying, 'She was clearly a chronic drug abuser and I find she came to her death as a result of an accident.'

Raymond's dark glasses failed to hide his tears as the verdict was announced.

With predictable indelicacy, at least one journalist buttonholed Raymond on his way out of the court and asked for a comment. None was forthcoming. From that moment onwards, he tended to shun the press attention he'd done so much to encourage.

Setting aside all the years of enmity between herself and Raymond, Maria tried to spare him further intrusion by throwing the press a few platitudes. 'It has been a very trying time for the family,' she said. 'They would like for Debbie to rest in peace now. It's been very sad and we would like to put it behind us.'

But that wasn't something Raymond was capable of achieving. As the months passed, the intensity of his emotion didn't lessen. Whenever friends or family raised the subject of his daughter's death, he'd turn so tearful that they learnt to avoid the subject. Perhaps hoping that the pain would recede if he didn't talk about what lay at its root, he adopted the same strategy.

# 51 VITAL STATISTICS

I N ONE OF THE FEW INTERVIEWS he granted after Debbie's death, Raymond declared, 'I've become a bit like Hoover. I have made myself a brand-name, only for adult entertainment.'

By 1993 Paul Raymond Publications was his most profitable vehicle for marketing this. Despite filing a pre-tax profit of £15 million, Raymond was already thinking of selling the company because he didn't want to embarrass Fawn and India by bequeathing them a pornography business. Not that he liked to admit to the true nature of his publishing firm. Even in the late 1980s, he was still feeding journalists that tired line about being an *entertainer* rather than a pornographer. His other favourite defence, freighted with spurious innocence, was that he was just 'celebrating beauty'.

As befitted the uncrowned King of Soho, the question of inheritance preoccupied Raymond. His experience with Debbie had, according to one of his friends, left him concerned about the potentially destructive effects of leaving so much money to Fawn and India. Those concerns were, however, offset by the pleasure he derived from knowing that they would, as he told that same friend, never have any material worries.

Around the end of 1993, he made an unexpected phone call to Jean, informing her that he was cutting her out of his will. 'I just laughed and told him I couldn't have cared less,' Jean later confessed. 'He said he wanted to become a recluse because people only liked him because of his money. He seemed so sad and lonely I ended up feeling sorry for him.'

Beyond his wealth, his twice-yearly trips to his house in Antigua and his warm relationship with Fawn, India and their father, Raymond's life had become unenviable, the cost of his single-minded pursuit of wealth increasingly apparent. Sessions in his office alternated with arid nights in his flat where the only other companionship was provided by his housekeeper and by visits from Howard and a handful of loyal friends.

Though his personal life remained in gloomy stasis, he carried on expanding his property empire. As soon as he heard that the so-called 'Island Site' near Piccadilly Circus – a block comprising the Rialto Cinema and substantial sections of Coventry and Rupert Streets – was going on the market, he moved to acquire it. His instinct for decisive action unhindered by recent woes, he instructed his chauffeur to drive him round to the offices of David Coffer, chairman of Earls Court & Olympia plc, which owned the Island Site. Raymond handed an envelope to Coffer, who assumed that it contained a letter detailing his bid. Instead, there was a cheque for £14.25 million inside the envelope.

Within forty-eight hours, contracts had been exchanged. When the deal was made public, Raymond gave the press what appears to have been a fabricated story about how he'd pursued the purchase for sentimental reasons. 'Years ago I queued up across the road at five in the morning at the kitchen entrance of Joe Lyons to work as a washer-up for 10 shillings a morning,' he claimed, consciously embellishing his image as a self-made man.

In an odd postscript to his failed attempt to buy Watford Football Club just over six years earlier, Raymond was contacted during June 1994 by Elton John's AIDS Foundation, a charity set up to support HIV prevention programmes and eliminate discrimination against HIV-positive people and AIDS sufferers. The foundation wanted him to donate premises in Soho where it could establish a charity shop.

Politely declining the request, Raymond expressed his surprise at being approached, given Elton John's previous disparaging comments about him. Raymond used the incident to exact revenge on the singer by leaking the story to the *Daily Mail*'s gossip columnist.

Elton John's low opinion of Raymond would have been lowered still further if he'd known about the deal Raymond had just struck. The deal was with Oscar Owide, someone with whom Raymond had been on good terms since the late 1940s. A sixty-something East End jailbird who possessed the accent of a country squire, 'Mr Oscar' had run a series of hostess clubs which had earned him the accolade of 'Britain's biggest pimp'. Raymond leased him the building that housed Paramount City. Since the place was no longer viable as either a theatre or a nightclub, Raymond let him turn it into a lap-dancing club – a relatively new phenomenon.

Years of smoking, drinking, late nights and lack of exercise had, by that stage, eroded Raymond's adamantine constitution and sapped his formidable reserves of energy. More specifically, his breathing had started to sound wheezy and effortful. Doctors diagnosed emphysema, a respiratory condition doubtless brought on by the thousands of hours he'd spent inhaling both his own and other people's cigarette smoke. He was prescribed daily pills and also advised to retire.

Disinclined to relinquish control of the business he'd built over five decades, he arrived at a compromise that sensibly staved off what would, for him, have been the emptiness of complete retirement. He'd stop going into the office every day, but remain executive chairman of the PRO and appoint a managing director who would take the routine decisions. The obvious candidate for that post was Carl Snitcher. Instead, Raymond appointed a friend of two of the board members of the trusts created in readiness for his death. The new managing director, who took over late that summer, was Joe Daniel. What made the appointment so bizarre was that Daniel hadn't stepped straight into the post from some high-ranking job in the City: he was merely the former senior business manager at the Russell Square branch of Barclays Bank.

Reservations were voiced within the organisation about Daniel's appointment as second-in-command. But there was no doubting the sagacity of Raymond's decision to reduce his workload. Nonetheless, his deteriorating health left him looking haggard and sunken-eyed, forgetfulness about taking his prescribed medication contributing to the decline. That October he was afflicted by severe stomach pains that led to him being hospitalised, then undergoing heart surgery. For someone accustomed to dispensing orders, Raymond must have found it frustrating to cede authority to his doctors. Spurning their advice that he wasn't yet well enough to cope with a transatlantic flight, he headed off for his usual end-of-year trip to Antigua.

When he got home early in January 1995, he collapsed in his flat. Partially paralysed, he was taken to the private Lister Hospital in Chelsea, from where he was discharged on the penultimate weekend of that month.

As part of the shift towards delegating responsibility for more aspects of his business, Raymond appointed Steve Bleach to the post of director of Paul Raymond Publications, a post similar to the one Debbie had occupied. Bleach was responsible for overseeing all the company's titles, produced for the British, French and American markets.

By late March, Raymond had recovered sufficiently to involve himself in his business again, staging meetings with key members of staff at his flat. He even ventured out to attend the memorial service for the comedian-turned-television-presenter Larry Grayson, who had died during Raymond's most recent hospitalisation. The service was held at St Paul's Church, the so-called 'Actors' Church', in Covent Garden, where the congregation, which included the Beverley Sisters, Danny La Rue, Russ Conway and Frank Fraser, heard tributes from Terry Wogan and Roy Hudd, along with a baritone rendition of 'Be Still, My Soul', set to piano music by Sibelius.

☆

A dramatic shift in the market for Raymond's form of publishing was in progress by the summer of 1997. His magazines now had to compete not only with rival softcore publications and increasingly accessible hardcore pornography but also with new, unforeseen rivals. The Internet represented one of these, though it hadn't yet developed into the threat that it would soon become. More immediate competition was offered by two softcore newspapers – the *Daily Sport* and the *Sunday Sport* – and by the emergence of so-called 'lad mags', high-circulation publications such as *Loaded*, which presented softcore pornography in a more widely tolerated format than Raymond's stable of magazines. As yet, though, his titles remained hugely popular.

It wasn't just the publishing side of Raymond's sex business which was looking jaded. With the boom in lap-dancing clubs, which offered the customers a one-to-one experience, the elaborate choreography and razzamatazz of the Revuebar seemed to belong to a different era. Raymond had, ironically, played a significant role in making the erstwhile cornerstone of his empire appear so anachronistic and incongruous. When he'd launched the Revuebar, there had been something illicit and disreputable about the sex industry. Over the intervening thirty-nine years, he'd probably done more than anyone else to turn nude entertainment, be it strip-shows or pornographic magazines, into an accepted – if arguably corrosive – ingredient of British life. He'd also contributed to transforming a large tract of Soho into a gay area, within which the Revuebar had become a besieged outpost of musky heterosexuality.

Sensing Raymond's waning interest in the venue that had provided the platform for his ascent from small-time impresario to big-time businessman, its long-serving forty-two-year-old choreographer Gérard Simi spoke to him about the possibility of taking it over. Raymond agreed to the proposal. He granted Simi a twenty-year lease on the Revuebar as well as the right to continue trading under its existing name. The lease, initially generating £150,000 a year rent, marked the end of Raymond's involvement in live entertainment, which stretched back more than half a century.

On Monday, 7 July that year, Simi launched the Revuebar's first show under his stewardship. 'I owed Raymond a lot, and I wanted to keep on flying the flag for him,' Simi said. 'I believed the Revuebar was important, something that should be immortal.'

The mortality of its founder couldn't be ignored. Illness had, as the journalist John Walsh put it, left him 'unrecognisable' from the dandy who had, only a few years earlier, been swanning round the West End. 'For all his wealth I don't think he is happy,' Howard said. 'He's done it all. There's nothing he craves. No goals left. He doesn't do much with his money.'

One source of consolation was the holidays he took with Fawn and India as well as their father and his new wife, Jilly. Recalling those trips, Fawn – who addressed him as 'Papa' – said he 'always had a sense of humour, especially when it came to practical jokes. On holiday we'd be walking past some villas and he'd ring a stranger's doorbell and run away and hide behind a tree.'

While the inheritance earmarked for Fawn and India continued growing, the pace of its growth hastened by the escalating value of West End property, other members of the Raymond clan were less fortunate. Recently parted from his wife Nerys and their three children, who were scraping by on state benefits, Derry confessed to having 'got into a mess'; Maria and Cheyenne were sharing a shabby bedsit in Chiswick; Boston and his mother, who subsisted on income support, had to make do with a housing association flat in Soho of all places; and Jean was still based in Tuxford, dependent on a £40-a-week state pension, plus £80-a-week interest from what remained of her divorce settlement.

Poor but far happier than Raymond, much of her time dedicated to her thriving dance troupe, Jean wanted nothing more to do with her first husband. To express her contempt for him, she'd had a 1950s black-and-white photo of Raymond – inscribed to 'My darling Jean' – framed with a lavatory seat. She hung this from the wall of her toilet. It was an arrangement which, she'd made sure, Raymond knew about.

Jean was only one of several excommunicated family members nursing intense grudges against Raymond. Most of those grudges had already been aired in the tabloid press, always eager to embellish his notoriety. In June 1998 he obtained warning of what promised to be the most uncomplimentary story so far printed about him. That warning came in the form of a stolen document, probably sold to him for a hefty fee. The document comprised a book proposal for a memoir by Maria, recounting her involvement with him, its title – *Paul Raymond: Devil's Disciple* – hinting at her less-than-complimentary opinion of her ex-father-in-law. 'Paul got very upset about it,' recalled Noel Botham.

Raymond's response was to initiate libel writs against both Maria and her publisher, John Blake. These were sufficient to suppress the proposed book.

# 52 THE WAY OF ALL FLESH

CONTINUING HIS GRADUAL disengagement from the day-to-day operations of his business, Raymond appointed John James to run Soho Estates Holdings, the arm of the PRO which dealt with his lucrative property business. Even though sales of the type of softcore magazines produced by his company were in decline, his publishing firm had so far resisted that trend, instead yielding large profits, its turnover in 1998 leaping from £26.4 million to £42 million.

Such were the proceeds from his property and publishing businesses that Raymond felt justified in awarding himself a generous pay rise, taking his salary from £790,000 to £3.5 million per year. His expanding annual income was, however, paralleled by the shrinking boundaries of his life. He began to exist under a form of self-imposed house arrest, exacerbated by increasing deafness that made him reluctant to venture into the bars and restaurants he used to frequent, where he now had trouble discerning what people were saying above the background hubbub. Seldom straying outside his own flat or visiting the purpose-built apartment which John and Jilly James had built for him in their home, he slid into a circumscribed routine symptomatic not just of old age and dwindling energy but also of depression. Behind perpetually drawn curtains that screened his flat from the neighbouring buildings, he'd get up late, have a bath, then change into a fresh pair of pyjamas and go back to bed, where he'd watch television, a glass of brandy often at his bedside. He'd also have phone conversations with Fawn on alternate days; study the latest correspondence and accounts shipped over from Archer

Street; make periodic calls to the PRO offices and hold weekly meetings with his senior staff. Whenever Howard, who visited him every ten days or so, tried to winkle him out of the flat, even for a walk in Green Park, he'd say, 'Maybe tomorrow.'

Newspapers that had once portrayed Raymond as an absurd, superannuated Lothario now took equal delight in running lushly embroidered stories depicting him as a trogladytic miser, as Britain's answer to Howard Hughes, bunkered down in the West End, his fingernails uncut, his once tight grip on his business slackened. Contrary to the impression of disconnectedness, of smouldering lunacy, projected by those stories, he still exercised judicious control over the most important moves undertaken by the PRO. Into that category fell the £12.5 million purchase of the former amusement arcade opposite the Windmill Theatre. He authorised John James to buy it only because they'd just discovered that their friend Mark Fuller had taken a £500,000-a-year lease on it with the intention of turning it into London's largest restaurant. 'Paul gave me six months' rent free,' Fuller recalled. 'I remember asking John why he was doing that when he knew I was opening in three months' time. And John said, "He wants to give your restaurant the best possible chance." Both Paul and I did very well out of it in the end.'

The success of Sugar Reef, Fuller's latest venture, bore out Raymond's enduring nose for a good deal. Just over six months after the restaurant had opened, Raymond appointed his nephew Mark Quinn, whom he liked and trusted, to the newly vacated managing directorship. A calm and reliable thirty-six-year-old, Quinn had been working for Raymond since the 1980s. Apparently under Quinn's influence, Soho Estates Holdings started to acquire freeholds outside its traditional territory, these acquisitions encompassing around £50 million-worth of commercial property in Hampstead, Kensington, Chelsea and Notting Hill.

Most of Raymond's property assets nonetheless remained in the

Soho area. Emphasising the perspicacity of these investments, Raymond reaped a twofold reward from them, concurrently benefiting from the soaring value of the freeholds and the sharp hike in rental prices in Soho. Over the previous two years rents on commercial premises had doubled. And even steeper rises were imminent, especially for tenants running sex shops. Owing to a decision by the Home Office to relax Britain's censorship laws, bringing them into line with the rest of Europe, the profits made by sex shops had been dramatically boosted. Their owners could now afford to pay a rental premium as high as £250,000 per year. No wonder Soho Estates Holdings had, by the latter stages of 2000, accumulated a bank balance of £50 million, much of it destined to be ploughed back into yet more freeholds.

Reluctant though Raymond had been to use the flat which John and Jilly James – father and stepmother of Fawn and India – had previously created for him, they'd also incorporated a spacious upstairs apartment for him in the house they'd just built near the Surrey town of Woking. Raymond took more of a liking to the new place, accessible via its own lift. 'John and Jilly made sure it was just his sort of thing. It was a monument to 1980s kitsch,' Mark Fuller remembered. 'He'd turn up there in the dead of night and send down little notes asking for roast beef and chips. Fawn and India would go up and see him quite a lot, but he tended to be very reclusive.

'After I'd sold Sugar Reef, I went round to see John and Jilly on Boxing Day. With the proceeds from the sale, I'd bought myself an Aston Martin. John and I were on the gravel driveway, revving up the car when an upstairs window opened. Paul, who was in his dressing gown, leant out and said, "I wish you a merry Christmas. However, I have a stone in my hand and I see you have a beautiful car. I understand that after the sale of my premises you still owe me £1,400 in service charges. And if you don't pay me I am going to throw this stone at your car." And I went,

"I'm afraid it was an oversight. Your company didn't mention it to me. Anyway, I settled it two days ago." And he said, "Thank you very much. I wish you a merry Christmas. And I will now drop the stone and let you and John carry on admiring your car…"'

Jean, now seventy years old, was still running the Groovy Grannies dance troupe, which had raised more than £15,000 for charity since its formation. During January 2002 she was diagnosed as suffering from terminal cancer. She died three weeks later in Bassetlaw Hospital. Her funeral took place on a chilly mid-February day at All Hallows, a thirteenth-century hilltop church in the village of Ordsall, six miles from her home. The setting couldn't have offered a sharper contrast to the racy, neon-etched West End world she'd once adorned. Howard and his two teenage children were among the large gathering of mourners who'd contributed the bouquets that were banked up against her coffin. In recognition of her work as a choreographer at the Revuebar, the Celebrité and the Bal Tabarin, her ex-husband sent one of his employees to represent the PRO.

Even in death she was unable to shake off the association with Raymond which assured the presence of a few reporters. Their coverage of the funeral initiated another wave of critical newspaper stories about Raymond – about his estrangement from his illegitimate son and from Howard's children.

Sustained by its south-east Asian clientele, the Revuebar – its red plush interior refurbished and remodelled – had initially thrived under Gérard Simi's new regime. Its takings had, however, since plummeted. Blame was heaped outside the bouncer-encrusted doors of Stringfellow's, Spearmint Rhino and other rival clubs which offered the brash, more fashionable attractions of pole- and lap-dancing. The Revuebar's problems were also attributed to the decline in tourism caused by post-9/11 fears of terrorism as well as potential avian flu and SARS pandemics.

Five years into his twenty-one-year lease, Simi faced a rent review. The substantial rise in the market value for leases in that area prompted Soho Estates Holdings to live up to its reputation by asking for a 120 per cent increase. After nine months of negotiations, the revised rent was reduced to £275,000 per year. Even so, when the second quarterly payment at the new rate was due, Simi didn't have the money to honour the agreement.

Raymond's involvement in the PRO had lately dwindled to the point where he no longer staged regular meetings in his flat, yet he was notified about the decision to send the bailiffs round to the Revuebar. His instincts as a businessman overriding his decades-long friendship with Simi, he made no objection. For Simi, the arrival of the bailiffs represented a callous act of betrayal – not just a personal betrayal but a betrayal of the institution Raymond had set up. 'I loved that place,' Simi recalled. 'I put thirty years of my life into it. I know business is business, but I didn't imagine Paul would do something like that. I thought he'd be more understanding. I thought he'd appreciate what I was doing.'

Early in February 2004, Simi placed the Revuebar, self-styled 'World Centre of Erotic Entertainment', into administration. Over the next few weeks, the venue stayed open while the administrators first sought potential investors and then, when that proved futile, hunted for someone willing to buy the remainder of Simi's lease.

In a doleful epilogue, tiny audiences – who'd been solicited by advertising that promised 'Personal Appearances of the World's Greatest Names in Striptease' – witnessed the final performances of *Erotica 2000*. Gold lamé, feather boas and high heels abounding, six women – supplemented by two men in leather jockstraps – worked through an intricately choreographed repertoire. This featured a stripping bride, a stripping policewoman and even striptease in a bank vault, surrounded by fake bullion, the cast's movements flickering across the tessellated surface of a revolving mirror-ball, suspended from the ceiling.

Stumbling out of one of the final performances, a beery lad in a sweatshirt gave his considered opinion of the show: 'It were shite.'

Just short of forty-five years after that nervous afternoon when Raymond had watched the customers filing up the main staircase for the first time, the Revuebar closed down and its famous neon sign was switched off. Simi calculated that more than two million tickets had been sold for his shows since he'd started working there.

His lease on the Revuebar was bought by Soho Clubs & Bars, which, pausing only to refit the venue in a style pertinent to the new clientele, reopened it as a gay club called Too2Much. There could be few more succinct expressions of the district's changing character.

*Forbes*, the prestigious American business magazine, provided Raymond with a premature eightieth birthday present. During the spring of 2005, he was named in thirteenth place on the 'Forbes British Billionaires' List'. Unlike the businessmen ahead of him, who included the motor racing mogul Bernie Ecclestone, he wasn't doing much with that fortune. Now wheelchair-bound, he was spending more time than ever in bed at Arlington House, the days enlivened by occasional visits from friends and family. One of those visitors was Howard, by then pursuing an entrepreneurial career so lacklustre that Raymond ended up loaning £166,500 to his businesses.

Ensconced in bed, Raymond drank brandy, watched television and read. Books – aside from those of the coffee-table variety – were still barred from his bedside table, meaning there was little chance of him reading *The Pornographer Diaries*, the latest novel by Danny King, a reformed burglar and car thief who'd been working for Paul Raymond Publications since 1999. Part of a surprisingly large contingent of PRP alumni establishing themselves in mainstream writing, graphic design and illustration, the humorist and *Guardian* contributor Harry Pearson among them, King had recrafted his own adventures in the skin trade into a scurrilous comedy, set in the offices of a PRP-like firm owned by the fictional London-based media and property magnate Philip Goss.

Raymond's chosen reading matter, which formed a collage across his bedspread, consisted of the paperwork from Archer Street, plus magazines and middle-brow newspapers. Perusing these, he'd inevitably have seen – and, perhaps, winced at – the extensive articles about the ostentatious pre-wedding party thrown by Elton John and partner at the aptly titled Too2Much. He'd also have seen the *Evening Standard*'s coverage of a story about himself, illustrated by an old photo of him.

The story described how Tara Stout, a former Sky Sports News and BBC Worldwide television presenter, had been evicted by him from her flat on Dean Street. In protest against Soho Estates Holdings' alleged failure to carry out vital repairs to her flat, she'd stopped paying her rent, triggering the arrival of bailiffs. To obtain publicity for her cause, she greeted the bailiffs in an outfit appropriate to Raymond's business – wearing nothing aside from a pair of bikini bottoms. The bailiffs called the police when she refused to get dressed. She did, however, put on a white coat. With this unbuttoned, she walked past the bailiffs and then down the street, provoking wolf-whistles and catcalls from the builders on the site across the road. In the end she was arrested outside – of all places – a strip-club and charged with disorderly behaviour likely to cause offence. When the case went to trial, the charge was dismissed. Outside Bow Street Magistrates' Court, Raymond's erstwhile tenant celebrated by stripping down to a bikini.

Back in his now distant heyday, Raymond would have instantly exploited the situation by offering her a contract to model for *Men Only* or *Club International*. He needed only to glance at the latest sales figures for these and his other magazines to realise that they too were well beyond their heyday. Under the dual onslaught of internet porn and lad mags, their sales were in steep, irreversible decline by 2006, annual pre-tax profits showing a 31 per cent drop from the £8.3 million announced the previous year.

As Steve Bleach, who had left his job at Paul Raymond Publications, recalled, 'I know he must've been worried by that trend because he asked if I'd like to work for his company again. That was the last time I went round to see him. Though the place was cleaned and maintained, it was starting to look a little tatty. I remember glancing at the curtains and they were all frayed and a bit dusty at the top. I just thought there was a feeling that everything was getting faded, which seemed a metaphor for other things in his life. He was still great company and fun to be with, but I felt as if he'd retreated into himself. He was out of touch with the world. He thought the Internet was a fad.'

However isolated Raymond became from the currents of the teeming city around him, he retained his engagement with the accounts he'd receive from Archer Street, with the immense roster of property he owned. During late June 2007 he was irked by an article he spotted in *Estates Gazette*, the leading journal of the property investment world. He was described in the article as owning the lease on the Greek Street building occupied by Soho House, a private members' club favoured by media smoothies. His annoyance stemmed from the fact that he didn't just own the lease. He owned the *freehold*. Paradoxically, given the secrecy of the PRO and his recent refusal to grant interviews to journalists, he wanted everyone to be aware of his status, to know that he wasn't a mere leaseholder, so he wrote to *Estates Gazette*, correcting their error. 'I own the freehold,' he informed them. 'Please print a correction.'

The breathing difficulties that had afflicted Raymond for at least a decade and a half worsened at the beginning of 2008. On Wednesday, 27 February an ambulance was summoned to Arlington House, from where he was taken to hospital, his speech rambling and often disjointed, his liver-spotted body now as desiccated as his lifestyle.

Howard, plus Fawn and her family, made regular visits to his private hospital room, during which he told Howard that he was quite contented.

If he had any regrets about his life, they remained unspoken, an opaque curtain of incoherence beginning to descend over him. He nevertheless mustered a reply when Fawn said, 'I love you.'

'I love you, too,' he responded.

Disorientation gradually setting in, his last words to Howard, who had turned forty-eight a few months earlier, were so unexpected that Howard assumed he'd misheard them at first. 'I want to see my wife,' Raymond kept repeating.

'I couldn't believe it,' Howard revealed. 'I said, "She won't be pleased. She's got the biggest frying pan waiting for you."'

When Raymond's condition worsened, a priest was summoned to give him the last rites. As these sonorous lines were recited, the many decades Raymond had lived without Holy Communion were effaced. Banking on divine forgiveness, he'd once confidently declared, 'I believe I will go Up There, if there is an Up There. God may decide to put me in purgatory for three or four months first.'

That Friday, at the age of eighty-two, what proved to be a fatal chest infection gave Raymond the chance to test this prediction. His long-standing fame ensured that British television and radio carried items about his death, but few of the youthful drinkers convening on the pavements of Brewer Street that night would have recognised his name.

Raymond's fifty-seven-year-old son, Derry, was listening to the news on a car radio when he heard what had happened. He was, he later admitted, so shaken that he had to pull over to the side of the road. With Raymond's demise, he could no longer daydream about establishing the father–son relationship he'd been denied.

Reporters scrambled for interviews with anyone who'd known Raymond, however tenuously. Between Monday and Wednesday of that week, often expansive obituaries of him appeared in most of the national newspapers, which were already speculating on the size of his estate and the contents of his will. The obituarists tended to lapse into glib formulations that shaped the truth into an existing template – clichés about a rags-to-riches journey, about material success masking personal tragedy, about the billionaire recluse who died alone and friendless. Transfixed by the details of his life and the scale of his wealth, the majority of them, however, failed to recognise the broader impact of what he'd achieved.

Far more than most government ministers, he'd played a prominent role in the transformation of British society, specifically British sexual mores. As a result of his relentless pleasure in wheeler-dealing which had enabled him to exploit the wave of permissiveness more effectively than his rivals, he helped to change the country in ways that weren't always positive. True, he and his ilk frogmarched many of the old hypocrisies to the exit and encouraged a more open attitude towards sex. Yet he also helped to turn the sex industry from an illicit enterprise into a vast, rapacious business, into a phenomenon that permeates and debases culture. Its influence can be found in advertising, television, newspapers, magazines, and on the high streets of most provincial towns, now home to the discreet façades of lap-dancing clubs with names that would've met with Raymond's approval – Teazers, Vamps, For Your Eyes Only.

Beyond a desire to be cremated, Raymond had left instructions for neither his funeral nor the destination of his ashes. Howard – who admitted to feeling bereft and alone – went ahead and arranged a Roman Catholic service at Wandsworth Cemetery, not far from Wimbledon, where they'd once lived. The guest list was restricted to Raymond's small family circle, including John James, Mark Quinn and two of Raymond's grandchildren, sixteen-year-old India and twenty-one-year-old Fawn, now studying social anthropology at St Andrews University. On the cold, drizzly morning of Monday, 12 March, the blustery wind making it seem even chillier, they made their way through the well-maintained, surprisingly rustic grounds of the late Victorian cemetery where Raymond was due to be cremated. His coffin had been laid in the central chapel, trimmed by wreaths. One of these carried a simple message from Fawn and India – 'Adored and loved'.

The subsequent reading of Raymond's will demonstrated just how intensely those feelings had been reciprocated. He bequeathed all but a fraction of his estate to them, making them two of Britain's richest women. Through what accountants euphemistically term 'Inheritance Tax planning', Raymond had placed the bulk of his money beyond the grasp of the Inland Revenue: in at least nineteen trusts, in offshore accounts, in companies that didn't fall within the ambit of his British estate. The value of that estate had consequently been whittled down to £74.5 million. Out of that, Fawn and India were given his Arlington House flat, his dying wish being that they should set up home there. Fawn was also given an immediate payment of £150,000. Raymond's will specified that India should receive the same amount on her twenty-first birthday. The rest of their inheritance was to be held in trust for them until they turned twenty-five.

Fawn and India aside, Raymond's will had only one other beneficiary – his long-serving secretary, who received £10,000. There was no mention of Derry, Cheyenne or Boston. Nor was there any reference to Howard, who inherited only a troubled past and a container filled with Raymond's ashes. Stoically insisting that his disinheritance made no difference to the affection with which he remembered his father, Howard made plans to scatter those ashes. One warm day that summer he envisaged distributing them round the streets of Soho where they'd uncoil like a grey genie, the breeze dispersing them across the West End, carrying them past buildings Raymond had owned, past people who remembered seeing him, past furtive customers darting out of sex shops, past the stallholders on Berwick Street Market, past preening young men drinking lattes at pavement tables, past Patisserie Valerie, past the Bar Italia, past Ronnie Scott's Jazz Club, past the site of the Revuebar, those ashes eventually settling, perhaps, as a fine dust on the surface of a car windscreen.

# ACKNOWLEDGEMENTS

B IOGRAPHIES ARE OFTEN touted as being definitive, yet the definitive biography is an unattainable ideal. The texture, the odd detours, the flow of someone's life remain no less elusive than the precise sensation of walking along a beach on a summer's day. However lengthy and detailed a biography becomes, it can offer only a *version* of that person's life, not an incontrovertible, all-encompassing portrait. Issue ten writers with identical raw material and you'd end up with the material being woven into ten different patterns.

Paul Raymond was suggested to me as a suitable subject by my friend and literary agent Matthew Hamilton of Aitken Alexander Associates. I was sceptical at first, but soon realised just how astute his suggestion had been. I hope I've done my subject justice and written the book Matthew envisaged when he first came up with the idea. I'd also like to thank him for steering the project so patiently through the protracted commissioning process and for many invaluable comments on the manuscript.

Once I'd started work on the book, I found myself the target of amiable joshing by friends and acquaintances about my 'research' which, by implication, consisted of watching striptease and browsing through old skin-magazines. Every time I tried to correct this misapprehension, I must've sounded like that stock figure of jest – the man who claims to buy *Playboy* for the beautifully written short stories. I hate to disappoint the mickey-takers, but researching *Members Only* differed little from researching any other biography. Mind you, I suspect that biographers of John Betjeman and his ilk are seldom required to interview retired strippers, showgirls, nightclub hostesses or wary-eyed ex-policemen. There was one conspicuous occasion, though, when scholarship collided with sleaze. That morning I had my library ticket temporarily confiscated while I inspected a tatty old Raymond Revuebar programme in the Rare Books section of the British Library, neighbouring academics meanwhile glancing up from their fragile antiquarian volumes to cast envious eyes over lurid photos of Pussy Divine and her fellow artistes.

Material for my book was, of course, harvested in a number of other libraries and archives: the University of Cambridge Library, Glossop Library, Jersey Heritage Trust, Companies House, the National Archives, UEA Library, the National Film Archive, Nottingham Central Library, Clacton-on-Sea Library, the BBC Written Archives Centre, Essex Record Office, and Islington Local History Centre.

Further raw material was gleaned through the assistance of the following ever-helpful staff at various institutions: Andrew Kirk, assistant curator of the Theatre Museum at the Victoria & Albert Museum; Robin Baker, Kathleen Dickson and Vic Pratt at the British Film Institute; Brother Peter and Adam Grace at St Francis Xavier College, Liverpool; Jo Playfoot in the Information Centre at IPC Media; Allan Tyler at the British Stammering Association; Natalie Whatmore at Channel 4 Television; David Capus of the Records Management Branch of the Metropolitan Police Service; Ruth Allen, information manager at the Metropolitan Police Directorate of Information; Cheryl Edwards at the Land Registry; Gordon Leith at the Department of Research and Information Services, Royal Air Force Museum, Hendon; Rebecca Spry at Condé Nast Publications; Steve Jebson at the Met Office; Roger Hull, researcher at Liverpool Record Office; Rob Lewis, information coordinator at Manchester Archives and Local Studies; as well as David Jenkins, duty archivist at Derbyshire Record Office.

I am, moreover, indebted to numerous friends, relatives, acquaintances and employees of Paul Raymond who agreed to be interviewed by me or to respond to written questions. They include Jonathan Hodge, Mark

Fuller, Steve Bleach, Noel and Lesley Botham, Fiona Richmond, Rusty Humphreys, Peter Richardson, Alexei Sayle, Nigel Planer, Gérard Simi, Marjorie Davies, Bob Amiss, Gerry Parker, Paul Lincoln, Frank Fraser, Miklos Matolsci, William Sinclair, Jo Sandilands (née Brooker), Murray Goldstein, Kenny Cantor, the late Pamela Green, Irma Kurtz, Clive Harris, Tony Klinger, Gerry Harrison, John Morell, Jenny Wilkes, Jenny Howe, Harry Pearson, Tim Walker, Michael Dillon, and Paul Cowan, not to mention Danny King who kindly volunteered a long list of useful contacts. Many other interviewees, among them former Metropolitan Police officers as well as friends and employees of Paul Raymond, insisted on me preserving their anonymity.

Yet more Raymond-related information and contacts were supplied by Alex and Stephanie Hamilton, David McGillivray, James Morton, David Kynaston, Lois Peltz, G.F. Newman, Jonathan Meades, Philip Howard, Paul Roy Goodhead, Tim Ewbank, Steve Chibnall, Max Décharné, John Williams, Peter Stanford, Norman Jacobs, Reg Young, Ken Rushton, Vaughan Thomas, Dr Sheldon Hall, Jon Smith, Mike Hallinan, Damon Wise and retired police sergeant John Allport, MBE, QGM, BEM. They were all tremendously generous with their time.

I'm similarly grateful to Iain Sinclair, Duncan Campbell, Judy Baines, Philip French, Tim Webb, Sparrow, Revel Barker, Ian Farrow, David and Judy Willetts, Keiron Pim, Liz Hodgkinson, Bob Fenton, Dave Fogarty, Andi Sapey, Mike Pentelow, Cathi Unsworth, Keith Davies, Andy Grocock, Alan Brownjohn, Arthur Ellis, Chris and Enid Stephenson, Terence Blacker, Bill Messom, Guy Myhill, Alan Byford, Yak Droubie, Pipa Clements from the Tombland Bookshop in Norwich, plus Anglo-Italian and Hack from www.wrestlingheritage.co.uk, all of whom made a significant contribution to my research.

Thanks are also due to Paul King, who devoted several days to helping me trawl through stacks of paperwork at the British Library and the National Archives; David Collard and Ailsa Montagu, who devised several of the chapter headings; Peter Krämer, who offered lots of incisive comments on the manuscript; Maurice Poole, who shared with me his impressive knowledge of the history of the Raymond Revuebar; Marc Glendening and Virginia Ironside, who provided me with accommodation and boundless encouragement; and my partner Jo Willingham, who selflessly endured regular updates on the antics of Mr Striptease.

Rounding off this gratitude marathon, I really appreciate the acute observations of my editor, John Williams, and the backing of Pete Ayrton of Serpent's Tail and Andrew Franklin of Profile Books, who commissioned *Members Only*. Gentlemen, your complimentary bottle of champagne and front row seats at the Soho Striperama await you.

# SELECTED BIBLIOGRAPHY

*The 1953 Guide to London Clubs* (A Regency Press Publication, 1953)

Adamson, Iain: *The Old Fox* (Frederick Muller, 1963)

Balon, Norman (with Bright, Spencer): *You're Barred, You Bastards! The Memoirs of a Soho Publican* (Sidgwick and Jackson, 1991)

Barfe, Louis: *Turned Out Nice Again: The Story of British Light Entertainment* (Atlantic Books, 2008)

Beeston, Trevor (edited by): *Priests and Prelates: The Daily Telegraph Clerical Obituaries* (Continuum, 2002)

Challenor, Harold (with Draper, A): *Tanky Challenor* (Leo Cooper, 1990)

Chambers, Peter and Landreth, Amy (edited by): *Called Up: The Personal Experiences of Sixteen National Servicemen, Told by Themselves* (Allan Wingate, 1955)

Cox, Barry; Shirley, John; Short, Martin: *The Fall of Scotland Yard* (Penguin Books, 1977)

Craig, Mary: *Longford: A Biographical Portrait* (Hodder and Stoughton, 1978)

Crookston, Peter: *Village London: The Observer's Guide to the Real London* (Arrow Books, 1978)

Davies, Hunter (edited by): *The New London Spy: A Discreet Guide to the City's Pleasures* (Anthony Blond, 1966)

Deighton, Len (editor): *Len Deighton's London Dossier* (Penguin, 1967)

Edmonds, Mark: *Inside Soho* (Robert Nicholson Publications, 1988)

Ewbank, Tim: *Olivia Newton-John: The Biography* (Piatkus, 2009)

Fabian, Robert: *London after Dark* (Naldrett Press, 1954)

Farson, Dan: *Soho in the Fifties* (Michael Joseph, 1987)

Faulks, Sir Neville: *No Mitigating Circumstances* (William Kimber, 1977)

Ferris, Paul: *Sex and the British: A Twentieth-century History* (Michael Joseph, 2003)

Fido, Martin and Skinner, Keith: *The Official Encylopedia of Scotland Yard* (revised edition, Virgin Books, 2000)

Fraser, Frank (with Morton, James): *Mad Frank: Memoirs of a Life of Crime* (Little, Brown, 1994)

Fraser, Frank (with Morton, James): *Mad Frank's London* (Virgin, 2001)

Fryer, Jonathan: *Soho in the Fifties and Sixties* (National Portrait Gallery Publications, 1998)

Glicco, Jack: *Madness after Midnight* (Elek Books, 1952)

Goldstein, Murray: *Naked Jungle: Soho Stripped Bare* (Silverback Press, 2004)

Grigg, Mary: *The Challenor Case* (Penguin Books, 1965)

Hamilton, Ian: *Walking Possession, Essays and Reviews, 1968–93* (Bloomsbury, 1994)

Hamilton, John: *Beasts in the Cellar: The Exploitation Career of Tony Tenser* (FAB Press, 2005)

Hanson, Dian: *The History of Men's Magazines*, Vols 1–4 (Taschen, 2004–5)

Hebditch, David and Anning, Nick: *Porn Gold: Inside the Pornography Business* (Faber and Faber, 1988)

Heery, Pat: *The History of St Francis Xavier's College, Liverpool, 1842–2001* (Self-published, 2002)

Heilpern, John: *John Osborne: A Patriot for Us* (Chatto & Windus, 2006)

Hennessy, Peter: *Never Again: Britain 1945–51* (Jonathan Cape, 1992)

Holden, Jack: *A Very Special School* (Self-published, 1994)

Jackson, Stanley: *An Indiscreet Guide to Soho* (Muse Arts Publications, 1947)

Jacobs, Norman: *Clacton Past* (Phillimore, 2002)

Kelland, Gilbert: *Crime in London* (The Bodley Head, 1986)

King, Danny: *The Pornographer Diaries* (Serpent's Tail, 2004)

Kynaston, David: *Austerity Britain. 1945–51* (Bloomsbury, 2007)

La Rue, Danny (with Elson, Howard): *From Drags to Riches* (Viking, 1987)

Lee, Gypsy Rose: *Gypsy: A Memoir* (André Deutsch, 1957)

Levy, Shawn: *Ready, Steady, Go! Swinging London and the Invention of Cool* (Fourth Estate, 2002)

Lord, Graham: *Just the One: The Wives and Times of Jeffrey Bernard* (Sinclair-Stevenson, 1992)

Luke, Michael: *David Tennant and the Gargoyle Years* (Weidenfeld and Nicolson, 1991)

McGillivray, David: *Doing Rude Things: The History of the British Sex Film, 1957–81* (Sun Tavern Fields, 1992)

Morton, James: *Bent Coppers: A Survey of Police Corruption* (Little, Brown, 1993)

Morton, James: *Gangland Soho* (Piatkus, 2008)

Morton, James: *Gangland: London's Underworld* (Little, Brown, 1992)

Morton, James and Parker, Gerry: *Gangland Bosses: The Lives of Jack Spot and Billy Hill* (TimeWarner, 2004)

Newburn, Tim: *Permission and Regulation: Law and Morals in Post-War Britain* (Routledge, 1992)

Norman, Frank: *Norman's London* (Secker and Warburg, 1969)

Norman, Frank and Bernard, Jeffrey: *Soho Night and Day* (Secker and Warburg, 1966)

*Pornography: The Longford Report* (Coronet Books, 1972)

Powell, Nosher: *Nosher* (Blake Publishing, 1999)

Randall, Lucian and Welchj, Chris: *Ginger Geezer: The Life of Vivian Stanshall* (Fourth Estate, 2001)

Richmond, Fiona: *Tell-Tale Tits* (Javelin Books, 1987)

Sandbrook, Dominic: *White Heat: A History of Britain in the Swinging Sixties* (Little, Brown, 2006)

Sharp, Neville T.: *Glossop Remembered* (Landmark Publishing, 2005)

Shellard, Dominic: *Kenneth Tynan: A Life* (Yale University Press, 2003)

Sheridan, Simon: *Keeping the British End Up: Four Decades of Saucy Cinema* (Reynolds & Hearn, 2001)

Shteir, Rachel: *Striptease: The Untold History of the Girlie Show* (Oxford University Press, 2004)

Sinclair, Iain (edited by): *London: City of Disappearances* (Hamish Hamilton, 2006)

Smith, D. J.: *Action Stations 3* (Patrick Stephens, 1990)

Smithies, Edward: *The Black Economy in England since 1914* (Gill & MacMillan Humanities Press, 1984)

Spinetti, Victor (with Rankin, Peter): *Up Front: His Strictly Confidential Autobiography* (Robson Books, 2001)

Stanford, Peter: *The Outcasts' Outcast: A Biography of Lord Longford* (Sutton Publishing, 2003)

Summers, Judith: *Soho: A History of London's Most Colourful Neighbourhood* (Bloomsbury, 1989)

Sutherland, John: *Offensive Literature: Decensorship in Britain, 1960–1982* (Junction Books, 1982)

Sweet, Matthew: *Shepperton Babylon: The Lost Worlds of British Cinema* (Faber & Faber, 2005)

Tames, Richard: *Soho Past* (Historical Society Publications, 2004)

Thomas, Donald: *Villains' Paradise: Britain's Underworld from the Spivs to the Krays* (John Murray, 2005)

Thomas, Donald: *An Underworld at War* (John Murray, 2003)

Thompson, W. and Annetts, J.: *Softcore* (Self-published, 1990)

Tomkinson, Martin: *The Pornographers: The Rise and Fall of the Soho Sex Barons* (Virgin Books, 1982)

Tossell, David: *Big Mal: The High Life and Hard Times of Malcolm Allison, Football Legend* (Mainstream, 2008)

Van Damm, Sheila: *We Never Closed* (Robert Hale, 1967)

Watts, Steven: *Mr Playboy: Hugh Hefner and the American Dream* (Wiley, 2008)

Webb, Duncan: *Crime Is My Business* (Frederick Muller, 1953)

White, Jeremy: *London in the Twentieth Century: A City and Its People* (Penguin, 2001)

White, Michael: *Empty Seats* (Hamish Hamilton, 1984)

Wilmut, Roger: *Kindly Leave the Stage! The Story of Variety, 1919–1960* (Methuen, 1985)

Wise, Damon: *Come By Sunday: The Fabulous, Ruined Life of Diana Dors* (Sidgwick & Jackson, 1998)

Wortley, Richard: *Skin Deep in Soho* (Jarrolds, 1969)

# FILMOGRAPHY

*Clubs Galore!* (Pathé News, 1958)

*Eddie Monsoon: A Life* (Channel 4, 1985)

*Soho Sex King: The Real Paul Raymond* (Channel 4, updated version broadcast in 2008)

# SOURCE NOTES

## 1      An Audience with the King

p. 1    'But these auditions... empty stage' (*Today*, week ending 31 December 1960)

p. 2    'Mr Striptease' (*Empire News*, 26 January 1958)

p. 2    'the King of the Keyhole Shows' (*Daily Mirror*, 27 April 1956)

p. 2    'Raymond claimed... her bath' (*Daily Star*, 19 September 1994)

p. 3    'I've never had... the first' (*Guardian*, 4 March 2008. Also quoted by one of Raymond's employees in conversation with the author)

p. 3    'I have read... sort of book' (*Guardian*, 4 March 2008. Also quoted by one of Raymond's employees in conversation with the author)

p. 3    'Reading could... street wants' (*Daily Express*, 29 November 1974. Also quoted by one of Raymond's employees in conversation with the author)

p. 3    'Not bad... his pocket' (Miklos Matolsci in conversation with the author)

p. 3    'There'll always... always' (*Sunday Times* colour supplement, 6 February 1970. Also quoted by one of Raymond's employees in conversation with the author)

p. 3–6    'It's simply... his patients' (*Today*, week ending 31 December 1960)

## 2      Educating Geoffrey

p. 9    'Much wants more...' (Steve Bleach in conversation with the author)

p. 9    'Public displays... "common"' (friend of Raymond in conversation with the author)

p. 9    'a terrible snob' (*BusinessAge*, December 1992, p. 53)

p. 9    'He said... forgiving' (*Daily Express*, 29 November 1974)

p. 9–10    'He and his... lighted windows' (*The Times*, 10 March 1990)

p. 10    'I think... all time' (*BusinessAge*, December 1992)

p. 12    'Whenever Geoff... material' (*The History of St Francis Xavier's College, Liverpool, 1842–2001*, p. 135)

p. 13    'Most evenings... Bear's Paw' (*The Times*, 10 March 1990)

p. 14    'Together with... public performance' (*St Francis Xavier's College Magazine*, Spring 1939)

p. 15    'The principals... full effect' (*St Francis Xavier's College Magazine*, Spring 1939)

p. 15    'He later claimed... Mass' (*Sunday Mirror*, 5 January 1969)

### 3    Phwoar and Peace

p. 18    'utterly unsatisfactory' (*A Special School*, p. 85)

p. 18    'Joe' (*Glossop Remembered*, p. 179)

p. 18    'It was a habit… atmosphere' (*Glossop Remembered*, p. 178)

p. 20    'these… 'wild'' (*The Times*, 10 March 1990)

p. 20    'Neither his mother… a girlfriend' (*The Times*, 10 March 1990)

p. 20–21    'Geoff was convinced… on him' (ex-schoolmate of Raymond's in conversation with the author)

p. 21    'The escapade… expel him' (*The Times*, 10 March 1990)

p. 22    'stewing with… Gauleiter' (*Glossop Remembered*, p. 179)

p. 22    'He was in a… adult life' (ex-schoolmate of Raymond's in conversation with the author)

### 4    Fiddler on the Hoof

p. 23    'he revealed… 'common drummer'' (*The Times*, 10 March 1990)

p. 23    'Withernsea's Brightest Spot' (*Holderness Gazette*, 22 July 1939)

p. 24    'he felt… settled on Geoff Raymond' (*Daily Express*, 29 November 1974, and *Guardian*, 24 May 1986)

p. 24    'Geoff had, by then… as a drummer' (*Evening News*, 8 January 1969)

p. 24    'Ladderstop' (*Evening Standard*, 13 April 1983)

p. 25    'I didn't like it…terrible' (*The Times*, 10 March 1990)

p. 26    'People like me… needed' (interview with the author)

p. 29    'hailed by… in the world' (*We Never Closed*, p. 90)

p. 29    'Shake it, sister!' (*We Never Closed*, p. 90)

p. 30    'We Never *Clothed*' (*We Never Closed*, p. 101)

p. 30    'It was not… ghastly' (*Guardian*, 24 May 1986)

### 5    Privates on Parade

p. 31    'According to… been ill' (*Evening Standard*, 1 April 1971)

p. 32    'Decades from then… the advice' (Miklos Matolsci in conversation with the author)

p. 33    'short haircuts… loathed' (*Business Age*, December 1992)

p. 34    'I was never… afterwards' (*The Times*, 10 March 1990)

p. 34    'We just… recalled' (*The Times*, 10 March 1990)

p. 35    'However easy… were due' (friend of Raymond's in conversation with the author)

p. 35    'Quinn later told… hidden' (*The Times*, 10 March 1990)

p. 37    'Back in… home town' (friend of Raymond's in conversation with the author)

p. 37    'The love of the theatre… money' (*Daily Mirror*, 27 April 1956)

p. 38    'it remained… own admission' (*Empire News*, 26 January 1958)

p. 38    'Quinn, sensing… commercial' (*Daily Herald*, 30 April 1963)

p. 59    'They said the... quite useless' (*Daily Mirror*, 10 November 1954)

p. 60    'The Web of... French bedroom' (*Daily Mirror*, 27 April 1956)

p. 60    'She would play... first place' (*Kindly Leave the Stage!*, p. 160)

p. 60    'the only moving nudes' (*Today*, week ending 7 January 1961)

p. 60    'The Eurasian... stark-naked reality' (*Daily Herald*, 18 August 1954)

p. 61    'In his eagerness... doting elders' (*Daily Herald*, 18 August 1954)

p. 61    'Called to give... to London' (*Daily Mirror*, 10–11 November 1954)

p. 62    'Even though... custody of him' (*Daily Mail*, 12 March 1998)

p. 63    'From Paris... de Montmartre' (*East Essex Gazette*, 20 May 1955)

p. 63    'she regarded... very good' (*Sunday Mirror*, 17 April 1983)

p. 63    'It's a bright... female form' (*East Essex Gazette*, 24 June 1955)

p. 64    'Three years... incoming tide' (*Clacton Past*, pp. 111, 113)

p. 64    'Musical Marie... non-stop pianist' (*Daily Express*, 14 November 1952)

p. 64    'Good thing... her today' (*East Essex Gazette*, 26 August 1955)

p. 65    'Half an hour... Ambulancemen' (*East Essex Gazette*, 2 September 1955)

## 10    Breast of British

p. 66    'Stopping for... a laugh' (Paul Lincoln in conversation with the author)

p. 66    'Home of the Stars' (photograph by Ronald Glendening, c. 1956)

p. 67    'Raymond asked La Rue... conducted themselves' (*From Drags to Riches*, p. 81)

p. 67    'Describing the... respectable' (*Daily Mirror*, 27 April 1956)

p. 67    'You'd never... doing that' (Miklos Matolsci in conversation with the author)

p. 68    'Asked about... the trainer?' (uncredited press cutting held at the IPC Information Centre, 22 January 1956)

p. 68    'I have just... in variety business' (uncredited press cutting held at the IPC Information Centre, 22 January 1956)

p. 70    'Nearly thirty... ostrich feather' (*The Times*, 19 August 1985)

p. 70    'A good show... nudes on TV' (*Daily Mirror*, 27 April 1956)

p. 71    'Look!... girl's underwear' (*Daily Mirror*, 27 April 1956)

p. 72    'It hailed... ever staged' (*Daily Mail*, 2 July 1956)

p. 73    'Don't move... murmured' (*Daily Mirror*, 2 July 1956)

p. 73–4  'I consider... the kill' (*Nottingham Guardian*, 2 July 1956)

p. 74    'Nikolai gave... think of' (*Daily Mail*, 2 July 1956)

p. 74    'Lamone cooed... high-heeled shoes' (*Daily Express*, 2 July 1956)

p. 75    'less welcome... her bikini' (*The Times*, 2 July 1957 and *Daily Herald*, 2 July 1957)

p. 75    'After the Raymonds... of the missing girl' (*The Times*, 2 July 1957)

p. 75    'Two Remanded... Comer' (*Southampton Evening Echo*, 4 July 1956)

p. 76    'Clegg's article... last night' (*Daily Sketch*, 5 July 1956)

p. 76    'she was infuriated... display her body' (*The Times*, 2 July 1957)

p. 76    'supported her by... correction' (*The Times*, 3 July 1957)

p. 76    'he refused to... barrister' (*News Chronicle*, 4 July 1957)

## 11    Crumpet Voluntary

p. 77    'A joke went round... bloody lot' (Donald Auty, *Moss Empires' Theatres in the Fifties* website)

p. 77    'Look, there's... audience' (*Daily Mirror*, 27 April 1956)

p. 78    'I did a trip... by that' (interview featured in Channel 4's *The Real Paul Raymond*)

p. 80    'advertising "non-stop striptease"' (*Naked Jungle*, p. 24)

p. 80    'billing itself... can move' (*Up Front*, p. 109)

p. 81    'executive-looking... Not Permitted' (*Empire News*, 29 May 1960)

p. 81    'Whenever the word... market value' (*Naked Jungle*, p. 26)

p. 82    'the Dance... Veils' (*What's On in London*, 12 July 1957)

p. 82    'According to Raymond... there and then' (*Daily Express*, 29 November 1974)

## 12    Gentlemen Prefer Nudes

p. 83    'The Old Fox' (*The Old Fox*, p. 218)

p. 83    'On behalf of... sequinned garment' (*The Times*, 2 July 1957)

p. 84    'You had better... fit me' (*Daily Sketch*, 2 July 1957)

p. 84    'Hilbery couldn't resist... choose to do it' (*The Times*, 2 July 1957)

p. 84    'These girls... called "indecent"' (*News Chronicle*, 2 July 1957)

p. 84    'Beyfus put it... more profitable' (*The Times*, 2 July 1957)

p. 85    'She added... well dressed offstage' (*Daily Herald*, 2 July 1957)

p. 85–6  'In a bid... *disgraceful* attack' (*The Times*, 2 July 1957)

p. 87    'Beyfus told the... of the witness' (*Daily Sketch*, 3 July 1957)

p. 87    'a speech in which... get it' (*The Times*, 3 July 1957)

p. 88    'He said the first... right-thinking people' (*The Times*, 4 July 1957)

p. 88    'The judge also... violin' (*Daily Sketch*, 4 July 1957)

p. 88    'They declared... choreographer' (*Daily Sketch*, 4 July 1957)

p. 88    'Hilbery dismissed... £1,500' (*News Chronicle*, 4 July 1957)

p. 88    'she mustered... that again' (*Daily Sketch*, 4 July 1957)

p. 89    'Raymond was also asked... have to pay' (*News Chronicle*, 4 July 1957)

p. 89    'But Jean... right to it' (*No Mitigating Circumstances*, p. 132)

## 13    A Room with a Revue

p. 90    'the Black Mile' (*Madness after Midnight*, p. 115)

p. 91    'Short time, dearie?' (*Norman's London*, p. 206)

p. 91    'Would you... sir?' (Conan Nicholas in conversation with the author)

p. 92    'Whatever you... the gangs' (Summers, *Soho*, p. 212)

p. 93    'he was told... *upstairs*' (*Sunday Times* colour supplement, 6 February 1970)

p. 94    'the refurbishment... £140,000' (*Today*, week ending 31 December 1960, *Daily Sketch*, 28 November 1958, and *Reynold's News*, 20 April 1958)

p. 95–6  'I'm here to... take his wife' (*Empire News*, 26 January 1958)

## 14    G-sting

2 May 1958, National Archives, MEPO2/10232, and statement by Superintendent Charles Strath, 28 November 1958, National Archives, MEPO2/10232)

## 15    Treasure Chests

p. 110    'extremely well run' (*The Times*, 24 September 1958)

p. 111    'But he regarded... around *plenty*' (*The Daily Mail*, 28 November 1958)

p. 111    'A glass of... To striptease' (*Daily Sketch*, 28 November 1958)

p. 111    'The face of... of skins' (*What's On in London*, 4 July 1958)

p. 112    'he admitted that... new-found wealth' (*Daily Telegraph*, 10 December 1989)

p. 112    'He didn't play... system' (*Sunday Times Magazine*, 17 August 2008)

p. 112    'In the hope of... City gents' (*Daily Mirror*, 28 November 1958)

p. 116    'The deluge... dependent father' (friend of Raymond in conversation with the author)

p. 116    'disgusted and shocked' (*People*, 26 June 1960)

p. 117    'In time... have chaplains' (*People*, 26 June 1960)

p. 117    'Yeardye – somewhat... life' (*Daily Telegraph*, 30 April 2004)

p. 117–18    'Raymond felt threatened... items of clothing' (*People*, 25 June 1961)

p. 118    'I don't like... need for it' (*Daily Mirror*, 16 September 1970)

p. 118    'He also tried... of staff' (*People*, 25 June 1961)

p. 118    'Gents' Hand-knitted... 36-24-36' (*News of the World*, 9 April 1961)

p. 118    'French Model Giselle' (*News of the World*, 16 April 1961)

p. 120    'he was interviewed... can object' (*Daily Herald*, 2 November 1959)

p. 120    'One day... twenty years?' (*Daily Mail*, 25 November 1959)

## 16    The Wages of Skin

p. 121    'At first he... disappointed," he remarked' (*Empire News*, 22 May 1960)

p. 122    'I think he... neighbour concluded' (interview with the author)

p. 122–3    'Consequently... church bazaar' (*Empire News*, 22 May 1960)

p. 123    'Never has so... so little' (*Skin Deep in Soho*, p. 156)

p. 124    'An informal... around £2.5 million' (*Empire News*, 22 May 1960)

p. 124 .    'more than quintuple... early 1960s' (figures held in the Kirk Douglas Collection at the University of Wisconsin-Madison, USA)

p. 124–5    'There were even... myself a fortune' (*Empire News*, 22 May 1960)

p. 125    'Whether you... to stay' (*Empire News*, 22 May 1960)

p. 125    'This girl... future husband' (*Today*, week ending 31 December 1960, and Miklos Matolsci in conversation with the author)

p. 126    'When you... rolls in' (*Empire News*, 22 May 1960)

p. 126    'in the region... £2,000-a-week' (*People*, 25 June 1961)

p. 126    'Probably via... six years' (*Sunday Dispatch*, 5 June 1960, and *Daily Sketch*, 5 June 1960)

p. 126    'Raymond later described... and police' (*Today*, week ending 31 December 1960)

p. 127    'he hoped... it the Bal Tabarin' (*Evening News*, 14 July 1960)

p. 128    'Dale quizzed him... put on' (*People*, 26 June 1960)

p. 128    'It's quite... disgusted me' (*People*, 26 June 1960)


## 17    The Men Who Would Be King of Clubland

p. 130    'the Square Mile of Vice' (*London after Dark*, p. 10)

p. 131–3  'Two months after... person there," he added' (*People*, 4 September 1960)


## 18    Storm in a D Cup

p. 135    'whispered... lurking in the wings' (Marjorie Davies in conversation with the author)

p. 135–6  'If Debbie wants... dark secret' (*Today*, week ending 31 December 1960)

p. 137    'Paul told me... sell the freehold' (Mark Fuller in conversation with the author)

p. 137    'Jack really didn't... came up' (e-mail from Tony Klinger to the author)

p. 137    'Jack – who... hiding it' (Rusty Humphreys in conversation with the author)

p. 138    'I remember... as clip-joints' (Miklos Matolsci in conversation with the author)

p. 138    'Paul Raymond: King of... female forms' (*Today*, week ending 31 December 1960)

p. 139    'Raymond and his wife planned... in the morning' (*Daily Mail*, 28 December 1960)

p. 139–40 'The presiding... good lines' (*The Times*, 30 December 1960)

p. 140    'The only complaint... with a tassel' (*News of the World*, 1 January 1961)

p. 140–41 'It acclaimed... and underworld' (*Today*, week ending 7 January 1961)

p. 141    'The outcome... sustain its success' (*Today*, week ending 7 January 1961)

p. 142    'With minor variations... Thank you' (*Striptease*, pp. 324–325)


## 19    Ding-dong

p. 143    'Opening for... High Seas' (*Evening News*, 10 April 1961)

p. 143    'suggestive movements' (*Daily Herald*, 13 April 1961)

p. 143    'in a very artistic fashion' (*Evening News*, 10 April 1961)

p. 144    'Raymond's barrister... yes – a little' (*Daily Mail*, 11 April 1961)

p. 144    'The first of them... decorum' (*Evening Standard*, 11 April 1961)

p. 144    'He also told... acts get?' (*Daily Telegraph*, 12 April 1961)

p. 144    'the detective was asked... very good' (*Daily Sketch*, 12 April 1961)

p. 145    'Addressing... respectable people' (*Evening Standard*, 12 April 1961)

p. 145    'Asked about the... parties at the Revuebar' (*Daily Sketch*, 13 April 1961)

p. 145    'When his barrister... book it' (*The Times*, 13 April 1961)

p. 145–6  'Clarke enquired... police allegations' (*Daily Telegraph*, 13 April 1961)

p. 146    'She testified... not that type' (*Daily Mirror*, 14 April 1961)

p. 146    'she explained... much to lose' (*Daily Sketch*, 14 April 1961)

p. 146–7  'We get royal... not vulgar' (*Daily Mirror*, 14 April 1961)

p. 147    'we would have to... cut it out' (*Daily Telegraph*, 13 April 1961)

p. 147–8 'I don't think anyone... so revolting' (*Daily Herald,* 14 April 1961)

p. 148 'never seen... offensive' (*Daily Telegraph,* 14 April 1961)

p. 148 'nothing indecent' (*The Times,* 14 April 1961)

p. 148 'never taken part... or obscene' (*Evening Standard,* 13 April 1961)

p. 148 'She said she'd been... am working' (*Daily Mail,* 13 April 1961, *Daily Telegraph,* 13 April 1961)

p. 149 'Strip Girl... To Court' (*Evening Standard,* 12 April 1961)

p. 149 'His speech was... should convict' (*Guardian,* 15 April 1961)

p. 149–50 'Before going... certain acts' (*Guardian,* 15 April 1961)

p. 150 'I am quite... some time' (*Daily Telegraph,* 15 April 1961)

p. 150 'The show goes... not finished' (*Daily Express,* 15 April 1961)

## 20     Impresario Lothario

p. 151 'If the evidence... revolting' (*Daily Herald,* 23 June 1961)

p. 151–2 'Because the... actor Harry H. Corbett' (Bob Amiss in conversation with the author)

p. 153 'Though not nearly... still indecent' (31 November 1961, National Archives, MEPO2/10168)

p. 153–4 'One woman danced... "John, John, John"' (22 November 1961, National Archives, MEPO2/10168)

p. 155 'A business run... for businessmen' (*Len Deighton's London Dossier,* pp. 165–6)

p. 155 'Something... sir?' (*Skin-Deep in Soho,* p. 165)

p. 155 'Known in the... single weekend' (*The Pornbrokers,* pp. 19 and 35)

p. 155 'He even received... of his shops' (*The Pornbrokers,* p. 173)

p. 156 'Tell them... I need' (*The Pornbrokers,* p. 36)

p. 156 'a new luxury Niterie' (back cover of a Revuebar programme held in National Archives, MEPO2/10168)

p. 157 'He liked to... "Let's Do It"' (*Come By Sunday,* pp. 183–4, 213)

p. 158 'Relentless... nice home' (*Sunday Mirror,* 17 April 1983)

p. 158 'he felt his... slow decline' (*Sunday Mirror,* 17 April 1983)

p. 158 'From an early... happy together' (*Daily Express,* 23 June 1977)

p. 158 'Raymond liked to... incompatibility' (*Sunday Mirror,* 17 April 1983)

p. 158 'You'd never hear... very discreet' (Marjorie Davies in conversation with the author)

p. 158–9 'I distinctly recall this... really embarrassed' (friend of the Raymonds' in conversation with the author)

p. 159 'Jean often... found someone else' (Marjorie Davies in conversation with the author)

## 21     The Bottom Line

p. 160 'I used to go... Richardson there' (Gerry Parker in conversation with the author)

p. 161 'If a man asked... nose for it' (interview with the author)

p. 161    'People must... behind them' (*The Times*, 6 January 1962)

p. 162    'To decent-minded... proceedings' (memo, 8 March 1962, National Archives, MEPO2/10168)

p. 162    'These were a... this is Mr Spillane' (Marjorie Davies in conversation with the author)

p. 164    'the sexiest girls I've seen' (*What's On in London*, 13 December 1963)

p. 164    'We counted... on television' (Marjorie Davies in conversation with the author)

p. 165    'I can't understand... reasonable price' (*Daily Mail*, 12 February 1962)

p. 166    'A fresh session... gentlemen' (*The Times*, 1 February 1964)

p. 167–8  'On the assumption... offer as well' (*Daily Herald*, 9 April 1962)

p. 168    'too good to refuse' (*Daily Mirror*, 9 April 1962)

p. 168    'People have been saying... want it' (*Daily Herald*, 9 April 1962)


## 22    Misleading Ladies

p. 169–70 'Just after 9 p.m... formal caution' (transcript supplied by Chief Inspector William MacKinnon, 4 May 1962, National Archives, MEPO2/10232)

p. 170    'None of the... the law' (memo from Police Sergeant Evans, 27 July 1962, National Archives, MEPO2/10168)

p. 170    'Our reputation... got on well' (Frank Fraser in conversation with the author)

p. 171    'He seemed... not to try' (Frank Fraser in conversation with the author)

p. 171    'like trying... sewage' (*Tanky Challenor*, p. 154)

p. 171    'I feel as if... my back' (*Villains' Paradise*, p. 387)

p. 172    'did not use... methods' (*The Challenor Case*, p. 103)

p. 172    'Raymond often... like Challenor' (Frank Fraser in conversation with the author)

p. 172    'Uncle Harry' (*The Challenor Case*, p. 13)

p. 172    'That's yours... for it' (*The Challenor Case*, pp. 16–17)

p. 173–4  'The show could... being extinguished' (memo from Police Inspector Hugh White, 30 October 1962, National Archives, MEPO2/10168)

p. 174    'told of... to his responsibilities' (National Archives, MEPO2/10168)

p. 175    'Please return...the rest' (*Daily Mail*, 20 February 1963)

p. 176    'Raymond contemplated... Area Council' (*Evening Standard*, 8 October 1963)


## 23    Tanky Panky

p. 177–8  'Rooum later recounted... biggest boy...' (*The Challenor Case*, pp. 49–51)

p. 178    'He didn't leave... arrested him' (*Evening Standard*, 13 August 1963, *The Times*, 14 August 1963, *Wimbledon Boro News*, 16 August 1963)

p. 183    'completely and utterly dog-tired' (*Wimbledon Boro News*, 11 October 1963)

p. 184    'The Playboy Room' (*What's On in London*, 13 December 1963)

p. 184    'good at social niceties' (*Skin-Deep in Soho*, p. 158)

## 24    Undressed to Thrill

p. 187    'He never... little offices' (Irma Kurtz in conversation with the author)

p. 189    'Life's much... tailor immediately' (*From Drags to Riches*, p. 135)

p. 189–90 'We'd run... in Hyde Park' (Paul Lincoln in conversation with the author)

## 25    The Sin Crowd

p. 191    'I'd seen him... impressive figure' (Rusty Humphreys in conversation with the author)

p. 192    'We'd go out... well with Paul' (Rusty Humphreys in conversation with the author)

p. 192    'too respectable' (*Naked Jungle*, p. 85)

p. 194    'It was my... shouldn't be seen' (Jo Brooker in conversation with the author)

p. 194    'In those days... stock it' (Bill Sinclair in conversation with the author)

p. 195    'Someone had left... shots of her' (Bill Sinclair in conversation with the author)

p. 196    'Raymond was so pleased... the stage' (Bill Sinclair in conversation with the author)

p. 196    'So inspired... at children' (*Daily Mirror*, 16 September 1970)

p. 197    'a nightclub tan' (*Madness after Midnight*, p. 123)

p. 197    'Howard remembered... his hands' (*Daily Mail*, 4 March 2008)

p. 197    'Raymond's tough... appearing at the Revuebar' (interview with the author)

p. 197    'she was impossible to control' (*Sunday Times Magazine*, 2 February 1986)

p. 198    'few friends... world' (*Sunday Times*, 15 November 1964)

p. 198    'As far back... an axe' (*Striptease*, p. 255)

p. 198–9  'For Olivia... you here' (*Olivia Newton-John: The Biography*, pp. 38–9)

p. 199    'I was off... it dissolve' (Miklos Matolsci in conversation with the author)

p. 200    'She's in... drowning!' (*Daily Mirror*, 17 April 1965)

p. 200–1  'She'd get it... petrified' (Pamela Green in conversation with the author)

p. 201    'Raymond approached... *piano*...?' (Pamela Green in conversation with the author)

p. 201–2  'In his relentless... the sweetener' (*Daily Mirror*, 24 August 1970)

p. 202    'We'd bring... on a pony' (Miklos Matolsci in conversation with the author)

p. 203    'The magazine... his investment' (Jo Brooker in conversation with the author)

p. 203    'He looked at... of thing' (interview featured in Channel 4's *The Real Paul Raymond*)

p. 204–5  'I said... about half an hour' (Jon Smith in conversation with the author)

## 26    Strip Special

p. 207    'It goes to... matters first' (*Sun*, 11 February 1966)

p. 208–9  'In June 1967... top brass' (*Daily Mail*, 13 October 1967)

p. 211    'The fathers of her... to the Revuebar' (*Sunday Times Magazine*, 2 February 1986)

p. 211    'playing her father' (*Mail on Sunday*, 16 June 1985)

p. 211    'Accustomed to... background' (*News of the World*, 15 November 1992)

p. 211–12  'Raymond agreed... own school' (*Sunday Times Magazine*, 2 February 1986)

p. 212  'outrageous pooftah jobs' (*Ginger Geezer*, p. 69)

## 27      Yes, We Have No Pyjamas

p. 216  'But it won't... like that' (*Daily Mail*, 31 January 1968)

p. 216  'He told me... unnecessary' (*Today*, 18 August 1994)

p. 217  'He said, "I've... arrangement' (*People*, 1 May 1988)

p. 217  'Once I had... common anymore' (*Today*, 18 August 1994)

p. 217  'Despite being... with his wife' (friend of Raymond in conversation with the author)

p. 217  'By November he'd... Downstage' (*Evening News*, 8 January 1969)

p. 218  'The main reason... five minutes' (interview with the author)

p. 218  'There are always... than I am' (*Evening News*, 8 January 1969)

p. 218  'In Hamburg... revolting' (*Evening News*, 8 January 1969)

p. 220  'He readily...entertain audiences' (*Sunday Telegraph*, 24 February 1974, *Daily Mirror*, 16 September 1970)

p. 220  'it is a long time... West End' (*Evening Standard*, 23 September 1969)

p. 220  'this strip-club... legitimate stage' (*The Times*, 13 January 1973)

p. 221  'What the... for years' (*Daily Mirror*, 16 September 1970)

p. 221  'Its adverse repercussions... different school' (*Daily Mail*, 28 June 1997)

p. 221  'At the annual... a belt' (*Sunday Times Magazine*, 17 August 2008)

p. 222–3  'Raymond invited... a contract' (Murray Goldstein in conversation with the author)

p. 223  'This caused... a living' (Miklos Matolsci in conversation with the author)

p. 224  'As far back... magical, "Soho"' (Quoted in *Skin-Deep in Soho*, p. 168)

p. 224  'Our respectable... exorbitant rents' (*Soho*, p. 157)

p. 225–6  'Raymond was in... us anything' (interview with the author)

p. 226  'On the night... "Get 'em off"...' (*Sunday Times* colour supplement, 6 February 1970)

## 28      The Naked and the Bed

p. 227  'Despite all this... fair risk' (*The Times*, 17 January 1970)

p. 228  'as flashily... candyfloss' (*The Times*, 4 April 1970)

p. 228–9  'I did a... fair enough' (Miklos Matolsci in conversation with the author)

p. 229  'the bosoms and buttocks show' (*Evening News*, 16 June 1970)

p. 229  'I think any... get home' (*Daily Mirror*, 16 September 1970)

p. 229  'finding... the moment' (*Daily Sketch*, 21 August 1970)

p. 229  'It would be... he left' (*People*, 6 September 1970)

p. 229  'So well... wedlock' (*Daily Mail*, 8 March 2008)

p. 229  'In many ways... without him' (interview with the author)

p. 230  'She said the call... rang off' (Metropolitan Police file CR203/72/33, viewed under the Freedom of Information Act)

## 29    Porn Again

p. 231–2    'Raymond was sitting… last either' (*Tell-Tale Tits*, pp. 76–80)

p. 233    'state handouts for filth' (*Offensive Literature*, p. 96)

p. 233    'so pornographic… being pornographic' (letter from Raymond Blackburn to the Attorney-General, Sir Peter Rawlinson, 2 October 1972, National Archives, DPP 2/5162)

p. 234    'I will make… great entertainment' (*Daily Mirror*, 16 September 1970)

p. 234    'Archie turned… for years' (e-mail from Fiona Richmond to the author)

p. 235    'Being the owner… sort of thing' (*Daily Mirror*, 16 September 1970)

p. 235    'enquiry into… always will' (*Daily Mirror*, 16 September 1970)

p. 235    'Even though… someone else?' (friend of Jean Raymond in conversation with the author)

p. 235–6    'Jealousy distilling… with a married man' (*Tell-Tale Tits*, pp. 179–81)

p. 236    'Through the… for a month' (*People*, 24 September 1970)

p. 236    'the Permissive Theatre of the Seventies' (*Daily Mirror*, 13 May 1971)

p. 236    'very seriously indeed' (*The Times*, 13 December 1972)

p. 237    'If Jean… durable form' (*Tell-Tale Tits*, pp. 180–81)

p. 237    'he *relished*… most alive' (*Sunday Times Magazine*, 17 August 2008)

p. 237–8    'If they carry… tropics in there' (*Daily Mirror*, 18 November 1970)

p. 238    'George Flowers reported… made a statement' (Metropolitan Police file CR203/72/33, viewed under the Freedom of Information Act)

p. 238    'Now I don't… aggravation' (*Sunday Times* colour supplement, 6 February 1970)

p. 239    'They liked… great relationship' (interview with the author)

p. 240    'crotch shots' (Keith Davis in correspondence with the author)

p. 240    'He didn't want… gold-digger' (*Tell-Tale Tits*, p. 161)

p. 241    'I used to get… with you' (*Sunday Times Magazine*, 2 February 1986)

p. 241    'About an hour and a half… explosive devices' (Metropolitan Police file CR203/72/33, viewed under the Freedom of Information Act)

p. 241    'Jean often rang… leant against it' (*Tell-Tale Tits*, p. 181)

## 30    Mr Striptease v. Lord Porn

p. 242    'who accused… and dirt' (*White Heat*, pp. 543–4)

p. 243    'I think until… of resistance' (*The Times*, 21 April 1971)

p. 244    'on the problems… Great Britain' (*The Times*, 19 April 1971)

p. 244    'Philip, does… non-committal reply' (*The Times*, 14 February 2004)

p. 245    'My Lords, I… aware of' (*Hansard*, 21 April 1971, column 369)

p. 245    'In discussing what… for years' (*Daily Mirror*, 4 May 1971)

p. 245    'flow of filth' (*The Times*, 11 May 1971)

p. 246    'I have a conscience… harm people' (*BusinessAge*, December 1992)

p. 246    'need W.H. Smith's… in the head' (*The Longford Report*, p. 315)

p. 247    'Speaking at the… year's time' (*The Times*, 11 May 1971)

p. 247    'a breakthrough… frankness' (*Daily Mirror*, 26 May 1971)

p. 247–8  'Raymond arranged… be recruited' (*Daily Mirror*, 26 May 1971)

p. 248    'a dirty magazine… bad name' (*Daily Mirror*, 26 May 1971)

p. 248    'Each morning… confront that day' (*Daily Express*, 14 December 1972)

p. 248    'His new-found fame… stop the strip-clubs?' (*Longford*, p. 168)

p. 249    'As part of… into a cab' (*Longford*, p. 170)

## 31    Filthy Lucre

p. 250–1  'Around 9.50 p.m… same conclusion' (Metropolitan Police file CR203/72/33, viewed under the Freedom of Information Act)

p. 251    'Doorstepped… with anyone' (Noel Botham in conversation with the author)

p. 252    'commercial sex-exploiters… of sex' (*White Heat*, pp. 551–2)

p. 252    'destructive and demoralising trends' (*The Times*, 16 June 1971)

p. 252    'love and… great nation' (*The Times*, 12 July 1971)

p. 253    'terms of reference… assist them' (Home Office memo, 8 October 1971, National Archives, HO 302/57)

p. 253    'that no help… given to de Boinod' (Home Office memo, 7 October 1971, National Archives, HO 302/57)

p. 253    'Stymied by… showed it to Longford' (Note for file, 8 October 1971, National Archives, HO 302/57)

p. 253    'Their products… BIG GAME' (Home Office memo, 7 October 1971, National Archives, HO 302/57)

p. 253    'Lord Porn's private eye' (*Longford*, p. 170)

p. 254    'Stung by accusations… to be desired' (*Guardian*, 13 November 1999)

p. 254    'Its author… to the police' (*Observer*, 15 August 1971)

p. 254    'Before boarding… to hell' (*Longford*, p. 16)

p. 254–5  'weapons of revolution' (*Offensive Literature*, p. 117)

p. 255    'He revealed that… dog's home' (*Evening Standard*, 1 April 1971)

p. 255    'Her father would have preferred… their will' (*Sunday Times Magazine*, 2 February 1986)

p. 255    'Rationalising… instruction' (*Sunday Mirror*, 12 August 1973)

p. 256    'At about 1.10 a.m… on Jean's home' (*Daily Mirror*, 28 October, 1 November, 21 November 1971, and *Daily Telegraph*, 28 October 1971)

p. 256–7  'I am told that… were corrupt' (*The Pornbrokers*, p. 66)

p. 257    'Distressed by… conclusive evidence' ' (*Longford*, pp. 170–71)

p. 257    'That changed… get back' (Metropolitan Police file CR203/72/33, viewed under the Freedom of Information Act)

## 32    Tonight's the Night

p. 259–60 'Concerned about… garage at her house' (Metropolitan Police file CR203/72/33, viewed under the Freedom of Information Act)

p. 260    'Further matters… into the facts' (*Daily Telegraph*, 28 October 1971)

p. 261    'Strip King… Court Riddle' (*Daily Mirror*, 28 October 1971)

p. 261    'Justice would… this case' (*Daily Telegraph*, 28 October 1971)

p. 261    'in a great state… guilty or not' (*Daily Telegraph*, 28 October 1971)

p. 261    'Now that… dropping the charges' (*Daily Mail*, 29 October 1971, and *Daily Telegraph*, 28 October 1971)

p. 261    'On Tuesday, 2… Remember Mrs McKay' (Metropolitan Police file CR203/72/33, viewed under the Freedom of Information Act)

p. 262    'That Friday… started yet' (Metropolitan Police file CR203/72/33, viewed under the Freedom of Information Act)

p. 262    'I appeal to… seven years' (*Daily Mirror*, 21 November 1971)

p. 262–3    'Raymond had to wait… to Mr Raymond' (Metropolitan Police file CR203/72/33, viewed under the Freedom of Information Act)

## 33    This Is Your Executioner Speaking

p. 264    'We think it's… of Barking' (*Evening News*, 11 April 1972)

p. 265    'nothing to suggest… the incidents' (Metropolitan Police file CR203/72/33, viewed under the Freedom of Information Act)

p. 265    'under consideration' (list of current OPS cases, 1 January 1972, National Archives, DPP 2/5162)

p. 266–7    'Until Monday… put the phone down' (Metropolitan Police file CR203/72/33, viewed under the Freedom of Information Act)

## 34    Greetings from Pornland

p. 268    'suitable for… family' (*The Longford Report*, p. 315)

p. 269    'I replied… been corrupted' (*Observer*, 24 April 1988)

p. 269    'Bob Guccione… exploited women' (*The Longford Report*, pp. 96–7)

p. 269    'They both stressed… itself and its readers' (*The Longford Report*, pp. 307–8)

p. 270    'Lord Longford?… specialise in' (*Evening News*, 4 January 1972)

p. 270–2    'Between the final… on stand-by' (Metropolitan Police file CR203/72/33, viewed under the Freedom of Information Act)

p. 272    'a big operation' (interview with the author)

p. 272    'Adams and a group… wait here' (Metropolitan Police file CR203/72/33, viewed under the Freedom of Information Act)

## 35     Money with Menaces

p. 273–7   'McGrath didn't... drove away' (Metropolitan Police file CR203/72/33, viewed under the Freedom of Information Act)

## 36     Room at the Top Shelf

p. 278     'As Raymond waited... collect a parcel' (Metropolitan Police file CR203/72/33, viewed under the Freedom of Information Act)

p. 278     'Abruptly shifting... from the box office' (*Daily Telegraph*, 13 December 1972)

p. 278–80 'When the man... now be dead' (Metropolitan Police file CR203/72/33, viewed under the Freedom of Information Act)

p. 280     'good witnesses' (Metropolitan Police file CR203/72/33, viewed under the Freedom of Information Act)

p. 281     'I'm something of... now' (*Evening News*, 11 April 1972)

p. 281     'To them... ex-missus' (*Daily Mail*, 29 October 1974)

p. 281     'They had a great... very normal' (Noel Botham in conversation with the author)

p. 282     'considerably more... than *Men Only*' (*The Longford Report*, p. 307)

p. 283     'During periods... boredom' (*Sunday Times* magazine, 17 August 2008)

p. 283     'Why bother... knickers?' (*The Times*, 13 January 1973)

p. 283     'What I have... *should* have' (*The Times*, 22 January 1971)

p. 283     'Two of the more... not wasted' ' (*John Osborne: A Patriot for Us*, p. 375)

p. 283     'Oates was... incident occurred' (interview featured in Channel 4's *The Real Paul Raymond*)

p. 284     'the most extreme... Publications Act 1959' (letter from Raymond Blackburn to Robert Mark, 16 September 1972, National Archives, DPP 2/5162)

p. 285     '*Men Only* had... obvious in *Club International*' (*The Longford Report*, p. 318)

p. 285     'The plain fact... ineffective' (*The Fall of Scotland Yard*, p. 193)

p. 285     'I see no... by the police' (*Daily Express*, 20 September 1972)

p. 285     'extreme pornographic... dog' (letter from Blackburn to the Director of Public Prosecutions, 8 November 1972, National Archives, DPP 2/5162)

## 37     Something Blue

p. 287     'Soon as the... with us' (Rusty Humphreys in conversation with the author)

p. 287     'It was probably... other crazy' (interview with the author)

p. 288     'I cannot... no one else' (*Daily Mirror*, 23 September 1972)

p. 289     'The law isn't... who draws it' (*Evening News*, 29 September 1972)

p. 290     'She was annoyed... Raymond's marriage' (*Tell-Tale Tits*, p. 179)

p. 290     'Raymond's lawyers... expropriated porn' (*Sun*, 9 December 1972)

p. 290     'I was in fear... children' (*Sun*, 13 December 1972)

p. 291     'Brian Leary... offending issue obscene' (*Evening Standard*, 14 December 1972, and *Evening News*, 14 December 1972)

p. 291    'their understandings' (*Evening Standard*, 14 December 1972)

p. 291    'excitement of the senses' (*Guardian*, 15 December 1972)

p. 292    'We concede that… trying to say' ([Watford] *Evening Echo*, 15 December 1972)

## 38    The Raymond Follies

p. 293–4  'All of a sudden… at Mr Raymond's office' (*The Times*, 16 December 1972)

p. 294    'the appalling violence… normal life' (*Daily Express*, 22 December 1972)

p. 294    'He couldn't understand… reconciliation' (interview with the author)

p. 294    'Another thing… troubled him' (friend of Raymond in conversation with the author)

p. 294    'On the eve… her petition' (*People*, 1 May 1988)

p. 294    'Noel Botham described… kid' (Noel Botham in conversation with the author)

p. 295    'This is a good day…enough for me' (*Daily Express*, 3 March 1973)

p. 295    'According to her… acceptable figure' (*Daily Express*, 11 August 1994)

p. 295    'Raymond expressed… £250,000' (*Sunday Mirror*, 17 April 1983)

p. 295    'In her account… short of cash' (*Daily Express*, 11 August 1994)

p. 297    'Raymond envisaged it as… Parisian cabaret' (*Sunday Telegraph*, 24 February 1974)

p. 297    'With luck, he… and sets' (*Guardian*, 30 March 1974)

p. 297    'Instead of being… *sex you up*' (*New Statesman*, 14 December 1973)

p. 298    'It's not right for me' (*Daily Express*, 23 June 1977)

p. 298    'Pure coincidence… bravely volunteered' (*Daily Mirror*, 15 March 1974)

p. 299    'Letting Debbie… in-jokes' (interview with the author)

p. 300    'It had an interior… hated' (*Tell-Tale Tits*, p. 89)

p. 300    'Richmond talked… in Latin' (*Tell-Tale Tits*, p. 89)

p. 301    'the judge delivered… *Tiger Tim's Weekly*' (*The Times*, 7 February 1974)

p. 301    'I'm not… entertainer' (*Sunday Times*, 24 February 1974)

p. 301    'Tits, bums… what *I* like' (*Sunday Times*, 24 February 1974)

p. 303    'Feigning… damned amateurs' (*Daily Mirror*, 15 March 1974)

p. 303    'tart-traps' (*London: City of Disappearances*, p. 27)

## 39    Let's Get Laid

p. 305    'Losers' Lounge', (*Just the One*, p. 189)

p. 305    'Raymond just… membership card' (Michael Dillon in conversation with the author)

p. 305–6  'I once asked… *deepest* sympathy' (Michael Dillon in conversation with the author)

p. 306    'Once the ring… for granted' (*Sunday Mirror*, 17 April 1983)

p. 307    Raymond had, by then… the police' (*Tell-Tale Tits*, p. 10)

p. 308    'When Fiona… it would show' (*Up Front*, p. 212)

p. 308    'to work up… hard way' (*Daily Express*, 23 June 1977)

p. 308    'Both her parents… a table' (*Sunday Mirror*, 3 November 1974)

p. 309    'As Jean walked… bye, Paul' (*Daily Mirror*, 29 October 1974)

p. 309    'I hope we are… the settlement' (*Daily Mirror*, 29 October 1974)

p. 309    'I'm numb… success it is' (*Daily Mirror*, 29 October 1974)

p. 309    'Stripped… of £250,000' (*Daily Mirror*, 29 October 1974)

p. 309    'I will not be… sort of money' (*Sunday Mirror*, 3 November 1974)

p. 310    'Paul was always… bloody useless' (Jonathan Hodge in conversation with the author)

p. 311    'Most investors… elbow room' (*Property Week*, 3 November 2000)

p. 312    'Watching Raymond… at that stage' (interview with the author)

p. 315    'We were talking… she agreed' (*News of the World*, 18 January 1976)

p. 316    'the Tamburlaine-like… lowest point' (*The Times*, 25 November 1976)

p. 317    'With a photographer… football field' (*Big Mal*, pp. 252–3)

p. 318    'We wouldn't… nobody's complained' (*The Times*, 28 June 1976)

p. 318    'Except for… family business' (*Daily Mail*, 12 March 1998)

p. 318    'Himself a… family business' (*Daily Mail*, 12 March 1998)

p. 318–19 'Back in London… was out' (*Sunday Times Magazine*, 17 August 2008, and *Daily Mail*, 12 March 1998)

p. 319    'Derry remembered… his nerves' (*Sunday Times Magazine*, 17 August 2008)

p. 319    'He portrayed… never notice' (interview featured in Channel 4's *The Real Paul Raymond*)

p. 319    'Derry was still… 8.30 p.m.' (*Sunday Times Magazine*, 17 August 2008)

p. 319    'If I had… coffee?' (*Daily Mail*, 12 March 1998)

## 40    A Captain of Skindustry

p. 320    'Now Britain's… Together' (Internet Movie Database)

p. 322    'We felt… pleasant experience' (*Daily Mirror*, 30 November 1976)

p. 322    'He used to say… proper friend' (e-mail from Fiona Richmond to the author)

p. 322–3  'Debbie was already… control of it' (*Daily Express*, 23 June 1977)

p. 324    'They get paid… exploiting men' (*BusinessAge*, December 1992)

p. 324    'Way-mon Wevue Bar' (former uniformed policeman in conversation with the author)

p. 324    'To his annoyance… being nude' (*Women's World*, November 1977)

p. 324–5  'when he said… the music hall' (*Guardian*, 21 January 1977)

p. 325    'the frankly… lady' (*Keeping the British End Up*, pp. 151–2)

p. 325–6  'Don't be… £100 a week' (*Daily Mirror*, 19 May 1977)

p. 326    'performance of… splendour' (*Daily Telegraph*, quoted in *The Times*, 29 October 1977)

p. 326–7  'I've been working… a worker' (*Daily Express*, 23 June 1977)

p. 327    'I became… turned up' (Jonathan Hodge in conversation with the author)

## 41    Playboy of the West End World

p. 328    'Each purchase… a thrill' (*Today*, 28 June 1986)

p. 329    'doing well' (*Daily Express*, 23 June 1977)

p. 329    'She was desperate... Raymond know' (Jonathan Hodge in conversation with the author)

p. 329    'Jean was... happy for Debbie' (friend of Jean Raymond in conversation with the author)

p. 330    'super' (*Daily Express*, 23 June 1977)

p. 330    'She subsequently... a musician' (*Daily Mirror*, 9 January 1978)

p. 330    'She called me... at my wedding!' (*News of the World*, 15 November 1992)

p. 330    'Jean later described... back to normal' (*News of the World*, 15 November 1992)

p. 330–1  'It was all... that morning' (Jonathan Hodge in conversation with the author)

p. 331    'By turning... being upstaged' (Jonathan Hodge in conversation with the author)

p. 331    'In the background... a portent' (Jonathan Hodge in conversation with the author)

p. 332–4  'We had a great... with laughter' (Jonathan Hodge in conversation with the author)

p. 334    'While we were... see me again' (*News of the World*, 15 November 1992)

p. 335    'Howard was a big... to Paul' (Noel Botham in conversation with the author)

p. 335    'Instead, Howard... own thing' (Jonathan Hodge in conversation with the author)

p. 335    'Debbie "did not... moved aside' (*Mail on Sunday*, 30 April 1995)

p. 335    'Until Howard... a businessman' (*Mail on Sunday*, 30 April 1995)

p. 335    'Paul was very... about it' (Jonathan Hodge in conversation with the author)

p. 336    'We met in the... proper existence' (*Mail on Sunday*, 30 April 1995)

p. 336    'rent-a-crowd' (*Evening Standard*, 24 April 1979)

p. 337    'a little bit... hard work' (*Daily Express*, 18 May 1979)

p. 338    'I always liked him... cave in' (Jonathan Hodge in conversation with the author)

p. 338–9  'Raymond told me... she was with' (interview with the author)

p. 339    'I'm sure they... liking him, though' (Jonathan Hodge in conversation with the author)

## 42    When the King of Porn Met the Queen of Clean

p. 341    'It was a perfectly... clothes off' (*News of the World*, 4 July 1979)

p. 342    'a violation of... privacy' (*Daily Mirror*, 17 April 1971)

p. 342–3  'Nattily... for Mary Whitehouse' (*Daily Mail*, 3 August 1979)

p. 344–5  'One night Paul... considerate lover' (*News of the World*, 30 August 1981)

p. 346    'he felt that... in particular' (friend of Raymond in conversation with the author)

p. 347    'like some action' (*Daily Telegraph*, 16 February 1980)

p. 347    'a very sincere... his country' (*BusinessAge*, December 1992)

p. 347    'We sincerely... team' (*The Times*, 16 February 1980)

p. 347    'Despite Downing Street... Raymond's offer' (*Daily Mirror*, 10 July 1981, and *Daily Express*, 11 March 1981)

p. 347    'Mr Raymond printed... rip-off' (*Daily Mirror*, 20 August 1981)

## 43     Paul Raymond Killed My Mother

p. 349    'I went round... all of it' (Peter Richardson in conversation with the author)

p. 349    'On the first... Comic Trip' (Peter Richardson in conversation with the author)

p. 349    'I remember... in the building' (Alexei Sayle in conversation with the author)

p. 350    'Keith Allen came... and run' (Peter Richardson in conversation with the author)

p. 350    'Turn right... Comic Strip' (Nigel Planer in conversation with the author)

p. 350    'That Willie... something "alternative"' (*Walking Possession*, pp. 260–61)

p. 351    'used to... funny haircut' (Nigel Planer in conversation with the author)

p. 351    'Just as... soft touch' (Peter Richardson in conversation with the author)

p. 352    'he claimed that... out the Maltese' (*Sunday Times*, 17 April 1983)

p. 352    'Beware of This Pair' (*News of the World*, 21 May 1978)

p. 353    'We used to... every morning' (interview with the author)

p. 353    'an all-day... centre' (*The Times*, 19 June 1981)

p. 354    'one of the most... in London' (sales brochure produced by Chesterton, Sturgis and Son)

p. 354    'a marvellous farce' (quoted on the cover of the script of *Anyone for Denis?*)

p. 355    'We didn't... both of us' (*Daily Telegraph*, 10 December 1989)

p. 356    'I am amazed... rotten money' (*Daily Mirror*, 20 August 1981)

p. 357    'I would certainly... added glamour' (*Evening News*, 31 October 1981)

p. 357    'I don't think... those displays' (*BusinessAge*, December 1992)

p. 358    'Mr Raymond was... you know' (*BusinessAge*, December 1992)

p. 359    'Raymond proclaimed that... £1.3 million' (*BusinessAge*, December 1992)

p. 359    'We want... Minnelli' (*Daily Express*, 13 November 1982)

p. 359    'an amicable agreement' (*The Times*, 15 October 1982)

## 44     Non-stop Erotic Cabaret

p. 360    'happy without... girlfriend' (*Daily Express*, 13 November 1982)

p. 361    'great mates' (*Evening Standard*, 13 April 1983)

p. 361    'He often used... been out with' (*Sunday Times Magazine*, 2 February 1986)

p. 362    'Remembering one such... I went home' (*Mail on Sunday*, 1 June 2008)

p. 362    'Debbie had arrived... serious about it' (*Sunday Times Magazine*, 2 February 1986)

p. 363    'When I first... please?' (*BusinessAge*, November 1992)

p. 363    'People get... go' (*BusinessAge*, December 1992)

p. 363    'Bending his... other staff' (*Sunday Times Magazine*, 2 February 1986)

p. 363    'by treating him... "Mr Raymond"' (ex-PRP employee in conversation with the author)

p. 363    'Very polite... smiling' (*Sunday Telegraph*, 13 July 1997)

p. 364    'Once the turkey... Debbie alone' (*News of the World*, 15 November 1992)

p. 364–5    'It was the top... cool cat' (John Morrell in conversation with the author)

p. 365    'After we'd all... the offer' (Alexei Sayle in conversation with the author)

p. 366    'I never found out... lot of fun' (Peter Richardson in conversation with the author)

## 45      Sugar and Spice and All Things Vice

p. 367     'You'll probably... lot of things' (*Sunday Times*, 17 April 1983)

p. 367–8   'I phoned... get with me' (e-mail from Fiona Richmond to the author)

p. 368     'I will go... shape or form' (*Sunday Times*, 17 April 1983)

p. 369     'launder money... of the mafia' (*Evening Standard*, 1 August 1985)

p. 370     'He always struck... than you' (interview with the author)

p. 370     'I drink far too much' (*Evening Standard*, 13 April 1983)

p. 372     'permitting... establishment' (*The Times*, 27 June 1983)

p. 372     'the lease... client's hands' (*The Times*, 6 September 1983)

p. 372     'Sex shops *should*... do not want' (*The Times*, 2 December 1983)

p. 374     'Maria later alleged... on coke' (*Mail on Sunday*, 30 April 1995)

p. 374     'When Jean became... He's alright' (*People*, 1 May 1988)

p. 375     'Soon enough... by Howard' (*Mail on Sunday*, 31 January 1994)

p. 375     'Raymond was disgusted... between them' (Noel Botham in conversation with the author)

## 46      Monte Carlo and Bust

p. 376     'a little goldmine' (*Guardian*, 24 May 1986)

p. 377     'He seemed... by me' (*Daily Express*, 18 July 1985)

p. 377     'Optimistic about... temporary' (*The Times*, 16 February 1985)

p. 377     'Among the few... insensitivity' (*Mail on Sunday*, 1 June 2008, and interview with the author)

p. 377     'I'm amazed... promise to her' (*Daily Express*, 18 July 1985)

p. 378     'the business he admitted... anything else' (*BusinessAge*, December 1992)

p. 378     'I've invested in... have thought' (*BusinessAge*, December 1992)

p. 379     'After she went... the pain' (*Mail on Sunday*, 1 June 2008)

p. 379     'I can phone... or listen' (*Sunday Times Magazine*, 2 February 1986)

p. 380     'When I die... the company' (*Today*, 28 June 1986)

p. 380     'He liked to tell... went awry' (former employee in conversation with the author)

p. 380     'he held... of the marriage' (friend of Raymond in conversation with the author)

p. 380     'Incensed... she'd done' (*Mail on Sunday*, 30 April 1995)

p. 381     'She always... cost a packet' (interview with the author)

p. 382     'Alarmed by... seeing Fawn' (*News of the World*, 15 November 1992)

## 47      Find the Lady

p. 382     'I love it... seeing him' (*Soho in the Fifties*, p. 175)

p. 383     'You never knew... West End show' (Clive Harris in conversation with the author)

p. 383–4   'As an editor... relished all that' (Steve Bleach in conversation with the author)

p. 385     'in danger... and shamed' (*Daily Mirror*, 4 January 1988)

p. 385     'I've always fancied... expansion' (*Daily Mirror*, 5 January 1988)

p. 386    'Paul Raymond is not... Maxwell *is*' (*Daily Mail*, 23 June 1994)

p. 386-7  'Most of the apparent... Wardour Street' (*Inside Soho*, pp. 215-16)

p. 388    'I just... overnight' (*Daily Mail*, 8 March 2008)

p. 388    'Looking back... problems' (*Mail on Sunday*, 31 January 1994)

p. 389    'An institution that... heritage today' (*BusinessAge*, December 1992)

p. 389    'Raymond assured the... few quid' (*Daily Mirror*, 20 April 1988)

p. 389    'Dubious about whether... his father' (*Daily Mail*, 28 June 1997)

p. 389    'I can't bear... of four years' (*People*, 1 May 1988)

p. 390    'He just turned... straight for it' (*BusinessAge*, November 1992)

p. 390    'I own that... that one' (*The Times online*, 9 March 2008)

p. 390-2  'The first time... you employ' (Steve Bleach in conversation with the author)

p. 392    'She was taking...drink or drugs' (interview with the author)

## 48    Hard Cash

p. 394    'I went into... multimillionaire' (Clive Harris in conversation with the author)

p. 394    'Q: 'Why do... customers *in*' (David Collard in conversation with the author)

p. 395-6  'I first met... page man' (Clive Harris in conversation with the author)

p. 396-7  'My wife... support he could' (Mark Fuller in conversation with the author)

p. 398    'backcombed mega-mullet' (e-mail from Jonathan Meades to the author)

p. 398    'If I was... last rites' (*BusinessAge*, December 1992)

p. 398-9  'My favourite... the car park' (Clive Harris in conversation with the author)

p. 399    'He seemed... two hundred decibels' (Steve Bleach in conversation with the author)

p. 399    'You may laugh... to confess' (*BusinessAge*, December 1992)

p. 399    'Look, I can't... down here' (*BusinessAge*, December 1992)

p. 399    'Women will let you... your own' (Steve Bleach in conversation with the author)

p. 400    'Howard got the... company' (*Daily Mail*, 8 March 2008)

p. 400    'Debbie said... an explanation' (*News of the World*, 15 November 1992)

## 49    Material Girl

p. 401    'have the sort... never retire' (*BusinessAge*, November 1992)

p. 401    'Hospitalisation... disapproved of it' (*Mail on Sunday*, 30 April 1995)

p. 402    'He noticed... her responsibilities' (*Daily Telegraph*, 27 January 1993)

p. 402    'Proud of... encountered' (*Sunday Times Magazine*, 17 August 2008)

p. 402    'She came to... clean it up' (*Mail on Sunday*, 30 April 1995)

p. 403    'Another recipient... Kerr's clinic' (*Speaking Out* newsletter, Autumn 1991)

p. 404    'Jean, I think... many charities' (*News of the World*, 15 November 1992)

p. 404    'They're giving... state of affairs' (*Sunday Telegraph*, 29 March 1992)

p. 404-5  'Late on the... lambasted him' (*The Times*, 12 June 1992)

p. 405    'Until Debbie... the phone down' (*News of the World*, 15 November 1992)

p. 405-6  'It's not... statement' (Mark Fuller in conversation with the author)

p. 406    'Debbie Raymond "has all the... empire to"' (*BusinessAge*, November 1992)

p. 406    'extremely good spirits' (*Daily Telegraph*, 27 January 1993)

p. 407    'Raymond was unaware... great form' (*Sunday Mirror*, 8 November 1992)

p. 407    'At 9.45 p.m... she was watching' (*Daily Telegraph*, 27 January 1993)

p. 407    'Raymond's housekeeper... drink probably' (*Daily Telegraph*, 27 January 1993)

p. 407    'absolutely devastated' (*Evening Standard*, 6 November 1992)

p. 408    'I'm a tough... understand it' (*Sunday Mirror*, 8 November 1992)

p. 408    'It was the most... his money' (Steve Bleach in conversation with the author)

## 50    Death Duties

p. 409    'It's not the... your fun' (*Sun*, 2 December 1992)

p. 409    'His indulgence... had occurred' (*Today*, 18 August 1994)

p. 409    'Paul hardly even... him again' (*News of the World*, 15 November 1992)

p. 409    'Her death... completely' (Noel Botham in conversation with the author)

p. 410    'He absolutely... *too* generous' (Mark Fuller in conversation with the author)

p. 411    'He became utterly... granddaughters' (interview with the author)

p. 412    'closing in on... wealth' (*BusinessAge*, December 1992)

p. 412    'If I'm not... to play' (*BusinessAge*, December 1992)

p. 412    'I'm incredibly... him happy' (*Sun*, 2 December 1992)

p. 412    'Some of... these pages' (*The History of St Francis Xavier's College, Liverpool, 1842–2001*, p. 108)

p. 412–14 'The uncertainty... behind us' (*Daily Telegraph*, 27 January 1993)

## 51    Vital Statistics

p. 415    'I've become... adult entertainment' (*Daily Star*, 19 September 1994)

p. 415    'Raymond was already... a pornographer' (ex-PRP employee in conversation with the author)

p. 415    'celebrating beauty' (a phrase mentioned by several journalists, including Tim Walker in an e-mail to the author)

p. 415    'I just laughed... sorry for him' (*Daily Express*, 11 August 1994)

p. 416    'His instinct... £14.25 million' (*The Times online*, 9 March 2008)

p. 416    'Years ago... shillings-a-morning' (*Guardian*, 2 July 1994)

p. 417    'Britain's biggest pimp' (*Evening Standard*, 6 January 2004)

p. 419–20 'Sensing Raymond's... be immortal' (Gérard Simi in conversation with the author)

p. 420    'unrecognisable' (*London: City of Disappearances*, p. 30)

p. 420    'For all his... with his money' (*Daily Mail*, 8 March 2008)

p. 420    'always had a... behind a tree' (*Evening Standard*, 1 April 2009)

p. 420    'Derry confessed... mess' (*Daily Mail*, 12 March 1998)

p. 421    'Paul got very upset about it' (Noel Botham in conversation with the author)

## 52    The Way of All Flesh

p. 423    'Maybe tomorrow' (*Daily Mail*, 8 March 2008)

p. 423    'Paul gave me... in the end' (Mark Fuller in conversation with the author)

p. 424    'John and Jilly made... your car' (Mark Fuller in conversation with the author)

p. 426    'For Simi... I was doing' (Gérard Simi in conversation with the author)

p. 427    'It were shite' (*Independent*, 11 March 2004)

p. 429    'I know he must've... a fad' (Steve Bleach in conversation with the author)

p. 429    'I own... correction' (*Evening Standard*, 7 March 2008)

p. 430    'I love... you, too' (*Evening Standard*, 1 April 2009)

p. 430    'I want to... waiting for you' (*Sunday Times Magazine*, 17 August 2008)

p. 430    'I believe I... months first' (*BusinessAge*, December 1992)

p. 430    'Derry, was... of the road' (Sunday *Times Magazine*, 17 August 2008)

p. 432    'Adored and loved' (*Mail on Sunday*, 9 November 2008)

p. 432    'Howard made plans... that summer' (*Sunday Times Magazine*, 17 August 2008)

# PICTURE CREDITS

Images featured in this book come from the following sources: St Francis Xavier College, Liverpool (p. 15); Rex Features (pp. 344, 410); Alamy.com (p. 147); the Ronald Grant Archive (p. 321); TopFoto (p. 193); Getty Images (pp. vi-vii, 127, 202); collection of the author (p. 92); Maurice Poole (pp. 28, 29, 47, 49, 69, 102, 141, 219, 228, 303); Jonathan Hodge (pp. 332, 333, 334, 368); Yak Droubie (pp. 53, 60, 71, 74, 115); Max Decharné (pp. 135, 156, 181); Roy Pearce (p. 209); and Marjorie Davies (pp. 152, 163, 165, 173). The author and publisher would like to thank John James of Soho Estates for granting permission to include images for which the Paul Raymond Organisation holds the copyright. Thanks are also due to Maurice Poole, Jonathan Hodge, Len Deighton, Roy Pearce, Yak Droubie, Max Decharné, Marjorie Davies and Brother Peter at St Francis Xavier College for their generosity in loaning material for use in this book. Another large consignment of gratitude is en route to Andi Sapey, ace photographer and Photoshop maestro, for helping with the reproduction and retouching of some of these images.

# INDEX